Collins

CW01646593

Key Stage 3
Science
Teacher Pack 1

Series editor: Ed Walsh
Authors: Sarah Askey
Tracey Baxter
Sunetra Berry
Pat Dower

William Collins' dream of knowledge for all began with the publication of his first book in 1819. A self-educated mill worker, he not only enriched millions of lives, but also founded a flourishing publishing house. Today, staying true to this spirit, Collins books are packed with inspiration, innovation and practical expertise. They place you at the centre of a world of possibility and give you exactly what you need to explore it.
Collins. Freedom to teach

Published by Collins
An imprint of HarperCollins*Publishers*
77 – 85 Fulham Palace Road
Hammersmith
London
W6 8JB

Browse the complete Collins catalogue at
www.collins.co.uk

10 9 8 7 6 5 4 3 2 1

ISBN 978-0-00-754020-4

Sarah Askey, Tracey Baxter, Sunetra Berry, Pat Dower and Anne Pilling assert their moral rights to be identified as the authors of this work.

British Library Cataloguing in Publication Data
A Catalogue record for this publication is available from the British Library

Commissioned by Letitia Luff
Project managed by Jane Roth
Series editor Ed Walsh
Managing editor Caroline Green
Project editor Amanda Redstone
Editorial assistant Lucy Roth
Edited by Elizabeth Barker, Hugh Hillyard-Parker, Sophia Ktori, John Ormiston, Kate Redmond, Jane Roth and Ros Woodward
Proofread by Tony Clappison and Nigel Rumble
Illustrations by Ann Paganuzzi and Ken Vail Graphic Design
Cover design by Angela English
Cover photograph by 1st Gallery/Shutterstock
Production by Emma Roberts
Printed and bound by RR Donnelley at Glasgow, UK

Health and Safety: All practicals in this book have been safety checked (but not trialled) by CLEAPSS (www.cleapss.org.uk) and the publisher and authors have made every reasonable effort to ensure that the experiments and activities in this book are safe when conducted as instructed. However, the publishers assume no responsibility for any damage or injury caused or sustained while performing the experiments or activities in this book to the full extent permitted by law.

Parents, guardians, and/or teachers should supervise students who undertake the experiments and activities in this book, and carry out full risk assessments before carrying out any practical work.
CLEAPSS is an advisory service providing support in science and technology for a consortium of local authorities and their schools including establishments for pupils with special needs.

Acknowledgements
Every effort has been made to trace copyright holders and to obtain their permission for the use of copyright materials. The publishers will gladly receive any information enabling them to rectify any error or omission at the first opportunity.

Contents

Extra resources on CD-ROM

All pages from this print book available as PDF and editable Word files

Student worksheets in 2 formats; reusable and write-on (all available as PDF and Word files)

Practical sheets (as PDF and Word files)

Technician's notes (as PDF and Word files)

Each type of resource sheet collated in chapter batches to enable easy printing

Scheme outline for Teacher Pack 2

Scheme outline for Teacher Pack 3

Introduction

Purpose of the Collins Key Stage 3 Science course

This course has been developed to provide support to teachers in planning and delivering exciting, engaging and effective lessons. The overarching priorities have been to:

- ensure that the requirements of the National Curriculum Programme of Study have been responded to
- support teachers in teaching lessons in which students make good progress and are on track to achieve well at the end of KS4
- offer ways of tracking, reporting on and responding to progress given the move away from levels in the National Curriculum
- enable schools to select the period of time they decide to devote to KS3 before starting on KS4 courses
- address the need to challenge and engage students working at different levels of attainment
- focus on the development of skills and processes as well as content
- provide teachers with clear guidance as to how learning can be managed during the lesson, from initial engagement to consolidation and application.

Overview of changes at Key Stage 3

Some concepts previously associated with GCSE are now in KS3, such as:

- the role played by Watson, Crick, Wilkins and Franklin in the development of the DNA model
- the chemical properties of metal and non-metal oxides with respect to acidity
- the properties of ceramics, polymers and composites
- heating and thermal equilibrium
- the superposition of waves
- resistance as the ratio of potential difference to current
- the concept of electrostatic fields
- the light year as a unit of astronomical distance.

How Science Works has been replaced with Working Scientifically, which covers a similar range of skills and processes but which moves away from the social and economic implications of scientific developments.

There are no levels or any descriptors of progression. Nevertheless, schools are expected to track progress, report accordingly and respond with further challenge or support.

Organisation of the Collins Key Stage 3 Science course

There are two biology, two chemistry and two physics chapters in each year. This means that science can be delivered as one subject or by subject specialists. A scheme of work shows both 3-year and 2-year routes though the course to aid long-term planning, see page 242. Support and strategies for building and assessing progress are embedded throughout. For more details please see *Planning the learning process* on pages 3-7.

How the lesson plans work

Chapter introductions

These:

- give an overview of the of the content and skills covered in the chapter
- help in assessing prior learning and identifying misconceptions
- list the overarching learning objectives to help medium-term planning.

Learning objectives and outcomes

- Learning objectives for each topic are shared with students in the Student Book for short-term planning.
- Learning outcomes at three levels are listed, and it is shown which learning activities contribute to achieving each outcome.

These help in tracking the progress of all students, identifying those making good progress and who are on the right trajectory for sound results at GCSE, those who are making better than expected progress and are headed for the top results at GCSE, and those making less progress and for whom some intervention is needed.

Skills development

Ensuring progression in skills has underpinned the development of the course. There are three skill sets used, developed from a range of sources including PLTS, SEAL and APP in Science:

- **Thinking scientifically** relates to the relationship between evidence, ideas and theories, and has a strong role to play in science generally and in KS4 courses. It includes asking questions, considering the quality of evidence, understanding how theories develop, evaluating risks, using units and nomenclature, using equations and analysing data.
- **Working scientifically** relates to conducting practical investigations and includes making predictions, designing investigations, recording evidence, presenting evidence, interpreting evidence, developing explanations and evaluating data.
- **Developing as learners** is not a science-specific set of skills, though science can play a strong part in developing the skills, and they are recognised by the Ofsted school inspection framework. They include planning progress, acting responsibly, developing resilience, asking questions, communicating effectively, respecting others and collaborating effectively.

Resources needed gives an overview of all the resources needed for a lesson. More detailed guidance for practicals is given in student practical sheets and technician's notes on the accompanying CD-ROM.

Common misconceptions highlight specific misconceptions for the topic.

Key vocabulary is highlighted throughout to support literacy.

Teaching sequence

The lesson plans all use the same learning sequence. This is based on the idea that learning develops in stages during a lesson and that different parts of the lesson have different functions.

Engage This section draws students in to thinking about the ideas, and includes possible starter activities. Here students encounter ideas that will make them want to find out more.

Challenge and develop Students meet something that will challenge their existing understanding. It might be questions, ideas, demonstrations or experiments that make them realise the inadequacy of a simpler explanation.

Explain Students are encouraged to develop a good explanation and supported in capturing ideas in words or graphically. Differentiation ideas are given for students making less or more than expected progress.

Consolidate and apply Students realise how the new learning is to be consolidated and applied, including real-world applications. Again, differentiation ideas are given for students making different levels of progress.

Extend Addresses how the ideas of the topic can be extended to stretch students able to progress further.

Plenary suggestions Varied activities help in gauging student progress.

Answers All answers to Student Book questions and worksheet questions are provided.

Extra resources on the accompanying CD-ROM

Every lesson has an associated differentiated worksheet to support written work. These are provided as write-on versions with lines for student responses, and reusable versions without lines that can be used again and again to reduce photocopying costs. Practical sheets are provided to give support for planning, carrying out and analysing practical work. Technician's notes are provided to explain the materials and setup and help with planning.

Collins Connect is a linked publication of digital resources to enhance lessons. The resources are listed by lesson in the scheme of work on page 242.

Planning the learning process: The thinking behind Key Stage 3 Science

Outstanding lesson plans

Each of the lesson plans is designed to support the delivery of high quality interactive lessons. They have a common structure that is transparent, making it easy for teachers to see what is suggested and make decisions about whether to use the plan as it stands or to customise. Sequences of lessons are planned to cover the requirements of the Programme of Study for Science (2013).

Objectives and outcomes

Each of the statements from the Programme of Study has been built into the plan and identified as 'overarching objectives'. From these authors have developed learning objectives for individual lessons; these draw upon processes as well as content. These objectives use the stem of 'we are learning how to' as it is important that students develop abilities as opposed to just learning facts.

From these, outcomes were developed; there is a strong relationship between objectives and outcomes. Outcomes use the stem 'what I'm looking for' (in which 'I' is the teacher) and indicate the evidence the teacher should see that indicates that learning has occurred.

The outcomes also play a critical role in the **assessment of progress**. The 2013 Programme of Study has no level descriptors but the importance of tracking progress hasn't diminished. Part of the function of the outcomes is to enable the teacher to decide if students are making good progress. The outcomes are differentiated; students who are making good progress will be, generally speaking, achieving at least two out of the three outcomes. Students regularly achieving all three may need, on occasions, more challenging activities. Those struggling to achieve more than one may need additional support. However the Teacher Pack materials are designed to be used in a flexible way, to be selected from and adapted to meet the needs of students.

Skills

Each lesson has two or three focus skills selected. The three sets of skills are as follows:

- **Thinking scientifically**. These are the skills that scientists use in a variety of contexts, such as asking questions, using equations and analysing data. Although these are used in practical activities their role is much wider than that. All lessons have such a skill identified; this skill will also be reflected in the learning activities and often feature in the objectives and outcomes.
- **Working scientifically**. These skills are strongly based on the 'Working Scientifically' aspect of the Programme of Study and are selected where practical activities form part of the lesson. Although students may well be developing and using a number of these skills there is always one in particular that is highlighted. This is designed to make it easier for teachers and students to focus upon particular aspects. Over a sequence of lessons the focus will change so that all are covered over a period of time. Obviously the teacher can select a different focus if their view is that this better serves students' learning needs. However what is less effective is a lesson in which a range of skills are ostensibly targeted but what happens in practice is that the same few (often gathering data and writing conclusions) are emphasised repeatedly.
- **Learner development**. Science has the power to develop a wider range of skills than those which are subject specific; it also draws upon these wider skills. In every lesson one of these is focused upon and reflected in the learning activities, providing an opportunity for the lesson to be placed in the wider context of the development of the student as a learner.

None of these skills are radical or original in nature, either in their form or function. Schools familiar with APP, PLTS or SEAL will recognise many of the components. However what the writing team have done is to present these in a form that is both manageable and integrated with the delivery of content.

The learning cycle

The main part of each lesson plan forms a common sequence as part of a 'learning cycle'. The basic idea behind this can be traced back to an inquiry lesson planning model developed for the Science Curriculum Improvement Study (SCIS) program in the USA, a K-6 science program in the early 1970s. In its original form the learning cycle model had 3 stages (exploration, invention and discovery). The idea was that the teacher would develop the science concept in the second stage, rather than defining it at the outset of the lesson as in the traditional approach. The introduced concept subsequently enables students to incorporate their exploration in the third stage and apply it to new examples. It thus has a strong link to a constructivist model of learning, in which students are challenged to develop ideas rather than being presented with a body of content to accept 'as is'. Many examples of learning cycles have since been developed; one current version is the 5E Learning Cycle, which is used in the new BSCS (Biological Sciences Curriculum Study) science programmes as well as in other texts and materials. The Collins KS3 Science sequence consists of the following stages:

- **Engage**, in which the teacher draws students into thinking about certain ideas. Here a student encounters ideas that will make them want to find out more.
- **Challenge and develop**, in which a student meets something that will challenge their existing understanding. It might be questions, ideas, demonstrations, experiments, etc., that make them realise the inadequacy of a simpler explanation.
- **Explain**, in which students are encouraged and supported to develop a good explanation. This draws upon the previous section and supports students to capture ideas in words or graphically.
- **Consolidate and apply**, where students realise how the new learning is to be consolidated and applied. Real world applications are often drawn upon at this point.
- **Extend**, in which ideas can be extended by students making greater than expected progress.

Throughout, the emphasis is upon students' active learning. Authors have identified what students should be doing to engage with each phase, and the purpose of the component, as well as the nature. This is designed to present the teacher with an open, easily assimilated structure which shows what is intended at each point. A teacher wishing to substitute their own activity will therefore be supported in knowing what it should do to support progress. Similarly a teacher using the plan as it is can see the reasoning behind what they are doing.

Encouraging discussion

Discussion is important for exploring ideas and evidence in science and for developing an understanding of concepts, as well as improving literacy. There is a wide variety of ways of organising small-group discussion. Eight of these are used extensively in the lesson plans:

- **Pair talk** This is easy to organise even in cramped classrooms. It is also ideal to promote high levels of participation and to ensure that the discussions are highly focused, especially if allied to tight deadlines. It can be used in the early stages of learning for students to recall work from a previous lesson, generate questions, work together to plan a piece of writing or take turns to tell a story. Pairs can also be used to work as reading partners with an unfamiliar text. It is also ideal for quick-fire reflection and review, and for rehearsal of ideas before presenting them to the whole class.
- **Pairs to fours** Students work together in pairs – possibly friendship, possibly boy/girl, etc. Each pair then joins up with another pair to explain and compare ideas.
- **Listening triads** Students work in groups of three. Each student takes on the role of talker, questioner or recorder. The talker explains something, or comments on an issue, or expresses opinions. The questioner prompts and seeks clarification. The recorder makes notes and gives a report at the end of the conversation. Another time roles are changed.
- **Envoys** Once groups have carried out a task, one person from each group is selected as an 'envoy' and moves to a new group to explain and summarise, and to find out what the new group thought, decided or achieved. The envoy then returns to the original group and feeds back. This is an effective way of avoiding tedious and repetitive 'reporting back' sessions. It also puts a 'press' on the envoy's use of language and creates groups of active listeners.
- **Snowball** Individuals explore an issue briefly; then pairs discuss the issue or suggest ideas quickly; then double up to fours and continue the process into groups of eight. This allows for comparison of ideas, or to sort out the best, or to agree on a course of action. Finally, the whole class is drawn together and a spokesperson for each group of eight feeds back ideas.
- **Rainbow groups** This is a way of ensuring that students are regrouped and learn to work with a range of others. After small groups have discussed together, students are given a number or colour. Students with the same number or colour join up, making groups comprising representatives of each original group. In their new group, students take turns to report back on their group's work and perhaps begin to work on a new,

combined task.

- **Jigsaw** A topic is divided into sections. In 'home' groups of four or five, students allocate a section each, and then regroup into 'expert' groups. In these groups, they work together on their chosen area, then return to original 'home' groups to report back on their area of expertise. The 'home' group is then set a task that requires the students to use the different areas of 'expertise' for a joint outcome. This requires advance planning, but is a very effective speaking and listening strategy as it ensures the participation of all students.
- **Spokesperson** Each group appoints a spokesperson. The risks of repetition can be avoided if:
  - one group gives a full feedback, and others offer additional points if not covered;
  - each group is asked in turn to offer one new point until every group 'passes';
  - groups are asked to summarise their findings on A3 sheets which are then displayed – the class is invited to compare and comment on them.

From: Literacy in Science, DfES © Crown copyright 2004

Starter and plenary toolkit

Authors have drawn on an varied selection of learning strategies, bringing ideas from lessons they have given or observed themselves, and drawing extensively from the following list:

- **Silent animation** Show students a short video clip without sound and ask them to say what they think is happening. They could either suggest the ideas or do a 'voice over' for it.
- **Ideas hothouse** Ask students to work in pairs to list points about what they know about a particular idea. Then ask the pairs to join together into 4s and then 6–8s to discuss this further and to come up with an agreed list of points. Ask one person from each group to report back to the class.
- **Where's the answer?** As students enter the room, give them a card with a word written on it. Then ask a question, ask them if they think they are the answer and why.
- **What's in the picture?** Have a complex picture such as the water cycle or a photo of an industrial process concealed by rectangles, each of which can be removed in turn. Ask for suggestions as to which tile should be removed and what the partially revealed graphic shows. Encourage speculation and inference; ask for suggestions as to which tile should go next and continue until a full explanation has been produced.
- **Learning triangle** At the end of a lesson ask students to draw a large triangle with a smaller inverted triangle that just fits inside it (so they have four triangles). In the outer three ask them to think back over the lesson and identify (and write in the respective triangles):
  - Something they've seen
  - Something they've done
  - Something they've discussed
  - Then to add in the central triangle: something they've learned
- **Heads and tails** Ask each student to write a question about something from the topic on a coloured paper strip and the answer on another colour. In groups of 6–8, hand out the strips so that each pupil gets a question and an answer. One student reads out their question. The student with the right answer then reads it out, followed by their question.
- **What do I know?** Ask students to each write down one thing about the topic they are sure of, one thing they are unsure of and one thing they need to know more about, being specific. Ask them to work in groups of 5–6 to agree on group lists, ask each group to say what they decided and agree as a class about what they are confident about, what they are less sure of and what things they want to know more about. This is a good way towards the end of a topic of identifying topics for revision.
- **Freeze frame** Ask students to create a 'freeze frame' of an idea in the topic. This involves 3–4 pupils arranging themselves as static image and other pupils to suggest what it represents.
- **The big ideas** Ask students to write down three ideas they learnt during the topic. Then ask them to share their facts in groups and to compile a master list of facts, with the most important at the top. Ask for ideas to be shared and find out which other group(s) agreed.
- **Ask me a question** Ask students to write a question about something from the topic and then a mark scheme for the answer. Encourage them to come up with ones worth more than 1 or 2 marks and to try out their questions on one another.
- **Hot seat** Ask each student to think up a question, using material from the topic. Select someone to put in the hot seat, ask students to ask their question and say at the end whether the answer is correct or incorrect.

Assessment of learning

There is a need for teachers to be able to assess the effectiveness of the learning and, indeed, for students to assess their own progress. This needs to be done for three reasons:

- Teachers need to gauge the effectiveness of a lesson, or sequence of lessons, to judge what the next steps should be.
- Student progress needs to be reported upon, both for accountability purposes but also to inform a whole school perspective on providing challenge and intervention.
- Teachers need to be able to assess whether the design of the lessons was effective for the next time they teach it.

This has, of course, been done previously using a system of levels. When the 2013 Programme of Study was published, it contained no level descriptors and the DfE indicated that it was dropping this calibration of progress. This doesn't mean that schools are not expected to assess progress, use it to plan next steps in learning or report on how individuals are doing. At the time of publication, levels are still being widely used, though this is likely to change as KS2 outcomes move to a new reporting system, GCSE outcomes move to a new set of grades and schools gain confidence in assessing progress.

Trajectories of Progress

Progress in KS3 Science can be represented by Trajectories of Progress based on what individual students need to achieve to be 'making good progress'. The three differentiated outcomes in each lesson plan (and the three coloured levels in the student book) correspond to three model trajectories for lower, average and higher attaining students.

An average student who studies the materials, encounters the ideas, tries the assessment activities and gains 40-70% of the marks is deemed to be progressing well. The materials enable the teacher to gather evidence to this effect, report accordingly and plan subsequent lessons effectively. Students gaining full (or close to full) marks may need additional challenge; those scoring half marks or under may need intervention.

However, schools may be using tracking systems still based on levels and it may be that data from the materials in these resources has to be used to support this. As a rule of thumb, assessment data from the books can be used to inform a levels based system as follows:

	Old NC level	KS3			KS4	
		Book 1	Book 2	Book 3	Yr 10	Yr 11
		10	10	10	10	A*
Student responses to broad range of assessment evidence, including Applying your ideas activities and end of topic Questions:		9	9	9	9	A
		8	8	8	8	B
		7	7	7	7	C
		6	6	6	6	D
Higher ToP: scores above 70%	**5**	5	5	5	5	**E**
Average ToP: scores 40–70%	**4**	4	4	4	4	**F**
Lower TOP: scores below 40%	**3**	3	3	3	3	**G**

FIGURE 1 Trajectory of Progress (ToP) the Collins Key Stage 3 Science progress tracking system

The Collins KS3 Science scheme has a number of assessment devices available to students and teachers. As well as questions in each spread which will give rise to written and spoken outcomes, there are also:

- **What you should already know** summarises ideas that students will have met previously at the start of each chapter. These provide an opportunity for discussions around prior learning so that the teacher can gauge what is already understood and plan teaching accordingly.
- **Applying your ideas** sections near the centre of each chapter. These provide an opportunity for students and teachers to assess how well key ideas from the earlier part of the topic has been mastered. The Teacher Guide suggests how additional support can be provided if responses are not as good as expected.

- **Checking progress** sections at the end of each chapter showing how the key ideas progress. This supports students in assessing their own progress and targeting areas they need to focus on. The teacher could get students to suggest why they've assessed themselves as they have.
- **Questions** at the end of each chapter, with a balance of style and focus. The styles of questions include objective test questions, short written answers and longer responses. The focuses include knowledge & understanding, application and evaluation. This means that responses can be analysed against these criteria as well as against area of content.

1.1 Introduction

When and how to use these pages

The Introduction in the Student Book indicates some of the ideas and skills in this topic area that students will already have met from KS2 or from previous KS3 work, and provides an indication of what they will be studying in this chapter. *Ideas you have met before* is not intended to be a comprehensive summary of all the prior ideas, but rather to point out a few of the key ones and to support the view that scientific understanding is progressive. Even though students might be meeting contexts that are new to them, they can often use existing ideas to start to make sense of them.

In this chapter you will find out indicates some of the new ideas that the chapter will introduce. Again, it isn't a detailed summary of content or even an index page; its purpose is more to act as a 'trailer' and a way of generating interest among students.

The outcomes, then, will be recognition of prior learning that can be built on and stimulation of students' interest in finding out more.

There are a number of ways these two pages can be used. You might, for example:

- Use the *Ideas you have met before* as the basis for a revision lesson as you start the first new topic.
- Use *Ideas you have met before* as the centre of spider diagrams, to which students can add examples, experiments they might have done previously or things they found interesting.
- Make a note of any unfamiliar/difficult terms and return to these in the relevant lessons.
- Use ideas from *In this chapter you will find out* to ask students questions such as:
  - Why is this important?
  - How could it be used?
  - What might we be doing in this topic?

Overview of the chapter

In this chapter, students will learn about the structure and function of specialised plant and animal cells, organisation in multicellular organisms, different types and adaptations of unicellular organisms and how plants and humans are adapted to reproduce. They will explore linked processes, including diffusion, pollination, seed dispersal, menstruation and fertilisation. They will consider environmental factors in discussing the role of insects and reasons for their demise.

This chapter offers opportunities for students to become familiar with the use of microscopes. They are encouraged to use 3-D models to explain the structures of different cell types. They will plan to collect evidence and present data on pollen-tube growth and evaluate the effectiveness of seed-dispersal mechanisms.They will explore validity and reliability of evidence in several contexts, including how different substances affect the developing foetus. They will discuss advantages and disadvantages of adapations in plants, encouraging reasoning, analysis and evaluation.

Obstacles to learning

Students may need extra guidance with the following terms and common misconceptions:

- **Nucleus** A common misconception is that the nucleus in a cell is the same as the nucleus of an atom.
- **Pollination and fertilisation** These may be used interchangeably by students to mean the same process.
- **Seed dispersal** Students may think that this only occurs by wind. They may also get confused between seeds and pollen.
- **Puberty** Students may think this consists of set changes at particular times.
- **Growth** A common misconception is that cells get bigger and bigger.

	Topic title	Overarching objectives
2	Historical ideas about living things	Cells as the fundamental unit of living organisms, including how to observe and record cell structure using a light microscope
3	Comparing plant and animal cells	Cells as the fundamental unit of living organisms, including how to observe and record cell structure using a light microscope The functions of the cell wall, cell membrane, cytoplasm, nucleus, vacuole, mitochondria and chloroplasts The similarities and differences between animal and plant cells
4	Describing cells	The functions of the cell wall, cell membrane, cytoplasm, nucleus, vacuole, mitochondria and chloroplasts The similarities and differences between animal and plant cells
5	Understanding unicellular organisms	The structural adaptations of some unicellular organisms
6	Understanding diffusion	The role of diffusion in the movement of materials in and between cells Diffusion in liquids and gases driven by differences in concentration
7	Understanding organisation in multicellular organisms	Hierarchical organisation of multicellular organisms: from cells to tissues to organs to systems to organisms
9	Comparing flowering plants	Reproduction in plants, including flower structure, wind and insect pollination
10	Knowing how pollination leads to fertilisation	Reproduction in plants, including flower structure, wind and insect pollination, fertilisation
11	Understanding the challenges facing pollinators	The importance of plant reproduction through insect pollination in human food security
12	Understanding how seeds are dispersed by the wind	Reproduction in plants, including seed and fruit formation and dispersal
13	Understanding how fruits disperse seeds	Reproduction in plants, including seed and fruit formation and dispersal, including quantitative investigation of some dispersal mechanisms
14	Understanding the male reproductive system	Reproduction in humans (as an example of a mammal), including the structure and function of the male and female reproductive systems
15	Understanding the female reproductive system and fertility	Reproduction in humans (as an example of a mammal), including the structure and function of the male and female reproductive systems, menstrual cycle (without details of hormones), gametes, fertilisation, gestation and birth
16	Learning about changes in puberty	Reproduction in humans (as an example of a mammal), including the menstrual cycle (without details of hormones)
17	Learning how a foetus develops	Reproduction in humans (as an example of a mammal), fertilisation, gestation and birth
18	Understanding factors affecting a developing foetus	Reproduction in humans (as an example of a mammal), to include the effect of maternal lifestyle on the foetus through the placenta

1.2 Historical ideas about living things

Lesson overview

Learning objectives

- Summarise some historical ideas about living things.
- Explain how evidence can change ideas.
- Select evidence to support or disprove ideas.

Learning outcomes

- Describe what people used to think about living things and how their ideas changed. [O1]
- Describe how early experiments were carried out and how new evidence changed people's ideas. [O2]
- Consider the quality of the evidence in different investigations and how good evidence can be used to refute or support ideas. [O3]

Skills development

- Thinking scientifically: understand how theories develop
- Working scientifically: interpret evidence
- Learner development: ask questions

Resources Worksheet 1.1.2 (the final page copied onto card)

Common misconceptions Not all living things are made from cells.

Key vocabulary organism, conclusion, microscope, cell, evidence

Teaching and learning

Engage

- Introduce the students to the theory of 'spontaneous generation', first proposed by Aristotle (see the Student Book), and ask them to **discuss** what investigation(s) they could carry out to prove or disprove this theory. Ask them to **consider** what evidence they would find from their investigations. How would they make this evidence reliable? Collect feedback and discuss their ideas. Is it harder to prove or disprove the theory through their investigations? [O1&3]

Challenge and develop

- Show the experimental set-up carried out by Redi (Figure 1.1.2b in the Student Book). Ask the students to **discuss** what Redi set out to do and what he found out using the questions in the Student Book, and to **identify** different aspects of his investigation. [O2]
- Ask them to **suggest** why people still believed in the spontaneous generation theory for 200 years afterwards, despite the evidence from Redi's investigation. Establish that evidence needs to be reliable in order to support or refute a theory, and discuss why the evidence from Redi's investigation was not reliable. [O2&3]
- Tell the students about the Pasteur investigation 200 years after Redi. Ask them to **compare** and **contrast** the two investigations. A range of questions about the nature of the investigations could be asked, such as 'What scientific question was being investigated?', 'What was the independent variable in the investigations?', 'Which variables were being controlled to make the test fair?' [O2&3]
- Show the students a timeline of the development of the microscope (Figure 1.1.2c in the Student Book). Discuss the impact of the microscope on ideas about living things. [O1&2]

Explain

- Ask the students to **complete** their own timeline of ideas, with annotations to **explain** the evidence that changed people's ideas using the Student Book to help. [O1&2]

Consolidate and apply

- **Pair talk** Ask the students to use the evidence cards from Worksheet 1.1.2 to **decide** which evidence can be used to support the theory of spontaneous generation, and which evidence refutes the theory. [O2&3]

  Higher-attaining students could **rank** the evidence in order of strength and **justify** their ideas.

Extend

- Ask students able to progress further which of the scientific studies they have learned about today had the most impact on ideas about living things and why. [O1, 2&3]

Plenary suggestions

Summarise learning Ask the students to work in pairs. Providing at least one example, one person tells their partner how they have met all the learning outcomes.

Answers to Student Book questions

1. a) support b) support c) disprove
2. For example swallows emerging from rafters; baby owls flying out of barns; woodlice coming out of wood
3. Does dead meat produce flies?
4. He used the same amount of dead meat; jars of the same size; left them for the same amount of time.
5. The sealed jars did not produce flies; if the theory had been correct, all the jars would have produced flies.
6. Life was only found in the bottles that had been left open to the air; life had come in from the air, not from the broth.
7. Pasteur's; because he used many bottles and kept them for over a year; this makes his investigation more reliable. He also had bottles especially made, so there was no chance of any air getting in.
8. People had believed in spontaneous generation for a long time; ideas are hard to change. Also Redi had carried out only one investigation, so the evidence was not very reliable.
9. We have discovered that living things are very complex; we have begun to understand how organisms work and how cells work. (This has been used to make discoveries about how to cure different cancers.)

Answers to Worksheet 1.1.2

1. a) cards 1, 5 and 6 b) cards 2, 3, 4 and 7
2. 1 Y People would think the corn stacks produced the mice.
   2 N If spontaneous generation were true, the broth would have produced bacteria.
   3 N When lambs are born, people would see them as coming from the mothers.
   4 N Cells are very complicated and couldn't just come from inanimate objects.
   5 Y People thought the eels could have come from the pools.
   6 Y People thought the dead meat produced the flies.
   7 N The dead meat should have produced the flies if the theory is true.
3. a) *Accurate* – the evidence is close to the truth.
   Valid – the evidence has been produced by a fair test and answers the scientific question being asked.
   Reliable – you can trust the evidence because the same results are given by many repeats.

   b)

	Accurate?	Valid?	Reliable?
1	Y	N	N
2	Y	Y	N
3	Y	Y	Y
4	Y	Y	Y
5	Y	N	N
6	Y	N	N
7	Y	N	N

   c) Card 1 describes the least reliable and valid evidence. To improve the quality of the evidence, several corn stacks should be tested, making sure they are all the same and there is nothing else but corn in them to start with. To prove the corn has made the mice, the stacks should be sealed so nothing can get in or out.

1.3 Comparing plant and animal cells

Lesson overview

Learning objectives

- Develop models to explain the differences between animal cells and plant cells.
- Record evidence using a microscope.
- Communicate ideas about cells effectively using scientific terminology.

Learning outcomes

- Label an animal cell and a plant cell. [O1]
- Compare and contrast the similarities and differences between plant cells and animal cells, and use a microscope independently to make observations. [O2]
- Describe the functions of the nucleus, cell membrane, mitochondria, cytoplasm, cell wall, vacuole and chloroplast. [O3]

Skills development

- Thinking scientifically: use models
- Working scientifically: record evidence
- Learner development: communicate effectively

Resources materials and equipment as detailed in the Technician's notes; overhead projector; Worksheet 1.1.3a; Worksheet 1.1.3b; Practical sheet 1.1.3a; Practical sheet 1.1.3b; Technician's notes 1.1.3

Common misconceptions Cells are two-dimensional, inert objects. The nucleus of a cell and the nucleus of an atom are the same.

Key vocabulary nucleus, cytoplasm, cell membrane, mitochondria, cell wall, vacuole, chloroplast

Teaching and learning

Engage

- Show the students the images of plant and animal cells in Figures 1.1.3a and b in the Student Book. Ask them to **identify** three facts about each image. [O1]
- Demonstrate how to use a microscope. Ask the students to **make observations** of a variety of different objects using the microscope – for example newspaper print, hair, a coin, a paper towel (see Technician's notes 1.1.3). Ask them to **discuss** their observations and the importance of the microscope in scientific discoveries. [O2]

Challenge and develop

- Ask half the students to follow the instructions on Practical sheet 1.1.3a and make up a slide of a cheek cell; ask the other half to follow instructions on Practical sheet 1.1.3b to make up a slide of an onion cell. Ask them to draw accurate diagrams of both types of cells on their sheets. [O1&2]
- Refer the students back to the different parts of the animal cell and the plant cell from the Student Book. Ask them to **relate** these to the corresponding parts of the diagrams of their slides, and to label them. If possible, link up a microscope to the overhead projector and point out the different parts from the prepared slides. [O1&2]
- Provide half of the students with the descriptions of different parts of an animal cell, and the other half with the descriptions of plant cells, found on Worksheet 1.1.3a. Ensure that they are clear about what the descriptions say. Provide the students with a range of different materials to select from. Ask them, in pairs, to **make a model** of their cells from the descriptions. [O1&2]
- **Pair swap** Ask one from each pair to join with someone who made the other model. Each should **explain** their model to the other. [O1&2]

Explain

- Select different students to show their cell models and to **explain** each part to the class. They should be able to **justify** why they chose certain materials to represent particular parts. Ask them to **identify** the features in a plant cell that are not in an animal cell. [O1&2]

Consolidate and apply

- Provide the students with Worksheet 1.1.3b. Ask lower-attaining students to complete task 1, **naming** each structure of the cell. Middle-attaining students should complete tasks 1 and 2. [O1]
- Higher-attaining students need to complete all three tasks **explaining** how the three cell parts are adapted to carry out their particular jobs. [O2&3]

Extend

- Ask the students to **research** how cells evolved in the first place. They should **prepare** a one-minute talk to deliver to the class. [O3]

Plenary suggestions

What am I? Play 'What am I?' Think of a part of a cell, and select students to provide a question to guess the part of the cell. Only 'yes' or 'no' answers can be given.

Answers to Student Book questions

1. under a microscope
2. yes
3. nucleus; mitichondria
4. oxygen; glucose; water, carbon dioxide; urea
5. cell wall; vacuole
6. plant cell; it has more structures in it
7. To provide them with extra strength and protection – many animals eat plants; to help with photosynthesis – chloroplasts absorb light.

Answers to Worksheet 1.1.3b

1. Refer to Figures 1.1.3b and 1.1.3c in the Student Book.
2. N = nucleus; C = chlorophyll; V = vacuole; C = cytoplasm; C = cell wall; C = cell membrane
   three structures in both: cell membrane; cytoplasm; nucleus
3. a) Very thin to help small substances transfer in and out quickly.
   b) Made of cellulose to give it strength.
   c) Packed with chlorophyll, which absorbs sunlight.

1.4 Describing cells

Lesson overview

Learning objectives

- Classify specialised cells as animal cells or plant cells.
- Describe different specialised animal cells and plant cells.
- Explain the structure and function of specialised cells using models.

Learning outcomes

- Identify different specialised animal and plant cells. [O1]
- Describe the structure of specialised cells. [O2]
- Use models to explain the function of specialised cells and how their structure enables them to do their job. [O3]

Skills development

- Thinking scientifically: use models
- Working scientifically: develop explanations
- Learner development: collaborate effectively

Resources selection of materials for making specialised cells – including red jelly, ready-made colourless jelly, cling film, cardboard boxes, lots of elastic bands, balloons, straws, scissors, sticky tape; Worksheet 1.1.4

Common misconceptions All plant cells contain chloroplasts. Cytoplasm is only found around the nucleus. In a nerve cell the cytoplasm extends the length of the axon.

Key vocabulary nerve cell, muscle cell, sperm cell, egg cell, root hair cell

Teaching and learning

Engage

- Show the students photographs or a video clip showing the wide range of different types of cell in the living world. Encourage students to **ask** questions about the variety of life on the planet. [O1]
- **'Pictionary'** Working in pairs, one student faces the board and the other has their back to the board. Display key words and ask those students facing the board to draw a picture of the word. The other student has to **guess** what it is. When one pair has guessed correctly, move on to the next word. This will help to recap ideas from the previous lesson. [O1&2]

Challenge and develop

Group the students in ability pairs.

- Provide each pair with the cards from Worksheet 1.1.4 illustrating different specialised cells. Ask them to **sort** the cards into animal cells and plant cells. Collect feedback and discuss the features that helped them with their classification. Then provide the pairs with the description cards and ask them to **match** these to the pictures of the specialised cells. [O1&2]
- Then provide students with the explanation cards for each of their specialised cells. Ask them to **match** them to the correct cells. Go through the answers. [O3]
- Set up tables with suitable materials for making models of specialised cells. Ask each pair of students to select one specialised animal cell and one specialised plant cell, according to the list below, and use the descriptions and explanations, as appropriate, to **make a model** of the two cells. [O2]

  Lower-attaining students – choose from red blood cell, egg cell, leaf cell

  Middle-attaining students – choose from ciliated epithelial cell, sperm cell, leaf cell

  Higher-attaining students – choose from muscle cell, nerve cell, root hair cell.

Explain

- **Pairs to fours** Link one pair with another, from different abilities. Now, working in groups of four, students should **explain** their models to each other, **describing** where the main structures are and how the cell is adapted to carry out its job. Select different pairs to **give explanations** about the other pairs' models. [O2&3]

Consolidate and apply

- Using the cards from Worksheet 1.1.4 with the diagrams of specialised cells, ask pairs of students to **rank** the cells in order from the most specialised to the least specialised. Can they **suggest** why some cells have to be more specialised than others? What implications might this have in terms of replacing these cells? [O1, 2&3]

Extend

- Provide students able to progress further with descriptions of other specialised cells, provided as 'Extension' on page 1 of Worksheet 1.1.4. Ask them to draw a labelled diagram of the cell from the description. They should **explain** how the structure helps the cell to carry out its job. This could be peer-assessed. [O3]

Plenary suggestions

Model work Select a range of models made by the class. Hold up each in turn and ask the students to **identify** the name of the cell, **describe** its essential features and **explain** how it is specialised to carry out its job.

Answers to Student Book questions

1. a) in the eye b) in the ear c) in the skin
2. sperm cell; nerve cell; muscle cell
3. a) nerve cell b) muscle cell c) sperm cell
4. *Leaf cell* has: many chloroplasts to capture sunlight; a thin cell membrane to allow water and carbon dioxide to enter quickly; a large vacuole to help the cell maintain its shape.

   Root hair cell has: an extended cytoplasm to enable as much water as possible to be collected; a large surface area for the extension; no chloroplasts so that maximum amount of water can be absorbed; a large vacuole to store water and sugars.
5. *Wind-transferred*: is very small and light so it can be blown long distances in the wind; has a hard, smooth coat for protection.

   Insect-transferred: has a spiky or sticky surface to stick to the fur of insects; is larger so it doesn't easily fall off insects.
6. Sperm cell; every part is highly specialised – head is large for genetic material; contains special enzymes for penetrating the egg cell; middle is packed with mitochondria for energy; tail is specially developed for swimming; no unnecessary additional structures.

Answers to Worksheet 1.1.4

1. a) *animal cells* A, B, C, D, G, H; *plant cells* E, F

   b) A5; B6; C2; D1; E3; F7; G4, H8
2. A8; B5; C7; D3; E2; F1; G6; H4
3. a) Any sensible order – for example, G, C, D, A, F, H, B, E

   b) Any sensible answer – for example, the nerve cell is more specialised than the root hair cell because it has a long extension with many more parts to it, such as the fatty insulation; the extension of the root hair is just an extension of the cytoplasm with no extra parts.

1.5 Understanding unicellular organisms

Lesson overview

Learning objectives

- Recognise different types of unicellular organisms.
- Describe differences in unicellular organisms.
- Compare and contrast features of unicellular organisms.

Learning outcomes

- Describe unicellular organisms – including yeast, bacteria, euglena, a paramecium and an amoeba – as being either prokaryotes or eukaryotes. [O1]
- Describe the functions of specialised parts of different unicellular organisms. [O2]
- Explain how different structures help organisms to survive. [O3]

Skills development

- Thinking scientifically: use units and nomenclature
- Working scientifically: develop explanations
- Learner development: collaborate effectively

Resources large poster paper and crayons; Worksheet 1.1.5

Common misconceptions All unicellular organisms are called bacteria.

Key vocabulary yeast, prokaryote, eukaryote, bacterium, protozoa

Teaching and learning

Engage

- Show the students images of fossils of early bacteria found in rocks. Encourage them to **ask questions** about the image. Discuss evidence like that found in rocks 3.8 million years ago, leading to the belief that life started with single-celled organisms. Introduce what is meant by a 'single-celled' organism. [O1]
- Show the students images of a simple prokaryote and a eukaryote (for example the bacterium and amoeba shown in Figures 1.1.5a and b in the Student Book). Ask them to **identify** similarities and differences between these two types of single-celled organism and see if they can **work out** how unicellular organisms are classified. Introduce the terms *prokaryote* and *eukaryote* and apply them accordingly to the images. Can students **identify** which is the first form of life from this classification? [O1]

Challenge and develop

- Group the students in ability groups of four. Give each group descriptions and diagrams of different unicellular organisms from Worksheet 1.1.5, choosing the organisms depending on each group's ability (see below). Ask each group to carry out tasks 1 and 2 from the worksheet for the organisms they have been given. [O1]
  - Lower-attaining students should be given images and descriptions of a bacterium and an amoeba (description cards 2 and 4). Ask them to **match** the description to the diagram (task 1). Then ask them to **complete** task 2 for these two organisms, **identifying** any interesting features in each organism that will help to classify it and features that help it to survive. [O1&2]
  - Middle-attaining students should be given images and descriptions of a euglena, a bacterium and an amoeba (description cards 2, 3 and 4). Ask them to annotate the diagrams from the descriptions to **explain** different features. [O2]
- Ask higher-attaining students to try task 3 on Worksheet 1.1.5. Ask them to produce their own drawings roughly drawn to scale to show the relative sizes of the different organisms. They can use the information in

the table and the descriptions given on Worksheet 1.1.5. They will need to use large poster paper. Ask them to annotate the diagrams accordingly and to **explain** how they think each of the features helps the organism to survive. [O3]

- Ask the students to swap their diagrams with another group of the same ability to **peer-assess** each other's work. They should add any missing parts and **identify** what the groups have done well and one thing they could improve on in the future. [O1, 2&3]

Explain

- Ask the students to draw up a table, such as this one, order to **compare** and **contrast** the organisms. [O2&3]

Name of organism	Is it a prokaryote or eukaryote?	Does it have a cell wall?	How does it feed?	How does it move?

Higher-attaining students should be able to **explain** how the different structures enable the organisms to survive. [O3]

Consolidate and apply

- Show the students video clips of the different organisms in action, or images of them. Ask them to **identify** each of the organisms and to **describe** three distinctive features of each. [O1, 2&3]

Extend

- **'Top trumps'**. Ask students able to progress further to devise some 'top trump' cards for each of the different organisms they have learnt about in the lesson. They should rate them for: their level of specialisation; how well they can move; how big they are; how easily they can find and absorb food; whether they are a prokaryote or a eukaryote; how likely they are to survive. [O3]

Plenary suggestions

Summarising Ask the students to write a paragraph to **summarise** what they have learnt about unicellular organisms. [O1, 2&3]

What am I? Ask the students to take it in turn to think of one unicellular organism. The rest of the class **ask questions**, which can only be answered by 'yes' or 'no', to find out what the organism is. They should try and guess within fewer than ten questions. [O1, 2&3]

Answers to Student Book questions

1. algae; protozoa; yeasts
2. They may have either tails, tiny hairs and/or chloroplasts.
3. Bacterium is a prokaryote; amoeba is a eukaryote.
4. Eukaryotes have a nucleus inside a membrane; prokaryotes do not.
5. Euglena contains chloroplasts to make its own food using sunlight; it has a tail to help it move towards the light.
6. The use of a tail enables euglena to move faster and manoeuvre more quickly.
7. *Similarities*: all have a cell membrane; all have cytoplasm; all have mitochondria; all contain genetic material; all can live independently

   Differences: some have a nuclear membrane (eukaryotes); others do not (prokaryotes); some have chloroplasts; some have cilia or a flagella, or move with flowing cytoplasm; some are very big; others are vey small; some contain protective slime layers

Answers to Worksheet 1.1.5

1. A3; B4; C5; D1; E2
2. a) *bacterium*: has no nucleus; *yeast*: has a nucleus and fixed spherical shape; *euglena*: has cilia around the cell membrane; *paramecium*: can change its shape and has a nucleus; *amoeba*: contains chloroplasts

   b) *bacterium*: has a layer of slime around the outside cell wall; *yeast*: has a cell wall; *euglena*: has a flagella (tail) so it can swim; *paramecium*: cilia help it to move and find food; *amoeba*: cytoplasm flows, enabling it to move
3. Appropriate diagrams correctly labelled and drawn to these scaled sizes: bacterium 5 mm; yeast 1 cm; euglena 5 cm; paramecium 20 cm; amoeba 50 cm

1.6 Understanding diffusion

Lesson overview

Learning objectives

- Describe the process of diffusion and its relation to the cell.
- Plan a fair test investigation to explore the factors affecting diffusion.
- Explain how the different factors speed up or slow down diffusion.

Learning outcomes

- Recognise that diffusion is the process by which materials move in and out of cells. [O1]
- Identify key variables to control, measure and change to investigate factors affecting diffusion. [O2]
- Explain the factors that affect diffusion. [O3]

Skills development

- Thinking scientifically: ask questions
- Working scientifically: design investigations/record evidence
- Learner development: collaborate effectively

Resources A3 paper; materials and equipment as detailed in the Technician's notes; perfume spray; Worksheet 1.1.6; Practical sheet 1.1.6a; Practical sheet 1.1.6b; Practical sheet 1.1.6c; Technician's notes 1.1.6

Common misconceptions Diffusion occurs only in liquids, not in solids and gases.

Key vocabulary glucose, diffusion, surface area, volume

Teaching and learning

Engage

- Carry out the following demonstrations to show the process of diffusion. Ask students to **record** their observations after each demonstration. [O1]
  - Spray some perfume in one corner of the room. Ask the students to put up a hand when they can smell it.
  - Use a 2-litre beaker or container of warm water. Add a crystal of potassium permanganate. Ask the students to draw and **describe** what they see.
  - Demonstrate removing a small disc from the centre of an agar plate, using a pipette. Put some food colouring in the middle gap.
- Ask the students to **explain** to a partner what is happening in all the demonstrations, and **describe** the similarities and differences. Collect feedback from selected pairs and discuss their ideas. [O1]
- Introduce the term *diffusion* as being the process in which molecules move from an area of high concentration to one of lower concentration, until the concentrations are equal. Use the Student Book here. Ask the students 'What do you predict will eventually happen to the perfume, potassium permanganate and food colouring?' [O1]
- Ask the students to **link** diffusion to their learning about cells. Discuss ideas about the speed of diffusion and its importance to the survival of the cell. Discuss how oxygen, glucose, nutrients and minerals enter the cell, and how carbon dioxide, urea and other waste leave the cell. [O1]

Challenge and develop

- **Group work** Group the students in ability groups of four. Students will **plan** and **carry out** three investigations to examine the effect of heat, concentration and type of liquid on the rate of diffusion. Provide each group with Worksheet 1.1.6, preferably copied onto A3, as a planning template. Differentiated practical instructions are provided on the three Practical sheets 1.1.6a, 1.1.6b and 1.1.6c. [O2]

Lower-attaining – provide each group with Practical sheet 1.1.6a, three agar plates, four pipettes, food colouring, methylene blue and potassium permanganate solution. They will also need a ruler and a timer. Ask them to **design** an investigation to find out how different liquids affect the rate of diffusion.

Middle-attaining – provide each group with Practical sheet 1.1.6b, six agar plates, four pipettes, food colouring, water, three small beakers and two 10 ml measuring cylinders. They will also need a ruler and a timer. Ask them to **design** an investigation to find out the effect of concentration on how fast diffusion takes place.

Higher-attaining – provide each group with Practical sheet 1.1.6c, six agar plates, a pipette, three bowls, some food colouring, ice cubes and three thermometers. They will also need a kettle, a ruler and a timer. Ask them to **design** an investigation in which they can demonstrate the effect of temperature on the rate of diffusion.

- Circulate around the groups. Ensure that they have thought carefully about each of the variables and corresponding values. All but lowest-attaining students should **consider** how to obtain reliable and valid evidence. All groups should **make a prediction**; higher-ability groups should use scientific understanding to support their prediction. Ask selected groups to **present** their plans and predictions. [O2]
- Ask the groups to **carry out** their investigations and **record** their results. [O2]

Explain

- Present the findings of each group on the board. Ask students to **describe** any pattern in the results. [O2]
- Ask the students to write an independent explanation of the results for the effect of temperature, size and concentration. [O3]

Higher-attaining students should be able to **use ideas** about particles and energy in their explanations.

Consolidate and apply

- Ask students to apply the ideas from their investigations to **predict** what will happen when a group of yeast cells is placed in a warm environment at 30 °C while another similar group is placed at a temperature of 5 °C. [O1&3]

Ask higher-attaining students to **explain** why many millions of bacteria are found in the small intestine of humans and not in the mouth. They may need some help in understanding how food is different in the mouth and in the small intestine. [O3]

Extend

- Provide students able to progress further with three prepared agar cubes of sides 1 cm, 2 cm and 3 cm, (Technician's notes 1.1.6). Ask them to **calculate** the surface area of each of the cubes and the volumes, and then the surface-area-to-volume ratio. What do they notice about the ratio in relation to the size of the cubes? This links with the third section in the Student Book. Put the cubes in three identical solutions of hydrochloric acid at the same time and ask the students to **observe** what happens. Can they **describe** the pattern of the speed at which diffusion occurs in relation to the size of the cube? How can they **relate** this to their study of unicellular organisms? Why are the majority of unicellular organisms microscopic? [O3]

Plenary suggestions

Summarising Ask the students to write a summary about their learning about diffusion, **explaining** the concept to another person of a similar age who has not studied this before. [O1, 2&3]

Answers to Student Book questions

1. (net) right to left
2. Outline should show animal cell (as in Figure 1.1.5a) with arrows labelled oxygen, water and sugar going from outside into the cell; and arrows labelled carbon dioxide and urea going out from the cell.
3. Two boxes; one with lots of circles (concentrated); only one or two circles in the other (diluted).
4. Temperature; because the particles have more energy.
5. As the size of the cell increases, the surface-area-to-volume ratio decreases:
   1 × 1 × 1: surface area 6; volume 1; ratio 6; 2 × 2 × 2: surface area 24; volume 8; ratio 3; 3 × 3 × 3: surface area 54; volume 27; ratio 2
6. The smaller they are, the higher the surface-area-to-volume ratio; and the faster the rate of diffusion.

1.7 Understanding organisation in multicellular organisms

Lesson overview

Learning objectives

- Define the terms tissues, organs and organ systems.
- Explain the organisational structure in multicellular organisms.
- Compare the strengths and weaknesses of multicellular organisms and single-celled organisms.

Learning outcomes

- Recognise the hierarchy of cell, tissue, organ and organ system; name some common tissues, organs and organ systems in humans. [O1]
- Explain the terms cell, tissue, organ and organ system, and the function of main organ systems in the body. [O2]
- Describe some benefits and disadvantages of multicellular organisms compared to single-celled organisms. [O3]

Skills development

- Thinking scientifically: use nomenclature
- Working scientifically: develop explanation
- Learner development: collaborate effectively

Resources Worksheet 1.1.7, with the second page copied onto card

Common misconceptions Organ systems are independent of each other and do not work together. All animals contain the same organ systems. Plants do not have organ systems.

Key vocabulary tissue, organ, organ system

Teaching and learning

Engage

- Show the students images of a unicellular organism, a sponge, a worm, a fish and a human. Ask them to **rank** the organisms in order of complexity. [O1]
- Ask them to **identify** how the complexity differs between the organisms. [O1]

Challenge and develop

- Use the analogy of a department store to help the students understand how organisation within an organism works. Ask them, working in pairs, to **make connections** between the department store organisation and the organisation of the human body. They should be able to **identify** the following: the department store is the organism; each individual department (e.g. clothing) is analogous to a body system within the organism (such as the nervous system or skeletal system); each type of clothing (e.g. shirts) in a department is analogous to an organ (e.g. brain within the body system); each type of clothing (e.g. casual or formal) is analogous to the tissue within the organ (e.g. white matter or grey matter); one particular shirt is analogous to a specialised cell within the tissue (e.g. nerve cell). [O1]

Explain

- Group the students in ability groups of four. Ask lower- and middle-attaining groups to use the cards from the previous task and correctly group together all the organ systems, their functions, organs, tissues and specialised cells (task 1 on Worksheet 1.1.7). Ask them to write an explanation of how cells 'connect' to tissues, tissues to organs etc. (task 2 on Worksheet 1.1.7). [O1&2]

  Ask higher-attaining groups to **complete** task 3 on Worksheet 1.1.7 to **compare** and **contrast** the organisation of a unicellular organism and a human and **explain** the advantages and disadvantages of each. [O3]

Consolidate and apply

- Ask the students to **describe** the organisation in a plant– can they **identify** different organs, tissues and specialised cells? [O1&2]

Extend

- For students able to progress further, return to the images used at the start of the lesson. Ask them to **research** the organ systems of each of the different organisms and **compare** them. Can they **conclude** whether all organisms have different forms of the same organ systems, or are some missing from more simple organisms? Which are the most vital organ systems for multicellular organisms? [O1&2]

Plenary suggestions

Devising analogies Ask the students to devise a different analogy to **explain** the organisation in a human, and also to describe how the analogy works and where it fails. [O1&2]

Answers to Student Book questions

1. For example: lungs – allow oxygen into the body and remove carbon dioxide; stomach – where digestion takes place; eye – enables us to see.
2. The skin is made from many different types of tissue; it has different layers; working together.
3. See answers to Worksheet 1.1.7 (task 1).
4. They are highly successful.
5. Being small carries has advantages – e.g. being able to adapt to a wider range of environments. However, it also has disadvantages – e.g. limited protection.
6. Multicellular organisms can grow to be larger than unicellular organisms; they are able to protect themselves better; they are more efficient at repairing themselves, obtaining food and reproducing; they can move in many more different ways to escape danger and find food.
7. Cells working in colonies could be more effective at catching and digesting food, or at defending themselves.

Answers to Worksheet 1.1.7

1.

Skeletal	To provide support for the organism and enable movement	Muscle cell	Muscle or bone tissues	Joint
Nervous	To send messages and so control movement and behaviour	Nerve cell	Nervous tissue	Brain
Respiratory	To allow oxygen to be absorbed by the blood and carbon dioxide to be removed from the body	Ciliated epithelial cells, alveoli	Lung tissue	Lungs
Digestive	To break down food so the nutrients can be absorbed by the blood	Cells which pass acid into the stomach	Lining of the small intestine	Mouth, stomach, intestines
Excretory	To help remove waste from the body	Sweat glands	Lining of the lungs	Lungs, kidneys, bladder
Reproductive	To make new individuals	Sperm cell, egg cell	Lining of the womb	Ovary, testes
Circulatory	To move blood around the body, delivering nutrients and oxygen, and removing waste from all cells	Red blood cell, white blood cell	Capillaries	Heart

2. a) Similar cells working together are known as tissues – for example, muscle cells work together to make muscle tissue.

   b) Similar tissues work together to make organs – for example, the brain is made of different nervous tissues working together.

   c) Different organs make up an organ system – for example the mouth, stomach and intestines make up the digestive system.

3. *Advantages of multicellular*: can grow bigger; more specialised cells so processes are more efficient; better ability to protect organism; more able to cope with environmental changes; usually live longer; complex functions possible.

   Advantages of unicellular: smaller so fewer resources are needed to survive; easier to reproduce; easier to repair itself if damaged; easier to hide from predators; can be a parasite on other organisms.

   Disadvantages of multicellular: many more resources needed to keep cells alive; harder to reproduce; if one system fails or becomes diseased, the whole organsism can fail; bigger so more difficult to hide from predators.

   Disadvantages of unicellular: can only grow to a restricted size; it's difficult to be protected from predators; can only remain very simple; life span is not long.

1.8 Applying key ideas

The skin is an organ

Objectives

- Extract ideas about the structure of plant cells and animal cells from earlier topics using the context of skin.
- Apply ideas about the adaptations of specialised animal cells using examples from cells in the skin.
- Use ideas and information to explain the structure and differences between multicellular and unicellular organisms.

Outcome

- Making clear and effective responses to questions, indicating understanding and the next steps in learning.

The purpose of this activity is to provide an opportunity to see how successfully students are grasping the key ideas so far. It isn't designed to be used as a formal test – it might be that students work on the questions collectively. It does provide an opportunity for you to look at written work, engage students in discussions and form ideas about progress being made.

The tasks are progressive. Lower-attaining students should be able to tackle the first two or three and higher-attaining students will find the later ones more challenging.

Resources cards of key words relating to cells; highlighters, sticky notes; Worksheet 1.1.8a; Worksheet 1.1.8b

Teaching & learning

Engage

- Challenge the students to think back over the last few lessons and **identify** some of the key ideas they have met. Draw out some responses about these ideas and say that it's important as learners that we develop a sense of our own progress.
- Put the students in groups of six. Provide each group with cards of all the key words relating to cells. Provide a series of closed questions relating to cells. Ask the students to **discuss** responses and agree on the correct key word.
- Ask the students to **organise** the key words into a mind map or categories that link together.

Challenge and develop

- Group the students in threes. Provide them with a set of illustrations of specialised cells and unicellular organisms, cut from Worksheet 1.1.8a. Ask them to **identify** each of the cells or organisms and to add a sticky note to each image to **explain** how it is adapted for its job.
- Ask the students to draw the outline of a human and a plant. They should **organise** the images in appropriate places to show where the cells can be found.

Explain

Ask the students to read *The skin is an organ* in the Student Book. Depending on their ability to **assimilate** text, you may need to adopt strategies such as:

- **Pair work** Using Worksheet 1.1.8b (a copy of the Student Book text) and highlighters, one student extracts key ideas by highlighting key words in the text and the other (with a different-coloured highlighter) highlights any words they don't understand.
- Work with students who have difficulty with reading to support them in decoding the text and accessing the ideas.

Consolidate and apply

- Now ask the students to attempt the tasks in the Student Book. They might do this individually or collaboratively. In each case, encourage them to **record** their ideas.

- Ask the students to **present** their responses to the various tasks, either orally or by displaying their work.

Extend

- The later tasks give opportunities for extension work for those students who are able to progress further.

Plenary

How well did we do? Ask the students for responses to questions such as:

- 'How well were you able to approach those tasks?'
- 'Did we manage to present some high-quality responses?'
- 'Are there some ideas that we need to strengthen in the latter part of this topic?'

Make a note of the responses and provide some overall feedback, indicating ideas that students have grasped effectively and those they may need to develop further.

Likely responses and next steps in learning

1 This task gives students an opportunity to recall the basic structure of a cell. They should be able to correctly identify the cell membrane, cytoplasm and nucleus. If students are struggling, recap the main parts and ask students to find them on their diagrams.

2 This task engages students in contrasting plant cells and animal cells. They should be able to show basic plant cell structures such as the cell wall, chloroplast, vacuole, cell membrane, nucleus, mitochondria and cytoplasm in both types of cell. This checks that the students know which parts are in plant cells and which are in both plant and animal cells. If they are struggling, elicit the names of the different parts of animal and plant cells from the group, and then ask them to apply them to the diagrams.

3 This task increases in challenge by asking the students to begin to explain terms using examples from the text. They should be able to identify an organ as being a group of tissues. The skin is an organ because it consists of epidermis, dermis and hypodermis. They should be able to identify a tissue as being a group of similar cells working together (e.g. the layer of fat cells in the hypodermis tissue). They should be able to describe a specialised cell as a single unit that has special features designed to carry out a particular job (e.g. the cells that store the pigment melanin, the heat receptor cells or the pain receptor cells). If the students are struggling with this, remind them of the department store analogy of what is meant by the terms *tissue* and *organ*. Use more concrete contexts to identify suitable examples, before applying these terms to the skin.

4 This task involves explaining the structure of particular specialised cells. The students should be able to label the three main parts of each cell – the cell membrane, cytoplasm and nucleus. They should be able to draw the basic outline of each these cells, drawing attention to their specialised features. They can use any of the speciailsed cells described in the skin. They should be encouraged to first identify the job of a particular specialised cell and then to draw attention to special features that enable it to do their job.

5 The students should be able to draw a basic bacterial cell and a fungal cell, comparing and contrasting their features. They should realise that paramecium and euglena both have to move to find food. The epidermis of animals and plants is waterproof, so there is little freely available moisture for them to inhabit.

1.9 Comparing flowering plants

Lesson overview

Learning objectives

- Describe the structures and functions of parts in the flowering plant.
- Explain why different plants have such diverse structures.
- Evaluate the differences between wind-pollinated and insect-pollinated plants.

Learning outcomes

- Identify and name the male and female parts of the flowering plant. [O1]
- Explain the differences in structure and function of a range of different flowering plants including wind-pollinated and insect-pollinated ones. [O2]
- Analyse the strengths and weaknesses of wind-pollinated and insect-pollinated plants. [O3]

Skills development

- Thinking scientifically: use nomenclature
- Working scientifically: record evidence
- Learner development: act responsibly

Resources projector; two different insect-pollinated plants; two different wind-pollinated plants; microscopes; scalpels; white tiles; microscope slides; Worksheet 1.1.9

Common misconceptions All plants are either male or female – they can't have both male and female parts.

Key vocabulary anther, filament, pollen, ovary, style, stigma

Teaching and learning

Engage

- Provide the students with Worksheet 1.1.9. The first task shows a diagram of a flowering plant and all the labels. Ask them to **identify** the parts of the diagram and to **describe** the functions of as many parts as they can, from prior learning. [O1]
- Use the Student Book to discuss how plant sexual reproduction evolved from asexual processes in mosses (where plants had to touch each other in order to reproduce) to the first wind-pollinated plants. Show images or video clips of different types of flowers to explore the diversity of different ways that plants have adapted. Explore why some flowers have male and female parts on the same plant, while others have separate male and female plants. [O1&2]

Challenge and develop

- Demonstrate how to dissect a flowering plant, using a projector if possible. Use images in conjunction with the real dissection to explain the different parts of the flowering plant and their functions. [O1&2]
- Group the students in threes. Provide them with two different insect-pollinated plants, two different wind-pollinated plants, microscopes, scalpels, white tiles and microscope slides. Ask the students to **dissect** each of the plants as you have shown. They can take photos or draw and label each dissection. They should draw up their own tables to **compare** each of the different structures in the wind-pollinated and the insect-pollinated plants. [O1&2]
- Ask the students to **discuss** their findings and **review** their ideas. [O1&2]

Explain

- Ask the students to **explain** why insect-pollinated plants are so different from wind-pollinated plants (the need to attract insects using large petals, nectar and scents). [O2]

Higher-attaining students will be able to **explain** about the position of the stamen in relation to the stigma in insect-pollinated flowers (so that pollen can be collected when insects gather nectar). They will also be able to **explain** how the structures of the anther and filament are adapted in wind-pollinated plants to enable the pollen to be effectively removed by the wind. They should be able to **identify** the advantages and disadvantages of each. [O3]

Consolidate and apply

- The second task on Worksheet 1.1.9 shows a range of different plants. Ask the students to **categorise** them into insect-pollinated plants and wind-pollinated plants. They should give reasons for their choices. [O2]
- Ask them to **explain** different adaptations of different insect-pollinated plants and different wind-pollinated plants. They should **identify** how different insect-pollinated plants differ from each other and suggest some reasons; and then do the same for the wind-pollinated plants (task 3 on Worksheet 1.1.9). [O2&3]

Extend

- Students able to progress further can **research** whether insect-pollinated plants or wind-pollinated plants are more highly adapted, **describe** some adaptations and **justify** their ideas on which plants are more successful. [O3]

Plenary suggestions

What am I? One student thinks of a part of a flowering plant. The other students then have to ask questions about what the part might be. Only 'yes' or 'no' answers may be given. [O1&2]

Spot the mistakes Show the students incorrectly labelled flowering plants and ask them to correct the errors. [O1]

Answers to Student Book questions

1. Discuss responses to this question.
2. The insect-pollinated flower has brightly coloured petals and flowers, with the stamen and stigma inside the flower. The wind-pollinated flower has very small flowers and dull, small petals; the stamen and stigma hang outside the petals.
3. The insect-pollinated flower has to attract insects; the bigger the flower, the more insects can visit it. The wind-pollinated flower needs to capture the wind to remove the pollen; so the stamen needs to hang outside the flower; the flower is small because it does not need to attract insects.
4. Some produce perfumes or scents that will attract particular insects; others make nectar for insects to feed on; some make their flowers into structures that resemble parts of the female insect.
5. To attract as many different pollinators as possible; or get reliability from just a few pollinators.
6. *Advantages of wind pollination*: pollen is sure to be dispersed; only small flowers needed so less energy wasted.
   Disadvantages of wind pollination: there's no guarantee that pollen will be transferred to other plants; lots of pollen needs to be made to increase the chances of successful transfer; lots of pollen wasted.
   Advantages of insect pollination: smaller amounts of pollen need to be made; there is a much higher success rate of transferring pollen to other plants.
   Disadvantages of insect pollination: elaborate mechanisms are needed to attract pollinators; if pollinators become endangered or extinct, pollination cannot occur.

Answers to Worksheet 1.1.9

1 Refer to Figure 1.1.9b in the Student Book – *petals* attract insects; *stamen* produces pollen; *stigma* receives pollen; *ovary* keeps the egg cell safe; and it is the place of fertilisation.

2 *Ragweed*: wind-pollinated – has small, insignificant flowers
Umbrella pine: wind-pollinated – pollen is very small and light, and can be released easily into the wind
Sweet pea: insect-pollinated – has a strong perfume smell to attract insects
Grasses: wind-pollinated – flowers hang down in the wind; stamen is on the ouside of the flower
Rapeseed: insect-pollinated – has brightly coloured flowers to attract insects
Passion flower: insect-pollinated – stigma is in a very prominent position to receive pollen from insects; brightly coloured and large petals so insects can land easily.

3 *Similarities in insect-pollinated plants*: the passion flower and the rapeseed have attractive flowers.
Differences in insect-pollinated plants: the stigma of the passion flower protrudes very prominently above the flower, whereas with the rapeseed it is more hidden.
Similarities in wind-pollinated plants: the grass and the ragweed have insignificant flowers.
Differences in wind-pollinated plants: the grass has stamens that hang down from the flower so the pollen can be easily caught by the wind.

1.10 Knowing how pollination leads to fertilisation

Lesson overview

Learning objectives

- Describe the processes of pollination and fertilisation.
- Analyse and present data on the growth of pollen tubes.
- Explain factors that affect the growth of pollen tubes.

Learning outcomes

- Describe how pollen is transferred to the ovary; follow instructions and plot simple data accurately. [O1]
- Explain how pollination leads to fertilisation; draw accurate graphs with lines of best fit where appropriate; describe trends in data. [O2]
- Explain how different factors such as sugar concentration and length of style can affect the length of pollen tubes; draw scales for graphs. [O3]

Skills development

- Thinking scientifically: analyse data
- Working scientifically: present evidence
- Learner development: communicate effectively

Resources A3 paper; graph paper; equipment and materials as detailed listed in the Technician's notes; Worksheet 1.1.10; Practical sheet 1.1.10a; Practical sheet 1.1.10b; Technician's notes 1.1.10

Common misconceptions The terms 'pollination' and 'fertilisation' describe the same process.

Key vocabulary fertilisation, pollen tube

Teaching and learning

Engage

- Show the students images of different types of pollen grains. Ask the students 'Can you predict whether the pollen grains are from insect-pollinated or wind-pollinated plants?'. Ask them to **summarise** the features that provide clues. [O1]
- Ask the students to **devise** five questions about pollen they want to ask and to write these on a sticky note. Come back to these questions at the end of the lesson. [O1]

Challenge and develop

- Show Figure 1.1.10a from the Student Book and ask the students to **explain** how a pollen tube is formed. Discuss how the pollen cell increases its cytoplasm once it lands on the stigma to produce a tube leading to the ovary. If possible, show the students a video clip of what happens when pollen lands on the stigma. Ask them to **identify** the structure called the pollen tube. [O1&2]
- Discuss the differences between the processes of fertilisation and pollination. [O2]
- Group the students in fours. Tell them they are going to **investigate** one of the following questions:
  - How does the concentration of sugar affect the number of pollen tubes formed?
  - Does the length of the style affect the length of the pollen tube formed? (more suitable for higher-attaining students).

  Ask the students to **follow instructions** from either Practical sheet 1.1.10a or Practical sheet 1.1.10b (higher-attaining students). [O1, 2&3]
- Students investigating the concentration of sugar should count the number of pollen tubes grown from pollen from one plant. [O1]

- Students investigating the length of style should be shown how to measure the length of pollen tube from given plants with the correct equipment. They should draw up a table to **compare** the average length of a pollen tube with the length of style. If necessary, the pollen tubes should be grown an hour or two before the lesson so they reach a measurable length during the course of the lesson. [O2&3]
- Discuss what makes a good graph. Ask the students to draw graphs of their data, and to **peer-assess** their graphs using criteria developed from class discussion. They should use, for example, correctly labelled axes with a sensible scale, and **decide** on a bar chart or line graph etc. [O2&3]
- Ask the students to **describe** and **explain** their results. [O3]

Explain

- Provide the students with Worksheet 1.1.10. The first task shows a cross-sectional diagram of a flower. You might want to copy this onto A3 paper. Ask the students to name each part and to annotate the diagram, **explaining** the process of pollination and how it leads to fertilisation, in particular the roles of the anther, stigma, style and pollen tube. They should include factors that affect the process and any adaptations to increase the chance of success of the process. [O1&2]
- Ask the students to share their explanations. Ask them to **read** other students' work and to use sticky labels to **peer-assess**, noting two good things about the explanations and one thing that needs improving.

Consolidate and apply

- Give the students some time to **make improvements** to their explanations and make any alterations.
- Ask the students to complete tasks 2 and 3 on Worksheet 1.1.10. [O2&3]

Extend

- Ask students able to progress further to **research** the methods used by different plants to avoid self-fertilisation and to maximise cross-fertilisation. Ask them to **evaluate** at least three methods, giving strengths and weaknesses. [O3]

Plenary suggestions

What have you learned? Review the questions that the students posed at the start of the lesson. How many can they now answer as a result of their learning?

True or false? Provide the students with ten statements about pollination. Read out the statements one by one, and ask the students to stand up if a statement is true, and to stay seated if it is false.

Answers to Student Book questions

1. *Pollination* is the transfer of pollen; *fertilisation* is the nucleus of a male cell fusing with an egg cell in the ovary.
2. An accurate line graph should be plotted; with a line of best fit.
3. As the sugar concentration increases, the growth of the pollen tube increases; up to a concentration of 15%; after which any increase in sugar concentration inhibits the growth of pollen tubes.
4. *Anomalous*: 15%, 200; 20%, 250 5. 5% = 250; 10% = 350; 15% = 450; 20% = 210
6. axes correctly labelled; correctly plotted points; two accurate lines of best fit
7. Temperature has the greater effect; longer growths are recorded.
8. The data in the effect of sugar concentration experiment is more reliable; the experiment has been carried out three times for each concentration.

Answers to Worksheet 1.1.10

1. A – ovary; B – ovule; C – carpel; D – style; E – stigma; F – pollen tube; G – anther; H – pollen grain; I – filament; J – petal a) anther makes pollen b) stigma captures the pollen c) pollen tube grows down the style to the ovary
2. Graph title: 'A graph to show how the concentration of sugar solution affects the growth of pollen tubes'; *x*-axis label: 'sugar concentration (% glucose); *y*-axis label: 'number of pollen tubes'.
3. a) 30% b) No; the pollen from different flowers needs different concentrations of sugar solution. Students should have identified this in their investigation.

1.11 Understanding the challenges facing pollinators

Lesson overview

Learning objectives

- Describe the role of insects in crop production, using data.
- Explain why bee populations are declining.
- Make suggestions for increasing insect populations, and hence crop production.

Learning outcomes

- Name some insects important in crop production. [O1]
- Explain some causes for CCD population decline in bees. [O2]
- Explain and evaluate methods used to increase insect populations. [O3]

Skills development

- Thinking scientifically: analyse data
- Working scientifically: develop explanations
- Learner development: communicate effectively

Resources news articles about the decline of bees; Worksheet 1.1.11

Common misconceptions Insects serve plants only as pollinators. Insects do not harm plants.

Key vocabulary adapted, colony collapse disorder (CCD), pesticide, insecticide, population

Teaching and learning

Engage

- Ask the students to draw up two columns. In one they should write the benefits of insects to plants, and in the other the problems that insects cause plants. Ask them to **reflect** on prior learning about insect pollination and to **describe** three important aspects. [O1]

Challenge and develop

- Provide the students with Worksheet 1.1.11, which has data on the percentage of crops that are pollinated by bees. Ask them to **present** the data using the correct type of graph and to **describe** what the graph shows. [O1]
- Show the students newspaper headlines or short video clips relating to the decline of the bee. Ask them to **summarise** all the reasons suggested for the decline of insect populations. Students can also refer to the Student Book. Ask them to **make links** with the information from the headlines/video clips and the graph they have drawn. Discuss the consequences of the decline of bees. [O2]
- Group the students in fours. Give them the cards from Worksheet 1.1.11. Ask the groups to **match up** the reasons for decline with the corresponding remedial actions, then to **arrange** the cards in order from the one with the most positive impact to the one with the most negative impact on bee populations. [O2&3]

Explain

- Ask the students to write a magazine article **explaining** the plight of pollinators using information and data from Topic 1.11 in the Student Book and from Worksheet 1.1.11. Set marking criteria for the task – students should:
  - **describe** the importance of the insects and bees as pollinators for crops (1 mark)
  - **describe** the reasons for their decline (1 mark for each point)
  - **explain** what methods are available to restore insect populations (1 mark for each point)

- **explain** what the consequences will be if we don't (1 mark for each point)
- **make decisions** on the most effective methods for restoring populations (1 mark for each point)
- **explain why** they think these are most effective (1 mark for each point). [O2&3]

Consolidate and apply

- Ask the students to read out their magazine articles and encourage the class to **peer-assess** them, using the marking criteria.
- Group the students in different groups of four. Return to the newspaper articles discussed earlier in the lesson. Ask the students to work in their groups and **discuss** the most appropriate actions to take in each scenario. [O3]

Extend

- Ask students able to progress further to imagine they are on an isolated island. They are responsible for growing crops to feed the villagers on the island. How would they manage the land and ensure the health of the insect populations, so that the crops can be successfully and sustainably pollinated? Ask them to draw up a management plan. [O2&3]

Plenary suggestions

True or false Provide the students with ten statements about the role of insects as pollinators and the decline of bees. Read out the statements one by one, and ask the students to stand up if a statement is true, and to stay seated if it is false.

Action planning Alternatively, ask them **identify** the three most important actions the world should take to avoid further loss of insect populations, and the three greatest barriers to carrying out these actions.

Answers to Student Book questions

1. For example, fruit and vegetables such as strawberries, raspberries, cucumbers, blackcurrants, marrows and peas.
2. Because they are specially adapted to collect pollen.
3. The plant species will die out because it cannot reproduce without transferring pollen.
4. Should show: pesticides are used; bees become confused; bees cannot return to the hive; less food and fewer bees; brought back to the hive; hive becomes smaller and weaker; weaker bees are more prone to infection; more bees die.
5. One suggestion is more intensive farming, which reduces the populations of wild flowers, important for nutrients. An alternative cause is the use of pesticides, affecting the ability of the bees to navigate back to the hives and making them weaker, so more prone to attack by infection.
6. Stop using pesticides, which affect the nervous systems of bees; grow more wild flowers on verges and around the crops; only use local hives; clean hives well to prevent spread of disease; increase the number of hives.

Answers to Worksheet 1.1.11

1. Correctly drawn bar graph a) apples and almonds b) grapes and strawberries
2. 1C; 2A; 3D; 4E; 5B
3. The order of the easiest solution to the hardest solution is debatable and several possibilities exist depending on the circumstances. One suggested answer is A, C, D, B, E.

   One solution with high impact would be to ban certain pesticides; this will stop the bees from being affected and increase their immunity to parasites.

   Another would be to allow roadside verges to grow; which would increase the number and variety of wildflowers growing near crops.

1.12 Understanding how seeds are dispersed by the wind

Lesson overview

Learning objectives

- Recognise the variety of different structures shown by different seeds.
- Describe the need for plants to disperse their seed.
- Plan an investigation into seed dispersal by wind.

Learning outcomes

- Describe some ways plants use to disperse their seeds; recognise dispersal methods by the structure of the seeds. [O1]
- Identify different reasons for a plant to disperse its seeds; identify key variables to change, control and measure in their investigation. [O2]
- Explain key variables to change, control and measure; explain how to collect accurate and reliable data in their plan. [O3]

Skills development

- Thinking scientifically: ask questions
- Working scientifically: design investigations
- Learner development: plan progress

Resources hand lenses; Worksheet 1.1.12a; Worksheet 1.1.12b

Common misconceptions Pollination and seed dispersal are the same thing.

Key vocabulary seed dispersal, germinate, independent variable, reliable

Teaching and learning

Engage

- Provide the students with a range of different seeds to examine using a hand lens – include fruits, wind-dispersed seeds, water-dispersed seeds and prickly seeds dispersed by animals. Ask them to draw up a table to **describe** the different characteristics of each seed and how each one might be transported. [O1]
- Ask the students to **summarise** their findings. Discuss why there are different mechanisms for transporting seeds and why it is important for seeds to germinate away from the parent plant. Include ideas relating to competition for light, water and nutrients.
- If possible, show video clips of mechanisms of seed dispersal, including exploding pods. [O1&2]

Challenge and develop

- Show the students different seeds dispersed by the wind, or images of them. Discuss different features of the seeds and draw up a list of their strengths and weaknesses through class **discussion**. Ask the students to **make predictions** about which seeds will be transported the furthest by wind. [O1&2]
- Group the students in fours. Provide each group with a copy of Worksheet 1.1.12a – an investigation planning template. Ask them to **plan** an investigation to answer one of these questions (split between the groups half and half):
  - How does the mass of a seed affect dispersal by the wind?
  - What is the most effective design for a seed dispersed by the wind?
- Encourage the students to **discuss** the success criteria for what makes an effective investigation plan.
- Either provide them with at least five different wind-dispersed seeds to investigate or ask them to make up their own five designs. In the latter case, make sure they are clear about aspects of their design that they

should vary – mass, wingspan or tail mechanisms – and ask them to make up sufficient 'seeds' to test, so that they can **collect** reliable evidence. [O2&3]

Explain

- Ask the groups to swap their plans and to **peer-assess** each other's using the success criteria discussed. Ask them to **identify** all the good points relating to the plan and one target for improvement. [O2&3]
- Provide them with improvement time, and then select one or two groups to **describe** and **explain** different features of their plan. With lower-attaining students, focus on the **identification** of variables; with higher-attaining students, focus on how to **collect** reliable and accurate data. [O2&3]

Consolidate and apply

- Provide students with Worksheet 1.1.12b. This describes a plan for an investigation about seed dispersal, but with several mistakes. Ask the students to work through the tasks listed correcting the mistakes, **assessing the quality** of the plan and making improvements. [O2&3]

Extend

- Students able to progress further should broaden their plan to answer the question 'Which is the most effective means of dispersing plants – wind, water, explosion mechanisms or animals/ insects?' Ask them to write a detailed account of how they would carry out this investigation and how they would collect reliable and valid evidence. [O3]

Plenary suggestions

Designing a 'super seed' Ask the students to **design** a 'super seed' that could be dispersed in many different ways. Ask them to annotate their design to **explain** its features, and give reasons why these features are effective. They should also **summarise** why it is important for plants to disperse seeds. [O1, 2&3]

Answers to Student Book questions

1. *Dandelion* is dispersed by wind; *coconut* by water; *cucumber* by animals.
2. *Dandelion seeds* have parachute structures to help them to glide on the wind. *Coconut seeds* are large, waterproof and able to float; the plants grow near the sea so the seeds can be transported by water. The *cucumber* has seeds inside a fleshy fruit, which can be eaten by animals.
3. The flowers from trees tend to be high up; making it ideal for seeds to be transported by wind; and enabling them to get as far away from the parent tree as possible.
4. *Advantages*: the ground is likely to be fertile; pollinators are already in the area; there is likely to be plenty of sunlight, water and nutrients because the parent tree has survived and reproduced here.

   Disadvantages: increased competition with parent plant for sunlight, water and nutrients; competition for pollinators; easy to catch a disease if the parent plant is affected.
5. the type of seed dispersal
6. The same area is sampled because conditions of light, humidity, temperature and nutrients are likely to be similar; samples are taken at the same time so that weather and seasonal conditions are the same.
7. using a large sample size
8. If plants become endangered, it may be important to know what the best conditions are for ensuring successful dispersal and germination.

Answers to Worksheet 1.1.12b

1. a) Description and values of variables; procedure to change the height; a diagram.

   b) Headings could include 'Independent variable and values'; 'Dependent variable';, 'Control of variables and values'; 'Prediction'.

   c) No; ten different seeds have been used; this has not been controlled.
2. a) Controlling the variables – *size of seed*: use the same size; *type of seed*: use the same type; *throwing the seed*: use a hairdryer on the same setting to supply the 'wind'; *amount of real wind*: do the test indoors.

   b) No; not all the control variables have been controlled.

   c) No; repeat readings at the same heights have not been made.
3. Assess the quality of a student's revised plans according to the criteria discussed.

1.13 Understanding how fruits disperse seeds

Lesson overview

Learning objectives

- Describe how fruits are used in seed dispersal.
- Compare evidence about seed dispersal by wind and by fruit formation.
- Use data to evaluate different seed dispersal mechanisms.

Learning outcomes

- Collect accurate and reliable evidence to answer a scientific question about wind dispersal. [O1]
- Describe the difference between a fruit and a seed, and give many examples of fruits and their seeds. [O2]
- Explain the advantages and disadvantages of different seed dispersal mechanisms. [O3]

Skills development

- Thinking scientifically: consider the quality of evidence
- Working scientifically: record evidence
- Learner development: collaborate effectively

Resources graph paper; for each group of six students – range of fruits; chopping board; knife for fruit dissection; scalpel; paper towels; tweezers; Worksheet 1.1.13

Common misconceptions Parts of the fertilised flower other than the ovary can become fruit.

Key vocabulary fruit, ovary, competition

Teaching and learning

Engage

- Read out a mix of true and false statements about seed dispersal and ask the students to stand up whenever they hear a true statement. [O1]

  Example statements:

  - 'Most plants use the wind to disperse their seeds.' (T)
  - 'Plants need to disperse seeds to improve their chance of survival.' (T)
  - 'Seed dispersal by fruits uses the least amount of energy.' (F)

- Review the terms 'reliable' and 'accurate'. Show the students explanations or provide them with statements to **discuss** as to whether they refer to accuracy or reliability. [O1]

Challenge and develop

- Ask the students to **review** their plans from the previous lesson and identify any further amendments that need to be made. Check that plans are suitable and suggest any amendments before they carry them out. Ask the students to follow their plans and **carry out** their investigations into wind dispersal, **collecting** accurate and reliable evidence. [O1]
- Discuss the students' results and ask them to draw conclusions about which are the most effective seeds to be dispersed by the wind. Ask questions relating to the strength of the evidence collected. Use the terms 'reliable' and 'accurate', and distinguish between them in relation to the students' own data. [O1]
- Group students in sixes. Provide each group with a range of different fruits, with three examples of each. Explain what is meant by the term 'fruit' and describe how fruits are formed. Ask the students to **discuss** the advantages and disadvantages of producing fruits for seed dispersal. Help them to **recognise** that the plant has to use a lot of energy in making a fruit, but that this is offset by the need to produce fewer seeds. [O2&3]

- Provide groups with the equipment to **dissect** each fruit (with appropriate safety warnings) and ask them to establish how many seeds are present in each. They should **record** their results in a table they **devise** themselves. Collect feedback and display the class results. Discuss variations between groups and reasons for these. Discuss how to produce reliable data relating to the number of seeds in each fruit. [O2]

Explain

- Show the students data in Table 1.1.13 in the Student Book on the number of seeds produced by plants that have wind-dispersed seeds. Ask them to write an explanation to **compare** this with their findings from the fruits they have investigated. [O2&3]

Consolidate and apply

- Ask the students to **compare** and **contrast** wind dispersal with fruit formation. They should **explain** reasons for the success of each and **justify** their ideas about which is the more successful method. [O1, 2&3]
- Students can then **complete** the differentiated tasks on Worksheet 1.1.13 according to their ability. [O1, 2&3]

Extend

- Ask students able to progress further to draw up a table to **suggest** the advantages and disadvantages of all the different seed-dispersal mechanisms and to **make predictions** about the average number of seeds likely to be produced from different mechanisms. [O3]

Plenary suggestions

Summarising Ask the students to **summarise** key points to review ideas about fruit formation.

Just a minute Select different students to speak for a minute on the topic of seed dispersal.

Answers to Student Book questions

1. The ovary of the plant after fertilisation.
2. the cauliflower
3. The fruits are eaten by animals; and the seeds are excreted with the animal's faeces; which contains many nutrients useful for growth. So the seed lands in a medium which will help it to germinate; thereby increasing the chance of successful germination.
4. Wind dispersal; to increase the success of germination in the right types of nutrient-rich soil.
5. Any suitable answer with a valid reason.
6. Seeds dispersed by wind produce the most seeds; water is able to transport the seeds the furthest distance from the parent plant.
7. Graphs of 'name of plant' against 'number of seeds'; and 'name of plant' against 'average dispersal distance'.

Answers to Worksheet 1.1.13

1. *Wind dispersal* – anything resembling a dandelion, sycamore helicopter seeds, or any plant with small, light seeds on the outside that the wind can easily catch. The seeds are the small object being carried by the wind; the tissue protecting and covering the seed is the ovary.

   Fruit dispersal – diagram should show a fruit with seeds inside; the fruit labelled as the ovary; the pips as the seeds.
2. a) A suitable scale should be drawn for the graph; the *x*-axis should be the number of seed; the *y*-axis should be the mass of the fruit.

   b) One hypothesis would be the larger the number of seeds, the more massive the fruit. This is because the more seeds there are, the more energy they will need when they germinate; or the more seeds there are, the larger the fruit to attract more animals so the seeds can be dispersed with the minimum amount of energy. The anomalous data is that for the avocado pear.
3. a) The data is not reliable; there is no sample size given for the numbers of seeds examined.

   b) A large sample of seeds needs to be examined (over 100); and a much wider variety of seeds tested

1.14 Understanding the male reproductive system

Lesson overview

Learning objectives

- Describe the structure and function of different parts of the male reproductive system.
- Compare plant and human male reproductive structures.
- Summarise the strengths and weaknesses of the human and plant male reproductive systems.

Learning outcomes

- Name the main parts of the male reproductive system; recognise sperm as the male sex cell. [O1]
- Describe the structure and function of the main parts of the male reproductive system; identify similarities and differences between human and plant reproductive systems. [O2]
- Explain why plant and human reproductive systems are so different; evaluate the strengths and weaknesses of both. [O3]

Skills development

- Thinking scientifically: use nomenclature
- Working scientifically: develop explanation
- Learner development: collaborate effectively

Resources Worksheet 1.1.14a; Worksheet 1.1.14b

Key vocabulary reproductive system, testes, scrotal sac, sperm duct, semen, urethra, penis

Teaching and learning

Engage

- Show the students a graph of human population over time. Ask them to **devise** five questions relating to the graph. Discuss the questions and ask the students to **suggest** possible answers. Establish all the factors that affect the population of a species.
- Now show the students a graph of bee population over time (fairly easy to find online), reminding them of earlier work on insect pollination. Ask the students to **compare** the two graphs and what effect one might have on the other over time. Ask them to **decide** which factors they think will influence human population more strongly – reproduction or crop production?

Challenge and develop

- Recap what is meant by the terms 'cell', 'tissue', 'organ' and 'organ system'.
- **Collective memory** Group the students in mixed ability groups of four. Provide them with a blank diagram of the male reproductive system, available as Worksheet 1.1.14a. First, see if they can name any of the parts and write the labels in pencil. Tell them that each student in their group will take in it turn to look at the correct names and descriptions of each part, which are with the teacher (Figure 1.1.14a in the Student Book) for 30 seconds and then label as much of the diagram as possible from memory. The group that completes the most correct labels on the diagram will win. Ask each group to plan a strategy to help them complete the labelling on the diagram. For example, give each student one part of the diagram to focus on. Carry out the activity, allowing each student about 30 seconds to look at the teacher's diagram and about one minute to record what they remember when they return to their group. Allow each student two turns before asking the groups to swap their diagrams and mark each other's. Ask them to fill in answers for parts that are missing or incorrect. [O1&2]
- Discuss each part of the male reproductive system in turn, using Figure 1.1.14a in the Student Book. [O1]
- Working with the cards from Worksheet 1.1.14b, pairs of students match the structures to the functions. [O1&2]

- The second part of the worksheet provides the names of different structures and asks students to write down the function. [O2]
- Recap the structures and functions of the system and ask students to correct any mistakes. [O1&2]

Explain

- Ask the students to look at the diagram of a flowering plant (Figure 1.1.9b in the Student Book). Ask them to **identify** corresponding parts of the plant and the human male reproductive systems. Ask them to write an explanation of how the parts are similar and how they are different. [O2&3]

  Lower-attaining students could write their answers in the form of a table.

  Ask higher-attaining students to **identify** additional parts in the male reproductive system and write why these parts are needed in the human but not in the plant.

Consolidate and apply

- Ask the students to **consider** what could go wrong with the male reproductive system and which parts are most likely to get infected. Ask them to **think of reasons** for their answers. [O3]

  Higher-attaining students could **research** how these problems might be remedied.

Extend

- Ask students able to progress further to **evaluate** the strengths and weaknesses of the plant male reproductive system and the human male reproductive system. They should **compare** which is more successful at making and transferring male sex cells and the limitations of each system. [O3]

Plenary suggestions

What am I? One student thinks of one part of the male reproductive system. The other students then have to ask questions about what the part might be. Only 'yes' or 'no' answers may be given. [O1&2]

Answers to Student Book questions

1. *male sex cell* is sperm; *female sex cell* is an egg cell.
2. to produce sperm; and deliver it to a female
3. *cell* = sperm; *organs* = testes, prostate gland
4. Correctly labelled diagram; path of sperm from testes; through sperm duct; past prostate; through urethra into penis.
5. *plants* = anther; *human* = testes
6. Plants have flowers to attract insects; female and male parts on the same plant so that pollen can be released and trapped;, pollen tubes to enable the pollen to reach the ovule.
7. Does not need to wait for an event like sexual intercourse to occur; pollen can be made and released at all times to increase the chance of fertilisation.
8. More plants are made each year than humans; so the plant reproductive system is more effective.

Answers to Worksheet 1.1.14b

1. A 4; B3; C1; D5; E2; F6
2. a) To carry the male genetic material and deliver it into the egg cell.
   b) To deliver the sperm to the prostate gland from the testes.
   c) To release sperm or urine out of the male.
   d) To supply vital nutrients to the sperm to enable them to survive.
   e) To make sperm cells.
3. Plants and humans have different ways of transferring the male sex cell to the female. Plants use wind or insects and are adapted for pollen to be transferred by eithe; humans rely on internal fertilisation.

1.15 Understanding the female reproductive system and fertility

Lesson overview

Learning objectives

- Describe the structures and functions of different parts of the female reproductive system.
- Explain the process of fertilisation.
- Explain problems of infertility and how they might be treated.

Learning outcomes

- Name the main parts of the female reproductive system; describe fertilisation as being a fusion of a male nucleus and a female nucleus. [O1]
- Describe the structures and functions of the main parts of the female reproductive system; describe some problems of male and female reproductive structures that lead to infertility. [O2]
- Explain how the male and female reproductive structures are designed for fertilisation; describe methods of combating infertility. [O3]

Skills development

- Thinking scientifically: use nomenclature
- Working scientifically: develop explanation
- Learner development: collaborate effectively

Resources Worksheet 1.1.14a; Worksheet 1.1.15a; Worksheet 1.1.15b

Common misconceptions Ovulation and fertilisation are the same thing.

Key vocabulary vagina, cervix, uterus, oviduct, ovary, ovulation, infertility

Teaching and learning

Engage

- Discuss some data on infertility (for example, about 17% of couples have a problem conceiving; about 11% of women aged between 15 and 44 are infertile) or a newspaper article or a case study. But emphasise that either or both of the man and the woman can have fertility problems because there are different causes.
- Introduce the term 'gametes' as the scientific word used for both male and female sex cells (sperm and egg).

Challenge and develop

- Introduce the female reproductive system using diagrams (Figure 1.1.15a in the Student Book). [O1]
- Hand out Worksheet 1.1.15b, which asks the students to **identify** the parts in a diagram of the female reproductive system and state their functions. [O1&2]

  Give lower-attaining students the cards from Worksheet 1.1.15b to help them match parts of the female reproductive system with their functions.

  Go through the students' responses and identify any misconceptions.
- Show the students web-based video clips of the process of ovulation and fertilisation – for example, from the BBC Knowledge and Learning Beta. Be clear about the distinction between the two processes. Stress that without ovulation, fertilisation cannot take place. [O1, 2&3]
- Provide the students with blank diagrams of the male and female reproductive systems from Worksheets 1.1.14a and 1.1.15a. Ask them to **annotate** both to show the journey of the sperm cells and the egg cells, including the processes of ovulation and fertilisation. Ask them to volunteer to show their responses. [O1&2]

- **Group work** Group the students in fours. Ask them to use their diagrams to **explore** possible reasons why fertilisation may not take place. They should compile their own table of factors, how they cause infertility and possible remedies. Ask them to check each other's answers. [O2&3]
- Discuss with the class the overall problem of fertility and its possible consequences for individuals, families and society. You could use web resources such as NHS Choices. [O3]

Explain

- Provide key words, relating either to the female reproductive system or to infertility problems. Ask the students to work in pairs taking turns to **explain** the words to each other. [O1&2]

Consolidate and apply

- Group the students in threes. Ask them to **role-play** being in a GP's surgery. One student will be the GP and the other two will be the couple who are infertile. The role of the GP is to **explain** how ovulation and fertilisation take place, using diagrams from earlier in the lesson, and outlining the possible causes and remedies for infertility. The 'man' and the 'woman' should try to ask some difficult questions for the GP to answer. When they have completed the role-play once, if there is time, ask them to swap roles so that each person has the opportunity of role-playing the GP. [O2&3]

  Select group(s) to show their role-play to the class.

Extend

- Referring to the third task on Worksheet 1.15b, ask students able to progress further to **consider** the adaptations of the female reproductive system. How is it adapted to maximise the chance of fertilisation? How successful is the system? They should **summarise** the strengths and weaknesses. [O3]

Plenary suggestions

Heads and tails Arrange students in groups of six. Ask each student to write a question about something from the topic on a coloured paper strip, and to write the answer in another colour. Hand out the strips so that each student gets a question and an answer. One student reads out their question – the student with the correct answer reads it out, followed by the question on their paper.

Answers to Student Book questions

1. in the ovary
2. to help push the baby out
3. Fertilisation takes place in the uterus; where the developing foetus will grow.
4. The egg cell contains nutrients essential for the early development of the foetus if the egg is fertilised.
5. *Ovulation* is the release of an egg from the ovary; *fertilisation* is a sperm cell fusing with the egg cell in the uterus.
6. External factors – don't drink alcohol, take drugs or smoke during pregnancy.
   Problems with ovulation – use hormone treatment to correct the imbalance.
   Endometriosis – surgery is needed to remove cysts.
   Blockages in the oviduct – surgery is needed to remove blockages.
   Male infertility – treat the testes for disease or cancer.

Answers to Worksheet 1.1.15b

1. 1C; 2A; 3D; 4E; 5B
2. Refer to Figure 1.1.15a in the Student Book.
3. Additional annotations should include:
   - The cervix is made of strong muscle to help push the baby out.
   - The oviduct is lined with ciliated epithelial cells that help push the egg to the uterus.
   - The uterus has a good blood supply so it is ready for fertilisation to take place.

   Problems that cause female infertility: blockages can occur in the oviduct; fertilisation can occur in the oviduct, which is dangerous for the foetus; cysts can occur around the ovary, preventing the egg from being released.

1.16 Learning about changes in puberty

Lesson overview

Learning objectives

- Recognise changes in male and female bodies during puberty.
- Describe the process of menstruation.
- Explain how some problems with menstruation occur.

Learning outcomes

- Name some changes that occur during puberty. [O1]
- Describe how the menstrual cycle works. [O2]
- Explain how and why some problems with menstruation occur. [O3]

Skills development

- Thinking scientifically: use nomenclature
- Working scientifically: present evidence
- Learner development: communicate effectively

Resources coloured crayons; Worksheet 1.1.16

Common misconceptions Puberty occurs at the same age in everyone. Everyone's experience of puberty is the same. Puberty and adolescence are the same thing.

Key vocabulary puberty, menstruation, period

Teaching and learning

Engage

- Discuss the changes that happen during puberty. Be sensitive to how self-conscious students will be at this age. Start with peripheral changes, such as increased sweating and the need for increased personal hygiene. Ask the students to **describe** the changes that occur during puberty in boys and girls. [O1]

  Higher-attaining students can **give reasons** for the changes. Discuss their answers, identifying and challenging any misconceptions.

Challenge and develop

- Provide the students with Worksheet 1.1.16 and ask them to complete the first section. [O1]
- Before they start on the second section of the worksheet, discuss the features of what makes an effective graph, and remind students of any earlier targets they had in presenting data from previous lessons. Ask the students to take these into account and to **present** the data from the table in graphical form. Ask questions about the data from the graphs. Use the graphs to establish that there is no exact order of events in puberty and some people will experience changes at different times. [O1]
- Discuss the menstrual cycle and how it works, using suitable video clips or Figure 1.1.16b in the Student Book. [O2]
- Explore the problems that can occur with the menstrual cycle, such as the absence of periods or very heavy periods (outlined in the Student Book). [O3]

Explain

- Ask the students to draw a flow chart to **explain** what is happening at each stage of the menstrual cycle. [O2]

Consolidate and apply

- Working in groups of three, the students prepare a leaflet for Year 6 students, **outlining** the likely changes that boys and girls undergo through puberty, and **describing** in simple terms how the menstrual cycle works. Ask them to include common problems and to say what could be done about them.
- Select different groups to share their leaflets and **communicate** their understanding of the changes in puberty. Ask the class to provide feedback on the clarity of their communication. [O1, 2&3]

Extend

- Ask students able to progress further to do the third activity on Worksheet 1.1.16. This provides images of the endometrium at different stages of the menstrual cycle, together with a timeline. Ask them to put the images in the correct places. They should be able to **identify** when ovulation takes place and the first day of the period. Students could also annotate the completed timeline to **explain** where and when problems with menstruation can occur. [O2&3]

Plenary suggestions

Correct the mistakes Present students with deliberate mistakes about the menstrual cycle and ask them to correct them. [O1, 2&3]

Hot seat Ask one student to sit in a chair and to pretend to be an 'agony aunt'. Ask the class to think up common problems during puberty and ask the person in the 'hot seat' to **suggest** with some solutions. [O1, 2&3]

Answers to Student Book questions

1. Height spurt; body hair develops in the armpits; and around the reproductive organs.
2. 8 years for a girl; 9.5 years for a boy.
3. No; the range of ages are wide; so any of the events can take place before another. The first period could start at 15.5 years with a height spurt at 8.5, or the opposite may occur. There is no fixed order for particular events.
4. Hormones cause the egg to mature and ovulation to occur; low levels of certain hormones can be responsible for an absence of periods; hormone imbalances cause very heavy periods and painful periods to occur
5. Correct annotations for normal cycle: day 14 – no ovulation/amenorrhea; days 1–5 – menorrhagia and dysmenorrhea.

Answers to Worksheet 1.1.16

1. Example answers:
   a) *Baby* is helpless/sleeps a lot.
   b) *Toddler* can crawl about.
   c) *Adolescent boy* begins to grow rapidly.
   d) *Adolescent girl* breasts begin to develop/starts periods.
   e) *Adult man* has hair on face/shaves/broad shoulders.
   f) *Adult woman* has fully formed breasts/large hips.
2. Graphs should be bar charts. Check that the correct values have been plotted. Check for suitable axes/use of space and labelling on the bar charts.
3. The correct order of the cut-outs is: D, C, B, E, F, A, G.
   Check that the timeline has been labelled correctly, as follows: menstrual flow/loss of blood: section D and/or C; the egg is released now: section F.
   a) 28th January b) 27th February c) 22nd December

1.17 Learning how a foetus develops

Lesson overview

Learning objectives

- Recognise the process of growth.
- Use data to show how the embryo grows during gestation.
- Compare and contrast the pregnant uterus with the non-pregnant uterus.

Learning outcomes

- Describe growth as reproduction of cells. [O1]
- Describe the difference between a foetus and an embryo; describe the structures and functions of different parts of a pregnant uterus. [O2]
- Choose scales to produce a line graph to show how a foetus grows during gestation; explain how a pregnant uterus is different from a normal uterus. [O3]

Skills development

- Thinking scientifically: analyse data
- Working scientifically: interpret evidence
- Learner development: communicate effectively

Resources petri dish; detergent; Worksheet 1.1.17

Common misconceptions Growth of cells involves the enlargement of cells, not the division of cells.

Key vocabulary cell division, stem cells, embryo, foetus, placenta, umbilical cord

Teaching and learning

Engage

- Show the students a video clip showing the moment of conception and subsequent division of cells as the embryo grows. Use a model of this, looking at bubble formation with detergent in a petri dish, so the students can see the bubbles multiplying to represent growth. Ask them to **discuss** the strengths and weaknesses of the model. In what way is it the same as cell growth? In what ways is it different? [O1]

Challenge and develop

- Show a video or models of a developing embryo from fertilisation to birth. Explore how the embryo starts with growing cells that are all the same (stem cells). After a few days, stem cells begin to differentiate and become specialised cells. Show an image of the embryo inside the womb after eight weeks. Ask the students to **discuss** the rate of its development and the difference between a foetus and an embryo. [O2]
- Introduce the term 'gestation' as the period of time from conception to birth. Discuss gestation, and periods of different organisms as a point of interest: elephants, 2 years; cat, about 30 days; mice, about 20 days; humans, 40 weeks. [O3]
- Show the students the illustration of a pregnant uterus in Figure 1.1.17c in the Student Book. Ask them to work in pairs to **compare** this with a non-pregnant uterus and to **describe** the functions of the different parts. [O2, O3]
- Talk about birth, discussing the main steps of the cervix relaxing and widening and the contraction of the strong muscles in the uterus to push the baby out during the birthing process.

Explain

- Show the students the diagram of the developing foetus in the Student Book (the same diagram is in Worksheet 1.1.17, task 2). Discuss the features of the developing foetus and ask the students to **explain** how it changes over time. Students could focus on how the size of the head changes compared to the body and write down the order of the development of different organs. [O2&O3]

Consolidate and apply

- Refer the students to the diagram on Worksheet 1.1.17, task 1 of the pregnant uterus. When students have **identified** all the lettered parts, ask them to **explain** the function of each part and to write why these are needed in a pregnant uterus but not in a non-pregnant uterus. [O2&O3]

  Lower-attaining students can complete the cloze exercise in the first section of the worksheet. [O1&2]

- Show the students the data relating to development of the human embryo (Figure 1.1.17b in the Student Book). Remind them of the features of a good graph and ask them to draw a graph from the data in Figure 1.1.17b (also included in Worksheet 1.1.17, task 2). Select different students to share their graphs and answers. Ask 'What is the most surprising thing you have learnt from the data?' They should then answer the questions on the worksheet. [O3]

  You may need to provide lower-attaining students with a ready-drawn axes and scales to help them to **present** the data.

  Higher-attaining students should draw a line of best fit.

Extend

- Referring to task 3 on Worksheet 1.1.17, ask students able to progress further to **research** the gestation of non-placental animals such as birds and frogs. Can they **suggest** some advantages and disadvantages of placental and non-placental foetal development? [O3]

Plenary suggestions

True or false? Present the students with some correct and incorrect statements about foetus development and ask them to stand up if a statement is true.

Learning triangle Ask the students to draw a large triangle with a smaller inverted triangle that just fits inside it (so they have four triangles). Ask them to think back over the lesson and to write in the three outer triangles something they have seen, something they have done and something they have discussed. Then, in the central triangle, ask them to write down something they have learned.

Answers to Student Book questions

1. Growth occurs when cells divide to make new cells.
2. They have the ability to become any cell in the body.
3. 9–12 weeks; 50 mm to 90 mm = 80% growth
4. The placenta transfers materials such as oxygen and glucose from the mother's blood to the baby's blood; and removes waste from the baby's blood to the mother's blood.
5. This stops the baby from bumping about in the uterus when the mother moves around.
6. The pregnant uterus contains a placenta, umbilical chord, amniotic sac and amniotic fluid. It has expanded to become about 16 times its normal size.

Answers to Worksheet 1.1.17

1. a) See Figure 1.1.17c in the Student Book.

   b) oviduct; reproducing; uterus; placenta; umbilical chord; oxygen; nutrients; amniotic fluid; protect.
2. a) *Placenta* – where blood from the mother exchanges oxygen, nutrients and carbon dioxide with blood from the foetus.

   b) *Umbilical chord* – carries the foetal blood to the placenta and blood with nutrients, oxygen and glucose from the mother to the foetus.

   c) *Amniotic fluid* – a fluid surrounding the baby that protects it from damage and harm, cushioning the movements of the mother.

   d) *Uterus* – the part where the developing baby grows; the muscles are the strongest in the body to help push the baby out of the womb during birth.

   Correctly drawn graph and line of best fit. The length of the foetus increases directly with age, with a very slightly higher rate of growth at the start of development compared to the end.
3. This allows students to apply their learning in new contexts by comparing the process of development in different organisms. Suitable illustrations of the structure of a bird's egg and the development of a tadpole will be easy to find either via the internet or in older, more traditional biology textbooks.

1.18 Understanding factors affecting a developing foetus

Lesson overview

Learning objectives

- Describe the effects of different factors on a developing foetus.
- Evaluate the strength of data.

Learning outcomes

- Name certain substances that will affect the development of the foetus. [O1]
- Describe the effects of different substances on the development of the foetus; describe whether or not there is enough evidence to draw conclusions. [O2]
- Explain the effect of different substances on the health and development of the foetus; explain whether or not given data are reliable and valid and suggest how to improve the quality of the data. [O3]

Skills development

- Thinking scientifically: analyse data
- Working scientifically: evaluate data
- Learner development: ask questions

Resources Worksheet 1.1.18

Key vocabulary premature, valid, reliable, sample size

Teaching and learning

Engage

- Show the students a labelled diagram of a pregnant uterus that includes some deliberate mistakes. Select students to **identify** the mistakes and to **correct** them.

Challenge and develop

- Discuss the role of the placenta in more detail, using images. Explain that any small molecules are able to pass through the placenta – including harmful ones such as alcohol, drugs and nicotine. [O1&2]
- Discuss the features of a good scientific survey. Include what is meant by 'sample size' and its importance in biological surveys, the terms 'validity' and 'reliability' and how they apply to scientific studies, and the need to collect unbiased evidence.
- **Group work** Working in groups of four, the students are provided with case studies of different scientific studies on factors affecting premature babies – these are in the second section of Worksheet 1.1.18. Ask the students to **analyse** these, **identifying** the questions being asked, the variables being controlled, how the evidence is collected, the sample size used and what was found out. They should use these to establish how valid and reliable the studies are. Collect feedback from the different groups and discuss their ideas. [O2&3]

Explain

- Ask the students to write a leaflet to pregnant mothers **explaining** how to ensure that their babies develop as well as they can, and what the consequences are if they take certain substances during pregnancy or if they omit essential nutrients. [O1, 2&3]

  Middle- and higher-attaining students should use data from the case studies in Worksheet 1.1.18 to support their ideas.

Consolidate and apply

- In groups of three, students should imagine they are conducting a survey to find out how exercise in pregnancy affects the growth of a developing foetus. Ask them to **devise** a plan to collect valid and reliable data. Select students to **feed back** their ideas. Ask the class to comment on the studies.

Extend

- Ask students able to progress further to **research** studies on other aspects of foetal development, such as the effects of taking nutrient supplements during pregnancy, e.g. folic acid. Ask them to **evaluate** the evidence, **describing** how valid and reliable the data are. [O3]

Plenary suggestions

- **Which is which?** Provide students with a list of substances such as alcohol, nicotine, folic acid, carbon monoxide, unhealthy drugs such as heroin, fish oils, carbon dioxide and oxygen, nutrients such as vitamins and minerals. Ask them to **identify** which substances can pass from the mother to the foetus, which can pass from the foetus to the mother and which are likely to be too big to pass. [O1, 2&3]

Answers to Student Book questions

1. The mother takes these chemicals into her body.
2. It would die; it would not be able to obtain oxygen, glucose or nutrients.
3. If the mother drinks alcohol, smokes, takes unsuitable drugs such as marijuana or cocaine, or has a poor diet lacking in nutrients in particular folic acid, the development of the foetus can be adversely affected.
4. Do not smoke, drink or use drugs during pregnancy; take folic acid.
5. Very confident; the scans shows a real picture of the foetus; so,for example, the height and weight can be measured accurately.
6. a) Not very reliable; only 127 babies were investigated; the amount of alcohol was not recorded.

   b) Not very reliable; the sample size is small; twice as many smokers were sampled as non-smokers.

   c) Not valid; questionnaires are not always completed accurately; the study is reliable because the sample size is large.

Answers to Worksheet 1.1.18

1. *Harm the foetus*: alcohol; nicotine; carbon monoxide; drugs like heroin

   Help the foetus: folic acid; fish oils; regular but moderate exercise; a healthy, balanced diet
2. Making mental connections; behavioural problems; lower intelligence and attention span; reduced ability to perform certain tasks
3. a) B, then A, then C; B has the largest sample size; C has the smallest.

   b) *Case study A*: How many mothers were binge drinkers? What were the backgrounds of the children?

   Case study B: How much alcohol did the mothers consume during pregnancy? How many children came from poor backgrounds?

   Case study C: Were children from the same background tested, where the same number of mothers did not drink? What was the actual performance of the children in the tests? Could other factors explain the fact they did not do as well?

1.19 Checking students' progress

The *Checking your progress* section in the Student Book indicates the key ideas developed in this chapter and shows how students progress to more complex levels. It is provided to support students in:

- identifying those ideas
- developing a sense of their current level of understanding
- developing a sense what the next steps in their learning will be.

It is designed either to be used at the end of a chapter to support an overall view of the progress, or alternatively during the teaching of the chapter students can self assess or peer assess using this topic as a basis.

It would be helpful if students can be encouraged to provide evidence from their understanding or their notes to support their judgments. In some cases it may be useful to explore the difference in the descriptors for a particular idea so that students can see what makes for a 'higher outcome'.

It may be useful with some descriptors to provide examples from the specific work done, such as an experiment undertaken or an explanation developed and recorded. If marking and feedback uses similar ideas and phrases this will enable students to relate specific marking to a more general sense of progress.

To make good progress in understanding science students need to focus on these ideas and skills:

Students who are making modest progress will be able to:	**Students who are making good progress will be able to:**	**Students who are making excellent progress will be able to:**
Recognise and label normal and specialised animal and plant cells; use a microscope to make observations.	Describe the functions of the nucleus, cell membrane, mitochondria, cytoplasm, cell wall, vacuole and chloroplast.	Compare and contrast the similarities and differences between normal and specialised animal and plant cells.
Describe unicellular organisms – including yeast, bacteria, euglena, paramecium and amoeba – as being either prokaryotes or eukaryotes.	Describe the function of specialised parts of different unicellular organisms.	Explain how different structures help organisms to survive.
Recognise the role of diffusion in living organisms.	Describe the process of diffusion, and name the materials needed by and those removed from the cell.	Explain the factors that affect diffusion.
Put the terms cell, tissue, organ and organ system in order of hierarchy, naming some common tissues, organs and organ systems in humans.	Explain the terms cell, tissue, organ and organ system and the function of all the main organ systems in the body.	Describe some benefits and disadvantages of multicellular organisms, compared to single-celled organisms.
Describe the role of different parts of the flowering plant in reproduction.	Explain the differences in insect-pollinated and insect-pollinated plants.	Discuss the strengths and weaknesses of wind-pollinated and insect-pollinated plants.
Recognise different seed-dispersal methods by the structures of the seeds.	Identify key variables that need to be controlled when investigating the effect of seed design on seed dispersal.	Explain the advantages and disadvantages of different seed-dispersal mechanisms.
Name the main parts of the male and female human reproductive systems.	Describe the structures and functions of the main parts of the male and female human reproductive systems; describe how fertility problems may arise.	Explain how the male and female reproductive structures are designed for fertilisation; describe methods to combat infertility.
Recognise changes that occur during adolescence.	Describe how the menstruation cycle works.	Explain how and why some problems occur with menstruation.
Identify substances passed on from a mother that will either help or harm her developing foetus.	Describe the structures and functions of different parts of a pregnant uterus, describing how substances pass into and from a developing foetus.	Explain how a pregnant uterus is different from a normal uterus, including the impact of different substances on the health and development of a foetus.

1.20 Answers to Student Book questions

This table provides answers to the *Questions* section at the end of Chapter 1 of the Student Book. It also shows how different questions assess attainment in terms of the focus and style of a question as well as the context. Question level analysis can indicate students' proficiency in approaching different aspects of scientific understanding and different types of answer.

Q	Answer		Focus			Style			Context			
		Marks available	Knowledge & understanding	Application	Evaluation of evidence	Objective test question	Short written answer	Longer written answer	Cells and unicellular organisms	Flowering plant and seed dispersal	Human reproductive systems	The developing foetus
1	c	1	x			x			x			
2	b	1	x			x			x			
3	c	1	x			x				x		
4	a	1	x			x						x
5	Living things come from non-living things. Any suitable example such as: • flies coming from dead meat • mice coming from corn stacks • eels swimming in shallow pools	2	x				x		x			
6	Pollen tube develops and grows towards the ovary. Nucleus of pollen tube enters egg cell in ovary.	1 1	x x				x x			x x		
7	Day 1: the lining of the uterus breaks down and first blood loss occurs Day 5: the lining begins to build up again; blood loss ceases Day 14: ovulation occurs; the egg moves from the ovary into the oviduct Day 21: the egg has now reached the uterus; if it is not fertilised, it will die and uterus lining will break down again	1 1 1 1	x x x x					x x x x			x x x x	
8	b	1		x		x				x		
9	d	1		x		x			x			
10	a	1		x		x				x		
11	b	1		x		x				x		

Q	Answer		Focus			Style			Context			
		Marks available	Knowledge & understanding	Application	Evaluation of evidence	Objective test question	Short written answer	Longer written answer	Cells and unicellular organisms	Flowering plant and seed dispersal	Human reproductive systems	The developing foetus
12	Is a eukaryote (has a nuclear membrane); contains chloroplasts	1 1		x x			x x		x x			
13	Any two from: • her mother started to menstruate late • hormonal imbalance • stress • not eating sufficiently well (anorexia) • defects in the ovary	2		x			x				x	
14	Any four from: • Farmers do not use pesticides • A wide variety of wild flowers grow in many areas • Not as much of the land is used for single crop cultures or building towns • Beehives are not shared around to pollinate crops • There is less infection due to disease	4		x				x		x		
15	Any two from: • How many men were sampled? • Were the men all a similar age? • Was the same volume of sperm tested? • Did the smokers smoke a similar number of cigarettes?	2			x		x				x	
16	Any four from: • Sketch should be a bar graph • Smoking mothers and non- smoking mothers on *x*-axis; weight of foetus on *y*-axis • Higher bar for non-smoking mothers • Carbon monoxide passes across the placenta of smoking mothers and reduces the amount of oxygen reaching the foetus • With less oxygen, the cells of the foetus do not grow as well	4			x			x				x
	Total possible:	**30**	**12**	**12**	**6**	**8**	**10**	**12**	**7**	**10**	**8**	**5**

2.1 Introduction

When and how to use these pages

The Introduction in the Student Book indicates some of the ideas and skills in this topic area that students will already have met from KS2 or from previous KS3 work, and provides an indication of what they will be studying in this chapter. *Ideas you have met before* is not intended to be a comprehensive summary of all the prior ideas, but rather to point out a few of the key ones and to support the view that scientific understanding is progressive. Even though we might be meeting contexts that are new to us, we can often use existing ideas to start to make sense of them.

In this chapter you will find out indicates some of the new ideas that the chapter will introduce. Again, it isn't a detailed summary of content or even an index page. Its purpose is more to act as a 'trailer' and generate some interest.

The outcomes, then, will be recognition of prior learning that can be built on and interest in finding out more.

There are a number of ways this can be used. You might, for example:

- Use *Ideas you have met before* as the basis for a revision lesson as you start the first new topic.
- Use *Ideas you have met before* as the centre of spider diagrams, to which students can add examples, experiments they might have done previously or what they found interesting.
- Make a note of any unfamiliar/difficult terms and return to these in the relevant lessons.
- Use *In this chapter you will find out* to ask students questions such as:
  - Why is this important?
  - How could it be used?
  - What might we be doing in this topic?

Overview of the chapter

In this chapter, students will learn about the human digestive system and breathing system; about the role of each of the organs involved and the way that each organ is adapted to its particular function. They will learn more about a healthy diet and the consequences of not having one, and about the effects of some lifestyle choices and diseases on the breathing system. They will also learn about the links between the digestive system, breathing system and circulatory system and study how the products of digestion and breathing are exchanged in our bodies. They will also start to learn about how we use some of the products of breathing and digestion to generate energy.

This chapter offers the opportunity for students to use and evaluate models of the digestive system and the breathing system. They will also analyse and evaluate primary and secondary data linked to digestion and breathing.

Obstacles to learning

Students may need extra guidance with the following terms and common misconceptions:

- **Diet** A diet is made up of all the food and drink that a person takes in. It does not refer to 'being on a diet' to lose weight, for example.
- **Breathing** Breathing is the process by which air moves in and out of the lungs. It should not be confused with respiration, which is a chemical process that takes place in cells to release energy from glucose. Oxygen from breathing is usually required for respiration.
- **Food groups** A food group is a set of foods that share similar nutritional properties. A common approach is to group foods as carbohydrates, proteins, fats, vitamins, minerals, fibre and water. A healthy diet includes all the food groups. An 'eatwell plate' gives an indication of the relative proportions of each required.
- **Energy requirements** The amount of energy needed from food varies with age, gender and activity. When working out how to meet energy requirements, data about the food groups and the nutrients needs to be looked at to ensure a balanced diet and to avoid deficiency diseases.

	Topic title	Overarching objectives
2	Exploring a healthy diet	Content of a healthy human diet: carbohydrates, lipids (fats and oils), proteins, vitamins, minerals, dietary fibre and water, and why each is needed
3	Testing foods	
4	Comparing energy needs	Calculations of energy requirements in a healthy daily diet Comparing energy values of different foods (from labels) (kJ)
5	Exploring obesity and starvation	The consequences of imbalances in the diet including obesity, starvation and deficiency diseases
6	Understanding deficiency diseases	
7	Understanding the human digestive system	The tissues and organs of the digestive system, including adaptations to function
8	Investigating the start of digestion	The tissues and organs of the digestive system, including adaptations to function and how the digestive system digests food (enzymes simply as biological catalysts)
9	Understanding the roles of the digestive organs	The tissues and organs of the digestive system, including adaptations to function
11	Introducing enzymes	How the digestive system digests food (enzymes simply as biological catalysts)
12	Recognising the role of bacteria	The importance of bacteria in the human digestive system
13	Understanding how we breathe	The mechanism of breathing to move air in and out of the lungs, using a pressure model to explain the movement of gases
14	Measuring breathing	The mechanism of breathing to move air in and out of the lungs, including simple measurements of lung volume
15	Evaluating gas exchange in humans	The structure and functions of the gas exchange system in humans, including adaptations to function
16	Investigating diffusion	The structure and functions of the gas exchange system in humans, including adaptations to function Diffusion in liquids and gases driven by differences in concentration Diffusion in terms of the particle model
17	Exploring the effects of disease and lifestyle	The impact of exercise, asthma and smoking on the human gas exchange system

2.2 Exploring a healthy diet

Lesson overview

Learning objectives

- Describe the components of a healthy diet.
- Examine the importance of each component of a healthy diet.
- Evaluate the quality of evidence contained in advertising about a healthy diet.

Learning outcomes

- Identify various components of a healthy diet. [O1]
- Explain the function of each of the components of a healthy diet. [O2]
- Critically evaluate diets with regard to health. [O3]

Skills development

- Thinking scientifically: consider quality of evidence
- Working scientifically: n/a
- Learner development: collaborate effectively

Resources needed an example of a 'healthy eating' advert; examples (or pictures) of foods representing each of the food groups; Worksheet 1.2.2

Common misconceptions Water is not a food or a food group. Diet means 'on a diet', rather than what we eat and drink.

Key vocabulary food group, nutrient, balanced diet

Teaching and learning

Engage

- Show the students a 'healthy eating' advert and ask them to focus on the heading. Use this as a starting point to discuss and identify what a healthy eating plan might include. [O1]
- Alternatively ask the students to **consider** and **justify** which foods we need in our diet (showing some examples of the food groups). [O1&2]

Challenge and develop

- Ask small groups to **consider** whether or not the discussion has changed their original views about what may be included in a healthy eating plan, and if so why. [O1&2]
- Present the students with examples of different foods and ask them to **suggest** which of the food groups (listed in Table 1.2.2 in the Student Book) they fit into. You could use food labels to inform discussion. Introduce the word *lipids* for fats and oils. [O1&2]
- Ask the students to **devise** ways of remembering the seven food groups, such as a mnemonic or a story that includes each group. [O1]

Explain

- **'Jigsaw' activity** Arrange the students in mixed groups of four to learn about the importance of each food group. Assign each student a number from 1 to 4. Student 1: vitamins and minerals; Student 2: proteins and carbohydrate; Student 3: water and fibre; Student 4: fats and oils. [O1&2]

  You may want to assign lower-attaining students number 3 or 4.

  Each group should then split into 'expert groups' made up of students assigned the same number across the class. Provide each group with the information relevant to their food group. Allow groups 5–10 minutes to assimilate the information and write notes using only 10 words, supported by diagrams. The original groups then re-form and each student spends 2 minutes teaching the group what they have learned. The rest of the group should **complete** Worksheet 1.2.2 as a summary of the work. [O1&2]

Consolidate and apply

- Focus on the additional text and pictures from the advert used in the engagement activity and ask the students to **evaluate** the material by asking questions such as: 'Where is the evidence that this is a good plan?'; 'How has the company tried to persuade us that we should buy into this plan?'. [O3]
- Ask the students to **devise further questions** to ask before deciding whether or not to sign up for the plan. [O3]

Extend

- For students able to progress further, introduce the ideas of *objectivity* and *validity*. Explain that we can judge objectivity by considering if the company has reason to give us inaccurate or misleading information. Explain that in order to determine whether or not data are valid, we must consider the methods used to collect the data. Ask the students to **relate these ideas** to the healthy eating plan advert and **respond to questions** to help them to assess whether or not the claims made are objective and valid. [O3]

Plenary suggestions

Role-play The students **role-play** the manager of a healthy eating company and a potential customer. The customer asks questions and the manager defends the company and explains why the customer should sign up. [O2&3]

Plan a diet Alternatively students **plan** a balanced and healthy diet for a day, **assess** each other's work, highlight reasons why the plan is good and **suggest improvements**. [O2&3]

Answers to Student Book questions

1. protein
2. two of: bread, pasta, biscuits, potatoes, fruit juice
3. protein and fats
4. Fat is a source of both energy and an insulating layer. Olive oil, a source of fat in the diet, is sometimes linked to a healthy heart. However, too much fat of some kinds can lead to obesity and heart disease.
5. The Mediterranean diet contains lots of fruit and vegetables. These contain lots of fibre and so help prevent constipation.
6. fruits, vegetables and carbohydrates; protein such as meat / eggs and dairy products; foods high in fats and sugar
7. The advert for a Mediterranean diet including olive oil gives evidence from a study about the reduced risk of heart disease and cancer in 1.5 million adults. The advert for a vegetarian diet states facts but does not cite evidence from a particular scientific study.
8. We might want to be cautious about trusting adverts because the advertiser will make money from selling the product or may want to persuade people in some ways, for example not to eat animals. Questions might include: 'What motives might these organisations have?' and 'What evidence is there for the claims made?'.

Answers to Worksheet 1.2.2

1. Carbohydrates: energy; protein: repair and growth; fats and oils: insulation and energy; vitamins: wide range of roles, e.g. repair of skin (vit. C), taking up calcium (vit. D); minerals: wide range of roles, e.g. calcium for healthy bones and teeth, iron for red blood cells; fibre: move food through the digestive system; water: prevent dehydration.
2. a) carbohydrates b) fibre c) protein
3. Letter including possible points such as: supplements contain specific vitamins or minerals but not such a good balance of food groups as can be obtained from eating a healthy diet; foods such as crisps are high in fat, also crisps are high in salt which can cause health problems.

2.3 Testing foods

Lesson overview

Learning objectives

- Test foods for starch, sugars, protein and fat.
- Predict the results of food tests for a range of foods.
- Evaluate the risks involved in carrying out food tests.

Learning outcomes

- Recall tests for some food groups. [O1]
- Predict results from food tests with a range of foods. [O2]
- Evaluate risks involved with food tests. [O3]

Skills development

- Thinking scientifically: evaluate risks
- Working scientifically: make predictions
- Learner development: act responsibly

Resources food packaging / labels; food samples, equipment and materials for food tests as detailed in the Technician's notes; Worksheet 1.2.3; Practical sheet 1.2.3 (second sheet copied onto card); Technician's notes 1.2.3

Common misconceptions No risks should be taken when carrying out practical work. Foods are made up of only one food group.

Key vocabulary starch, sugar, protein, fat, risk

Teaching and learning

Engage

- Hand out some examples of food labels or packaging. Ask the students to **consider** what these labels tell us.
- **Pair talk** Ask the students to **discuss ideas** about why manufacturers provide these labels. Share ideas across the class. [O1]

Challenge and develop

- Ask the class to **suggest** how manufacturers might obtain information for labelling. [O1]
- **Pair talk/pairs to fours** Give each pair a set of cards from Practical sheet 1.2.3. Students **compare** the methods for testing for sugars, starch, protein and fats to **identify the risks** and **evaluate** the methods by placing them in rank order from highest risk to lowest risk. Pairs form fours to **discuss** their findings. [O1&3]

Explain

- Give each pair one or two foods from all four food groups, depending on the time available. Ensure that a range of foods is tested by each group. Ask the students to **predict** the results first. [O2]
- Pairs carry out each of the tests and **record** their observations in a results table. Encourage the students to **assess** and minimise risks. (There is a risk in testing for fats because of the ethanol used. Other risks include the possibility of hot water spilling and glassware breaking.) [O1&3]

Consolidate and apply

- Ask pairs to **consider** whether their predictions were correct or not. [O2]
- Pairs **record** a conclusion about what each food contains. [O2]

- **Pairs to fours** Pairs share their results, and then form different fours to collect more results. Alternatively conclusions about each food could be shared centrally.
- A final question on the Practical sheet asks students to use their results to recommend a food:
  - containing protein, for a patient who needs to build up muscle
  - containing high energy, for a pregnant woman
  - containing no fat, for an inactive, overweight person. [O2]
- Students attempt Worksheet 1.2.3. [O2]

Extend

- Ask students able to progress further to **evaluate the risks** involved in testing foods to decide whether or not those risks are worth taking. They should make alternative **suggestions** about how the process could be made safer. [O3]

Plenary suggestions

Learning triangle Students work individually to construct a learning triangle (draw a large triangle with a smaller inverted triangle that just fits inside, so that they have four triangles). In the outer triangles, students write: something that they have seen; something that they have done; something that they have discussed. Finally, in the central triangle, something that they have learned. [O1, 2&3]

Answers to Student Book questions

1. The Government – the Foods Standards Agency carries out the work on behalf of the Government.
2. food groups present; types of vitamins and minerals (e.g. salt); amounts or percentages of each food group
3. allows people to make healthy food choices; allows people with allergies to avoid certain foods
4. Chicken also contains fats.
5. Iodine solution would show a colour change from orange to black to show presence of starch. Biuret solution would show a colour change from blue to mauve. No colour change would be seen with Benedict's solution and no white solution would be seen with ethanol.
6. Milk would give a positive result for sugar (Benedict's solution turn orange), a positive result for protein (Biuret solution turn mauve) and a positive result for fats (milky-white solution when ethanol added). Iodine would not change colour, giving a negative result for starch.
7. risks such as: ethanol is flammable; glass could be broken; water could scald
8. use a water bath; keep ethanol away from a naked flame; crush the food gently with the glass rod in the glass tube; position boiling tubes so that they do not roll off the bench; tie long hair back; wear goggles
9. There is a significant risk associated with ethanol near a naked flame because it is flammable; so students using the apparatus shown in Figure 1.2.3c should not take the risk.

Answers to Worksheet 1.2.3

1. a) i) low sugar ii) high saturated fat b) cheese
2. a) four from: saturated fat (0 g, 0%), cholesterol (0 mg, 0%), sodium (250 mg, 10%), potassium (530 mg, 15%), dietary fibre (1 g, 4%), protein (8 g)

   b) four from: calories, calories from fat, total fat, total carbohydrate, sugars

   c) i) meal 1 (fewer calories) ii) either (both 0 g saturated fat)

   d) The first labelling system is clearer to see; it is easier to compare foods.
3. Explanation should include avoidance of certain foods that may cause food allergies; losing weight by controlling calories and fat; planning a specific diet (such as an iron-rich one).

Answers to Practical sheet 1.2.3

Applying what you know about foods: high-protein diet for body builder; more carbohydrates for pregnant woman but not sugar; sugar should be avoided by the overweight person.

2.4 Comparing energy needs

Lesson overview

Learning objectives

- Describe how we use energy from food.
- Compare the energy requirements of people of different ages and with different lifestyles.
- Analyse numerical data about energy contents of foods.

Learning outcomes

- Describe how we use energy. [O1]
- Compare and explain the energy requirements of different people. [O2]
- Suggest how to meet energy requirements healthily using numerical data. [O3]

Skills development

- Thinking scientifically: analyse data
- Working scientifically: present evidence
- Learner development: respect others

Resources food packets and labels showing energy in different foods; graph paper; Worksheet 1.2.4

Common misconceptions We only need energy when we are moving.

Key vocabulary energy, respiration, kilojoule (kJ)

Teaching and learning

Engage

- Show pictures of people using energy in different ways – such as running, swimming, lifting something, someone huddled up trying to keep warm. Ask the students to write down how energy is being used in each picture, and then form pairs to **discuss** their ideas. [O1]
- Ask the students to sit very still. Then ask them how their bodies are using energy. [O1]

  You may wish to mention respiration briefly at this stage. Explain respiration as the way that we transform energy in the food that we eat into useful energy inside the cells of our bodies.

Challenge and develop

- Arrange the students in groups of three and assign each student a role based on the people shown in Figure 1.2.4b in the Student Book. Ask them to **discuss** the energy requirements of each of the three people. [O1&2]
- Pairs of groups join up to **compare** their ideas. [O1&2]

Explain

- Ask the students to work individually to answer the questions on Worksheet 1.2.4. Support them as necessary to complete the task. [O1&2]

Consolidate and apply

- Present the students with food packets and labels. Ask them to work in (mixed ability) pairs to match foods that contain similar amounts of energy per portion. [O3]
- **Pair talk** Ask the students to **consider** which of the foods they would recommend to someone who is trying to get enough energy in a healthy way. [O3]

Extend

- Ask students able to progress further to devise an eating plan for one day for a 16-year-old boy, resulting in an energy intake of approximately 12 000 kJ. [O3]

Plenary suggestions

Loop card game Students prepare to take part in a loop card game. Each student writes out a question on a piece of card and writes the answer on a card with a different colour. Collect, shuffle and redistribute the cards so that each student has one question and one answer. The first student reads out their question and the student with the correct answer answers the question. This second student then reads out the question on the other side of their card, and so on.

Answers to Student Book questions

1. food
2. to grow; to repair; to move; to keep warm
3. for basic body functions – such as the beating of the heart; contraction of muscles involved in breathing; to help circulation
4. A pregnant woman needs more energy than an adult woman because she needs energy for her baby to grow, feed and move.
5. Males have more muscle and less fat than females; muscles need energy to contract.
6 a) An elderly male probably needs less energy than an average adult man; an elderly man is likely to be less active and probably has less muscle.
   b) An elderly woman probably needs less energy than an elderly man; females have less muscle than males.
7. Butter and jam have similar energy content; chocolate and banana have similar energy content.
8. The jam and the banana are the healthier choices. Butter is high in (saturated) fats, which can be bad for the heart and may contain high levels of salt, whereas jam contains natural sugars and vitamins from fruit. Chocolate is high in fats whereas bananas are low in fat. Both contain contain vitamins and minerals, but chocolate is high in added sugar.
9. 20 bananas. This would not be advisable because the man would not be eating a balanced diet.

Answers to Worksheet 1.2.4

1. a) very little movement; smallest mass to move
   b) physical activity requires more energy; lots of muscle movement requiring energy
   c) has to provide energy for her baby to feed and grow; extra energy to carry the baby around
2. a) bar chart with four bars, daily energy needs (kJ) on the *y*-axis
   b) bar drawn for an elderly man at a slightly smaller value than an adult female
3. a) The boys need 3200 kJ more per day (12 000 − 8800).
   b) Teenage boys generally are more active than teenage girls; they have more muscle; they have larger bodies; they may be growing at a faster rate.

2.5 Exploring obesity and starvation

Lesson overview

Learning objectives

- Describe the physical effects of eating too much and eating too little.
- Explain the physical effects of obesity and starvation.
- Compare how deaths from starvation and obesity have changed over time.

Learning outcomes

- Describe some of the physical effects of obesity and starvation. [O1]
- Explain some of the physical effects of obesity and starvation respectively. [O2]
- Interpret data about deaths from starvation and obesity. [O3]

Skill development

- Thinking scientifically: analyse data
- Working scientifically: interpret evidence
- Learner development: respect others

Resources Worksheet 1.2.5 – pages 2 and 3 copied onto card

Common misconceptions Obesity is linked only with overeating. Hunger and starvation are the same things.

Key vocabulary obesity, starvation, malnutrition

Teaching and learning

Engage

- Write the words 'respect' and 'empathy' on the board. Ask the students to **discuss** with a partner what each word means to them. Collect some feedback. [O2]
- Ask the students to look at Figures 1.2.5a and 1.2.5b in the Student Book and **consider** why the lesson started with these. [O2]

Challenge and develop

- In pairs, students sort the 'symptoms' cards from page 2 of Worksheet 1.2.5 into 'physical effects of eating too much' and 'physical effects of eating too little'. [O1]

Explain

- Ask the students to keep the cards from the previous activity. Give each pair a set of 'explanations' cards from page 3 of Worksheet 1.2.4. Pairs match up the explanations to four of the physical effects from the previous activity. [O1&2]

  You may need to tell lower-attaining students which effects are included. Starvation: muscle loss, cold extremities, lack of menstruation in females, fatigue; Obesity: breathing problems, joint problems, fatigue, heart disease.

- **Pairs to fours** Students **compare** and **discuss ideas**. [O1&2]

Consolidate and apply

- Ask the students to **discuss** what the graphs in Figure 1.2.5d in the Student Book show. Ask them to answer questions 6–8 and then review answers as a class. [O3]
- Ask the students to **consider** and **discuss** what data from the UK only might show, or data from an underdeveloped part of the world only. [O3]

Extend

- Ask students able to progress further to **consider** different causes of obesity and starvation. This could include medical conditions such as thyroid problems and anorexia nervosa, causing obesity and starvation, respectively. Ask them then to **consider** how a low income can contribute to both conditions. [O1&2]

Plenary suggestions

Plenary dice Arrange the students in groups of four. Display the following key linked to the sides of a dice:

- (1) Name one thing that you have seen today
- (2) Name one thing that you have done today
- (3) Name one thing that you have learned today
- (4) Ask the rest of the group a question about what they have learned today
- (5) Give an example of how working with others helped you today (or could have helped you)
- (6) Say how what you have learned today is important to real life

Students take turns to roll the 'plenary dice' and to make a comment that relates to the number they roll.

Answers to Student Book questions

1. body mass index; a measure of body fat based on the height and weight of an individual
2. not taking in enough energy and nutrients over a prolonged period
3.

Obesity	**Starvation**
high blood pressure	muscle loss
aching and swollen joints	fatigue
breathing problems	infertility
heart disease	dry skin and hair
	severe weight loss

4. obesity – the body tires easily due the large mass that is being moved; starvation – the body tires due to lack of energy intake
5. joint problems due to large mass being carried; dry skin and hair due to lack of vitamins and fats

6 a) Deaths from obesity increase between 1990 and 2010.
  b) Deaths from starvation decrease between 1990 and 2010 (larger decrease from 2000 to 2010).

7. Deaths from obesity are: about 14 million higher than from starvation in 2010; are about 2.75 times more than number of deaths from starvation.
8. Deaths are not always recorded accurately (particularly in underdeveloped countries). Conditions caused by obesity are often recorded as cause of death (e.g. heart disease).

Answers to Worksheet 1.2.5

1. eating too much: high blood pressure; type 2 diabetes; fatigue; swelling and pain in joints; excessive sweating; high cholesterol; breathing problems; weight gain; heart disease

   eating too little: huge weight loss; fatigue; muscle loss; cold extremities; low blood pressure; constipation; lack of menstruation; eyes and face appear sunken; dry skin and hair
2. obesity: the body is easily tired due to the large mass being carried; carrying a large mass puts pressure on hips and knees; the breathing system struggles to provide enough oxygen for the large mass; the heart is overworked due to supplying blood to the extra fatty tissue

   starvation: the body is easily tired due to lack of energy from food; heat is diverted away from the extremities; hormone production is disrupted; muscles are used as an energy store.

2.6 Understanding deficiency diseases

Lesson overview

Learning objectives

- Identify the causes and effects of some deficiencies in the diet.
- Suggest which foods could prevent well-known deficiencies.
- Plan ways of communicating ideas about preventing deficiency diseases.

Learning outcomes

- Describe the cause of some deficiency diseases. [O1]
- Describe and explain several deficiency diseases and suggest foods that could prevent them. [O2]
- Creatively communicate ideas about prevention. [O3]

Skills development

- Thinking scientifically: ask questions
- Working scientifically: n/a
- Learner development: communicate effectively

Resources information about deficiency diseases (see Engage below); Worksheet 1.2.6 (second page copied onto card)

Common misconceptions Obese people cannot be deficient. Malnutrition does not occur in developed countries.

Key vocabulary deficiency disease, vitamin, scurvy, rickets, anaemia

Teaching and learning

Engage

- Show pictures of some deficiency diseases and ask the students to **suggest** what the lesson is about. Then take some feedback across the class, ensuring that students **give reasons** for their ideas. [O1]

Challenge and develop

- Working in pairs, students should sequence the paragraphs cut out from page 2 of Worksheet 1.2.6 to make sense of the causes, effects and treatment of scurvy. [O1&2]

Explain

- Provide the students with information about the deficiency diseases rickets, vitamin K deficiency and anaemia. As a class, read the information. Ask the students to work individually to **devise questions** based on the information. [O1&2]
- **Pairs to fours** Working in pairs, the students **discuss ideas** and agree on some questions. Refer them to the Student Book if they need help. Ask the pairs to form fours – each pair then tests out their questions on the other. [O1&2]

Consolidate and apply

- Ask the students to create an annotated poster aimed at educating new mothers about deficiency diseases. Lead a short discussion about the types of things this audience will need to know and how they will make their poster appealing. [O1, 2&3]
- Students could attempt tasks 2 and 3 of Worksheet 1.2.6. [O1&2]

Extend

- Ask students able to progress further to work together to **peer assess the leaflets** from the previous activity. Students should assess using 'two stars and a wish' whereby they identify two positive features and also a point for improvement. The students then make amendments to improve their work. [O3]

Plenary suggestions

Assessing significance Students work in groups of four to write down the significance of each image from the engagement activity. Ask groups, one at a time, to **explain the significance** of an image of their choice. Each group must choose a different image until all are explained. Finally, ask the groups to plan two more images that you could add if delivering this lesson to another class. [O1, 2&3]

Answers to Student Book questions

1. They ate no fresh fruit.
2. Children are growing, adults are not.
3. Sunlight is needed to convert vitamin D into a useful form. Children who stay indoors are more prone to rickets because they do not get enough sunshine.
4. They contain high levels of iron.
5. scurvy – oranges and kiwi fruit; rickets – milk formula and oily fish ; anaemia – liver and spinach
6. Fresh fruit and vegetables contain other nutrients as well as vitamin C.

Answers to Worksheet 1.2.6

1. 6, 2, 1, 4, 5, 3
2. a) tiredness;, muscle weakness; bleeding gums

   b) One of the sailors who ate the fruit was fit enough to go back to work in only six days. The other sailor was fit enough to act as a nurse to the other sick men.
3. He fed all patients the same food and drink; the activity of all patients was similar (lying down); there was similar level of sickness to start with; the same number of men were consigned to each group.

2.7 Understanding the human digestive system

Lesson overview

Learning objectives

- Identify the organs of the human digestive system.
- Explain the role of digestion.
- Analyse links between digestion and the circulatory system.

Learning outcomes

- Identify some of the organs of the digestive system. [O1]
- Explain the role of digestion and the location of several organs of the digestive system. [O2]
- Interrogate by questioning of the links between the digestive system and circulatory system. [O3]

Skills development

- Thinking scientifically: ask questions
- Working scientifically: n/a
- Learner development: ask questions

Resources sample of food, such as a sandwich; torso model or poster; large sheets of (flipchart) paper; different-coloured pens; mini whiteboards; Worksheet 1.2.7

Common misconceptions Eating is the same as digestion. Digestion is the process that releases usable energy from food.

Key vocabulary digestion, digestive system, chemical energy, respiration, circulatory system

Teaching and learning

Engage

- **Group work** Ask groups of three to **construct a mind map** about digestion using a large sheet of paper and three pens. It will be useful to give the students different coloured pens so that you can monitor the input from each. Do not correct anything on the maps at this point – the students will be revisiting them in Topic 2.9. [O1, 2&3]

Challenge and develop

- Show an item of food – for example a sandwich. Ask questions such as 'Why do we need to eat?', 'How do we release energy from this sandwich?', 'What do we mean by digestion?'. Students could use mini whiteboards for this. [O1&2]

Explain

- Talk about each of the digestive system organs in the logical order that the food would take using a torso model. [O1]
- Ask the students to work individually on Worksheet 1.2.7 to **identify** the parts of the diagram. Allow the students to take turns to explore the torso model/poster. They can check their answers using Figure 1.2.7b in the Student Book. [O1]
- Arrange the students in small groups. Ask the groups to **discuss** what happens to the digested food in the gut. Ask them to consider where it leaves the gut, where it is transported to and how it is transported. [O2&3]

Consolidate and apply

- **Pairs** Ask the students to **devise two questions** based on what they have learned today. Show them a list of common command words:
  - calculate
  - compare
  - complete
  - describe
  - evaluate
  - explain
  - state/give/name/write down
  - suggest
  - use the information in the passage/graph/table.

  You could differentiate by directing certain groups to use specific command words (such as 'describe' for the lower-attaining, 'compare' for the higher-attaining).
- Pairs then carry out reciprocal question-and-answer sessions with two other groups. [O1, 2&3]

Extend

- Ask students able to progress further to look at the equation for respiration:

  glucose + oxygen → carbon dioxide + water + ENERGY

  Ask them to **consider the relationships** between the digestive system, the circulatory system and the breathing system. [O2&3]

Plenary suggestions

What have I learnt? Draw an outline of the human body on the whiteboard and ask the students to add the organs of the digestive system. [O1&2]

Answers to Student Book questions

1. mouth; oesophagus; stomach; small intestine; large intestine; anus
2. Undigested food would not be able to pass through (constipation).
3. chemical energy
4. Only small food molecules are absorbed into the bloodstream through the wall of the small intestine
5. undigested food; faecal waste passes out of the anus
6. in the bloodstream
7. thin; rich
8. Without the circulatory system, the products of digestion could not be carried to other parts of the body. This would mean that respiration could not take place in cells and we would not release energy from food.

Answers to Worksheet 1.2.7

1. A–H: mouth; oesophagus; stomach; pancreas; small intestine; large intestine; appendix; anus
2. a) anus b) large intestine c) mouth d) stomach e) small intestine
3. Statement similar to: Food contains chemical energy. Digestion breaks down large food molecules into smaller food molecules. These smaller molecules are then carried to cells by the circulatory system, where chemical energy is released.

2.8 Investigating the start of digestion

Lesson overview

Learning objectives

- Describe what is meant by chemical and physical digestion.
- Explain how teeth and saliva are adapted to digestion.
- Suggest how results can demonstrate that digestion begins in the mouth.

Learning outcomes

- Describe in simple terms what is meant by physical and chemical digestion. [O1]
- Describe precisely what is meant by physical and chemical digestion and explain the results of chewing starch. [O2]
- Interpret the results of chewing starch and suggest improvements to a demonstration to show that chemical digestion occurs in the mouth. [O3]

Skills development

- Thinking scientifically: consider the quality of evidence
- Working scientifically: interpret evidence
- Learner development: collaborate effectively

Resources drinking water; plastic cups; plain crackers; model of teeth or a skull with teeth; iodine solution and dropper; glass rod; Worksheet 1.2.8

Common misconceptions Digestion takes place only in the stomach.

Key vocabulary physical digestion, saliva, enzyme, chemical digestion

Teaching and learning

Engage

- Ask the students to rinse their mouth with water, and then chew a piece of dry cracker for about a minute without swallowing it (***check for allergies first***, for example to wheat or gluten). Ask the students to be aware of any change in taste or texture, and then to **discuss** what they noticed with a partner. Collect feedback across the class. [O1&2]

Challenge and develop

- If possible, show a web-based video clip of digestion in the mouth. Ask the students to watch for explanations about how digestion takes place in the mouth. Show the video clip again and ask them to make notes on this. Students then **discuss their ideas** in pairs and produce a list of ways that digestion is supported in the mouth. [O1&2]
- As a class, agree whether each observation from the 'Engage' activity is linked to teeth or to saliva. Introduce the terms 'physical digestion' and 'chemical digestion'. [O1]

Explain

- Demonstrate a model of the teeth to show the different types of teeth in a human and the role of each in physical digestion. Alternatively ask students to look at Figure 1.2.8a in the Student Book. [O1&2]
- Read 'Why is saliva so important?' as a class. Students then answer questions 1–6 individually. [O1&2]
- The students then work in pairs to **write a conclusion** for the cracker experiment. [O1&2]
- Students could then attempt Worksheet 1.2.8. [O1]

Consolidate and apply

- Ask the students, working in groups of three or four, to **consider** how we improve our evidence that chemical digestion starts in the mouth. You could direct them back to the cracker experiment and give them a clue to think about food tests that they carried out previously. [O3]
- If the idea arises to test the cracker for starch after chewing for different lengths of time, and if time allows ask the students to carry out the investigation. Ask a volunteer to chew a cracker for one minute, spit the chewed cracker into a plastic cup and add iodine solution. As a control, crush a cracker, add a little water and then iodine. Compare the changes in colour. [O2&3]

Extend

- Ask students able to progress further to think about using the test for glucose. They could **plan an investigation** to show how the amount of glucose varies with the length of time that a cracker is chewed for. [O2&3]

Plenary suggestions

Sentence summaries Ask small groups of students to **devise a sentence** summarising something that they have learned today. Then groups share their statement with the class. [O1, 2&3]

Answers to Student Book questions

1. mechanical crushing of food
2. makes food easier to swallow; easier for chemicals to digest food
3. a) molars and pre-molars b) canines
4. softens the food; contains enzymes to chemically digest food
5. contains enzymes (to digest starch)
6. starch digestion would not begin in the mouth; food would be more difficult to swallow
7. The one who described food going soft.
8. The one who described food tasting sweet.
9. Yes; one student stated that the bread tasted sweet – evidence that starch was broken down to glucose.

Answers to Worksheet 1.2.8

1. a) A incisors; B canine; C molars
   b) incisors; canines; molars
2. a) physical and chemical b) physical and chemical c) chemical
3. Paragraph similar to: Saliva softens our food and makes it easier to swallow, so it would be difficult to swallow food without it. Saliva contains an enzyme (that breaks down starch, so couldn't start digestion (of starch) without saliva.

2.9 Understanding the roles of the digestive organs

Lesson overview

Learning objectives

- Describe the roles of the oesophagus, stomach, intestine and pancreas in digestion.
- Explain how the structure of each of the organs is adapted to its function.

Learning outcomes

- Describe the roles of some of the organs of the digestive system. [O1]
- Explain how the structure of each digestive system organ relates to its function. [O2]
- Apply the structure and function of the digestive system organs to creative writing. [O3]

Skills development

- Thinking scientifically: ask questions
- Working scientifically: n/a
- Learner development: plan progress

Resources diagram or large cut-out parts of the digestive system; ball; food items, materials and equipment to make a model of the digestive system as detailed in the Technician's notes; mind maps from Topic 2.7; sticky notes; Worksheet 1.2.9; Technician's notes 1.2.9

Common misconceptions All foods are digested. The oesophagus and the windpipe are the same tube.

Key vocabulary faeces, adaptation, oesophagus, stomach, pancreas, small intestine

Teaching and learning

Engage

- Stick large cut-outs of the organs of the digestive system on the classroom floor. Ask volunteers to walk the journey (with a ball representing food) and ask other students to **identify** the organs as they go. [O1]

Challenge and develop

- Demonstrate a digestion model using the instructions in the Technician's notes 1.2.9. At each stage, ask the students to **discuss** what happens and how well the organ is designed to do its job. Facilitate discussion with questions and answers. [O1&2]

Explain

- Students work individually to match each organ with its role in Worksheet 1.2.9. Students can check their answers against Figure 1.2.9a in the Student Book. [O1]
- Ask the students to read 'Adaptations of the organs' in the Student Bookand to answer questions 7–9. They could then attempt section 2 of Worksheet 1.2.9. [O1&2]

Consolidate and apply

- Ask the students to write a creative piece. Set the scene by asking them to close their eyes and to imagine that they are a piece of food. Recap the sequence of the digestive organs as they listen. Students then imagine that they are the piece of food and **describe** their journey. [O3]

  Direct lower-attaining students to Figure 1.2.9a in the Student Book for support.

Extend

For students able to progress further:

- Worksheet 1.2.9 section 3 asks students to **predict the effects** if they had no teeth, if their stomach did not produce acid, and if they had no large intestine. [O1&2]
- You could then ask the students to **predict the consequences** of a malfunctioning of each organ of the digestive system. They could **record their ideas** in a table. [O1&2]

Plenary suggestions

Mind mapping Ask the students to revisit the mind map they constructed in Topic 2.7. Working in the same groups, students amend or add to their maps as necessary, based on what they have learned over the last three lessons. Groups then **identify questions** that they still have about digestion. These are **recorded** on sticky notes and displayed. The students will revisit them at the end of Topic 2.12. [O1&2]

Answers to Student Book questions

1. small intestine
2. mouth; stomach
3. The liver produces bile, which helps with fat digestion.
4. rectum
5. You would see it in faeces approximately 1–2 days after eating.
6. diarrhoea (or dehydration)
7. The pancreas produces enzymes that digests fat (lipase); may also mention that liver produces bile to break fats into droplets.
8. The stomach secretes (hydrochloric) acid.
9. The larger surface area allows more nutrients to be absorbed across the small intestine wall.

Answers to Worksheet 1.2.9

1. oesophagus – C; stomach – E; small intestine – B; liver – F; large intestine – A; anus – D
2. a) Made of muscle which contracts and mixes food.
   b) Contains the enzyme that breaks down protein (protease).
   c) Contains villi, which increase the surface area of small intestine so more nutrients can pass; these have a thin wall; and a good blood supply.
3. a) You would not be able to physically digest food well; enzymes would not be able to break food down (chemically) as efficiently if food was not broken down physically.
   b) The enzyme that breaks down protein in the stomach would not work (as efficiently); bacteria may survive in the stomach and make us ill.
   c) Water would not be absorbed from the waste; resulting in diarrhoea.

2.10 Applying key ideas

Can you stomach it?

Objectives

- Extract ideas from the text about diet and digestion in other animals.
- Use information about the structure of other digestive systems to explain how they are adapted to their function.
- Apply ideas about digestive systems to the efficiency of digestion in different animals.

Outcome

- Clear and effective responses to questions, indicating understanding and the next steps in learning.

The purpose of this activity is to provide an opportunity to see how successfully students are grasping the key ideas so far. It isn't designed to be used as a formal test; it might be that students work on the questions collectively. It does provide an opportunity for you to look at written work, engage students in discussions and form ideas about progress being made.

The tasks are progressive. Lower-attaining students should be able to tackle the first two or three, and higher-attaining students will find the later ones more challenging.

Resources needed Pictures of different animals; grass; bowl; large sheets of paper; pens; highlighters; Worksheet 1.2.10

Teaching and learning

Engage

- Challenge the students to think back over the previous few lessons and identify some of the key ideas they've met. Draw out some responses about these ideas and say that it's important as learners that they develop a sense of their own progress.
- Show pictures of different animals such as birds, big cats, bears. Ask the students to discuss what they know about the diets of these animals and the ways that they digest foods.

Challenge and develop

- Show a bowl of grass and tell the students that you are going to have a diet of just grass from now on. Take some immediate responses but do not validate answers at this point.
- Ask the students to think about any benefits or drawbacks of eating such a diet. They should work in groups to record their thoughts on a large sheet of paper in any way they choose.

Explain

As a class, read the passage 'Can you stomach it?'. Clarify the meanings of any new or unfamiliar words. It may help to show an image of the stomach of a cow.

Students work in pairs to read the text again. You can hand out Worksheet 1.2.10, which has a copy of the text, and ask the students to highlight:

- examples of different digestive systems (in one colour)
- explanations of how parts of the digestive system are adapted to their function (in a different colour).

Consolidate and apply

- Now ask the students to attempt the tasks – they can do this individually or collaboratively.
- Ask the students to present their responses to various tasks – either orally or by displaying their work.

Extend

- For some students the later tasks are an opportunity for extension work.

Plenary

How did you do? Ask the students for responses to questions such as:

- How well were you able to approach those tasks?
- Did you manage to present some high-quality responses?

Ask the students to note down any ideas that need strengthening in the later part of the topic. Provide the class with some overall feedback and share the ideas that may need developing further.

Likely responses and next steps in learning

1. This gives the students an opportunity to assimilate information from the text and to display it in another format. This also encourages them to reflect on the role and process of digestion.
2. This involves recalling that some foods are more difficult to digest than others. The students also have the opportunity to demonstrate what they understand of a balanced diet and why it is important. A better response would relate a balanced and healthy diet to a greater yield of milk and beef.
3. This recalls, from a knowledge of body systems, that organs are adapted to their function. This allows the students to apply their understanding of adaptations to an unfamiliar context. The students also demonstrate their ability to display data in a logical form.
4. This recalls information from the text and also encourages the students to work independently to find information. This allows them to demonstrate the ability to relate structure to function in an unfamiliar situation.
5. This requires the students to consider ideas used throughout the topic so far. Their understanding is checked as they devise questions to ask others. A better response would include questions directed at a whole range of ideas and would also include questions with unambiguous answers.
6. The animal with the longest digestive system would generally have the most efficient digestion. This allows the students to consider why there is sometimes a compromise in body design. The students discuss the advantage of a shorter digestive system having smaller mass and allowing for more rapid acceleration. A better response would identify that the increase in speed is a bigger advantage than the disadvantage from a loss of efficiency .

2.11 Introducing enzymes

Lesson overview

Learning objectives

- Describe the role of different enzymes in digestion.
- Analyse a model of the digestive system.
- Explain observations of a practical activity to explore the role of enzymes.

Learning outcomes

- Describe the roles of some of the digestive enzymes. [O1]
- Explain the results of an enzyme investigation. [O2]
- Analyse a model of the digestive system used in an enzyme investigation. [O3]

Skills development

- Thinking scientifically: analyse data
- Working scientifically: develop explanations
- Learner development: communicate effectively

Resources equipment as listed in the Technician's notes; Worksheet 1.2.11; Practical sheet 1.2.11; Technician's notes 1.2.11

Common misconceptions Enzymes are alive and therefore killed by high temperatures. Enzymes are harmful because they break things down.

Key vocabulary amylase, starch, sugar, catalyst

Teaching and learning

Engage

- Ask the students to **build a molecule** of starch by joining together several small building bricks (or beads that click together) of the same colour. Then ask them to **model** starch being broken down into glucose by amylase enzyme. Ask them to **compare the sizes** of starch and glucose molecules. [O1]
- Repeat the activity for proteins (made from several different-coloured bricks) broken down into amino acids by peptidase enzyme and for fats (made from two different-coloured bricks per molecule) broken down into fatty acids and glycerol by lipase enzyme. [O1]

Challenge and develop

- Give out Practical sheet 1.2.11. **Discuss** the model of digestion included in the investigation. Students work in pairs to set up the experiment up and leave it to incubate for 20 minutes. [O3]
- Demonstrate that the starch solution added to the visking tubing does contain starch (using iodine) and does not contain glucose (using Benedict's solution). [O3]

Explain

- **Pair talk** Ask the students to **predict** what will happen in the investigation. They must predict whether or not starch and/or sugar will be found in the tubing and around the tubing after incubation. [O1&2]
- Ask the students to read 'Enzymes in digestion' and 'More about enzymes' in the Student Book and answer questions 1–6. [O1]

Consolidate and apply

- The students test the liquids for starch and glucose and **record** the results on Practical sheet 1.2.11. They **explain** the results using prompts on the worksheet and say whether their prediction was correct or incorrect. [O2&3]
- The students **complete** the questions about enzymes on Worksheet 1.2.11. [O1]

Extend

- Ask students who are able to progress further to **compare** the model to the digestive system. They should list things that the model and the digestive system have in common and things that are different. Ask the students to **consider** whether they can suggest any improvements to the model. [O3]

Plenary suggestions

Enzyme loop cards Arrange the students in groups of five. Ask each student to write a question about enzymes on a piece of card and the answer to their question on a different colour of card. The cards are collected and redistributed so that each student has one question and one answer. They then play a loop card game – one student reads out a question, the student with the correct card answers, then asks their question, and so on. [O1, 2&3]

Answers to Student Book questions

1. starch to glucose; protein to amino acids
2. starch: mouth and small intestine; protein: stomach and small intestine; fats: small intestine
3. A diagram illustrating: large fat molecules (triangles); an arrow showing digestion by lipase cutting up of bonds in the small intestine; fatty acids and glycerol (smaller triangles).
4. Nothing would happen – enzymes are specific and amylase only breaks down starch.
5. Molecules must be broken down into smaller molecules so that they can be absorbed into the blood through the walls of the small intestine.
6. Not much digestion takes place in the small intestine. Digestion can still take place in the mouth (starch) and stomach (protein).
7. Starch is broken down to glucose by amylase.
8. a) small intestine b) undigested food c) blood
9. Glucose molecules are smaller than starch molecules. The visking tubing has holes that glucose can pass through but starch molecules are too big.

Answers to Worksheet 1.2.11

1. chemical; larger; smaller; specific; saliva, starch
2. amylase – starch – mouth; protease – proteins – stomach; lipase – fats – small intestine
3. Drawings or models to represent starch broken down into sugar, proteins broken down into amino acids, fats broken down into fatty acids and glycerol.

Answers to Practical sheet 1.2.11

Explanation: Amylase enzyme breaks down starch so, after incubation, the liquid inside the visking tubing should contain glucose but no starch (or very little). This models the situation with food in the intestine. Starch cannot pass through the visking tubing membrane but glucose can so, after incubation, the liquid around the visking tubing should contain glucose but no starch. This is because the large starch molecules are unable to pass through the wall of the intestine, but when broken down to small glucose molecules, these can pass through and be absorbed into the blood.

2.12 Recognising the role of bacteria

Lesson overview

Learning objectives

- Describe the role of bacteria in our digestive system.
- Explain how the natural flora of bacteria can be disturbed.
- Analyse data about the effects of antibiotics on gut bacteria.

Learning outcomes

- Describe some roles of bacteria in digestion. [O1]
- Explain how the natural flora may be disturbed. [O2]
- Analyse data related to the disturbance of the natural flora. [O3]

Skills development

- Thinking scientifically: analyse data
- Working scientifically: interpret evidence
- Learner development: collaborate effectively

Resources mind maps from Topic 2.7; sticky notes from Topic 2.9; ten pictures (or stickers) of smiley faces and ten pictures (or stickers) of sad faces; whiteboard; advert for or information about probiotic drinks; graph paper; Worksheet 1.2.12

Common misconceptions All bacteria are bad for us. Bacteria and viruses are the same. It is dirty to have bacteria in or on our bodies.

Key vocabulary gut, flora, probiotic, antibiotic

Teaching and learning

Engage

- Read out the 'True or false' statements about bacteria from section 1 of Worksheet 1.2.12 and ask the students to answer by moving to one side of the room or the other, labelled 'True' and 'False'. Alternatively they could answer using whiteboards. [O1&2]

Challenge and develop

- Ask the students to look at Figure 1.2.12a in the Student Book. Read 'How bacteria help with digestion' as a class. [O1]
- Ask about ten volunteers to come to the front of the class. Give each volunteer a picture of a smiley face to represent helpful bacteria. Line the students up against the whiteboard and say that this is the lining of the large intestine. Now give two more volunteers a picture of a sad face to represent disease-causing bacteria. They should stand by the helpful bacteria – but cannot attach to the intestine because they are outnumbered. Next, tell the helpful bacteria volunteers that some of them have been killed off and ask eight of them to move away. The disease-causing bacteria then move in and attach to the intestine and start to replicate. More volunteers with 'sad face' pictures now attach to the intestine wall. Ask students to **comment** about the effects of killing off the helpful bacteria. [O2]

Explain

- Ask the students to look at Table 1.2.12 in the Student Book and to **discuss** in pairs what the data shows. They then draw a graph and answer questions 7–9. [O2&3]

Consolidate and apply

- Show the students an advert for probiotic drinks, or hand out some information. Working in groups of three, they write a script for a TV advert promoting probiotic drinks. If time allows, groups read their scripts. [O1&2]

Extend

- Ask students able to progress further to **analyse the graph** drawn in more depth. Ask them to **predict** the number of bacteria after 0.75 days and after 8 days. Then ask them to draw another line on the graph to show the effect of drinking probiotics starting after 0.5 days following the antibiotics. [O3]

Plenary suggestions

Mind mapping Ask the students to refer back to their mind maps about digestion that was started in Topic 2.7 and continued in Topic 2.9. The original groups work to amend and add to their maps. Return to the sticky notes and check whether the questions are now answered or not. Distribute any unanswered questions for the students to **research**. [O1, 2&3]

Answers to Student Book questions

1. large intestine
2. fermenting carbohydrates; producing enzymes; protecingt from harm by disease-causing bacteria
3. Acid in the stomach kills bacteria.
4. There are more helpful bacteria than disease-causing bacteria.
5. Because the disease-causing bacteria are outnumbered and they cannot attach to the intestine.
6. Dehydration can occur (possibly leading to death).
7. The number of bacteria stays level up to 0.25 days after starting the antibiotics; then drops to its lowest after 2 days; then it starts to increase; gradually at first and then more rapidly.
8. Antibiotics cannot distinguish between good and bad bacteria; they eliminated some good bacteria from the gut.
9. 0.5 days; because by this time the number of disease-causing bacteria has decreased

Answers to Worksheet 1.2.12

1. a) T b) F c) F d) T e) F f) T g) T h) T
2. a) Break down complex food molecules so that energy can be released.

   b) i) Enzymes break down large food molecules in digestion (also important in many other processes – e.g. respiration).

   ii) Vitamins play many roles in keeping us healthy –, e.g. vitamin C for healthy skin and the immune system, vitamin D to help absorb calcium.

   c) They would pass out of the body; they would be wasted.
3. If useful bacteria are present in large numbers, disease-causing bacteria are less likely to be able to survive (they compete for resources with useful bacteria).

2.13 Understanding how we breathe

Lesson overview

Learning objectives

- Describe the mechanism of breathing in and out.
- Evaluate a model of breathing.
- Calculate changes in pressure and explain how these help us breathe.

Learning outcomes

- Describe the movement of the ribs and the diaphragm during breathing. [O1]
- Evaluate a model of the breathing system. [O2]
- Calculate changes in pressure and explain how these changes bring about breathing. [O3]

Skills development

- Thinking scientifically: analyse data
- Working scientifically: n/a
- Learner development: develop resilience

Resources large sheets of paper and pens; torso model; equipment to make a bell-jar model of the breathing system, as detailed in the Technician's notes; Worksheet 1.2.13 ; Technician's notes 1.2.13

Common misconceptions We 'suck' the air in when we breathe. Respiration takes place in the lungs.

Key vocabulary lungs, diaphragm, pressure

Teaching and learning

Engage

- Ask the students to write down one thing that they know about breathing and one thing that they would like to know, or are unsure of. [O1]
- Then, in groups of five or six, the students should agree a list between them and **record their ideas** on large sheets of paper in a grid with three headings – **K**now, **W**ant to know and **L**earned (KWL). The 'Learned' section will be blank now but will be revisited. Display the KWL grids. [O1]

Challenge and develop

- Use the torso model to describe the parts of the breathing system and to show that the lungs are in a cavity, surrounded by the ribcage and diaphragm. Ask the students to feel their ribs move up and out as they breathe in, and down and in as they breathe out. At this point you could ask the students to **discuss** why we breathe and dispel any myths about breathing and respiration if these arise. [O1]
- Ask the students to **complete** tasks 1 and 2 of Worksheet 1.2.13. [O1]

Explain

- Demonstrate a bell-jar model of the breathing system (see Technician's notes 1.2.13). Question students – ask them to **identify** what each part of the model represents. [O1&2]
- Ask the students to **discuss** in pairs what happens to the volume of the lungs as the diaphragm moves. [O1&3]

  Higher-attaining students should also **discuss** what happens to the pressure in the chest as the volume changes.

- Ask the students to **summarise** what happens to the volume and pressure in the chest to bring about breathing in and out (as outlined in task 3 of Worksheet 1.2.13). They can **assess** their work against Figure 1.2.13bin the Student Book. [O1&2]

Consolidate and apply

- Working in pairs, ask the students to **evaluate** the bell-jar model of the breathing system, considering what is good about the model and what is bad in terms of how it matches the real breathing system. [O2]
- Ask the students to share any ideas of how the model could be improved. [O2]

Extend

- Ask students able to progress further to look at the information in question 9 in the Student Book. Introduce the idea of 'mmHg' as another unit of pressure. Ask the students to convert the pressure just before breathing out (0.4 kPa) to mmHg (1 mmHg = 133.32 Pa). [O3]

Plenary suggestions

Breathing sequence Give each student a piece of paper or card holding one statement – for example:

- The ribs move up and out
- The diaphragm contracts and moves down
- The volume inside the lungs increases
- The pressure inside the lungs decreases
- Air rushes into the lungs

Ask them to work as fast as they can to complete a correct sequence with four other students. They must stand in the correct order to show the stages of breathing in. [O1]

Answers to Student Book questions

1. trachea
2. down
3. The volume increases before breathing in, and decreases on breathing out.
4. a) balloons b) bell jar c) elastic membrane d) glass tubing
5. inflate
6. matches – diaphragm moves up and down; trachea allows air in and out; lungs inflate and deflate
   not match –ribcage cannot move (our lungs cannot deflate completely)
7. highest just before breathing out; lowest just before breathing in
8. Air would not automatically pass in our out of the lungs.
9. 0.8 kPa

Answers to Worksheet 1.2.13

1. A–E: trachea; ribs; alveoli; lung; diaphragm
2. B / A; D; C; E
3. They should link increased volume with decreased pressure of air in the lungs as the air molecules have more space to spread out. When the pressure inside the lungs becomes less than the pressure outside the lungs, air rushes into the lungs (or converse). Diagrams should show air particles more spread out in a larger volume.

2.14 Measuring breathing

Lesson overview

Learning objectives

- Describe what is meant by lung volume and identify some simple methods to measure it.
- Identify independent, dependent and control variables in a lung–volume investigation.
- Interpret and evaluate data linked to lung volume.

Learning outcomes

- Describe simple ways of measuring lung volume. [O1]
- Plan a simple lung–volume investigation considering variables. [O2]
- Interpret and evaluate data from a lung–volume investigation. [O3]

Skills development

- Thinking scientifically: analyse data, use equations
- Working scientifically: design investigations
- Learner development: communicate effectively

Resources materials and equipment as detailed in the Technician's notes; graph paper; KWL sheets from Topic 2.13; Worksheet 1.2.14; Practical sheet 1.2.14; Technician's notes 1.2.14

Common misconceptions We breathe in oxygen and breathe out carbon dioxide. The lungs are full of just air, like balloons.

Key vocabulary vital capacity, independent variable, dependent variable, control variable

Teaching and learning

Engage

- Demonstrate a lung dissection. You may wish to show the lungs inflating by careful use of a pump. Use the dissection to show the students the parts of the breathing system, including cutting the lung to show the cross-section of bronchioles. [O1]

Challenge and develop

- Ask the students to **estimate** the volume that they can expel from their lungs. Explain that this is the *vital capacity* and is measured in litres. Record some of the estimates to refer to later. [O1]
- Demonstrate measuring lung volume by water displacement. Use a volunteer and then compare the result with earlier estimates. Tell the students that an average male has a vital capacity of approximately 6 litres. [O1]

Explain

- Arrange the students in groups of five or six and ask them to **discuss** factors that might affect lung volume. Explain that they are going to plan and carry out an investigation into lung volume. Support groups in choosing one factor to investigate, such as student height or shoulder width. [O2]
- Stop groups at this point and show them a lung-volume bag. Demonstrate how to use the bag by standing still, taking a deep breath in and blowing as hard as possible into the bag. Show the students that they must then hold the bag tightly just under the mouthpiece to prevent the air from escaping. Demonstrate how to press against the bag to move the air to the bottom of the bag. Once the air is collected at the bottom, ask a student to read the volume of air in the bag. [O1]

- Students then **plan an investigation**, agreeing on the dependent variable, the independent variable and control variables. They will need to control factors such as whether they stand or sit, use the same method to measure lung volume each time and always taking a deep breath in before measuring the breath out. Students can use Practical sheet 1.2.14 for guidance. [O2]
- Ask the groups to **discuss** what they **predict** the results will show. They then **collect** and **record** data. They should find a positive correlation between height and lung volume, and between shoulder width and lung volume, if other factors have been controlled well. [O2]
- Ask the students to display their results as a scatter graph. Groups then **discuss** what the results show and whether or not this matched their predictions. [O3]

Consolidate and apply

- Ask the students to **analyse** and **evaluate** their results, using the prompts on Practical sheet 1.2.14 if necessary. [O3]

  Higher-attaining students should try to **suggest** improvements to the investigation.
- Students further apply their understanding using Worksheet 1.2.14. [O3]

Extend

For students able to progress further:

- Introduce the idea of *residual volume* (volume of air remaining in the lungs). Ask them to write an equation for the total lung volume using vital capacity and residual volume.
- Assuming that the residual volume is approximately 1.2 litres, ask the students to **calculate total lung volume** for an average male (vital capacity 6 litres). [O3]

Plenary suggestions

KWL Ask the students to revisit the KWL grids from Topic 2.13 in their original groups. They should share what their groups found from the investigation and how they evaluated it. Ask the groups to agree on things that they have learned today and select one student to add to the 'L' column of the grid. [O1, 2&3]

Answers to Student Book questions

1. lung volume – the amount of air that can be breathed out after a big breath in
2. 2.4 litres
3. He has not finished growing yet.
4. lung volume; litres
5. height; metres
6. all either stand or sit; force air out of the bag each time
7. as height increases, lung volume increases
8. 180 cm
9. more data collected; bigger sample (possibly more accurate methods)

Answers to Worksheet 1.2.14

1. lung volume: B; breathing rate: C; peak flow: A
2. a) i) Muscles become stronger with exercise, including those between the ribs and diaphragm; so the ribs move out more; and the diaphragm moves down more.

   ii) Athletes gain more oxygen with every breath, which is used in respiration to release more energy.

   b) i) Breathing rate will decrease.

   ii) lung cancer; emphysema
3. a) The patients are likely to have similar lung and chest sizes if they are the same height and weight.

   b) Patient 2: lower peak flow; more breaths per minute

   c) Patient 1: larger lung volume; lower breathing rate

   d)160 l/min (640 − 480); or patient 2 has a 25% lower value [(480 ÷ 640) × 100]

2.15 Evaluating gas exchange in humans

Lesson overview

Learning objectives

- Describe the features of the human gas exchange system.
- Explain how the features enable gases to be exchanged.
- Evaluate how well adapted the human gas exchange system is to its function.

Learning outcomes

- Describe some of the features of the human gas exchange system. [O1]
- Explain how the alveoli and blood capillaries are adapted to function. [O2]
- Organise group discussion and communicate effectively to evaluate the human gas exchange system. [O3]

Skills development

- Thinking scientifically: ask questions
- Working scientifically: n/a
- Learner development: collaborate effectively

Resources torso model; five balloons blown up partially to approximately the same size and fastened together tightly on a stick; one balloon blown up much bigger and fastened to a stick; A4 paper and pens; Worksheet 1.2.15; KWL sheets from Topic 2.13

Common misconceptions Breathing and respiration are the same. Respiration takes place in the lungs.

Key vocabulary alveoli, respiration, capillaries

Teaching and learning

Engage

- Show the students the large balloon you have inflated and tell them that this is a model of an alveolus in the lung. Next show a different model using several smaller balloons partially inflated and tied together tightly. Tell the students that the sticks represent the bronchi. Point out that the second model is more realistic than the first model. [O1]

Challenge and develop

- Arrange the students in small groups and ask them to **discuss** why we need a gas exchange system. They should **record their ideas** on sticky notes. They then **consider** what our gas exchange system needs to do. Ask the groups to share their ideas by asking each group to give a new idea, one at a time, until all groups 'pass'. [O1]

Explain

- As a class, read 'Our gas exchange system' from the Student Book. Refer back to the starter activity and ask for comments about why the second model is the better design. [O1&2]
- Arrange the students in groups of four and ask them to read 'Designed to perfection?' in the Student Book and then **discuss** question 5. [O2]
- Ask the groups to **summarise** the structure of the human gas exchange system and how it is adapted to its function. All the students should make notes. Assign students within each group a number from 1 to 4. The students then rearrange themselves into groups made up of same-number students. They take turns in sharing what their group discussed. [O1, 2&3]

Consolidate and apply

- Ask the new groups to write a 'school report' for the human gas exchange system. You may wish to discuss the format briefly asking for suggestions as to what to include – such as good features of the human gas exchange system and what could be improved. Worksheet 1.2.15 (sections 1 and 2) could help to prepare students for this activity. [O2&3]

Extend

- Ask students able to progress further to **research** the gas exchange systems of other animals, such as a frog, a fish and a worm. The students should **consider** if these systems are well designed for each animal. Worksheet 1.2.15 section 3 provides some structure for this activity. [O2]

Plenary suggestions

Breathing system 'freeze-frame' Ask groups to produce and act out a 'freeze-frame' linked to the breathing system topic. Other students try to work out what the group is showing. [O1, 2&3]

What have you learned? Groups who worked together on the KWL grid should **discuss** the new things that they have learned. One student is selected to add to the 'What we have learned' section of the grid. [O1, 2&3]

Answers to Student Book questions

1. carbon dioxide
2. for respiration
3. thin; moist; 'bumpy'
4. oxygen; carbon dioxide
5. a) Gases diffuse across moist surfaces more efficiently than across dry surfaces.
   b) Oxygen is constantly removed to allow more to pass through the alveoli.
   c) A large area allows more gases to pass across.
6. lungs; ribcage; trachea; bronchi; bronchioles; alveoli
7. all the cells in the body
8. Respiration involves all the cells in the body, not just the lungs etc. The breathing system is the way that we get air into the body, not the way we use it.

Answers to Worksheet 1.2.15

1. a) We need to take oxygen…from the lungs and into the blood.
   We need to take carbon dioxide…from the blood and into the lungs.
   Oxygen is…transported to cells for respiration.
   Carbon dioxide is…a product of respiration in cells.
   b) Oxygen and carbon dioxide are exchanged across the alveoli walls in the lungs.
2. a) alveolus wall is only one cell thick; capillary wall is very thin; alveolus wall is moist; lots of blood capillaries close to the alveoli walls
   b) The discussion should describe blood picking up oxygen from the lungs and exchanging carbon dioxide back into the lungs.
3. a) worms: carbon dioxide passes out directly though the skin
   fish: carbon dioxide passes from blood to water across the gills and water is passed out of the mouth
   b) Comparison to include: humans have lungs; fish have gills; worms have neither
   Fish exchange oxygen and carbon dioxide in water; humans and worms exchange in air.
   Small size and limited movement of worms means they don't need a developed gaseous exchange system.

2.16 Investigating diffusion

Lesson overview

Learning objectives

- Explain how diffusion makes breathing possible.
- Observe the effects of diffusion.
- Apply diffusion to our breathing system and ask questions to develop understanding.

Learning outcomes

- Define diffusion, giving examples. [O1]
- Explain observations in terms of the diffusion of particles. [O2]
- Demonstrate an understanding of role of diffusion in gas exchange in the lungs. [O3]

Skills development

- Thinking scientifically: ask questions
- Working scientifically: n/a
- Learner development: ask questions

Resources equipment as detailed in the Technician's notes; A3 paper and pens; Worksheet 1.2.16; Technician's notes 1.2.16

Common misconceptions Oxygen is breathed in and carbon dioxide is breathed out. Particles break up during diffusion.

Key vocabulary particles, concentration, semi-permeable membrane

Teaching and learning

Engage

- Engage the students in a **role-play** of a model of the breathing system. Follow the instructions provided in Technician's notes 1.2.16. Avoid using the word 'diffusion' at this stage. [working towards O1]
- Ask the students to work in pairs to **complete** the tasks on Worksheet 1.2.16. [working towards O1]

Challenge and develop

- Demonstrate several examples of diffusion. These include the diffusion of copper sulfate in water, the diffusion of perfume particles across the room, the diffusion of food colouring in water projected onto a whiteboard (see Technician's notes 1.2.16). Ask the students to **consider** what is happening and then to form pairs to **discuss** the observations. [O2]

  You may want to remind students at this point that in Chapter 1 they learnt about diffusion into and out of cells.

Explain

- Draw a simple diagram on the whiteboard showing some particles on one side of a membrane and none on the other. Then add to the diagram the membrane as an alveoli wall and the particles as oxygen. Arrange the students in mixed ability groups of four. Ask them to draw a similar diagram on a large sheet of paper to show the diffusion of the oxygen particles. [O1,O3]
- Ask the students to **consider** when the diffusion would appear to stop; ask them to add to the diagram to show this point. [O1]
- Next, ask them to **consider** what would happen if the starting concentration in the alveoli was higher. They can **record** this in note form or as a diagram. [O3]

- Finally, remind the students that the blood is on the other side of the membrane. Ask the groups to **consider** how diffusion would be affected by the blood moving quickly. [O3]
- Each groups now selects an envoy. These travel to other groups to listen to their ideas and to share their own group's ideas. The envoys return to their own group and a final discussion takes place. [O1&3]

Consolidate and apply

- Working in the same groups, ask the students to **devise two questions** about diffusion. You could direct the students to the command words used in Topic 2.7. The groups collaborate to share questions and aim to answer them. [O1, 2&3]

  Encourage higher-attaining students to link diffusion to the breathing system.

Extend

- Ask students able to progress further to **devise a mark scheme** for the questions set and to set questions worth more than 1 or 2 marks. Command words such as 'apply' and 'analyse' could be suggested as stems for questions. [O1, 2&3]

Plenary suggestions

Prize question Each group chooses their 'best question' to try out on the rest of the group (and the teacher). [O1, 2&3]

Answers to Student Book questions

1. They spread out from an area of high concentration to one of lower concentration.
2. Particles spread out from the food through the air to your nose.
3. The concentrations would stay the same; no (net) movement would take place.
4. alveoli
5. thin; moist; bumpy
6. diffusion would happen more slowly; gases could not dissolve
7. all the cells in the body; for respiration
8. the larger the gradient, the higher the rate of diffusion

Answers to Worksheet 1.2.16

1. a) i) oxygen ii) carbon dioxide
   b) students as air particles; cells, alveolus wall and blood (and possibly yellow beanbags as nitrogen)
2. a) red beanbags; oxygen passing across an alveolus wall to blood
   b) blue beanbags; carbon dioxide passing across an alveolus wall to air in the lungs
   c) to students labelled 'cells'; representing oxygen being carried to cells
   d) blue beanbags; representing carbon dioxide being passed from cells to blood
3. The discussion should describe what the model does and explain what each part showed, in a logical order.

2.17 Exploring the effects of disease and lifestyle

Lesson overview

Learning objectives

- Describe the physical effects of disease and lifestyle on the breathing system.
- Explain the physical effects of disease and lifestyle on the breathing system.
- Describe how our understanding about the effects of smoking has changed over time.

Learning outcomes

- Identify some of the physical effects of exercise, asthma and smoking. [O1]
- Explain the physical effects of exercise, asthma and smoking. [O2]
- Explain how the understanding of the effects of smoking has developed over time. [O3]

Skills development

- Thinking scientifically: understand how theories develop
- Working scientifically: n/a
- Learner development: act responsibly

Resources smoking machine as detailed in the Technician's notes; KWL sheets from Topic 2.13; Worksheet 1.2.17; Technician's notes 1.2.17

Common misconceptions Smoking relieves stress. Smoking only harms the smoker.

Key vocabulary asthma, nicotine, tar, cilia

Teaching and learning

Engage

- Ask the students to work in small groups to write down effects of smoking on 'smokers', 'friends and family' and 'society as a whole' in three separate lists. [O1]
- Next, ask the students to **discuss** other factors that affect the breathing system and to **classify** each as either a 'lifestyle factor' or a 'disease factor'. [O1]

Challenge and develop

- Demonstrate a smoking machine (see Technician's notes 1.2.17). Run the machine first without a cigarette and ask students to note the appearance of the glass wool and the universal indicator solution. Then use a cigarette to show the effects on the glass wool and on the universal indicator. [O1]

Explain

- Arrange the students in mixed-ability groups of three for a jigsaw activity. Label the students in a group as 'smoking', 'asthma' or 'exercise'. [O1&2]

  You may want to assign higher-attaining students 'smoking' and lower-attaining students 'exercise'.

- The groups then split to form 'expert' groups of three with others who were assigned the same label. Provide each group with relevant information – for example from the Student Book. Allow 10 minutes for groups to **assimilate** the information about the physical effects of their assigned factor into notes and diagrams, using a maximum of 20 words. [O1&2]
- The students return to their original groups and take a few minutes each to teach the rest of the group what they have learned. The rest of the group should **summarise** what they have learned. [O1&2]

Consolidate and apply

- Discuss how attitudes to, and evidence about, smoking have changed over time. Emphasise that smoking was not always thought to be bad for health (or for those around us). [O3]
- Ask the students to work in pairs to complete the tasks on Worksheet 1.2.17. [O3]

Extend

- Ask students able to progress further to **consider** the smoking machine again. They should work out how the model is similar to, but different from, a real person smoking. Ask them to **decide** whether it is a good model or not. [O1&2]

Plenary suggestions

KWL Ask students to re-form their original KWL groups from Topic 2.13 and to add anything relevant from this lesson. Each group then **agrees and shares** a favourite fact, idea or strategy used during the work on the breathing system. [O1, 2&3]

Answers to Student Book questions

1. lifestyle: e.g. exercise; smoking disease: e.g. asthma; lung cancer
2. bronchioles tighten and thicken, and decrease in width; mucus is produced
3. increases lung volume; increases strength of intercostal muscles; increases size and number of capillaries
4. nicotine; tar; carbon monoxide
5. damages the cilia; can cause cancer
6. The chemicals in cigarette smoke can enter the lungs of non-smokers around them and cause similar damage.
7. Research proved a link between smoking and lung cancer. This evidence led to the banning of advertising.
8. Nicotine is addictive making it difficult to stop; some may choose not to believe the evidence.

Answers to Worksheet 1.2.17

1. a) Table to show: tar causes cancer; nicotine is addictive and increases cholesterol; carbon monoxide reduces oxygen in the blood

   b) Asthma sufferers often inherit the condition or the cause is unknown, whereas smoking is a choice.
2. Poster to include: text and pictures; information about the negative effects of smoking such as lung disease, increased cholesterol, wrinkled skin and, coughing, for example.
3. a) Timeline to show: 1954: Nobel prize for linking smoking and cancer

   1970s: evidence of link between passive smoking and the possibility of damage to unborn babies

   2007: smoking baned in public places

   b) 53 years

   c) Research provided evidence for the harmful effects of smoking, which people didn't understand previously. There was a long time between the discovery and the ban because: the research was not widely known about; the link may have not been believed; evidence about the harmful effects on those around smokers was not recognised until the 1970s.

2.18 Checking students' progress

The 'Checking your progress' section in the Student Book indicates the key ideas developed in this chapter and shows how students progress to more complex levels. It is provided to support students in:

- identifying those ideas
- developing a sense of their current level of understanding
- developing a sense what the next steps in their learning are.

It is designed either to be used at the end of a chapter to support an overall view of the progress, or alternatively during the teaching of the chapter. Students can self assess or peer assess using this as a basis.

It would be helpful if students can be encouraged to provide evidence from their understanding or their notes to support their judgements. In some cases it may be useful to explore the difference in the descriptors for a particular idea so that students can see what makes for a 'higher outcome'.

It may be useful with some descriptors to provide examples from the specific work done, such as an experiment undertaken or an explanation developed and recorded. If marking and feedback uses similar ideas and phrases this will enable students to relate specific marking to a more general sense of progress.

To make good progress in understanding science students need to focus on these ideas and skills:

Students who are making modest progress will be able to:	**Students who are making good progress will be able to:**	**Students who are making excellent progress will be able to:**
Describe the components of a healthy diet (food groups). Recall the tests for starch and sugar. Suggest some foods that contain starch and sugar.	Explain the role of some of the components of a healthy diet. Recall the tests for protein and fats. Suggest several foods that contain proteins and fats.	Explain the role of all of the components of a healthy diet. Predict the observations of food tests for several foods for starch, sugar, protein and fats.
List groups of people who need different amounts of energy from food. Describe some of the physical effects of obesity and starvation. Describe the cause and symptoms of scurvy and suggest foods to treat it.	Compare the energy requirements of different people such as men and women, teenagers and the elderly, pregnant and non-pregnant women. Explain some of the physical effects of obesity and starvation.	Explain why different groups of people have different energy requirements. Use data on packaging to plan how individuals could meet their energy requirements.
Name some of the organs of the digestive system. Describe what is meant by physical digestion and chemical digestion.	Locate the organs of the digestive system on a diagram. Recall where physical digestion takes place and where chemical digestion takes place. Explain how teeth and saliva are adapted to digest food.	Name the organs of the digestive system in the order that food passes through them. Explain the link between digestion and circulation.
Describe the role of the stomach and small intestine in digestion. Recall the names of some digestive enzymes.	Describe the role of the oesophagus, pancreas and large intestine. Describe some adaptations of the organs of the digestive system. Explain the role of three digestive enzymes.	Explain how the structure of each of the organs of the digestive system supports its function. Explain how visking tubing can be used to model the digestive system.
Describe the movements of the ribs and diaphragm during breathing in and out. Describe what is meant by lung volume.	Explain how changes in pressure in the chest bring about breathing in and out. Describe two ways of measuring lung volume.	Compare the pressure in the chest before breathing in and breathing out with atmospheric pressure.
Describe which gas from the air is used in the body. Describe where gases are exchanged between the lungs and the blood. Describe examples of disease and lifestyle choices that affect the breathing system.	Describe four features of the alveoli that help gas exchange. Explain how each feature of the alveoli supports gas exchange. Explain the effects of exercise, asthma and smoking on the breathing system.	Explain the difference between breathing and respiration.

2.19 Answers to Student Book Questions

This table provides answers to the Questions section at the end of Chapter 2 of the Student Book. It also shows how different questions assess attainment in terms of the focus and style of a question as well as the context. Question-level analysis can indicate students' proficiency in approaching different aspects of scientific understanding and different types of answer.

Q	Answer		Focus			Style			Context		
		Marks available	Knowledge & understanding	Application	Evaluation of evidence	Objective test question	Short written answer	Longer written answer	Healthy diet	Digestion	Breathing
1	c	1	x			x			x		
2	a	1	x			x			x		
3	d	1	x			x				x	
4	b	1	x			x					x
5	Any two body processes involving muscles such as breathing, heart beating	2	x				x		x		
6	Volume increases	1	x				x				x
	Pressure decreases	1	x				x				x
7	Chemical digestion involves chemicals (enzymes)	1	x					x		x	
	Reasonable example such in mouth/by saliva, in small intestine, in stomach or specific example of enzyme	1		x				x		x	
	Physical change is the mechanical breakdown	1	x					x		x	
	Reasonable example, such as by teeth or in stomach	1		x				x		x	
8	b	1		x		x			x		
9	c	1		x		x			x		
10	d	1		x		x				x	
11	c	1		x		x					x

Q	**Answer**		**Focus**			**Style**			**Context**		
		Marks available	Knowledge & understanding	Application	Evaluation of evidence	Objective test question	Short written answer	Longer written answer	Healthy diet	Digestion	Breathing
12	Description of effect of smoking such as damages cilia, dust particles irritate airways, tar clogs lungs	1		x			x				x
	Asthma sufferers have inflammation of/ narrower airways already	1		x			x				x
13	Scurvy is caused by a lack of vitamin C	1		x			x		x		
	Lemon juice contains vitamin C	1		x			x		x		
14	Alveoli exchanges gases (oxygen, carbon dioxide), whereas	1		x				x		x	x
	villi allows digested food through	1		x				x		x	x
	Reasonable adapatations specified such as, large surface area, thin wall, good blood supply, moist lining	2		x				x		x	x
15	Any two from: • Antibiotics kill bacteria causing infection • Also may kill good/other bacteria • Some bacteria useful in digestion • Example of role in digestion	2			x		x			x	
16	Any four from: • Lipase enzymes break down fats • Digested fats/ fatty acids absorbed (through small intestine) • Fats travel around body/ to cells (in blood) • If not broken down, not absorbed • Blocked enzymes do not work	4			x			x		x	
	Total possible	**30**	**10**	**14**	**6**	**8**	**10**	**12**	**8**	**16**	**10**

3.1 Introduction

When and how to use these pages

The Introduction in the Student Book indicates some of the ideas and skills in this topic area that students will already have met from KS2 or from previous KS3 work, and provides an indication of what they will be studying in this unit. *Ideas you have met before* is not intended to be a comprehensive summary of all the prior ideas, but rather to point out a few of the key ones and to support the view that scientific understanding is progressive. Even though we might be meeting contexts that are new to us, we can often use existing ideas to start to make sense of them.

In this chapter you will find out indicates some of the new ideas that the chapter will introduce. Again, it is not a detailed summary of content. Its purpose is more to act as a 'trailer' and generate some interest.

The outcomes, then, will be a recognition of prior learning that can be built on and interest in finding out more.

There are a number of ways this can be used. You might, for example:

- Use *Ideas you have met before* as the basis for a revision lesson as you start the first new topic.
- Use *Ideas you have met before* as the centre of spider diagrams, to which students can add examples, experiments they might have done previously or what they found interesting.
- Make a note of any unfamiliar/difficult terms and return to these in the relevant lessons.
- Use ideas from *In this chapter you will find out* to ask students questions such as:
  - Why is this important?
  - How could it be used?
  - What might we be doing in this topic?

Overview of the chapter

In this chapter, students will extend and further develop their ideas on separation from KS2 – for example revisiting the use of sieving and developing this to include filtration. New separation techniques – chromatography and distillation – are introduced. Students investigate dissolving, consider solubility and apply the Law of Conservation of Mass. They are asked to apply their knowledge of changes of state and of solubility to explain their uses. Students are introduced to ideas about atoms, compounds and mixtures, including the use of simple circle models. At this stage students have yet to apply the particle model to solids, liquids and gases or the kinetic theory. The models are very much part of the students' visualisation of atoms and their behaviour. There is a focus on developing and extending the students' use of technical language to describe processes – for example solvent, solute, solution.

This chapter offers a number of opportunities for students to develop their practical skills across a range of contexts, and they should be encouraged to recognise and reduce risks by working safely. Students should start to recognise, name and choose appropriate apparatus for practical activities.

Obstacles to learning

Students may need extra guidance with the following terms and common misconceptions:

- **Materials** Misconceptions include: all materials are fabrics/clothing.
- **Dissolving** Misconceptions include: dissolving is a chemical reaction. There will also be potential for confusing very similar terms such as solute, solvent and solution.
- **Pure water** Some students will have an 'everyday' understanding of 'pure' water as opposed to chemically pure water.

	Topic title	**Overarching objectives**
2	Working safely in a laboratory	
3	Recording experiments	
4	Recognising materials, substances and elements	Differences between atoms, elements and compounds Chemical symbols and formulae for elements and compounds The concept of a pure substance
5	Understanding water	The concept of a pure substance
6	Dissolving	Mixtures, including dissolving
7	Separating mixtures	Mixtures, including dissolving Simple techniques for separating mixtures: filtration
8	Dissolving and evaporating	Mixtures, including dissolving Simple techniques for separating mixtures: evaporation
9	Extracting salt	
10	Understanding distillation	Simple techniques for separating mixtures: distillation
12	Finding out what air is made of	Simple techniques for separating mixtures: distillation The composition of the atmosphere
13	Exploring chromatography	Simple techniques for separating mixtures: chromatography The identification of pure substances
14	Using chromatography	Simple techniques for separating mixtures: chromatography
15	Finding the best solvent	Mixtures, including dissolving Simple techniques for separating mixtures: chromatography
16	Modelling mixtures and separation	Mixtures, including dissolving Conservation of mass, changes of state and chemical reactions

3.2 Working safely in a laboratory

Lesson overview

Learning objectives

- Recognise and reduce risks when working in a laboratory.
- Name and select appropriate equipment.

Learning outcomes

- Give simple explanations of potential risks in the laboratory and name common equipment. [O1]
- Give effective explanations of simple safety precautions and select suitable equipment. [O2]
- Give really effective explanations of how to reduce risks and choose the most appropriate equipment for a practical task. [O3]

Skills development

- Thinking scientifically: evaluate risks
- Working scientifically: develop explanations
- Learner development: act responsibly

Resources needed examples of laboratory equipment, including Bunsen burner, boiling tube and test-tube holders/rack, or beaker, gauze, tripod; Worksheet 1.3.2

Key vocabulary risk, laboratory, hazard, apparatus, Bunsen burner

Teaching and learning

Engage

- Ask the students, working in pairs, to name sports and jobs that require protective equipment. [O1]
- **Pair/small group talk** The students should **explore the reasons** for the use of protective equipment – i.e. identify the hazards and risks to health. [O2&3]

Challenge and develop

- Ask the students to **identify potential risks** and hazards in the laboratory. Figure 1.3.2b in the Student Book may help with this task. [O1]
- Students should **discuss** in their pairs possible safety precautions to reduce the risks identified – e.g. gas, fire, keep gas taps turned off; water, slip hazard, clear up spillages; bags and stools, trip hazard, move out of the way; glass, breakages, put where they are least likely to be damaged. [O2]

  Higher-attaining students should be encouraged to **explain** how these precautions reduce the risk. [O3]

Explain

- Show the students examples of the most common laboratory equipment and give their names and uses. [O1]
- Ask them to **identify potential risks** and possible precautions to follow when using each piece of equipment. The students should **consider** the advantages and disadvantages of glass and plastic for making measuring cylinders and beakers – e.g. reduced breakages but cannot be heated. [O1&2]
- Demonstrate lighting a Bunsen burner and ask the students to **explain** the safety precautions being used to reduce risks – e.g. yellow safety flame, do not turn gas on until you have a flame to light it with. [O2&3]
- The exercises on Worksheet 1.3.2 will help the students to understand the steps in using a Bunsen burner safely, and encourage them to think about safe practice in the laboratory. [O1, 2&3]

Consolidate and apply

- Ask the students to heat some water in a boiling tube using test-tube holders/rack or a beaker on a gauze and tripod. Different groups should use different equipment so that techniques can be compared for possible risks and safety benefits. While one student performs the task their partner observes and **identifies risks and precautions**; then they reverse roles and repeat the experiment, adopting the identified safety precautions. [O1&2]
- Discuss the risks and identified precautions from different activities. Link these conclusions to the need for risk assessment of practical activities before they take place. [O3]

  Higher-attaining students should be challenged to **suggest** and **explain** precautions that should be in place before an activity begins. They can then refine their ideas during the activity, or **consider** changes to the precautions that would be necessary if alternative equipment or chemicals were used. [O3]
- **Group talk** Students **discuss** and choose which equipment to use to ensure that the safest procedure is used when carrying out an experiment. Experiments could include heating 20 cm^3 of acid (see Figure 1.3.3a in the Student Book); boiling 500 cm^3 water; heating a piece of metal. [O3]

Extend

- Ask students who are able to progress further to **identify risks and precautions** for alternative procedures – e.g. filtering a hot solution, heating a substance in a conical flask/evaporating dish, measuring the volume of a solution of a strong acid. [O3]

Plenary suggestions

Risk reduction Show the students equipment or pictures of equipment and ask them to **suggest** how it can be used to reduced risk – e.g. test-tube rack, clamp and stand, test-tube holders, heatproof mat. [O1, 2&3]

Answers to Student Book questions

1. Three examples such as builders, welders, engineers, firemen, soldiers.
2. To stop the transfer of bacteria/germs/diseases from/to patients.
3. a) helmet,

   b) helmet: protects head/brain; knee pads, elbow pads, shin guards, gloves (wrist guards): protect bones/joints from falls, scrapes and breaks
4. At least six hazards should be identified from: eating, drinking, no goggles, glass container on edge of table, spillages, flames unattended/near inflammable liquid/under flammable materials on shelf, blue rather than yellow flame, hair not tied back, bags in middle of floor, stool behind student, exposed wires, using hands rather than equipment to hold containers when pouring possibly hazardous substances.
5. Any sensible answer linked to the hazards identified in question 4.
6. Any appropriate laboratory safety rules – e.g. no running, goggles on, stool/bag under bench, stand up, hair tied up, report breakages/spillages, do not mess about with gas/water taps, do not enter laboratory without a teacher present.
7. a) heat resistant, so it will not melt b) any sensible answer – e.g. do not need to hold it in flame, stable, will not fall over
8. a) stops test tubes rolling off the desk; no need to hold hot tubes while they cool

   b) avoids holding equipment in flames; will not fall, spill/tip over
9. Use a test-tube holder or clamp and stand; point away from the face; hold test-tube holders at the end.
10. Keeps hot Bunsen base off the table; catches any sparks/ash that could fall; can put hot tongs/object directly on it.

Answers to Worksheet 1.3.2

1. a) A explosive; B flammable; C oxidising; D corrosive; E toxic; F harmful to the environment; G moderate hazard; H long-term health hazard; I contains gas under pressure

   b) petrol – flammable (several others also appropriate); X-ray room – long-term health hazard; dusty smoky environment – long-term health hazard

   c) People can understand regardless of language; less confusion or ambiguity.
2. a) ii, iv, vi, viii, iii, vii, v, i b) Any reasonable ideas – e.g. positioning and use of the Bunsen burner for heating; use of goggles; securing loose clothing/ long hair.
3. a) Supervision, organisation, clear instructions b) Follow instructions, behave responsibly, ask if in doubt, help others c) Good facilities and equipment, proper training for teachers and technicians

3.3 Recording experiments

Lesson overview

Learning objectives

- Represent scientific experiments clearly.
- Make and record accurate measurements.

Learning outcomes

- Name and draw common practical apparatus. [O1]
- Select, name and draw practical apparatus accurately; record measurements appropriately. [O2]
- Accurately record measurements and justify the choice of practical apparatus using appropriate scientific terms. [O3]

Skills development

- Thinking scientifically: use units and nomenclature
- Working scientifically: record evidence
- Learner development: communicate effectively

Resources needed evaporating dish; measuring cylinder; balance; pictures of apparatus and/or volume of liquid in a measuring cylinder; Worksheet 1.3.3

Common misconceptions The scale and level of detail required in diagrams is not important. 3D diagrams are more accurate. Volume is measured from the top of the liquid.

Key vocabulary experiment, line diagram, measuring, meniscus, data

Teaching and learning

Engage

- **Quiz** Show the students a series of practical apparatus and ask them to name each item – e.g. Bunsen burner, measuring cylinder, beaker, conical flask, gauze. [O1]
- Encourage the students to be as specific as possible when naming apparatus by introducing different sizes and scales – e.g. 10 cm^3 measuring cylinder, 100 cm^3 beaker. Ask them to **identify the differences** between test tubes and boiling tubes. [O2]

  Higher-attaining students may **consider** when/why the size of equipment may be important.

Challenge and develop

- Ask pairs of students to draw pictures of a common piece of apparatus – e.g. test tube, beaker, Bunsen burner (Worksheet 1.3.3 task 1) and **compare** their drawings (mini-whiteboards could be used). [O1]
- Ask them to **consider key features** of the apparatus and why it is important that scientists have an agreed convention for drawing them. Ask 'Is it important that all the features are recorded?' Use the apparatus to aid discussion. [O2]

Explain

- Show the students the most common laboratory apparatus, and the corresponding line drawings. They will get a chance to draw these for themselves when they carry out the tasks on Worksheet 1.3.3. Emphasise the clarity, size and conventions of line drawings – e.g. evaporating basin showing no top line as described in the Student Book. [O1&2]

- Demonstrate a simple combination of apparatus and show the students how to combine line drawings in a practical context – e.g. heating a test tube with a Bunsen burner flame; heating a beaker on a gauze and tripod with a Bunsen burner and using a heatproof mat. [O2]

Consolidate and apply

- Ask the students to measure a given volume of liquid in a measuring cylinder – e.g. 35 cm^3 in 50 cm^3 measuring cylinders and **compare** with their neighbours – are they all at the same mark? How do they know? [O2]
- Introduce and explain the importance and technique of measuring volume using the meniscus. [O2]
- Students should **compare** the accuracy of measuring volumes of liquid in beakers/conical flasks using appropriate measuring cylinders. For example, they could pour 50 cm^3 water from a beaker into a measuring cylinder and record the accurate volume using the meniscus (note: coloured water will help with clarity and visibility). [O2&3]
- Collate the results centrally via sticky notes or directly into a table for comparison and discussion.

  Higher-attaining students could be challenged to **suggest** a suitable method for recording their results and to **make a prediction** as to the outcome of the experiment. [O3]
- **Group talk** Ask the students about the clarity of their results using questions such as 'How can the data be recorded clearly?' Establish the conventions for table drawing and recording units/numbers/headings. [O2&3]
- Worksheet 1.3.3 task 2 provides consolidation for reading volumes of liquids in measuring cylinders and considering the accuracy required. [O2&3]

Extend

Ask students able to progress further:

- to write the rules for measuring liquids/recording data in tables [O3]
- to **identify**, draw and **justify** the most appropriate apparatus for a procedure – e.g. reacting 5 cm^3 of an acid with 45 cm^3 of an alkali; heating 150 cm^3 of water to 60 °C and adding 10 g of salt until it dissolves. [O3]

Plenary suggestions

Apparatus match Show the students different pictures and ask them to identify the apparatus or the volume of liquid in a measuring cylinder (could be true/false). [O1&2]

Answers to Student Book questions

1. So that it is easy for anybody to draw the apparatus and explain the experiment to other scientists clearly.
2. Only the direction of heat being applied is important/other heating apparatus could be used.
3. a) 10 cm^3 measuring cylinder – closest size to volume b) 25 cm^3 measuring cylinder – closest size to volume
   c) normal balance/weighing scale – no decimal places required d) accurate balance – two decimal places required/more precise measurement e) thermometer or similar as no precision needed f) stopwatch or any suitable device to measure whole seconds
4. It affects the accuracy/precision of the measurement; it could affect outcome of a reaction/experiment.
5. *Good* – clear headings, rows/columns; volume units in heading; shows repeats and the average clearly
   Improve – mass units/g should be in the heading; all numbers should have same number of decimal places
6. Answers could include: clear structure/use ruler, clear headings, correct units in headings, all numbers easy to read, numbers to appropriate/same number of decimal places
7.. 100 cm^3 cylinder would have been less accurate/precise for measuring the smaller volumes; there might be bigger errors in the smaller readings, e.g. 5 cm^3.

Answers to Worksheet 1.3.3

1. Check use of ruler, sharp pencil, curved corners, cross-section view with no top on open vessels.
2. a) i) 45 cm^3 ii) 23 cm^3 iii) 31.5 cm^3 iv) 6 cm^3 v) approx 110 cm^3
   b) For iii) use a smaller measuring cylinder, e.g.50 cm^3, so that the scale is finer. For v) use a bigger cylinder or pour some of the liquid into a second cylinder and add the two measurements together.

3.4 Recognising materials, substances and elements

Lesson overview

Learning objectives

- Recognise the difference between materials, substances and elements.
- Identify elements by their names and symbols.
- Explain what is meant by a chemically pure substance.

Learning outcomes

- Classify substances as materials, pure substances, compounds or elements. [O1]
- Interpret the names and symbols of common elements and compounds. [O2]
- Explain the difference between pure and chemically pure substances. [O3]

Skills development

- Thinking scientifically: use units and nomenclature
- Working scientifically: develop explanations
- Learner development: ask questions

Resources needed range of substances (or pictures), some pure; labels from orange juice and bottled water showing their composition; objects labelled with chemical symbols; large Periodic Table; Worksheet 1.3.4a; Worksheet 1.3.4b

Common misconceptions Materials are all fabrics/clothing. Water/orange juice are chemically pure.

Key vocabulary material, compound, element, symbol, molecule, pure

Teaching and learning

Engage

- Identify prior knowledge by giving the students a series of different materials or pictures – e.g. bottle of water/pure orange juice carton, metal, plastic, glass, charcoal or graphite, wood, sodium chloride/salt, fabric. Ask them to **identify** what the items are made of and then **classify** them into groups. [O1]
- **Group work** Ask the students to produce a list of the substances present in the different materials. [O1]

  Higher-attaining students may **make links** to particles of materials from prior knowledge of solids, liquids and gases.

Challenge and develop

- Ask the students to **identify** the substances that are pure using questions such as 'How do you know that substances are pure?'. [O3]
- Use the labels from water and orange juice packaging to **make observations** about the number of substances they contain and conduct simple experiments – e.g. evaporate water to show residue of salts. [O1, 2&3]
- Ask the students to **list observations** about the names and symbols of materials – e.g. iron nail (Fe), graphite (C), salt/sodium chloride (NaCl) using questions such as 'Are they single pure substances?'. Discuss how the names and symbols give clues to their composition. Introduce the idea of elements being the simplest pure substances. [O1&2]

Explain

- Show a large Periodic Table and explain that it includes all the chemical elements (as symbols). Everything in the Universe is made up of a combination of these and most are compounds – e.g. sodium chloride. [O2]

- Orientate students with the Periodic Table by choosing element symbols for them to find and interpret – e.g. Al, N, He, Pb. Ask 'Which elements have you heard of?', 'What are their symbols?'. The numbers (atomic number and atomic mass) need not be referred to at this stage – these will be introduced in Chapter 4. [O2]

  Higher-attaining students may be able to **predict symbols** from names of elements and **identify elements** that have symbols not linked to their English names –, e.g. lead (Pb); gold (Au).

- **Pair talk** Students should study the Periodic Table provided on Worksheet 1.3.4a and **identify similarities/differences** and rules about symbols – always a capital letter at start; one or two letters; none the same as another. [O2]

Consolidate and apply

- Ask the students to **classify** substances, compounds and elements using symbols and **record** their observations. Worksheet 1.3.4b can support or supplement this activity. This will help to orientate and familiarise students with common names and symbols. [O1]

  Higher-attaining students should be challenged to **explain**, with correct terms and examples, the differences between a) substance, element and compound; b) chemically pure and naturally pure substances.

- **Pair talk/Pairs to fours** Students should test each other on symbols or take turns to list as many element names as they can in 30 seconds. [O2]
- Ask them to **explain** why every element has a different symbol by asking 'How would you recognise whether a substance was an element or a compound?' [O1]
- Ask the students to **identify elements** they think may be present in a human body. They should check their ideas against Table 1.3.4b in the Student Book and collaborate to answer the questions. [O1&2]

Extend

For students able to progress further:

- Ask questions about the relative sizes of elements, encouraging students to **explain**: 'Which are bigger – elements/compounds or cells?'; 'What are cells made of?'. [O1]
- Consolidate understanding by making it clear that cells are made up of chemical elements, therefore elements and compounds are much smaller than cells. (Particles as atoms are introduced later.) [O1]

Plenary suggestions

'I think that is…because…' Name various substances and ask the students to **identify** them as materials, pure substances, compounds or elements.

Answers to Student Book questions

1. C 2. CO is a compound of carbon and oxygen; Co is an element (cobalt). 3 carbon, hydrogen and oxygen
4. Chemically pure water contains only one substance/is a compound (H_2O); bottled water is a mixture of safe substances.
5. It is a compound/single chemical substance made of three different elements joined together/has three 'capital letters', and therefore is not a single element.
6. 'Pure' makes things sound natural, safe, clean and good for us.
7. Blood is a mixture of water, salts and haemoglobin; haemoglobin is a compound/contains only one type of substance.
8. Graph (pie chart or bar chart) appropriately scaled (0%–70%) and containing symbols

Answers to Worksheet 1.3.4b

1. a) O b) S c) N d) Ni e) Mg f) Hg g) Na h) K i) P j) Pb
2. a) C b) H_2O c) CO d) CO_2 e) Pt f) H_2O_2 g) $CaCO_3$ h) Co i) MgO j) Ca
3. *copper*: single element, material, pure substance; *orange juice*: material; *oxygen* (O): single element, material, pure substance; *copper carbonate*: single compound, material, pure substance; *sparkling mineral water*: material; *soil*: material; *concrete*: material

3.5 Understanding water

Lesson overview

Learning objectives

- Recognise the importance and different sources of water.
- Explain the differences between types of water.

Learning outcomes

- Give simple differences between tap water and other water sources, e.g. seawater. [O1]
- Explain the differences between types of water such as tap, bottled and seawater. [O2]
- Explain the need for and importance of a clean water supply. [O3]

Skills development

- Thinking scientifically: evaluate risks
- Working scientifically: interpret evidence
- Learner development: communicate effectively

Resources needed evaporating dish; Bunsen burner; materials and equipment as detailed in the Technician's notes; Worksheet 1.3.5; Practical sheet 1.3.5; Technician's notes 1.3.5

Common misconceptions Tap/bottled water is pure water.

Key vocabulary mixture, water, limescale, purifying

Teaching and learning

Engage

- **Pairs to fours** Working in pairs, ask the students to **identify** as many sources of water on Earth as they can. [O1]
- Then they should join with another pair and collate and **classify** the sources of water identified – e.g. natural, artificial, weather, liquid/solid/gas. [O1&2]

  Higher-attaining students may **consider** the sources of water in different countries – e.g. UK v. Africa, reservoirs, underground wells, clean/processed water via pipes in homes, collection of 'dirty' water from rivers etc. They should then **make links** between conditions in each country – e.g. weather, economic/social/cultural differences, city/rural locations.

Challenge and develop

- Ask pairs of students to **identify potential risks and hazards** of drinking water from the different sources identified by the class. Encourage them to answer questions such as 'Would they drink this type of water?' and 'What are the reasons for your answer?' [O3]
- Discuss the concept of pure water by asking 'If water needs to be pure to be drinkable, just what is 'pure' water?' Link back to Topic 3.4. [O3]

Explain

- The students should perform a simple practical task to **investigate** the residue left by different types of water using Practical sheet 1.3.5. [O1&2]
- Ask pairs of students to **summarise** their findings. They should **explain** what happened to the water and say what the residue might be that is left behind.[O1&2]
- Discuss limescale and its advantages/disadvantages with respect to health and the maintenance of appliances such as dishwashers and washing machines or residues in water pipes, central heating systems and hot-water tanks etc. [O1&2]

Consolidate and apply

- **Group talk/Jigsaw activity** Students should **compare** and **consider** the issues surrounding the quality and availability of the water supply in the UK compared to that of, for example, Africa and the impact of this on health, food supplies and way of life. The questions on Worksheet 1.3.5 will consolidate the students' understanding of how we obtain water, how much we use and what health risks may be associated with drinking contaminated water. [O1, 2&3]
- Students can present the key issues and be prompted to **contrast** the situations in each country, and the impact it has on how we live. [O1, 2&3]

Extend

For students able to progress further:

- Ask them to **investigate** the work of charities/agencies in relation to providing safe and clean water in the least-developed countries – e.g. Water Aid, Oxfam, UNICEF, Pump Aid, Water for Africa, Action Water. [O3]
- The students should **discuss** why it is crucial to supply and restore water supplies as soon as possible after natural disasters or for refugees who flee war zones. [O3]

Plenary suggestions

Ask the students to **explain** the differences between pure water, tap water, bottled water and seawater, and **consider** why it might not be a good idea to drink water taken from a river. [O1, 2&3]

Answers to Student Book questions

1. It is not just water; there are other things in seawater (e.g. salt, minerals, substances dissolved from rocks/atmosphere)
2. Evaporate the water and a residue will be left behind.
3. fluoride; chlorine compounds
4. It was dissolved out of rocks.
5. Different minerals/salts/compounds/amounts of calcium are dissolved in it.
6. So people do not get diseases/poisoned/ill from chemicals/bacteria in the water.
7. *Clean water* is safe to drink but not pure; it can have salts/minerals in it, it is a mixture. *Pure water* has nothing dissolved in it.
8. a) Cleaner water can be obtained from underground – it is safer to drink, does not evaporate in heat/does not get contaminated as easily as surface water.

   b) Reservoirs store/capture rain water which can be cleaned for drinking; always have a supply all year round

Answers to Worksheet 1.3.5

1. a) B – little rain but abundant supply of seawater b) C – this may be the only option unless water is transported in

   c) A – reservoirs can hold lots of water for periods when there is less rain

   d) D – cheaper than building reservoirs, but essential to purify the river water due to possibility of disease
2. a) 600 litres, but may be less if there is shared use b) washing and toilet flushing

   c) SE and Midlands; due to low rainfall and high population

   d) Discourage unpleasant and unrealistic options – e.g. not flushing toilets, drinking less. Credit ideas such as low volume toilet flushers; normal showers rather than power; don't leave taps running; usingmore efficient appliances such as washing machines.

   e) Examples include installing water meters so that people pay for what they use; education campaigns.
3. a) Examples include cholera (bacteria that cause sickness, diarrhoea, dehydration, death); dysentery (as for cholera plus person may pass of vomit blood; typhoid (as for bacteria plus severe fever, liver damage, death).

   b) Examples include chlorination, boiling, ozone treatment, microfiltration, ultraviolet treatment.

   c) Microbes may be able to survive boiling temperatures briefly; water could be re-contaminated before it is drunk; toxic substances present may be unaffected by boiling.

3.6 Dissolving

Lesson overview

Learning objectives

- Explain the terms solvent, solution, solute and soluble.
- Identify factors that affect dissolving.
- Explain the difference between a dilute solution and a concentrated solution.

Learning outcomes

- Describe what happens when substances dissolve. [O1]
- Use the correct terms to describe dissolving. [O2]
- Consistently use the correct terms to explain factors that affect dissolving. [O3]

Skills development

- Thinking scientifically: use units and nomenclature
- Working scientifically: develop explanations
- Learner development: communicate effectively

Resources needed salt, spoon/spatula; measuring cylinder; rice; peas; materials and equipment as detailed in the Technicians notes; Worksheet 1.3.6; Practical sheet 1.3.6; Technician's notes 1.3.6

Common misconceptions Things 'disappear' when they dissolve and have no mass. New substances form when things dissolve. Water is the only solvent/things only dissolve in water.

Key vocabulary solvent, solution, soluble, solute, concentration

Teaching and learning

Engage

- The students should work in pairs to **classify** examples or pictures of substances that dissolve and those that do not – e.g. salt, sugar, oil, sand, tea leaves, coffee, butter, soil etc. Challenge could be provided by including ice (melts not dissolves) or orange juice (liquids mix but don't dissolve). Worksheet 1.3.6 introduces the concept that some substances will dissolve in only certain types of solvent. [O1]
- Ask students to **explain** how they know that something dissolves and collate their key ideas – e.g. it disappears, there is no solid left, the liquid changes colour. [O1]

  Higher-attaining students could be asked to **consider** where a solid goes when it dissolves, or to draw a diagram to **explain** what they think happens when something dissolves.

Challenge and develop

- Using the Student Book introduce the key terms solute (solid), solvent (liquid) and solution (mixture). [O2]
- **Group work** Students should work together to **investigate** the mass of salt that will dissolve in water, using Practical sheet 1.3.6. Allocate different masses/spoons of salt to the different groups. All the groups should add the same volume/temperature of water to the salt samples. Collate the class results. [O1&2]
- Compare the results through class discussion. The students should **identify** that the amounts of solute and solvent are important. Encourage students to use the correct terms – solute, solution, dissolved, solvent, solution. [O1&2]

Explain

- Explain that substances (solutes) that dissolve are described as soluble. Demonstrate dissolving using a simple model with different-sized 'molecules' – e.g. rice and peas. The demonstration should show that the solute particles mix with and 'hide' between the particles of the solvent. Draw a simple diagram to show this. Ask the students to **explain** why the model shows a mixture. Ask 'What would happen if more rice were added?' [O1, 2&3]

Higher-attaining students should start to link this idea to increasing concentration – i.e. more solute in the same volume of solution.

Consolidate and apply

- Students should **interpret data**, such as that in Table 1.3.6 in the Student Book, that relates to the dissolving of different types of sugar. Ask the students, in pairs, to **consider** why the size of the sugar crystals affects how they dissolve. [O3]
- Discuss the idea that the movement of the liquid/solvent helps to break down the crystals and separate the tiny molecules. An analogy could be used such as a group of friends trying to stay together in a crowd – e.g. in a corridor at break/home time or a football crowd. [O1, 2&3]
- Ask the students to **consider** other factors that might affect how quickly sugar dissolves – e.g. temperature, stirring to make the solvent particles move faster. Discuss the impact these factors may have. The effect of temperature is explored further in Topic 3.8. [O3]

Extend

- Ask students able to progress further to use a simple circle model diagram to represent the differences between solvent and solution; high and low concentrations; soluble and insoluble. [O2&3]

Plenary suggestions

'Disappearing' salt Ask the students to independently draw and label a diagram to support an explanation of why salt looks as though it disappears when it dissolves. Peer assess against the outcomes. [O1, 2&3]

Answers to Student Book questions

1. It dissolves/it is soluble. 2. You can taste it/it tastes sweet.
3. A mixture of a solute (solid) and a solvent (liquid) 4.The solute was sugar, the solvent was water.
5. white cubes, coffee lumps, granulated, caster; larger lumps needed more stirs to dissolve (or vice versa)
6. same volume of water (100 cm^3); same mass (1.5 g except granulated, 1.45 g); all sugar/same solute
7. The solute (sugar) crystals are broken apart by the movement of and collisions with the solvent (water) molecules and are separated.
8. Stirring makes the water molecules move faster and so it breaks up the sugar crystals and spreads them out quicker than if the water was still.
9. Faster; the crystals are smaller in icing sugar so they will break apart/dissolve faster.
10. Two diagrams similar to that shown in Figure 1.3.6d: one with a few sugar molecules, evenly distributed among a larger number of water molecules; the other with a larger number of sugar molecules, evenly distributed among a similar number of water molecules to those shown in the first diagram.

Answers to Worksheet 1.3.6

1. a) solution – a mixture of a solvent with a solute dissolved in it b) solute – a substance that is dissolved in a solvent

   c) concentration – the mass of solute dissolved in a particular volume of solvent d) soluble – substances that will dissolve e) solvent – a liquid in which another substance will dissolve
2. a) Because it will not dissolve in water. b) For uses like children painting it is useful to wash in water; for protective paint it must be alble to withstand e.g. rain.

   c) Accept any reasonable suggestions – e.g. i) does not dissolve on beaches ii) dissolves in drinks iii) is dissolved in fizzy drinks iv) does not wash off cars
3. a) Shows a dilute solution with only a few sugar particles dissolved. b) Shows a more concentrated solution.

   c) Shows a solution that cannot hold any more sugar; some sugar has collected at the bottom.

3.7 Separating mixtures

Lesson overview

Learning objectives

- Recognise the differences between substances and use these to separate them.

Learning outcomes

- Describe how to separate simple mixtures. [O1]
- Choose and explain appropriate separation techniques. [O2]
- Clearly explain the choice and method of separation using the correct terms. [O3]

Skills development

- Thinking scientifically: ask questions
- Working scientifically: develop explanations
- Learner development: collaborate effectively

Resources needed picture of fruit salad; filter paper; salt solution; sand; cordial; water; oil; separating funnel; sawdust; flour; gravel; iron; aluminium pins; vinegar; Worksheet 1.3.7 (the second page copied onto card)

Common misconceptions All liquids are soluble. Liquids are soluble. All metals are magnetic.

Key vocabulary filter, mixture, filtration, insoluble, immiscible

Teaching and learning

Engage

- Revise the difference between a pure substance and a mixture, drawing a diagram to illustrate the idea – Figure 1.3.6d in Topic 3.6 of the Student Book could be used as the basis for the diagram.
- Show the students a picture of a fruit salad asking question such as 'How do we know this is a mixture?', 'How can the components be separated?' The introduction in the Student Book answers this question.
- Extend the discussion by asking further questions to link the discussion to Topic 3.6 on solubility – 'Can we separate salt and water in the same way?', 'Why not?'. [O1&2]

Challenge and develop

- Ask the students to **describe** and **explain** to a partner how a mixture of rock and sand could be separated. Focus on clear language – ensure that they know the difference between 'describe' and 'explain' (this is because…). [O1&2]
- **Pairs to fours** Pairs of students explore an issue briefly, and then double up to fours to share and **identify** the best answer from their group to feedback to the class.
- Share the rules for mixtures with the students (Table 1.3.7 in the Student Book). Explain that separations by physical methods do not involve chemical reactions because they exploit the differences in *physical* properties (e.g. magnetic) of the substances in the mixture. [O1]
- Ask the students to **consider** iron filings and sand, asking questions such as 'What properties do they have in common?', 'What is the difference between them?', 'How can they be separated?'. [O1&2]

  Higher-attaining students could **consider** the differences between iron and sulfur and iron sulfide, if appropriate.
- Ask the students to play the pairs card game on Worksheet 1.3.7 (task 1) to consolidate their thinking about the different methods that can be used to separate mixtures of substances. [O1, 2&3]

Explain

- Through **discussion** with a partner, students should **suggest** a method for the separation of salt and sand by **identifying the differences** between them. [O1, 2&3]
- Demonstrate folding a filter paper and explain that the soluble substance (filtrate) passes through while the insoluble substance (residue) remains. This is shown in Figure 1.3.7c of the Student Book. [O2&3]
- The students should separate salt solution from sand by filtration. Follow the experiment with a class discussion, asking students to **suggest** how the salt could be separated from the water – e.g. by boiling the water to leave a residue. Extracting salt commercially is covered in Topic 3.9. [O1, 2&3]

Consolidate and apply

- Show mixtures of cordial/water and oil/water. Explain the difference between 'miscible' and 'immiscible'. Ask students to **consider** different mixtures of liquids. Ask questions such as 'Do liquids dissolve liquids?'. Students need to appreciate the difference between dissolving solids (soluble/insoluble) and mixing liquids (miscible/immiscible). [O1&2]
- **Discuss** how immiscible liquids can be separated. Demonstrate and explain the use of a separating funnel. Figure 1.3.7d can be used to support the demonstration. [O2&3]

Extend

- Ask students able to progress further to **explain the difference** between insoluble and immiscible; physical properties and chemical properties; mixtures and compounds. [O2&3]

Plenary suggestions

Separating substances Give the students a range of substances and ask them to **identify** and **explain** a suitable separation technique – e.g. sawdust and water; flour and gravel; iron and aluminium pins; vinegar and olive oil. [O1, 2&3]

Answers to Student Book questions

1. Sieves have visible holes/larger holes; filters have very small holes/holes are not visible; filters are often made of paper that is folded; sieves can be used to separate solids of different-sized particles; filters can separate soluble and insoluble substances.
2. Separate the tea leaves/ground or solid coffee from the liquid you drink; remove the solid tea/coffee from the drink.
3. No; just the iron filings.
4. No nickel chloride is a compound and is not magnetic (pure nickel is magnetic); lead is not magnetic.
5. Physical methods of separation use differences in physical properties, which are unaffected when things are mixed together.
6. sieving 7. Vinegar and oil are immiscible/do not mix/separate out.
8. Sugar is soluble and will pass through the filter paper with the water.
9. Diagram showing these separation choices: both substances are solids of different-sized particles – sieving; one is magnetic – magnet; one is an insoluble solid, the other is a liquid – filtration; a soluble substance – evaporation; both substances are liquids: if immiscible – separating funnel (if miscible – distillation, covered in Topic 3.10).

Answers to Worksheet 1.3.7

1. Students may need some discussion time to match the cards on the first run through, so they may benefit from additional plays of the game. The cards should pair up as follows: *magnet* – iron powder and talcum powder; *evaporation* – sugar and water; *sieve* – stones and sand; *shake and leave to settle* – carbon dioxide from a fizzy drink; *filter paper* – water and sand
2. a) Neither metal is magnetic; so neither is attracted.

   b) They are miscible; a separating funnel works for liquids where one floats on top of the other.

   c) The sand and ink will both pass through the sieve; if the grains of sand are small enough.

   d) The water in both types of milk would evaporate; and leave the other components behind.
3. a) Oil floats on water so even if it is vigorously mixed it will float back to the top.

   b) Contain and concentrate the oil using a floating boom. Use buckets or pumps to remove the oil. If water is still present use a separating funnel.

3.8 Dissolving and evaporating

Lesson overview

Learning objectives

- Separate a soluble substance from water.
- Form crystals from solutions.
- Explain solubility.

Learning outcomes

- Describe the effect of temperature on dissolving. [O1]
- Describe methods for producing crystals. [O2]
- Use data to draw conclusions about solubility. [O3]

Skills development

- Thinking scientifically: analyse data
- Working scientifically: interpret evidence
- Learner development: act responsibly

Resources needed copper sulfate (or alum); water; beakers; spatulas/spoons; Worksheet 1.3.8

Common misconceptions All crystals are the same shape. Crystals do not contain any water.

Key vocabulary soluble, solubility, crystallisation, crystal, saturated

Teaching and learning

Engage

- **Quiz** Ask the students to **recall**, **define** and exemplify the key words – soluble, solute, solution, solvent, mixture, dissolve. [O1]
- Explore the students' understanding of the terms by giving more abstract clues – e.g. not soluble, not a liquid, not a mixture. [O1]

Challenge and develop

- **Pair talk** Show the students the data on temperature and sugar solubility in Table 1.3.8 of the Student Book. Ask them, working in pairs, to compile a list of things that can be **inferred** from the table. [O1]
- **Snowball activity** Ask the pairs to form larger groups to **discuss** and list their responses. Turn this into a class discussion, so that groups can **compare** lists, ticking off or adding points they did not pick up. [O1&3]
- Review and highlight the quality of student responses in terms of descriptions, explanations and analysis/conclusions. [O1&3]
- Draw up and share with the students a progressive list of criteria for marking the quality of responses later in the lesson. [O1&3]

Explain

- Ask the students to **consider** if the sugar would continue to dissolve if even more were added. What would they see? Explain the idea of saturated solutions and that crystals start to reform at this point. [O2&3]
- Students make a saturated solution of copper sulfate or alum (or work with a ready-prepared solution) and **compare** the crystal formation both by evaporation at room temperature and by heating. [O1, 2&3]

Consolidate and apply

- Ask the students to **recall** and **explain** what happens to crystals during dissolving. Reinforce the concept, explaining that crystal formation is the reverse. [O2]
- Discuss what happens when the water evaporates from a solution. Model evaporation using students /counters/ animation – i.e. the solute particles get closer together (there are fewer water particles in the solution as it evaporates). [O2]

  Higher-attaining students could be challenged to **suggest** what will happen if the water is evaporated more quickly or more slowly.

Extend

- Ask students able to progress further to **interpret the solubility graphs** in Figure 1.3.8d in the Student Book and then answer questions 7–11. To carry out their analysis they should use the criteria identified in *Challenge and develop* above as a checklist or mark scheme for their analysis. [O3]

Plenary suggestions

Creating crystals Show the students pictures of natural crystals – e.g. amethyst geodes or the Naica giant crystals in Mexico (see Student Book Figure 1.3.8b). Ask them to write down an explanation of how they were formed. The students should then use the criteria identified in *Challenge and develop* to peer mark their work – e.g. description, explanation, analysis/conclusions. [O1, 2&3]

Answers to Student Book questions

1. More sucrose dissolves at higher temperatures.
2. as a (line) graph
3. 380–420 g 4. One in which no more solute will dissolve.
5. Stages should include preparation of saturated solution and evaporation of water to grow crystals.
6. Less solute can be dissolved at lower temperatures/less soluble.
7. sodium nitrate 8. Yes, because up to about 80 g will dissolve at 20 °C.
9. As the solution cooled below about 80 °C crystals would start to form.
10. 100 g

Answers to Worksheet 1.3.8

1. Dissolving is involved in the household activities a), c), d), e) and g).
2. a) For example:

Temperature (°C)	0	20	40	60	80
Mass of potassium nitrate dissolved (g)	13	47	77	103	125
Mass of sodium nitrate dissolved (g)	73	88	102	122	148

   Ensure that a ruler is used, and that quantities and units are labelled.

   b) Check that students have already done this style of graph in Maths. The activity may need to be modified or adapted by providing scaffolding and concentrating on one particular aspect of graph drawing.

3. a) Both compounds increase in solubility as temperature increases; $NaNO_3$ is more soluble at all temperatures; the solubility of KNO_3 increases faster as temperature rises.

   b) From Topic 1.3.4, it is a material made from a combination of chemical substances.

   c) Plants absorb water and dissolved substances through their routes; they have no ability to 'eat' solids.

   d) They could all be 'washed' away and wasted when it rains heavily; thus could pollute rivers and lakes.

3.9 Extracting salt

Lesson overview

Learning objectives

- Identify sources of salt and describe how it is extracted.
- Recognise the uses and importance of salt.
- Obtain pure salt from a mixture.

Learning outcomes

- Identify sources and uses of salt. [O1]
- Describe how salt is extracted. [O2]
- Recognise the advantages and disadvantages of salt-extraction methods. [O3]

Skills development

- Thinking scientifically: ask questions
- Working scientifically: present evidence
- Learner development: respect others

Resources needed materials and equipment as detailed in the Technician's notes; picture of the Dead Sea; Worksheet 1.3.9; Practical sheets 1.3.9a, b and c; Technician's notes 1.3.9

Common misconceptions All salt comes from the sea.

Key vocabulary salt, evaporate, sodium chloride, rock salt, brine

Teaching and learning

Engage

- Show the students a range of types of salt – e.g. table salt, sea salt, large rock salt crystals (cubic shape). Ask them to examine the samples and then pose questions such as 'What is (sea) salt used for?', 'Where does (rock) salt come from?' Explain that sodium chloride is a compound we commonly use as 'salt', but that there are many other salts. [O1]

  Higher-attaining students may **make links** to the elements/compounds/mixtures they have met up to this point – e.g. chloride, sulfate, nitrate; identify elements from use of formulas to represent them etc.

Challenge and develop

- Split the class into groups to **explore** the three different ways of extracting and purifying salt highlighted in the Student Book (and on Worksheet 1.3.9):

  - extraction from rock salt
  - evaporation of brine/seawater
  - solution mining.

  Students may raise the point that these methods don't result in pure salt. Acknowledge this point and say that this will be explored later in the lesson as the method is evaluated.

- Students should follow Practical sheet 1.3.9a, 1.3.9b or 1.3.9c to **model** one of these three industrial methods for obtaining salt.

  Allocate roles to ensure that all students contribute to the activities – e.g. timekeeper (ensures task is completed on time and that the team works together), resource manager (collects and manages all the apparatus and resources), chief scientist (responsible for the quality of the science/explanation), reporter (responsible for recording and reporting group findings). [O2]

Explain

- Students need to be prepared to **demonstrate** and **explain** their process. Support students in using key terms and in highlighting the key processes. [O2]
- **Group work/jigsaw** Ask the students to present their findings so that they hear information about all three methods. These presentations could be run as a jigsaw group activity rather than a whole class activity (depending on class size). Members of each group (e.g. chief scientist/reporter) swap groups and present/teach their findings to a different group; they then return to their original groups to be taught about the other methods by the remaining team members (timekeeper/resource manager) who heard the other presentations. [O2]

Consolidate and apply

- During others' presentations, the students collate information and produce their own spider diagram/list of key points in order to **feed back** to their original teams and to allow comparison between the methods. [O2&3]

  Higher-attaining students should be challenged to **explain** clearly the scientific reasoning behind the processes.
- Students should **identify** the similarities and differences of the three processes as well as pros and cons. [O3]

Extend

- Show a picture of the Dead Sea to students able to progress further and ask them to design a series of demonstrations for the rest of the class to explain density/buoyancy – e.g. salt solutions (add food colouring to differentiate them) that will 'float' on top of each other; an egg floating at different levels in 'water/brine'. [O1]

Plenary suggestions

3–2–1: Ask the students to list three methods of extracting salt, two uses of salt, one disadvantage of salt mining. [O1, 2&3]

Answers to Student Book questions

1. flavour food; preserve food; make chlorine 2. chlorine; it kills bacteria in drinking water
3. They trapped sea water in shallow ponds and waited for it to evaporate.
4. Climate not hot enough/not enough sunshine/too much rain in Britain.
5. makes ice melt; provides grip/friction/stops slipping 6. clay
7. does not dissolve/not soluble 8. crush, dissolve, filter, evaporate
9. *Rock salt* – red/brown/sandy/grit/crystals/solid
   Solution mining – colourless solution (brine)/white crystals/purer salt/less impure
10. Purer/less impure; cheaper/quicker to produce; only need to evaporate water rather than remove sand/impurities
11. *Advantages*: less impure/rock/clay; quicker/easier to separate pure salt from just water
    Disadvantages: leaves holes underground; unstable ground/land sinks/buildings may collapse

Answers to Worksheet 1.3.9

1. Three processes: a) dissolving b) filtering c) evaporation
   Substances: i) rock salt ii) clay/sand/rock iii) salt solution iv) clay/sand/rock v) salt solution
   vi) water vapour vii) concentrated salt solution or salt viii) salt
2. Diagrams should make salt, sand and water particles distinct; show the mixtures present in i), iii), v) and vii); pure substances in ii), iv), vi) and viii). Higher-attaining students should show the higher concentration of the solution in vii) compared to vi).
3. a) Diagram should include: pumping of water into rocks; dissolving; salt solution brought to the surface; separation of salt from salt solution.
   b) *Positives*: new facilities; jobs; more economic activity in the area to benefit other businesses such as shops.
   Negatives: more traffic; visual, noise and other pollution; have to wait for new facilities; not enough detail or guarantees; exploitation of local area for potentially marginal benefits.

3.10 Understanding distillation

Lesson overview

Learning objectives

- Use distillation to separate substances.
- Explain why distillation can purify substances.

Learning outcomes

- Describe distillation. [O1]
- Explain the physical processes involved in distillation. [O2]
- Identify the advantages of distillation. [O3]

Skills development

- Thinking scientifically: evaluate risks
- Working scientifically: develop explanations
- Learner development: develop resilience

Resources needed evaporating basin; watch glass/tile; materials and equipment as detailed in the Technician's notes; boiling water; boiling tubes; delivery tubes; salt solution; condenser; ink; Worksheet 1.3.10a, Worksheet 1.3.10b copied onto card; Practical sheet 1.3.10, Technician's notes 1.3.10

Common misconceptions Boiling and evaporation are the same. The water in the condenser mixes with the substances being separated.

Key vocabulary vapour, condense, distillation, Liebig condenser, purify

Teaching and learning

Engage

- Ask the students to **recall** and **demonstrate** their understanding of the three states of matter and changes of state by working in pairs to produce/complete a simple flow diagram – e.g. solid → liquid → gas → liquid → solid and labelling appropriate stages – i.e. freeze, boil, condense, melt. [O2]
- Review the results and explore the students' understanding of melting and boiling points being the temperatures at which the changes of state occur and link these to freezing and condensing points (i.e. same point/temperature in reverse). [O2]

Challenge and develop

- Demonstrate the evaporation of a salt solution in an evaporating basin. Ask the students to **explain** the processes using questions such as 'Why does separation work?', 'Where does the water go?', 'How could the water be captured?' [O2]
- Demonstrate the condensation of steam from the evaporating basin by holding a watch glass/tile above the basin. Highlight the fact that steam is the name we give to water vapour and that it is a gas. Ask the students to **identify** the disadvantages and safety implications of the process – e.g. hot steam, spitting salt. [O3]

Explain

- Ask the students to perform a simple distillation using boiling tubes and a delivery tube to separate salt and water – they can use Practical sheet 1.3.10. During the process students should **consider** what happens and also how the method differs from the evaporating basin method. [O1, 2&3]
- Ask the students to **feed back** their observations – e.g. salt does not spit/dry out as quickly/can collect the water in distillation but cannot in evaporation basin method/may appear to be quicker to complete.

- Support the students in drawing accurate line diagrams to model and demonstrate the processes – i.e. heating, boiling, cooling, condensing (label solution, liquid, solid, gas/water vapour/steam etc.). [O1&2]

Consolidate and apply

- Demonstrate the use of distillation to separate two liquids using a condenser – e.g. ink and water – or have groups of students **observe** the process from a number of sets of apparatus set up around the room. [O1&2]
- Ask the students to label the equipment on Worksheet 1.3.10a, **explain** the processes involved and the advantages over the previous methods – e.g. larger scale, condenser cools vapour more efficiently etc. [O1, 2&3]

Extend

- Ask students able to progress further to develop a model, cartoon or 'drama' to explain the processes that take place during distillation. Use counters or circles to show differences in the distribution and movement of solute and solvent particles in the starting flask, the vapour, the condenser and collecting vessel. [O2]

Plenary suggestions

Distillation cards Give the students the set of cards from Worksheet 1.3.10b to sequence the processes that occur during distillation. [O1&2]

Answers to Student Book questions

1. perfume; petrol; vodka; (essential oils, fuels, alcoholic drinks)
2. The window is colder than the steam/water vapour; so the gas condenses/turns back to liquid/water.
3. It stops the steam/vapour/water escaping; captures the steam/vapour/gas and turns it back/ condenses it to water/liquid.
4. The condenser has water to keep the tube cold; which makes condensation happen more quickly; because it is colder.
5. Any reasonable safety precautions linked to Figure 1.3.10c – clamp flask above heat source; joints/bungs are tight and leak free/nothing can escape; glass not cracked/broken; not too much liquid in distillation flask to boil over; heat source not too near condenser; cold water for condenser is on and does not leak; collection beaker is in the right place/no spills.
6. It is quicker; collects the water and the salt; no spitting salt; less water/salt is lost.
7. The thermometer gives the temperature of the vapour/boiling point; so you know which substance is being separated – i.e. which is a gas (in the condenser) and which is still liquid (in the flask).
8. They are flammable liquids; a direct flame cannot be used.
9. They have different boiling points/ethanol has a lower boiling point/turns to vapour/gas first; and can be condensed and collected before the water boils.

Answers to Worksheet 1.3.10a

1. a), b) A seawater, solution or mixture that is to be separated
   B thermometer; to check the boiling point of the vapour
   C condenser; to cool the water to make it condense back into a liquid
   D cold water; cools the condenser
   E beaker; collects the product – the solvent from the original mixture
   F distilled water; one of the products
   G heat; speeds up evaporation of the water/solvent
2.

Mirror method	Simple; much of the water is lost as it escapes into the air; mirror gets warm and less condenses
Alchemists still	Captures more water than mirror method; some vapour is still lost
Liebig condenser	More elaborate/expensive equipment; most efficient of the three due to effective cooling of water vapour by a flow of cold water; stays efficient indefinitely so long as cold water is supplied

3. Any sensible, scientifically correct ideas

Answers to Worksheet 1.3.10b

The correct sequence is B, E, D, C, A, F.

3.11 Applying key ideas

How hard is your water?

Objectives

- Extract ideas about water being hard from the text.
- Extract ideas about solubility to explain some of the implications of the concept.
- Use ideas and information about elements, compounds and formulas to explain the properties of chemicals.

Outcomes

- Making clear and effective responses to questions, indicating understanding and the next steps in learning.

The purpose of this activity is to provide an opportunity to see how successfully students are grasping the key ideas so far. It is not designed to be used as a formal test; it might be that students work on the questions collectively. It does provide an opportunity for you to look at written work, engage students in discussions and form ideas about progress being made.

The tasks are progressive. Lower-attaining students should be able to tackle the first two or three, and higher-attaining students will find the later ones more challenging.

Resources needed test tubes; samples of hard and soft water; liquid soap

Teaching and learning

Engage

- Ask the students to unscramble some anagrams to identify the different sources of water – e.g. airnewtar (rainwater), clearig (glacier), seanco (oceans), irservero (reservoir), ngripss (springs), versir (rivers) etc.

Challenge and develop

- Provide the students with samples of hard and soft water (labelled anonymously A and B) and ask them to add a little soap to each, shake and **observe** the effect.
- Ask them to **suggest** what might cause the difference in the behaviour. Collect the responses but do not validate ideas at this stage.

Explain

- Ask the students to read the text 'How hard is your water?' Depending on their ability to assimilate text, you may need to adopt strategies such as:
  - Students work in pairs with copies of the text and highlighters. One student highlights key ideas and the other (with a different colour) any words they are not comfortable with.
  - Using the text as a source of ideas, ask the students to draw a spider chart with 'hard water' at the centre and its properties and applications around it.
  - Work with a group of students who have difficulty with reading to support them in decoding the text and accessing the ideas.

Consolidate and apply

- Now ask the students to attempt the tasks in the Student Book. They might do this individually or collaboratively, but encourage them to **identify** and **record** their ideas.
- Ask students to present their responses to various tasks, either orally or by displaying their work.

Extend

- The later tasks give opportunities for extension work for those students able to progress further.

Plenary

Ask the students for responses to questions such as:

- 'How well were you able to approach those tasks?'
- 'Did we manage to present some high-quality responses?'
- 'Are there some ideas that we need to strengthen in the latter part of this topic?'

Make a note of the responses. Provide some overall feedback, indicating ideas that students have grasped effectively and those they may need developing further.

Likely responses and next steps in learning

1. This task gives students an opportunity to place the context within their own experience and to think about the idea that not all drinking water supplies are, or taste, the same. It also encourages them to start drawing ideas from text, such as the evidence for water being hard (limescale in kettles and deposits in central heating systems) and dissolved chemicals causing a distinctive taste.
2. This task involves extracting ideas from the text about water being hard because of chemicals being dissolved in it. Also about the nature of the chemicals causing temporary or permanent hardness and the chemicals getting there as a result of water flowing over and reacting with certain rocks, such as limestone. They should identify that bicarbonates cause temporary hardness, sulfates and chlorides cause permanent hardness and that only the former can be removed by boiling.
3. This is a recall task from prior knowledge ideas about solubility. Students need to extract information about the specific chemicals from the text, but then relate it to their understanding of the concept and how it could be demonstrated using a simple experiment, such as adding the chemical to water and observing the lack of solubility.
4. This prompts the students to apply knowledge of elements and symbols to understanding what a formula indicates and also how formulas are constructed.
5. This also involves looking at a formula, albeit a more complex one, and decoding it. It also explores the relationship between the name of a chemical and the elements present in the compound. Students should identify the 'bi' prefix, indicating 'two' (as in HCO_3 groups) in the old name. They should also notice the presence of hydrogen in the formula and the new name.

3.12 Finding out what air is made of

Lesson overview

Learning objectives

- Describe the composition of air.
- Separate gases from air.

Learning outcomes

- Describe the composition of air. [O1]
- Identify sources of air pollution and their impact. [O2]
- Explain why distillation can be used to separate the gases in air. [O3]

Skills development

- Thinking scientifically: analyse data
- Working scientifically: interpret evidence
- Learner development: communicate effectively

Resources needed images relating to air pollution; candle; white tile; incense stick; Worksheet 1.3.12

Common misconceptions Air is mostly oxygen. Air pollution only comes from cars. Air pollution is not harmful.

Key vocabulary gas, air pollution, boiling point, compressed

Teaching and learning

Engage

- Show the students the pie chart of air composition (Figure 1.3.12b in the Student Book) and ask them to answer related questions, such as question 1 in the Student Book. Reinforce the idea that oxygen is not the most abundant gas, but it is the one we need to breathe and to burn fuels. [O1]

  Higher-attaining students should **consider** how the composition of the air might be known. Ask questions such as, 'Can air be separated?', How might this be done?' This information is provided in the 'Boiling cold' section of the Student Book and also relates to the 'Extend' section in this lesson plan.

Challenge and develop

- Ask the students to **consider** what else is present in air and how it might have got there. Demonstrate burning a candle and holding a white tile close to the flame. The students should **observe** the release of particles/soot. This demonstration could be repeated with an incense stick to model the spread of 'smell' particles as they mix with air. [O2]
- Students could **consider** the different composition of air in different places – e.g. roadside/countryside, near a volcano/the middle of the ocean, inside a house/outside. [O1&2]

  Higher-attaining students may be able to **make the link** between the composition of the air and the origin of pollutants.

Explain

- Show the students images relating to air pollution – e.g. 1956 smog in London, mask-wearing in China, buildings being cleaned, newspaper headlines relating to pollution – and share their ideas and concerns about pollution. [O2]
- Students **analyse data** relating to air pollution in Worksheet 1.3.12 and **draw conclusions** about the sources and impact of common pollutants. [O1&2]

Consolidate and apply

- Ask the students to **consider evidence** in relation to global carbon dioxide levels relating to the data in Worksheet 1.3.12. [O1&2]
- Discuss ways in which pollution could be reduced – what actions can individuals, communities, manufacturers, governments take? [O2]

Extend

- Ask students able to progress further to **explain** how distillation can be used to separate the components of air. This exercise relates to the 'Boiling cold' section of the Student Book. [O3]

Plenary suggestions

Hot seat Give the students the name of a substance present in the air and ask for facts about it – e.g. *oxygen*: a gas, makes up 20% of the air, we breathe it; *sulfur dioxide*: a gas, a pollutant, a compound, it irritates the lungs. [O1&2]

Answers to Student Book questions

1. nitrogen; oxygen
2. … oxide
3. burning carbon compounds; animals breathe it out
4. Pollutants make lung conditions such as asthma worse.
5. Accurate information is needed from different areas/things may change during day and night.
6. fine particles; sulfur dioxide and nitrogen oxides; burning fuels; traffic
7. The cryogenic distillation of air; compressed air is cooled and then heated slowly in a fractionating column until oxygen boils and is separated at −183 °C.
8. The need to compress the gas/use high pressures;and to keep it at very low temperatures.
9. Compressed gases take up less space/can fit more in a small container.

Answers to Worksheet 1.3.12

1. a) particles; sulfur dioxide; ozone

   b) Fuels such as oil, coal, gas, petrol, diesel that have formed over millions of years from the remains of living things.

   c) Any activities that use fuel – driving, air travel, using electricity, heating homes, industry

   d) Ideas about insulating homes, more efficient transport
2. a) Little change before 1800; slowly rising at first after that; more rapid rise through the 20th century.

   b) Increase in industrial activity; much greater use of mechanised transport that burns fuel; wider use of electricity.

   c) Not completely because the gas is also produced in natural processes.

   d) They predicted the increase in world population, industry, use of electricity and mechanised transport; they assumed that the cause of carbon dioxide rise is due mainly to human activity.

   e) climate change; more frequent extreme weather; more desertification, rise in sea level
3. a) e.g. cars, air travel, high electricity consumption, fossil fuel used for heating

   b) Any reasoned argument which reflects social conscience/responsibility.

   c) Ideas around negotiation and incentives – e.g. through trade agreements, sharing knowledge and technology to reduce pollution.

3.13 Exploring chromatography

Lesson overview

Learning objectives

- Use chromatography to separate dyes.

Learning outcomes

- Identify mixtures using chromatography. [O1]
- Describe how to separate a mixture using chromatography. [O2]
- Use evidence from chromatography to explain the composition of mixtures. [O3]

Skills development

- Thinking scientifically: use units and nomenclature
- Working scientifically: interpret evidence
- Learner development: ask questions

Resources needed sugar-coated sweets/felt-tip pens/food colouring; water; pipette dropper; filter paper; beaker; pencil; Worksheet 1.3.13

Common misconceptions Paper chromatography is the only type of chromatography. Substances have to be coloured to be separated.

Key vocabulary mixture, separate, paper chromatography, chromatogram, dye

Teaching and learning

Engage

- Give the students some sweets with sugar-coated coloured shells, felt-tip pens or food colouring and ask them to put the sweet or a dot of colour on a piece of filter paper. The students should then slowly drop water onto the sample using a pipette. Ask questions such as 'What has happened?', 'Why do you think that is?' and encourage them to **explain** their answers and use the correct terms – e.g. dissolve, soluble. The 'Separating colours' section in the Student Book supports this exercise. [O1&2]

  Tips for carrying out successful chromatography:

  - Use water soluble dyes/pens.
  - Several applications of the pen/dye, allowing each to dry before the next is applied, gives a more intense colour.
  - Allow each drop of water to spread fully before the next is applied.

Challenge and develop

- Explain to the students that they need to be able to reproduce what you do exactly, so as they observe the demonstration they need to make notes/diagrams etc. using the correct terms.
- Demonstrate two methods of paper chromatography – dropping, and using a wick standing in water. Emphasise the terms and processes. [O2]

Explain

- Students should **investigate the composition** of coloured inks and dyes using the two methods. [O1, 2&3]
- They will need to **produce evidence** that they have listened to you and followed instructions carefully by producing quality chromatograms. You might want to initiate a competition. [O1, 2&3]

Consolidate and apply

- **Pairs to fours** Student pairs **present** their chromatograms and explanations to each other. [O1, 2&3]
- **Peer assess** The students should **discuss** who has provided the best evidence best and say why. Give feedback for areas of improvement – e.g. smaller dot of ink, put dots further apart, have less water in the beaker, put the dot further up the filter paper away from water line, find a better method of keeping the filter paper straight; do not leave in the water too long.
- Identify and summarise the key things to remember when performing paper chromatography – e.g. pencil line, ink dots as small as possible, ink dots above the water line etc. [O2]
- The students should answer the questions on Worksheet 1.3.13 to help consolidate their learning, and understand how mistakes and carelessness will affect the results. [O2]

Extend

- Ask students able to progress further to **interpret chromatograms** and **draw conclusions** from them, for example:
  - whether the same/different inks/dyes were used
  - why different inks spread different distances up the filter paper. [O3]

Plenary suggestions

Chromatography quiz Ask the students to **justify** why: pencil lines are used; the water level must be below the ink spot; chromatography would not work for a permanent marker pen/oil-based paint; same dye in a different pen would always be in the same place on the same type of filter paper. [O1, 2&3]

Answers to Student Book questions

1. It can be separated into different colours (as shown by the blue and yellow circles in Figure 1.3.13b).
2. It dissolves and spreads with the water.
3. It is a way of separating mixtures/a separation method.
4. chromatogram
5. The pencil line will not dissolve in water.
6. Salt is white/will not show up/ is a solid.
7. This stops the dyes washing down into the water.
8. They are the same dye/same mixtures of dyes.
9. Both are mixtures of three components; both contain the same blue dye; both contain a yellow dye, but not the same one; the R_f of the blue dye is $3 \div 7 = 0.43$; the yellow dye travelled further than the blue one (is more soluble than the blue dye).
10. Make the chromatogram in the same way but look at the results under a ultraviolet light so that the spots show up.

Answers to Worksheet 1.3.13

1. a) The colours in the line would move up the paper with the dyes being analysed (if the ink used is water soluble).
   b) The permanent marker does not move because it is not soluble in water.
   c) The water, ink/dye might not soak up the paper, or might do so very slowly.
   d) The dyes could all travel to the top of the paper.
   e) The dye is washed across the paper, rather than its components separating gradually.
2. Look for clear communication, correct terminology, avoidance of mistakes such as in Q1. The students should describe or illustrate clearly how the results would show identical or non-identical food colourings.
3. a) The dye was soluble in the water/soap and could transfer from the towel into the shirt.
   b) The red dye of the towel was probably made of a mixture of several different dyes which had different solubilities.
   c) Some of the dye may be bonded to the cloth and not washed off, or is not water/soap soluble.
   d) During manufacture a lot of dye is used so some will wash off. In an old towel, unbonded, water-soluble dye has already been washed away in previous washes.
   e) It depends on whether or not the dye has bonded to the material of the shirt.

3.14 Using chromatography

Lesson overview

Learning objectives

- Use chromatography to identify unknown substances.
- Draw conclusions from evidence.

Learning outcomes

- Identify patterns and evidence using chromatography. [O1]
- Interpret chromatograms and draw conclusions. [O2]
- Identify similarities and differences between chromatography and DNA analysis. [O3]

Skills development

- Thinking scientifically: consider the quality of evidence
- Working scientifically: present evidence
- Learner development: collaborate effectively

Resources needed filter paper; pens/dyes; water; materials and equipment as detailed in Technician's notes; Worksheet 1.3.14; Practical sheet 1.3.14; Technician's notes 1.3.14

Common misconceptions Paper chromatography is used in police forensics.

Key vocabulary forensic, reliable, chromatography, accurate, evidence

Teaching and learning

Engage

- Discuss with the students why it is important that police collect forensic evidence to catch criminals and what precautions police/forensic teams need to take to ensure that the evidence is reliable enough to convict criminals. [O1&2]
- Remind the students that chromatography is one of a number of separation techniques that might be used in different situations, including gathering evidence for criminal investigations, which they will think about in Worksheet 1.3.14. [O1&2]

Challenge and develop

- **Set the scene**: Referring to the scenario in the Student Book, or another of your choice, tell the students that they will act as police forensic teams gathering evidence to identify a criminal. The evidence must be **recorded** carefully and to satisfy a judge that there is enough reliable evidence. [O1&2]

Explain

- Teams of students perform chromatography on a series of pens/dyes etc. to compare materials from a crime scene in order to gather reliable evidence to make the right conviction. They can use Practical sheet 1.3.14. You might want to allocate roles to ensure that all students participate – e.g. resource manager, quality-control manager, reporter, chief scientist etc. [O1&2]

Consolidate and apply

- Students gather and present their evidence to the 'judge'. [O1&2]

  Higher-attaining students could act as lawyers cross-examining the 'chief scientists' from different groups and scrutinising their findings, methods and quality/quantity of evidence etc.

- Discuss the merits of each case and identify areas that need improvement to guarantee prosecution – e.g. number of repeats, elimination of all other possible matches, no cross-contamination from other samples, accurate measurements and fair tests to get exact matches etc. [O1&2]

Extend

- Ask students able to progress further to **discuss** ways in which DNA evidence is used in criminal investigations using the section 'Special separation' in the Student Book as a model. Students **explain** the similarities and differences between this technique and chromatography to the rest of the class (question 7 in the Student Book). [O3]

Plenary suggestions

Where's the evidence? Show the students two chromatograms and ask them to **draw conclusions** about the evidence. You could use the chromatograms in the Student Book. [O1&2]

Answers to Student Book questions

1. The paint came from the gang's car.
2. Analyse paint from another part of the car.
3. No; further evidence is needed to prove that the car was at the crime scene and that no other car could match the same paint pattern produced due to possible repaint/repair; look at layers of paint rather than just surface layer; transfer of evidence from the wall/gate to the car, e.g. brick dust, paint from gate posts.
4. The inks separate out into different components/colours/spots.
5. The pattern from the graffiti matches up with those from the suspect's marker pens.
6. Repeat the test/do it more than once; to make sure the results were repeatable.
7. It separates/identifies components of mixture; produces a pattern; identical components travel the same distance under the same conditions
8. Chromatography uses a liquid/solvent/solubility; electrophoresis uses a gel and electric current to separate components.
9. Any reasonable answer to illustrate they should avoid contamination; such as: gloves, masks, overalls, sealed containers/bags.

Answers to Worksheet 1.3.14

1. a) Distillation; the water evaporates and leaves the salt behind; the water vapour is condensed to give pure water.

   b) Chromatography; if they are not the same they should show up differently on a chromatogram. (In reality more detailed analysis of proteins can be carried out.)

   c) Sieve; provided the mesh is of a suitable size, the soil can pass through and the stones are retained in the sieve.

   d) Chromatography; if it is pure, only one mark would be visible on a chromatogram; if it is a mixture and at least one component is soluble, two or more marks would be visible.

   e) Very fine filter; the particles of the gases of the air must be able to pass through; but the tiny particles of pollutant are trapped.
2. a) four in each

   b) Only the genuine medicine contains the active ingredient; the toxin is present in the suspect medicine.

   c) The suspect medicine would not make them better (no active ingredient); and could poison them (contains a toxin).

   d) Criminal deception to make money; or intent to harm.
3. Explanation covering: collection of samples from crime scenes; analysis of samples by chromatography and electrophoresis; comparison with samples from the suspects; need to avoid contamination; need for other evidence.

3.15 Finding the best solvent

Lesson overview

Learning objectives

- Choose the best solvent.
- Recognize hazards when using solvents.

Learning outcomes

- Identify hazard symbols. [O1]
- Select appropriate solvents for different uses. [O2]
- Link the uses of solvents to their properties. [O3]

Skills development

- Thinking scientifically: evaluate risks
- Working scientifically: interpret evidence
- Learner development: communicate effectively

Resources needed nail varnish remover (optional); fabrics with stains; stain removers; materials and equipment as detailed in the Technician's notes; Worksheet 1.3.15; Technician's notes 1.3.15; (Practical sheet 1.3.14 can be made available to support students as they set up their chromatography experiments)

Common misconceptions All solvents are dangerous. Water is the best solvent.

Key vocabulary insoluble, solvent, dissolve, hazard, volatile

Teaching and learning

Engage

- Show the students a collection of common symbols and ask them to **suggest** their meaning – e.g. road symbols, shop/brand signs. [O1]
- Explore why symbols are used in chemistry, using the chemical hazard symbols that are shown in Table 1.3.15 in the Student Book (but without showing this table to the students at this stage – the discussion should begin simply with the names and symbols flammable, moderate health hazard, dangerous for the environment, harmful to long-term health. [O1]
- Students could either **suggest** symbols for the names or be given the opportunity to match the names and symbols. [O1]

Challenge and develop

- Ask pairs of students to set up a chromatography experiment using permanent marker pens. They should **explore** the use of different solvents to see how the substances separate – e.g. water, alcohol/water, acetone/water. The procedure is the same as that used in the previous topic (Practical sheet 1.3.14). See Technician's notes 1.3.15; care is needed with the solvents used – there should be no naked flames and adequate ventilation. Ask the students to label their chromatograms and retain them. [O2]

Explain

- Demonstrate the volatility and flammability of acetone and alcohol. The students could **observe** the 'cold' effect of blowing a solvent such as nail varnish remover (acetone) from the back of their hand. CAUTION: only one very small drop is required – do not use on dry/broken skin. [O3]
- Make links between volatility and smell. Ask the students to **suggest** why alcohol is often used as a solvent in perfumes. This links to the section 'Clean and smelly' in the Student Book. [O3]

- The students should now review Table 1.3.15 in the Student Book. Ask them to **identify the names** of different solvents, their uses and the hazards associated with these. Worksheet 1.3.15 will help with this. You could ask the students if they are aware of any other hazards relating to solvents – e.g. solvent abuse. [O1]

Consolidate and apply

- Return to the results of the chromatography experiment in 'Challenge and develop'. Ask the students to **discuss their findings** in pairs by answering a series of questions such as 'What are the differences?', 'Which is the best solvent?', 'What is the evidence?' This could include the degree of separation, if any – the solvent that gave the best separation of components implies a better solubility for that application if conditions were the same (fair test). [O2]
- Discuss the findings asking 'Why does the solvent affect the pattern in chromatography?' Students need to be able to **identify** and **explain** the importance of solubility in chromatography. [O2&3]

Extend

For students able to progress further:

- ask them to **explain** how a knowledge of solvents is useful for cleaning clothes – this relates to the 'Careful choice' section in the Student Book. [O2&3]
- provide several fabrics and stains for them to **investigate** with stain removers/solvents. [O2&3]

Plenary suggestions

True or false Show the students hazard symbols and give correct/incorrect names. [O1]

Answers to Student Book questions

1. All paints are not soluble in water.
2. a) acetone/propanone b) alcohol/ethanol c) water
3. flammable; irritant; harmful; harmful to the environment
4. *Advantages*: hard-wearing; waterproof; good grip
   Disadvantages: have to heat it; sticky; smelly; dangerous; hard to remove from cars
5. The solvent used might remove the car paint as well as the tar.
6. Some damage dyes and fabric; a single solvent does not dissolve every type of stain; different substances need different solvents.
7. The vapours are cooled and condensed so they can be collected.
8. Some solvents are toxic and harmful to the environment.
9. *Advantages*: evaporates; can be removed quickly; dries quickly
   Disadvantages: smells; spreads quickly; may be flammable; harmful to breathe

Answers to Worksheet 1.3.15

1. a) i) toxic; long-term health hazard; flammable; dangerous to the environment
   ii) moderate health hazard; long-term health hazard; flammable
   b) It will not dissolve in water.
   c) White spirit; water will not work; turpentine is expensive and more dangerous.
2. a) emulsion; easy to use
   b) acrylic; intense colour; quick drying so can keep adding to the painting
   c) gloss paint; protects the wood from rain; easy to wipe clean
3. Any good examples that show the student appreciates the following: different substances require particular solvents; solvents must not cause unwanted damage; solvents should be non-hazardous where possible; safety procedures and equipment may be needed in some cases.

3.16 Modelling mixtures and separation

Lesson overview

Learning objectives

- Explain what happens to mass during dissolving.
- Use a circle model to explain dissolving and separation.

Learning outcomes

- Recognise pure substances and mixtures. [O1]
- Use a simple model to explain what happens to mass during dissolving. [O2]
- Use a simple model to explain dissolving and separation. [O3]

Skills development

- Thinking scientifically: understand how theories develop
- Working scientifically: develop explanations
- Learner development: communicate effectively

Resources needed coloured card circles as models of atoms; beaker of red water; beaker of blue water; salt; tiddlywinks/plasticine/modelling clay; Worksheet 1.3.16

Common misconceptions Mass decreases during dissolving because a substance disappears.

Key vocabulary model, atom, molecule, pure, Law of Conservation of Mass

Teaching and learning

Engage

- Show the students a series of simple circle models and ask them to **identify** atoms, compounds, mixtures, pure substances. [O1]
- Ask the students to draw a diagram to represent a mixture of two of the previous pictures and adapt the diagram to represent 'soluble' and 'insoluble'. Questions 1 and 2 in the Student Book support this. [O1&2]

Challenge and develop

- **Pair talk** Show the students two beakers – one containing red water and the other blue water. Weigh them and record the masses. Working in pairs, ask the students to **predict** and **explain** what will happen to the mass if the liquids are mixed. [O1]
- Show them the same experiment, but this time use salt and water. Ask 'Will the same thing happen?' Students should **explain** their reasons for the similarities or differences in the expected outcome. This exercise relates to the 'Conservation of mass' section in the Student Book. [O1&2]
- Discuss the findings as a class and aim to remove misconceptions around mass changes during dissolving. Remind the students that dissolving is NOT a chemical change – solutions are mixtures. [O2]

  Encourage higher-attaining students to develop the depth of their explanations and use the correct terminology.

Explain

- Model the process of dissolving using students/counters/balls to represent the particles in the water and the salt mixing together. Explain dissolving as a process of mixing – i.e. a physical process. [O3]
- Demonstrate knocking down skittles or the movement of snooker balls etc. by collisions – this provides a model for the way that solvent molecules collide with solids/crystals such as salt and break them apart/dissolve them. The more collisions, the faster the crystal breaks apart – and dissolves faster when stirred or the solvent is at a higher temperature. [O3]

Consolidate and apply

- **Pair talk** Students should work in pairs to produce a series of circle models, a poster, cartoons or models (tiddlywinks, plasticine, modelling clay) to represent a series of scenarios – e.g. dissolving, filtering, crystallisation, evaporation. Refer to the Student Book section 'Modelling' to introduce this activity. [O2&3]
- Discuss what makes a good model. Agree points with the students and list success criteria for the activity – e.g. different types of substance represented by different colours/sizes; changes are clear between steps in the process; changes are explained well using appropriate terms; model explains what can be/is observed. [O2&3]
- Discuss with students other physical processes, such as chromatography, distillation, freezing, filtering and evaporation. Encourage students to **consider** how the models they use to understand mixing and dissolving can be used to understand these as well. Worksheet 1.3.16 can be used to support and embed this. [O1, 2&3]

Extend

Students able to make further progress should:

- **observe** closely the breakdown of salt crystals during dissolving [O3]
- **consider** the importance of the movement of the solvent and the impact of temperature (this relates back to the Topics 3.6 and 3.8 on dissolving). [O3]

Plenary suggestions

Review Peer-mark the posters/models using the success criteria agreed and identify things that could be improved. [O1, 2&3]

Answers to Student Book questions

1. Circle models help scientists to understand the composition of substances, explain their observations and explain processes simply, or explain things that cannot be seen directly.
2. a) one circle; any colour b) two identical circles touching; any colour c) two circles touching; different colours d) random pattern of joined circles; any colour combinations, any pairings
3. a mixture of a solvent and a solute
4. It has the same total mass as the solute and solvent together/there is no change in mass.
5. Two circle models needed:

   a) Separate solvent and solute diagrams; solvent circles spread out; solute circles clustered more tightly (can be atoms or molecules; single or groups of circles).

   b) The same number of circles as the solute and solvent in (a); in one diagram; randomly mixed together.
6. Some of the salt or water was spilled; some water evaporated.
7. The salt particles get smaller; and mix with the water particles.
8. The water particles could be smaller; there could be more of them; could imply movement; salt particles could show that they are made of lots of particles stuck together.
9. a) A model similar to that shown in Figure 1.3.16d with some of the smaller water circles above the level of the solution.

   b) A model to show a magnet with iron 'circles' attached; and sand 'circles' still in a pile.

Answers to Worksheet 1.3.16

1. a) Evaporation; shows a liquid and a few particles escaping into the air as a gas.

   b) Dissolving; shows the particles of the solid spreading out through the solvent.
2. a) Diagram should show closely packed, random solvent particles that have soaked up the paper. At different positions, two or more blobs of particles to represent the different inks from the pen. The particles should be distant from each other and from the solvent particles.

   b) As the solvent moves upwards the inks in the mixture are carried upwards also. Different inks move different distances compared to the solvent and each other. This depends on the size of the particles of the ink and the ink's solubility.
3. Diagram should show: liquid state with a dissolved substance; evaporation of liquid to form a gas with none of the dissolved substance present; condensation of gas particles to form a pure liquid.

3.17 Checking students' progress

The 'Checking your progress' section in the Student Book indicates the key ideas developed in this chapter and shows how students progress to more complex levels. It is provided to support students in:

- identifying those ideas
- developing a sense of their current level of understanding
- developing a sense of what the next steps in their learning will be.

It is designed either to be used at the end of a chapter to support an overall view of the progress, or alternatively during the teaching of the chapter students can self assess or peer assess using this topic as a basis.

It would be helpful if students can be encouraged to provide evidence from their understanding or their notes to support their judgements. In some cases it may be useful to explore the difference in the descriptors for a particular idea so that students can see what makes for a 'higher outcome'.

It may be useful with some descriptors to provide examples from the specific work done, such as an experiment undertaken or an explanation developed and recorded. If marking and feedback uses similar ideas and phrases this will enable students to relate specific marking to a more general sense of progress.

To make good progress in understanding science students need to focus on these ideas and skills:

Students who are making modest progress will be able to:	**Students who are making good progress will be able to:**	**Students who are making excellent progress will be able to:**
Name and draw equipment and explain obvious laboratory risks.	Select and draw apparatus accurately; explain safety precautions.	Justify equipment choice and measurements; explain how to reduce risks.
Use 2D images to represent a range of laboratory equipment.	Use laboratory equipment safely to gather evidence.	Record evidence in an effective way.
Describe how to separate mixtures.	Select and explain appropriate separation techniques.	Explain the choice and method of separation using correct terms.
Describe the process of dissolving and the effect of temperature.	Describe methods for producing crystals of different sizes.	Use data to draw conclusions about solubility.
Understand that seawater is a mixture.	Explain why most water is not pure, and why this is not necessarily a problem.	Explain why contaminated water is a problem and identify what can be done about it.
Identify sources and uses of salt.	Describe how salt is extracted.	Recognise advantages and disadvantages of salt extraction methods.
Describe the process of distillation.	Explain the physical processes involved in distillation.	Identify the uses and advantages of distillation.
Describe the composition of air.	Identify sources of air pollution and their impact.	Explain how distillation can be used to separate gases in air.
Identify mixtures using chromatography.	Explain how to separate a mixture using chromatography and interpret chromatograms.	Use chromatograms to explain the composition of mixtures; compare chromatography and DNA analysis.
Explain the idea of a solvent.	Explain mass changes during dissolving; select solvents for different uses.	Use a model to explain dissolving and separation; link the uses of solvents to their properties.

3.18 Answers to Student Book Questions

This table provides answers to the *Questions* section at the end of Chapter 3 of Student Book 1. It also shows how different questions assess attainment in terms of the focus and style of a question as well as the context. Question-level analysis can indicate students' proficiency in approaching different aspects of scientific understanding and different types of answer.

Q	Answer		Focus			Style			Context			
		Marks available	Knowledge and understanding	Application	Evaluation of evidence	Objective test question	Short written answer	Longer written answer	Practical techniques	Solubility	Chemicals and reactions	Separation techniques
1	d	1	x			x				x		
2	a	1	x			x					x	
3	b; d	2	x			x					x	
4	Any two from: • observe carefully • wear goggles • point away from yourself and others • stop heating if it boils over • any other reasonable response	2	x				x		x			
5	Any two from: • different solvents dissolve different substances • not all solvents dissolve all substances • you need to use a solvent that does not mark or stain the fabric • some solvents are safer than others	2	x				x			x		
6	Procedure to include: • heating of water to evaporate • examination of crystals formed • appropriate equipment used • safety procedures such as goggles	 1 1 1 1	x					x	x			
7	a	1		x		x						x
8	d	1		x		x					x	
9	b	1		x		x						x
10	b	1		x		x					x	

Q	Answer		Focus			Style			Context			
		Marks available	Knowledge and understanding	Application	Evaluation of evidence	Objective test question	Short written answer	Longer written answer	Practical techniques	Solubility	Chemicals and reactions	Separation techniques
11	a) 'Acme was the least soluble and Delightful the most' gets 1 mark; the order of solubility from least to most being Acme, Carefree, Bonzo, Delightful gets 2 marks	2		x			x			x		
	b) 'Keep other factors the same (such as temperature)' gets 1 mark. Realising that even though the masses and volumes are different, the ratio (even if not explained using that term) is the same gets the second mark	2		x			x		x			
12	Description of chromatography experiment including:			x				x				x
	• setting up filter paper	1										
	• applying inks	1										
	• putting in solvent	1										
	• examining and comparing positions of colours	1										
13	'The hotter the water, the bigger the mass' gets 1 mark; reference to 'solubility increasing' gets 2 marks	2			x		x			x		
14	Relevant points include: • horse C had drug Y • none of the horses had drug X • horses A, B and D had neither drug	4			x			x				x
	Total possible:	**30**	**12**	**12**	**6**	**8**	**10**	**12**	**8**	**7**	**5**	**10**

4.1 Introduction

When and how to use these pages

The Introduction in the Student Book indicates some of the ideas and skills in this topic area that students will already have met from KS2 or from previous KS3 work, and provides an indication of what they will be studying in this unit. *Ideas you have met before* is not intended to be a comprehensive summary of all the prior ideas, but rather to point out a few of the key ones and to support the view that scientific understanding is progressive. Even though we might be meeting contexts that are new to us, we can often use existing ideas to start to make sense of them.

In this chapter you will find out indicates some of the new ideas that the chapter will introduce. Again, it isn't a detailed summary of content. Its purpose is more to act as a 'trailer' and generate some interest.

The outcomes, then, will be a recognition of prior learning that can be built on, and interest in finding out more.

There are a number of ways this can be used. You might, for example:

- Use *Ideas you have met before* as the basis for a revision lesson as you start the first new topic.
- Use *Ideas you have met before* as the centre of spider diagrams, to which students can add examples, experiments they might have done previously or what they found interesting.
- Make a note of any unfamiliar/difficult terms and return to these in the relevant lessons.
- Use ideas from *In this chapter you will find out* to ask students questions such as:
  - Why is this important?
  - How could it be used?
  - What might we be doing in this topic?

Overview of the chapter

In this chapter, students will learn about the ideas of atoms, elements and compounds, and ways that scientists represent them using symbols and formulas. They will learn how scientists have developed the Periodic Table and will start to learn about its groups, patterns and trends. Various elements are explored with regard to their different chemical and physical properties. Students will learn how to understand chemical reactions in terms of a rearrangement of atoms and how to represent these using circle diagrams, formulas and equations. They will study metals, non-metals and oxides.

This chapter offers a number of opportunities for students to investigate materials and reactions at first hand and use evidence to construct explanations. They explore evidence that reactions have occurred and how the properties of materials determine their applications.

Obstacles to learning

Students may need extra guidance with the following terms and common misconceptions:

- **Atoms and elements** Misconceptions include: elements were 'invented'; they can all be dug up from the ground; they all have symbols with the same letters as their English names; elements and atoms are different substances; elements are all different, but all atoms are the same; atoms are like cells and of a similar size.
- **Metals and non-metals** Misconceptions include: all metals are silver-coloured, magnetic and strong; all metals can be dug up from the ground; metals all melt at very high temperatures; the melting point and freezing point of a substance are different; non-metals are all solids; gases have no mass (do not weigh anything); air is an element; water is an element; all gases are poisonous.
- **Reactions** Misconceptions include: any elements can combine in any order or quantities; atoms change when compounds form, e.g. H_2O is a new atom; atoms change size; you can only join two atoms together side-by-side, like holding hands (linear); when things burn they disappear or are destroyed forever; heating and burning are the same; dissolving is a chemical change; heating always causes chemical changes.

	Topic title	Overarching objective
2	Finding elements and building the Periodic Table	Chemical symbols and formulas for elements and compounds
3	Looking at the Periodic Table of elements	The principles underpinning the Mendeleev Periodic Table The Periodic Table: periods and groups; metals and non-metals
4	Understanding elements and atoms	Differences between atoms, elements and compounds Chemical symbols and formulas for elements and compounds
5	Understanding metals	The varying physical and chemical properties of different elements The properties of metals and non-metals
6	Understanding non-metals	
7	Identifying metalloids	The varying physical and chemical properties of different elements
8	Discovering the origin of metals	The varying physical and chemical properties of different elements The properties of metals and non-metals Chemical symbols and formulas for elements and compounds
9	Choosing elements for a purpose	The varying physical and chemical properties of different elements
11	Combining elements	Differences between atoms, elements and compounds Chemical symbols and formulas for elements and compounds
12	Using models to understand chemistry	
13	Understanding what happens when an element burns	Chemical reactions as the rearrangement of atoms Representing chemical reactions using formulas and using equations Combustion
14	Observing how elements react in different ways	The varying physical and chemical properties of different elements Representing chemical reactions using formulas and using equations The chemical properties of metal and non-metal oxides with respect to acidity
15	Identifying the special features of carbon	The varying physical and chemical properties of different elements
16	Understanding oxidation	Representing chemical reactions using formulae and using equations Oxidation
17	Investigating carbonates	Conservation of mass changes of state and chemical reactions Combustion, thermal decomposition, oxidation Chemical symbols and formulae for elements and compounds Thermal decomposition
18	Explaining changes	Differences between atoms, elements and compounds Chemical symbols and formulae for elements and compounds Conservation of mass changes of state and chemical reactions Chemical reactions as the rearrangement of atoms Thermal decomposition, oxidation

4.2 Finding elements and building the Periodic Table

Lesson overview

Learning objectives

- Identify where and how different elements were found.
- Recognise differences between elements.
- Recognise that the Periodic Table has changed over time.

Learning outcomes

- Give examples of common elements and suggest where they may be found. [O1]
- Explain why the most ancient elements were found first. [O2]
- Outline a timeline of discovery of the elements. [O3]

Skills development

- Thinking scientifically: understand how theories develop
- Working scientifically: interpret evidence
- Learner development: communicate effectively

Resources needed sample/photo of haematite; timeline for students to add their cards to; Worksheet 1.4.2 – page 2 copied onto card and cut up

Common misconceptions Elements were 'invented' or 'made' rather than discovered. Elements can all be dug up from the ground.

Key vocabulary element, native element, compound, atom, Periodic Table

Teaching and learning

Engage

- Ask the students to **interpret the data** in Table 1.4.2 in the Student Book to prepare a bar chart, ordering the top 10 most abundant elements in the Earth's crust. [O1]
- Extend the task by asking them to **identify the symbols** of the elements – Al, C, H, Fe, Mg, O, K, Si, Na and Ti. [O1]

Challenge and develop

- Explain that most elements cannot simply be dug up in pure form (native metals) and that most are found as combinations of elements – compounds in rocks – that need to be extracted before we can use them (covered in more detail in later lesson). Refer back to the bar chart and clarify that these elements are found in the Earth's crust, i.e. rocks. Ask students to **suggest** 'Where else might oxygen be found on Earth?', 'How is the oxygen in the atmosphere and that in the rocks different?' (the element is a gas in air and occurs as solid compounds in rocks). [O1&2]
- Show a sample/photo of haematite (iron oxide) and ask groups/pairs of students to **suggest** how life would be different if our ancestors had not learned how to separate the iron from the rock. Gather feedback and reinforce the idea that our lives change as a result of new discoveries in chemistry – e.g. weapons, building materials, transport, silicon chip technology etc. [O2]

Explain

- Give the students a set of element cards from Worksheet 1.4.2 and ask them to **consider**:
  - Which are more likely to be native metals? Why? [O1]
  - What are 'synthetic' elements? [O1]

- Reinforce the idea that electricity and technology have made a big difference to what we can do and discover, and that through the work of one scientist, other scientists make further discoveries. [O2]

Consolidate and apply

- Set up a research activity in which the students **investigate the history** of some of the elements (access to the internet will be needed). This could be a card completion activity that is then presented as a Periodic Table by the class – e.g. collect the name, symbol, year of discovery, who/where discovered, how it got its name, its basic properties and uses. (Simplify or extend the detail required to meet the ability of the students.) [O2&3]

Extend

- Ask students able to progress further to **investigate** and outline the classification of elements that were named after people/places/words that have symbols that do not match their English names – e.g. mendelevium, einsteinium, curium; germanium, francium, polonium, americium; lead, tin, gold, silver, potassium, sodium, tungsten. [O3]

Plenary suggestions

Sequence cards Produce a timeline of the discovery of elements. Do this as a group activity and then play 'snap' to compare answers.

Answers to Student Book questions

1. In the Sun the elements are in their natural elemental states; on Earth they are mostly found as compounds.
2. a) water b) earth c) fire d) air – although it is hot, wet and is visible in the air
3. They are native elements that do not have to be extracted from rocks/ores like iron; they are easier to find.
4. Unlike the ancient Greeks, Davy used evidence from experiments that can be repeated to verify his discoveries.
5. They needed electricity to extract them so they could not have been discovered sooner.
6. There are no gaps in the Periodic Table; all the heavy elements (after U) are man-made.
7. They are man-made or produced in the radioactive decay of existing elements.
8. ununpentium – Uup

4.3 Looking at the Periodic Table of elements

Lesson overview

Learning objectives

- Navigate the Periodic Table and identify some of the elements.
- Identify features of the Periodic Table and describe how it is organised.
- Explain why the Periodic Table is useful.

Learning outcomes

- Identify an element from its symbol and atomic number. [O1]
- Explain how the Periodic Table is organised using the correct terms. [O2]
- Explain and exemplify trends and patterns in the Periodic Table. [O3]

Skills development

- Thinking scientifically: analyse data
- Working scientifically: develop explanations
- Learner development: communicate effectively

Resources needed samples or photos of zinc, sodium, sulfur, carbon, mercury; materials and equipment for a practical demonstration of alkali metal reactions as detailed in the Technician's notes; graph paper; Worksheet 1.4.3a; Worksheet 1.4.3b; Practical sheet 1.4.3; Technician's notes 1.4.3

Common misconceptions All elements have symbols with the same letters as their 'English' names.

Key vocabulary Periodic Table, period, group, atomic number

Teaching and learning

Engage

- Ask the students to use element symbols to spell hidden words or vice versa, e.g. WAtEr, STaB, SHIP, LiNK, MoNeY, CuBiClEs, PAuSe, FlOWErS, NoISe, PaLaCe, PrINCeEsS, HoUSe, HeLiCOPtEr, PoLiCe, ReVErSe, TaSTe, SURfEr, NOBODy, HeAt, BrOThEr, ArTiClEs, STaTiON. [O1]

Challenge and develop

- **Pair talk** The students should examine the Periodic Table and **describe** what they see – e.g. symbol, name and atomic number. Point out that atomic numbers are sequential and that there are no gaps – there are more in rows at bottom than at the top, e.g. 2, 8, 8, 18. [O2]

  Higher-attaining students could be asked to **consider** the lanthanide and actinide series and **develop an explanation** for why their positions are not strictly correct.

- Introduce the ideas of metals, non-metals, groups and periods. Ask the students to label or colour the Periodic Table on Worksheet 1.4.3a. Identify an element and ask the students to **predict** whether it is a metal or a non-metal. [O2]

  Higher-attaining students should encounter group and period numbers when answering questions such as 'How many metals are there in Group 1?'

Explain

- Explain that Mendeleev put his elements into groups (chemical families) of elements that have similar reactions. At this point you could demonstrate some reactions of alkali metals (Technician's notes 1.4.3) or show videos of these. Ask the students to **make observations** and recognise the similarities between these elements. They can use Practical sheet 1.4.3, which also has some questions. [O3]

- Introduce names of common families of elements – alkali metals, transition metals, halogens and noble gases. Introduce the positions of solids, liquids and gases on the table – the students can then label their Periodic Table. [O2]
- The students **make observations** about some elements and then **compare** them – e.g. zinc, sodium, sulfur, carbon, bromine. Introduce another element – such as copper – and ask 'How is it like the others?', 'Where should it go in the table?'. [O3]

  Early Periodic Tables were organised by atomic mass. Higher-attaining students may be asked to **calculate** the average of the masses of lithium and potassium, showing that it equals the mass of sodium $\frac{6.9 + 39.1}{2} = 23$. This doesn't always work out perfectly (especially with non-metals) so it was decided that reactivity was a better way to organise the table.

  Higher-attaining students can **consider** why atomic masses were known before atomic numbers – the early elements were discovered before ideas about atomic structure were developed.

Consolidate and apply

- Refresh the concept of melting point and boiling point being the temperatures at which substances change state. Give an example of a solid, a liquid and a gas at room temperature, for example carbon, mercury and oxygen – ask the students to **explain** what this tells us about their relative melting and boiling points. [O3]
- **Group work** Ask the students to **analyse data** about the elements to **describe** and **explain** their states and changes at different temperatures. [O3]
- Provide examples of statements and explanations (emphasising the correct terminology) as models, e.g. 'at room temperature (20 °C) the element has melted but not boiled so it must be a *liquid*.' The students can compose similar statements and peer mark. [O3]

Extend

- Ask students students able to progress further to plot and **analyse data** for a graph of melting points of elements across Period 2 using the data in the table on Worksheet 1.4.3b. [O3]

  Higher-attaining students may be able to **predict the pattern** – temperatures increase from Group 1 across the transition metals, and then decrease across the non-metals and gases.

Plenary suggestions

Who am I? Give the students details of common elements to increase their confidence in using and navigating the Periodic Table. Details could include names, symbols, atomic number, atomic mass and uses.

Answers to Student Book questions

1. 18
2. alkali metals; halogens; noble gases; transition metals
3. metals; metalloids; non-metals
4. left to right in rows called periods; vertical groups have similar properties; metals are on the left, non-metals on the right; metalloids in between; transition metals are in the middle; the lanthanides/actinides at the bottom
5. a) Group 14 b) Period 3
6. a) V b) Y c) W
7. W; X, Y and Z are already solids and V is a gas; W is the only liquid that freezes at −7 °C; V does not freeze until −210 °C
8. V

Answers to Worksheet 1.4.3b

1. a) It melts and becomes a liquid. b) It boils and becomes a gas.
   c) Melting is going from solid to liquid; freezing is from liquid to solid.
   d) There is no difference.
3. a) They gradually increase to a maximum; then drop sharply and stay below 0 °C.
   b) They increase; drop a little; then increase to a maximum; then drop sharply and stay below 0 °C.
   c) Boron is the anomaly; its boiling point is lower than that of beryllium.

4.4 Understanding elements and atoms

Lesson overview

Learning objectives

- Interpret chemical symbols.
- Explain what is meant by 'element' and 'atom'.
- Work out the composition of different substances based on their names.

Learning outcomes

- Describe substances using the terms atom, element and compound. [O1]
- Use the Periodic Table to identify and provide information about elements. [O2]
- Use the Periodic Table to calculate the mass of elements and compounds. [O3]

Skills development

- Thinking scientifically: analyse data
- Working scientifically: interpret evidence
- Learner development: develop resilience

Resources needed 2 g of carbon; cards with chemical symbols; materials and equipment for the practical demonstration of a chemical reaction as detailed in the Technician's notes; Worksheet 1.4.3a; Worksheet 1.4.4; Practical sheet 1.4.4; Technician's notes 1.4.4

Common misconceptions Elements and atoms are different substances. Elements are all different but all atoms are the same. Atoms are like cells and are of a similar size.

Key vocabulary atom, atomic number, atomic mass, compound

Teaching and learning

Engage

- **Pair talk** Using the Periodic Table on Worksheet 1.4.3a, ask the students to devise clues to **identify** the name of an element. More points should be awarded for the least number of clues needed. Encourage the students to use clues relating to group/period/atomic mass/atomic number, saving the symbol for the final clue. You can award bonus points for creative clues. [O1&2]

Challenge and develop

- Using the Student Book, introduce the idea of each element consisting of tiny particles called atoms. Explain that all atoms in an element are the same, but that different elements are made up of different types of atoms. Also point out that the atomic mass and atomic number describe the atoms that make up the element. [O1&2]
- Show a drop of water and 2 g of carbon. Ask the students to **predict** if there is a higher number of atoms in the water/carbon than the number of people on Earth. The carbon and water have roughly the same number of atoms (1×10^{23}), although the atoms are different. There are approximately seven billion people on Earth (7×10^{9}) so there are more atoms in one drop of water than there are people on Earth!

  Another example to give is 'If a grapefruit was the size of the Earth, each atom in the grapefruit would be the size of a blueberry'. Ask the students to imagine filling the Earth with blueberries! [O3]

Explain

- Ask the students to **complete** a table of data to collate the symbol, atomic number and atomic mass of elements, based on Table 1.4.4 in the Student Book but using different elements. Ask them to state which is the bigger/smaller number. Ask 'Is this always true?' [O1&2]

- Make it clear that an atomic mass is not the mass in grams of each atom in an element. Tell the students that an atomic mass is 'relative' – it allows us to compare atoms with other atoms – e.g. a carbon atom is 12 times heavier than a hydrogen atom. [O3]

Consolidate and apply

- Ask the students to **predict** what happens when atoms combine. Use a practical demonstration or a video clip to show a reaction such as sodium with chlorine (see Technician's notes 1.4.4), or a video clip of aluminium reacting with iodine, or copper with chlorine. Students can use Practical sheet 1.4.4 to guide them in recording their observations. [O2]
- Introduce the idea that not many atoms exist as single atoms , but join to other atoms to form molecules. If the atoms in a molecule are the same then it is an element; if they are different it is a compound. Reintroduce the idea of a formula (briefly presented in Chapter 3) with the small numbers representing the number of atoms of each element. Show the students the formula of an oxygen molecule, O_2, and a water molecule, H_2O, to demonstrate the concept. [O1]
- **Group work/Envoys** Distribute cards showing various chemical symbols – e.g. Ca, He, O_2, CO_2. Ask the students to **identify the elements** and to **explain** the difference between 'atom', 'molecule', 'element' and 'compound'. [O1]

Extend

Ask students able to progress further to:

- **explore** the Periodic Table and discovery of various elements using Worksheet 1.4.4 [O2]
- **interpret** more complex structures such as cisplatin in Figure 1.4.4d in the Student Book, $PtCl_2(NH_3)_2$ [O2]
- use atomic masses to **identify** the idea of molecular mass – e.g. oxygen, zinc oxide, water, methane, carbon dioxide, calcium carbonate [O2&3]
- answer question 8 in the Student Book and use the responses to explore the concept of mass of atoms. [O3]

Plenary suggestions

The Periodic Table quiz Read out period/group/atomic number/atomic mass/symbol and ask the students to either list their responses or 'show and tell' with mini-whiteboards after each question. [O1&2]

Answers to Student Book questions

1. to identify them; to tell them apart; to form a common international language; as a shorthand way of writing elements
2. an atomic number identifies the element ; different numbers = different elements
3. a) 6 b) 40 c) 7
4. atoms; each element has a different type of atom
5. An element contains one type of atom; a compound contains more than one type of atom, joined together.
6. nitrogen × 2; hydrogen × 6; chlorine × 2; platinum × 1
7. Indium-tin oxide is a transparent electrical conductor made of a combination of two compounds, indium oxide and tin oxide; these compounds contain the elements indium, tin and oxygen.
8. a) carbon b) bromine c) iron d) calcium

Answers to Worksheet 1.4.4

1. a) Metals that are found as metal elements (or alloys) in nature.
   b) For example gold (Au), silver (Ag), platinum (Pt), copper (Cu) and iron (Fe) (there are others that are alloys).
   d) They didn't need to be extracted from a compound but were seen to be metals.
2. a) lithium (Li); sodium (Na); potassium (K); rubidium (Rb), caesium (Cs); francium (Fr); beryllium (Be); magnesium (Mg); calcium (Ca); strontium (Sr); barium (Ba); radium (Ra)
   c) They are only ever found in compounds, so needed to be extracted.
   d) They are difficult to isolate because the technology to do so had not previously existed.
3. a) neon (Ne); argon (Ag); krypton (Kr); xenon (Xe); radon (Rn) c) They only exist in small quantities and are unreactive.

4.5 Understanding metals

Lesson overview

Learning objectives

- Recognise the properties and uses of metals.
- Identify differences between metals.

Learning outcomes

- Identify some common properties of metals and their uses. [O1]
- Identify similarities and differences between metals and how these relate to their uses. [O2]
- Select metals most appropriate for a particular use and justify the selection. [O3]

Skills development

- Thinking scientifically: consider the quality of evidence
- Working scientifically: present evidence
- Learner development: ask questions

Resources needed materials and equipment as detailed in the Technician's notes; Worksheet 1.4.5; Practical sheet 1.4.5; Technician's notes 1.4.5

Common misconceptions All metals are silver-coloured, magnetic and strong.

Key vocabulary ductile, malleable, sonorous, conductor

Teaching and learning

Engage

- Ask the students 'What do we use metals for?'. Working in pairs, students take turns listing answers and **identifying** as many uses of metals as they can. [O1]
- **Group work** Encourage the students to look around the room and to think about what they have done today that may involve a metal. In groups, they present their thoughts as a list of ideas. [O1]

Challenge and develop

- Ask 'Why do we use metals?'. The students use prior knowledge and awareness of why we use metals and the properties of metals to propose answers. [O1]
- Demonstrate the thermal conductivity of metals (see Technician's notes 1.4.5), possibly contrasting with non-metals. [O1]
- Working in pairs, the students **investigate** the conduction of electricity by different metals, and possibly again non-metals for comparison (see Practical sheet 1.4.5 and Technician's notes 1.4.5). [O1&2]
- **Group work** Introduce the various properties of metals to provide appropriate terminology. The students can then **justify** each of the uses in their lists from the starter activity, **identifying** the main reasons for the use of each metal (the properties) – such as strong, shiny, high melting point. [O1, 2&3]

Explain

- **Envoys** Students collaborate to produce a spider diagram **recording the properties** of metals with examples for each. Using envoys, they should then **compare their findings** with other groups and give feedback (e.g. as two stars and a wish). [O1, 2&3]

Consolidate and apply

- Demonstrate the differences between sodium and iron – for example shiny/dull, hard/soft, scratchability, magnetic or not, density, reactivity in water. Explain that not all metals are the same, even though they have common properties such as density, magnetism, and sheen lasts if it doesn't react with air (rusting). Point out that the properties dictate the uses, for example we couldn't use sodium instead of iron for making a car. [O1&2]

- **Group work** The students should select the best material to use for a given purpose, **justifying their choices** using the correct terms. They should then **peer-assess responses** with another group. [O2&3]
- Ask the students to **consider** if it is just the properties of a substance that dictate what we use it for. [O2&3]

  Higher-attaining students may be able to **consider** the cost of the metals and perhaps link to the need to extract them from compounds.

Extend

For students able to progress further:

- Introduce the idea of alloys by examining the need to produce new substances that have the advantages of a number of metals.
- The students **compare the uses** of the original metals and of their alloy for a particular application – iron .v. steel (rusting, strength); copper .v. brass (discolouration, strength); aluminium .v. duralumin (light, unreactive, strong) for the construction of cars, aeroplanes, buildings. You could demonstrate a smart alloy returning to its original shape to illustrate an application such as 'bendy' spectacle frames. [O1, 2&3]

Plenary suggestions

Which property is most important? Show the students a metal object for them to **identify the property** most relevant to its use. Ask them to **justify their choices**; examples include kettles, bath taps, a concert stage, necklaces, barbecues. [O1, 2&3]

Answers to Student Book questions

1. malleable; conduct heat well;, conduct electricity well; shiny (when freshly cut); strong; ductile
2. a) conduct heat; high melting point; non-toxic; unreactive b) don't corrode with water; non-toxic c) light; non-toxic;don't corrode with water
3. For example: iron/cobalt/nickel is magnetic; mercury is a liquid at room temperature; uranium is radioactive
4. a) iron is grey, magnetic and rusts; copper is orange, not magnetic and doesn't rust

   b) iron goes dull, rusts; is relatively weak (*also accept* less malleable/doesn't bend easily); stainless steel stays shiny, doesn't rust and is stronger than iron (*also accept* more malleable/bendy)
5. An alloy is a mixture of metals that has different properties from the metals it is made from; e.g. may be stronger.
6. a) Sodium reacts with water; would react with sweat and burn the neck; it is soft; would break easily; wouldn't stay shiny

   b) Rhodium is rare and valuable; it would be prohibitively expensive.
7. Pt at £28 × 31 g = £868 is less than Rh at £21 × 42 g = £882; the rhodium ring is more valuable

Answers to Worksheet 1.4.5

1. a) All the atoms in it are identical.

   b) Melt two (or more) metals together; mix them and let the mixture solidify.

   c) elements: iron, aluminium, gold, silver, zinc, copper; alloys: steel, brass, bronze
2. iron gate: strong, cheap; steel bridge: strong; aluminium foil: can be made very thin, won't react with food easily, high melting point; brass clock: strong, attractive, won't rust; gold ring: attractive, won't rust or tarnish; silver necklace: attractive, won't rust or tarnish; zinc coating on bucket: strong, won't rust; bronze sword: strong, won't rust; copper base on saucepan: good conductor of heat
3. a) zinc coated: strong; won't corrode b) brass or stainless steel: strong; won't corrode

   c) zinc coated: strong; won't corrode d) copper: very good conductor of electricity; cheap

   e) aluminium: light; bends; won't corrode f) silver or brass: attractive; malleable; won't corrode

   g) copper, gold or silver: attractive; malleable; won't corrode h) steel or aluminium: strong; won't corrode

4.6 Understanding non-metals

Lesson overview

Learning objectives

- Identify the uses of common non-metals.
- Describe the properties of non-metals.

Learning outcomes

- Identify elements as non-metals using their properties. [O1]
- Explain why substances are classified as non-metals. [O2]
- Compare and constrast the properties of metals and non-metals. [O3]

Skills development

- Thinking scientifically: ask questions
- Working scientifically: record evidence
- Learner development: collaborate effectively

Resources needed hand lenses; materials and equipment for demonstrations and class practical as detailed in the Technician's notes; Worksheet 1.4.3a; Worksheet 1.4.6; Practical sheet 1.4.6; Technician's notes 1.4.6

Common misconceptions Non-metals are all solids. Gases have no mass. Air and water are elements. All gases are poisonous.

Key vocabulary halogen, salt, noble gas, inert

Teaching and learning

Engage

- Ask the students to **recall** properties of metals and then **predict** those of non-metals. [O1]

Challenge and develop

- Using the Periodic Table (Worksheet 1.4.3a), ask the students to **identify** some non-metals. The students add information to their predictions and **explain** these additions, supporting the explanation with evidence. [O1]
- Ask the students to **explain** the link between the states of different non-metals at room temperature and their melting/boiling point. [O2]

Explain

- Demonstrate hydrogen burning with a squeaky pop, oxygen relighting a splint and a helium balloon floating. The students can use Practical sheet 1.4.6 to guide them in their observations. They should **identify** similarities and differences between the gases, using appropriate terminology. Ask if this is something that metals could do. Show a video clip or photos of fluorine, chlorine, bromine and iodine before asking the students to **compare** them and **identify** why they are classified as non-metals. [O1, 2&3]
- The students should **observe** the appearance of sulfur, iodine and carbon and **compare** them to each other and to gases and metals, answering the questions on Practical sheet 1.4.6. [O1&3]
- The students can then **research** (using books and the internet) the properties of non-metals, and **identify** the common properties highlighting any odd ones out. [O3]
- Emphasise that carbon is a special element with properties of both metals and non-metals. [O1, 2&3]

  Higher-attaining students may appreciate that both carbon and sulfur exist in different forms called allotropes – e.g. graphite and diamond.

Consolidate and apply

- The students **collaborate** to record all the properties on cards and organise them into lists of metals and non-metals plus any that are common to both. [O1, 2&3]
- They should individually construct a Venn diagram to show the properties of metals and non-metals with carbon in the middle with 'bits of both'. [O1&3]

It may make it easier for lower-attaining students to **consider** individual elements in order to construct their Venn diagram – e.g. iron, sulfur and carbon.

Higher-attaining students could increase the complexity of their diagram by creating additional sections – e.g. solid/liquid/gas, magnetic; then **identify elements** that fit the categories. Alternatively they could create a key to identify an element.

- Ask the students to **compare** and **contrast** sodium, chlorine and sodium chloride (see Technician's notes 1.4.6). They can answer the questons in sections 1 and 2 of Worksheet 1.4.6. Point out the fact that the elements sodium and chlorine are not very useful and are dangerous in their element form – but as a salt/compound, sodium chloride is one of the safest and most useful chemicals we have. [O1&3]

Extend

- Students able to progress further could **research** the uses of non-metal elements and of their compounds with metals. Introduce the idea that non-metals change their names when in a compound, e.g. sulfur – sulfide, oxygen – oxide etc. The students can do task 3 on Worksheet 1.4.6. [O2&3]

Plenary suggestions

What am I? Read out the properties of a substance and challenge the students to **predict** what it could be. [O1]

Answers to Student Book questions

1. Metals tend to be stronger, shinier, denser and better conductors. Many non-metals are unreactive gases at room temperature; some have special properties and some are vital to life.
2. salts
3. It sublimes; it appears not to melt; just turns straight from a solid to a gas
4. *Helpful*: rubber; gunpowder; sulfuric acid; essential to life *Harmful*: toxic gas; acid rain
5. a different form of the same element; different arrangement of the same atoms
6. It produces sulfur dioxide; a choking gas that attacks lungs and throat.
7. It is brittle; can be crushed into a powder; it doesn't conduct electricity or heat.
8. they are inert; don't react or form compounds
9. Reward any reasonable comparison and challenge higher-attaining students to use the Periodic Table.

   a) Both are gases; helium is lighter and inert; chlorine is harmful and forms compounds.

   b) Both are halogens and kill bacteria; iodine is a solid at room temperature and chlorine is a gas.

   c) Bromine is a liquid at room temperature and forms compounds. It's atoms are twice as heavy as argon, which is an inert noble gas. Both non-metals are used in making light bulbs.

   d) Metals are shiny and are good conductors of heat and electricity; most are sonorous and ductile. They are found towards the left of the Periodic Table. Non-metals are on the right; they are less dense.

4.7 Identifying metalloids

Lesson overview

Learning objectives

- Describe semi-metals and their properties.
- Identify some common uses of semi-metals.

Learning outcomes

- Identify the semi-metals (metalloids) using the Periodic Table. [O1]
- Explain why these elements are called semi-metals. [O2]
- Link and explain the uses of semi-metals using their properties. [O3]

Skills development

- Thinking scientifically: understand how theories develop
- Working scientifically: present and interpret evidence
- Learner development: act responsibly

Resources needed photos comparing old and new technologies; Worksheet 1.4.7

Common misconceptions Silicone is an element (they may recognise its use in surgical implants or as plastic/rubber sealants). All radioactivity is deadly.

Key vocabulary metalloid, semi-metal, semiconductor, crystalline, radioactive

Teaching and learning

Engage

- **Pair work** The students **identify** the semi-metal elements from word clues such as anagrams and/or missing letters – e.g. nlosici (silicon), -rs-n-c (arsenic). Increase the challenge by giving:
    - direction clues from a known element – e.g. next to/underneath/count three on from …
    - crossword-style questions using period/group information – e.g. held up by tin (Ge); I live at 5:15 and am known by another name (Sb, antimony). [O1]

Challenge and develop

- **Pair work/Envoys** Ask the students to **consider** the question 'These elements fit between the metals and the non-metals – what properties might they have?' Pairs of students should **discuss** and share with another group, and then present their top five predictions. Once you have collected feedback, ask the students to **justify their choices**. Show the students photos of the semi-metals and ask if they want to modify their predictions and, if so, why. [O1&2]

Explain

- Show the students a photo comparing old and new technologies – e.g. televisions, mobile phones, computers. Ask them to consider and to **explain** what is happening to technology over time, drawing out points about developments leading to products and devices being smaller, smarter and faster. Explain that semi-metals are responsible for this revolution microchips or silicon chips and that semi-metals are semiconductors. Ask the students to **consider** what they think this means. [O2&3]

Consolidate and apply

- **Group work/jigsaw** Ask the students to conduct a research activity to link and **explain** the properties and uses of some semi-metals. Worksheet 1.4.7 can be used. This could be run as a group activity with presentation of work to the rest of the group, or as a jigsaw group activity in which each group becomes an expert on a particular element, with each member of the group being responsible for learning as much as possible in order to pass on this knowledge. One member from each group then forms a new group and they teach each other about their element – all students **summarise** what they have heard about each of the elements in a report. [O2&3]

Extend

For students able to progress further:

- Ask them to **assess their predictions** about the properties of semi-metals and to **predict** what the world would be like if we hadn't discovered the properties of semi-metals. [O3]
- The students should **apply** what they have learned to reverse time and **predict** what life would be like without various inventions and knowledge – e.g. having modern technology, knowing arsenic is a poison, knowing that some elements are radioactive. [O3]

Plenary suggestions

'3–2–1' activity Ask the students to **reflect on** their learning by responding to the following three statements: 'Three things I have learned are…'; 'Two things I found interesting were…'; 'One thing I am going to tell someone else is…'.

Alternatively they could **reflect on** alternative statements: 'Things I did well today…'; 'Things I need to remember…'; 'Things I need to improve…'.

Answers to Student Book questions

1. *Useful*: (used to be) used in pesticides and as a 'cure-all' tonic; used in glass and semiconductors
   Harmful: toxic poison that can be transported in water and via food
2. from mining works, rocks and soils; from pesticides (cigarettes is an unlikely source)
3. Sand and clay are used to construct building materials such as cement, glass, concrete, steel; silicon chips use pure silicon and make electrical items tiny and speedy.
4. Both elements are in Group 14; elements in the same group have similar properties.
5. For example, uranium and polonium; invisible radiation causes cell damage/cancer over time
6. in making electricity in nuclear power stations; in medicine to identify and treat cancer

Answers to Worksheet 1.4.7

1. a) silicon (Si) b) germanium (Ge) c) arsenic (As) d) antimony (Sb) e) polonium (Po) f) tellurium (Te)
2. The students should pick out features such as: being bright in appearance like metals; having moderate conductivity; brittle.
3. a) They have some metallic properties, e.g. appearance; some non-metallic properties, e.g. brittle; and some intermediate properties, e.g. conductivity.
   b) Other elements close by on the Periodic Table have some similar properties, so the division is not clear.

4.8 Discovering the origin of metals

Lesson overview

Learning objectives

- Recognise that metals have to be extracted from ores.
- Evaluate the impact of extracting metals from the Earth.

Learning outcomes

- Identify different ways of extracting metals. [O1]
- Explain what is meant by metal 'extraction' and metal 'ore'. [O2]
- Evaluate the effects of mining metals. [O3]

Skills development

- Thinking scientifically: ask questions
- Working scientifically: interpret evidence
- Learner development: respect others

Resources needed photos of mines from the gold rush to the present day; materials and equipment for demonstrations of extracting copper from copper oxide and copper sulfate as detailed in the Technician's notes; Worksheet 1.4.8a; Worksheet 1.4.8b; Practical sheet 1.4.8; Technician's notes 1.4.8

Common misconceptions All metals can be dug up from the ground. All mines are underground.

Key vocabulary extraction, ore, electrolysis, reduction

Teaching and learning

Engage

- Provide pairs of students with cards from Worksheet 1.4.8a in order to **identify metal ores** and match them to their chemical names and formulas – e.g. malachite, which is $CuCO_3$, copper carbonate. They can find some clues in the Student Book. [O1]

Challenge and develop

- Ask the students to **explain** the difference between native metals (such as gold) and other metals that are only found in ores. [O2]
- Outline the two extraction methods featured in the Student Book – thermal reduction and electrolysis – and ask the students to **recall ideas** from earlier in the chapter. They should **explain the method** Davy used in the extraction of potassium and sodium using electricity. [O1]
- Ask the students to **compare** iron and aluminium extraction, and **consider** why we need the metals to be separated from their compound form in rocks. This should involve them in **interpreting evidence** that they have been presented with during the chapter relating to the properties and uses of metals and compounds. [O2]

  Higher-attaining students may link the uses to reactivity or stability mentioned in previous lessons.

- Demonstrate two different extraction processes – extracting copper from copper oxide (or carbonate) using carbon, and the electrolysis of copper sulfate. See the Technician's notes 1.4.8. The students can use Practical sheet 1.4.8 to guide their observations. [O1]

Explain

- Show photos of mines ranging from the Californian gold rush to modern-day super pits and ask the students to **discuss** what it would be like to work and live there; what the pros and cons would be. Ask them to

consider why we create these huge mines (emphasise that this is a world that uses metals for building, electronics, transport etc). [O1]

Consolidate and apply

- Ask the students to extract information about coltan mining in the Democratic Republic of the Congo using Worksheet 1.4.8b. They then **interpret the evidence** to compare mining in Australia and the DRC **identifying** similarities and differences. Ask the students to **consider** whether or not they would give up their mobile phones and MP3 players to save a gorilla. [O1, 2&3]

  Challenge the higher-attaining students to **justify the reasons** for the differences between mining in Australia and the DRC – e.g. economic, political, social considerations.

Extend

For students able to progress further:

- Ask them to select a medium (flyer, poem, poster, TV news article or newspaper article) to publicise the issues around mining in the DRC and the link to mobile phones
- They should then collaborate to produce the chosen piece of work. [O3]

Plenary suggestions

'Give one, get one' activity Ask the students to write down a key word and a definition for a different key word. They then swap with a partner who provides the keyword for the definition and definition for the key word. The students then swap back the completed exercise and **peer assess**.

Answers to Student Book questions

1. Native metals like gold can be found in the ground or in watercourse beds; they don't need to be extracted from ores.
2. Water helps in separating denser gold pieces from rock and sand.
3. It is a rock with enough metal in it to make it worthwhile extracting.
4. electrolysis as for aluminium/potassium/sodium; (thermal) reduction as for copper/ iron
5. It is the properties of the pure metal that makes it useful.
6. Answers could include: children don't go to school but earn money; working conditions may be dangerous and could cause injury/death; loss of homes/land/farmland for food/crops; loss of animals and habitats could affect food sources/ecology; fighting/violence
7. *Advantages* – jobs, puts money in the community (shops, fuel, supplies); *Disadvantages* – noise, dust, traffic, ruins the landscape, pollution, habitat damage
8. health and safety rules; working conditions; use of child labour; consideration of environmental impact
9. Our demands could have a negative impact on local people's lives, on the environment, on wildlife; if there was no demand/value/market for the metal fewer people may have died.

Answers to Worksheet 1.4.8a

malachite – $CuCO_3$ – copper carbonate	bauxite – Al_2O_3 – aluminium oxide
haematite – FeO_3 – ferric (iron)oxide	galena – PbS – lead sulfide

Answers to Worksheet 1.4.8b

1. a) To extract metals like tantalum and niobium for use in modern technologies.
   b) poor workers' rights; damage to the environment; no benefit to the country as a whole
   c) good for workers; wider benefits for the country
2. They should list the differences in practice; the only similarity is that large quantities of coltan are mined from the ground.
3. They should suggest positives and negatives for each strategy and make a judgement about each.

4.9 Choosing elements for a purpose

Lesson overview

Learning objectives

- Recognise elements and their differences from physical data.
- Use data and the properties of elements to choose suitable materials.

Learning outcomes

- Identify metals and non-metals using physical data. [O1]
- Explain the properties of elements using physical data. [O2]
- Use physical data to select the most appropriate element for a specific purpose. [O3]

Skills development

- Thinking scientifically: analyse data
- Working scientifically: interpret evidence
- Learner development: develop resilience

Resources needed data of melting points and boiling points and other physical data for a variety of elements, from the internet or reference texts; Worksheet 1.4.9

Common misconceptions All metals melt at very high temperatures. The melting point and the freezing point of a substance are different. Big negative numbers (e.g. temperatures below zero) are larger than smaller negative numbers.

Key vocabulary melting point, toxic, density

Teaching and learning

Engage

- Ask the students to order pictures or descriptions of objects according to their temperature – e.g. Arctic/Antarctic, ice cube, a chilled can of cola, a human body, a cup of tea, a pan of boiling water, an oven baking a cake, a blow torch melting iron, the Sun. Then provide corresponding temperatures so that they can present their findings on a number line. Emphasise the significance of negative values. [O1&2]

Challenge and develop

- Ask the students to **consider** the cup of tea or the can of cola and the properties important for the containers. Ask 'Could it be made from a different material to that used to make the cup, and if so, why?'. Introduce the ideas of unreactive, non-toxic and weight, and encourage students to **recall the properties** of metals and non-metals. The students should produce a quick poster/spider diagram to select the properties needed for a cola can. [O3]

Explain

- Explore the students' understanding of the melting and boiling points of water at 0 °C and 100 °C. Ask students to indicate at what temperature water is solid, liquid and gas and appreciate that the melting point and the freezing point are the same, as are the boiling point and condensing point. [O1&2]
- Present the students with examples of melting points and boiling points for other substances (e.g. gallium m.p. 30 °C, b.p. 2403 °C; mercury m.p. –39 °C, b.p. 357 °C; cobalt m.p. 1495 °C, b.p. 2870 °C) and ask them to **identify** when it freezes/condenses; and changes from gas to liquid. Ask 'If it was 20 °C in a room, what state the substance would be in?'. [O1&2]

  For lower-attaining students observations could be limited to melting points only.

- Tell the students the melting point and boiling point of oxygen (–218 °C and –183 °C respectively) and ask in what situations it is gas, liquid and solid. Challenge the students' understanding with questions:

- The average temperature on Pluto is −234 °C, so would oxygen be a solid, liquid or gas there?
- On Mercury the average daytime temperature is 465 °C, but at night it is −184 °C, so what would happen to the oxygen over a day? [O2]

Consolidate and apply

- Ask the students to consider Table 1.4.9 in the Student Book, showing some physical data for a selection of elements. This is repeated on Worksheet 1.4.9, which has some differentiated questions on the data for studnets to answer. [O1, 2&3]
- Again referring to the table of elements data, ask the students to select a material suitable for making a drink can, **explaining** their choice (question 6b in the Student Book). [O3]

  Higher-attaining students should be able to approach this task without support. Most students will require scaffolding via questions or sentence starters, e.g. 'The can cannot be made of X because…' ; 'This is important because…';, 'The can should be made from X instead of Y because it is a better…,which is important because…'.
- Students should share their choices and reasons, and **peer/self-assess** the quality of the evidence. [O3]

Extend

- Give students able to progress further physical data from the internet or reference texts for another three substances and a proposed use for each substance. They should **discuss** whether or not the best choices have been made. [O3]

Plenary suggestions

Traffic light and target The students rate their performance and confidence in using the skills and set a personal target – for example:

- I understand what is meant by melting point and boiling point.
- I can predict whether a substance is a solid, a liquid or a gas using its melting point and boiling point.

Answers to Student Book questions

1. Gallium would melt in your hand and make any drink held in it toxic.
2. light/low density; malleable/flexible; non-toxic; withstand cold temperatures; unreactive/not corrode
3. Lead is too heavy (high density) and toxic. Mercury is liquid at room temperature and toxic.
4. Iron is heavy and rusts and wouldn't stay attractive. Gold would stay shiny, but be quite heavy and is non-toxic; it is unreactive, but is soft and very expensive.
5. helium; hydrogen
6. a) *For*: cheap; light (low density); stay cool because it is a poor conductor of heat.; *Against*: brittle; would make marks

   b) Aluminium; it is cheap, light, has a high melting point and is non-toxic.

   c) aluminium, copper, graphite, silver, iron – sodium, helium, hydrogen, lead, gallium are all completely unsuitable

Answers to Worksheet 1.4.9

1 a) T b) F c) F d) T e) F f) T

2. a) Students should create a linear scale. b) He; Pb; Al; Ag; Ga; Cl; Cu

   c) The second; lead is a liquid only above 327 °C.
3. a) Agree: conducts electricity; disagree: high cost

   b) Agree: good at withstanding high temperatures; disagree: brittle

   c) Agree: reasonably cheap and strong; disagree: rusting would affect the food unless the iron was protected

   d) Agree: it is reasonably strong and less dense than some other metals so the bike is light; disagree: it is relatively expensive and the protective layer that aluminium forms looks unattractive

   e) Agree: it is inert/unreactive; disagree: its low density means it could easily float away instead of smothering the flames.

4.10 Applying key ideas

How tinny is a tablet?

Objectives

- Extract ideas about tin and other elements from the text, including earlier sections of the chapter.
- Apply ideas about the properties of tin to explain some of its applications.
- Use ideas and information about elements, compounds and formulas to explain the properties of chemicals.

Outcome

- Clear and effective responses to questions, indicating understanding and the next steps in learning.

The purpose of this activity is to provide an opportunity to see how successfully students are grasping the key ideas so far. It isn't designed to be used as a formal test; it might be that students work on the questions collectively. It does provide an opportunity for you to look at written work, engage students in discussions and form ideas about progress being made.

The tasks are progressive. Lower-attaining students should be able to tackle the first two or three, and higher-attaining students will find the later ones more challenging.

Resources needed information about the history of the canning of food; soldered circuit board or photo of one; magnets; empty cans; highlighters; Worksheet 1.4.10

Teaching and learning

Engage

- Challenge the students to think back over the last few lessons and **identify** some of the key ideas they've met. Draw out some responses about these ideas and say that it's important as learners that we develop a sense of our own progress.
- Tell the story of the development of the canning of food from the time of the Napoleonic Wars, when the French government offered a prize for an effective way of preserving food for troops. Pass round some clean empty tin cans and ask the students to **suggest** what they are made of and **explain** why they are useful.
- Display a photo of a soldered circuit board or pass round an example and ask the students to **consider** what the metal is that is used to make the joints.

Challenge and develop

- Provide the students with magnets and ask them to test the cans. Ask them to speculate why a tin can is magnetic, even though tin isn't.
- Ask them to **suggest** what properties you might look for in a material used to solder components together. Take responses but don't validate any ideas at this stage.

Explain

Ask the students to read the passage called *How tinny is a tablet?* in the Student Book. Depending on their ability to assimilate text you may need to adopt strategies such as:

- **Pair work** Using Worksheet 1.4.10 and highlighters, one student extracts key ideas by highlighting key words in the text and the second student (using a different-coloured highlighter) indicates any words they don't understand.
- Using the text as a source of ideas, you can draw a spider chart with tin at the centre and its properties and applications around it.

  Work with a group of students who have difficulty with reading to support them in decoding the text and accessing the ideas.

Consolidate and apply

- Now ask the students to attempt the tasks in the Student Book. They might do this individually or collaboratively. In either case, encourage them to **record their ideas**.
- Ask the students to present their responses to various tasks, either orally or by displaying their work.

Extend

- The later tasks are an opportunity for extension work for those students able to progress further.

Plenary

Ask the students for responses to questions such as:

- How well were we able to approach these tasks?
- Did we manage to present some high-quality responses?
- Are there some ideas that we need to strengthen in the later part of this chapter?

Make a note of any responses.

Provide the class with some overall feedback, indicating ideas that they have grasped effectively and those they may need to develop further.

Likely responses and next steps in learning

1. This gives the students an opportunity to recall experiences and to recall or research the definitions of the terms. They should be able to describe tin as being a soft and silvery metal and may add that it doesn't discolour in air. They should explain that 'ductile' means it can be stretched or shaped and 'malleable' means that it can be hammered into sheets or other shapes. This checks that key words are being used effectively.
2. This involves recalling that an alloy is a mixture of two metals made by melting them together. Copper alloyed with tin is much stronger than either metal, making it more useful for certain applications. The making of bronze often required trade because the metals generally occur in different areas and had to be bought or exchanged. The complete question checks understanding of the concept of alloying and the ability to apply information.
3. This recalls from wider common knowledge that some metals corrode in sea water and then requires students to deduce that bronze doesn't corrode. A better response will indicate that bronze is strong and even that it can be cast. The skills needed for a complete answer require students to draw on wider ideas and experiences and to apply ideas about suitability to applications.
4. Solder needs a low melting-point so it can be easily melted (but not so low that it would melt in typical living conditions) and run into joints. A better answer would include that it is a good conductor of heat (and electricity), and an even better one that it doesn't corrode. Successful answers show the ability to link properties to applications.
5. Its neighbours in the group are germanium and lead. A correct answer shows the ability to navigate the Periodic Table and to identify a column as the group. Germanium is a metalloid and lead is a metal, relatively soft and malleable like tin.
6. Ores are compounds of metals 'trapped' inside rocks in sufficient quantity to be worth extracting. The formula shows that each molecule of tin ore contains one atom of tin and two of oxygen. Arsenic and sulfur, when heated, form arsenic oxide and sulfur dioxide – both elements are hazardous. A complete answer shows the ability to understand formulas, an understanding of oxides (though the name 'sulfur dioxide' may be unfamiliar to some students) and the recall of, or ability to refer to, information about elements from earlier in the chapter.

4.11 Combining elements

Lesson overview

Learning objectives

- Explain what is meant by a compound.
- Recognise how compounds are formed and named.
- Interpret the ratio of atoms and formula of compounds.

Learning outcomes

- Correctly classify elements and compounds, describe and give an example of a compound. [O1]
- Explain how and why compounds may be formed. [O2]
- Accurately describe compounds including the ratio of atoms via chemical formulas. [O3]

Skills development

- Thinking scientifically: use units and nomenclature
- Working scientifically: develop explanations
- Learner development: communicate effectively

Resources needed building bricks; photos of constructions using building bricks; building-brick combinations to illustrate elements/compounds; materials and equipment for demonstrations of compound formation as detailed in the Technician's notes; Worksheet 1.4.11; Practical sheet 1.4.11; Technician's notes 1.4.11

Common misconceptions Any elements can combine in any order or quantity. Atoms change when compounds form, for example H_2O is a new atom. Atoms change size.

Key vocabulary model, ratio, formula

Teaching and learning

Engage

- Ask the students to construct something using building bricks and to **identify the rules** they have used – e.g. only fit bricks in the available holes. They should **compare** their building with those of other students and **discuss** what is the same and what is different – e.g. *same*: bricks, colours, size of bricks; *different*: final shapes, the way bricks are connected.
- Show some photos of amazing creations made using building bricks, discussing that the same bricks are used but the combinations and numbers of bricks makes a difference. Explain that this principle works in the same way with elements – the building blocks are the same, but how they fit together is different and that this is called *bonding* (the word chemists use to describe the joining of atoms and the reason they stay together). [O2]

Challenge and develop

- Ask the students 'If each building brick represents an atom and each colour a different element, how would we show a compound?' Discuss what the difference is between bonding two bricks of the same colour (element), and bonding bricks with different colours (compound). [O2]

Explain

- Demonstrate, or show a video clip of, the formation of a simple compound – e.g. copper oxide/magnesium oxide/iron sulfide (see Technician's notes 1.4.11; there are health and safety issues here), and ask the students to make and **record observations**. They can use Practical sheet 1.4.11 to guide them. Ask 'How do you know that something new has been made? What has changed?'. The students should then **model** the formation of the compound using the bricks. [O1&2]

- Ask the students to **explain** how the symbols of the elements could be used instead of bricks. Introduce the term 'formula' and explain that a formula represents the ratio of atoms in molecules of a compound – e.g. CH_4 (ratio 1 : 4) is not the same as C_2H_4 (ratio 2 : 4 or simplify to 1 : 2). Remind the students of the importance of capital letters at the start of each element – e.g. CO is not the same as Co, Cs is not the same as CS. Avoid using circle/particle models because this is introduced in Topic 4.12. [O2&3]

Consolidate and apply

- Students practise and **apply their knowledge** to answer Student Book questions 7, 8 and 9 and Worksheet 1.4.11 about formulas. [O2&3]

Extend

- Ask students able to progress further to **consider** the number of pins on the building bricks and the possible combinations of one-, two-, four- and eight-pin bricks that can be joined to another eight-pin block without overlap. This is a good model to show how the ratio of atoms works – e.g. hydrogen, Groups 1 and 17 are like the one-pin bricks; Groups 2 and 16 are like the two-pin bricks, Group 14 elements are like the four-pin bricks. Ask the students to **apply** this idea to work out the formula for given compounds such as CCl_4, CO_2, H_2O, $MgBr_2$, K_2O etc. [O1&3]

Plenary suggestions

Element or compound? Show the students diagrams/photos of building-brick combinations and ask them to **classify** the 'substance' as an element or compound. Extend the activity by asking them to **predict** the name of a substance that it could represent and to **explain** how they made the decision. [O2&3]

Answers to Student Book questions

1. An element consists of one kind of atom; but there are two or more elements in a compound. Elements combine to form compounds.
2. The model is made of building blocks put together in different combinations. Elements are joined in different ways to create different compounds.
3. The compound's name includes the names of the elements it is made from.
4. Oxygen is the element (gas); an oxide is a compound consisting of oxygen combined with other element(s).
5. any appropriate model to show carbon monoxide, CO and carbon dioxide, CO_2
6. a) potassium chloride b) nickel oxide c) lead iodide
7. a) 1 : 2; sulfur dioxide b) 1 : 1; nitrogen monoxide c) 2 : 3; aluminium oxide d) 1 : 4; carbon tetrachloride
8. SiO_2; 'dioxide' means two oxygen atoms to one of silicon
9. atoms of carbon, hydrogen and oxygen; 6 : 12 : 6 but the simplest ratio is 1 : 2 : 1

Answers to Worksheet 1.4.11

1. a) i) sodium iodide ii) calcium oxide iii) magnesium chloride iv) lithium bromide
   b) i) copper sulfate ii) calcium carbonate iii) copper nitrate
2. i) hydrogen, oxygen ii) carbon, oxygen iii) sodium, chlorine iv) magnesium, chlorine
   v) hydrogen, sulfur, oxygen vi) calcium, copper, oxygen vii) hydrogen, nitrogen, oxygen
   viii) copper, sulfur, oxygen
3. i) 1 : 1 ii) 1 : 2 iii) 1 : 2 iv) 1 : 2 v) 1 :1: 3 vi) 2 : 1 : 4

4.12 Using models to understand chemistry

Lesson overview

Learning objectives

- Use a simple model to show the differences between atoms and molecules.
- Use models to represent compounds.

Learning outcomes

- Represent atoms and diatomic molecules using a simple circle model. [O1]
- Explore the value of a simple circle model for representing compounds. [O2]
- Make links between simple circle models and chemical formulas. [O3]

Skills development

- Thinking scientifically: understand how theories develop
- Working scientifically: interpret evidence
- Learner development: ask questions

Resources needed simple circle models as particle diagrams; building-brick model (as in Topic 4.11); circular coloured stickers, tiddlywinks, modelling clay or coins and paper; commercial models if available; Worksheet 1.4.12; Practical sheet 1.4.12

Common misconceptions Atoms change size. All atoms are the same. You can only join atoms together side-by-side, like holding hands.

Key vocabulary atom, element, molecule, compound, ratio

Teaching and learning

Engage

- **Pair talk/Pairs to fours** Show the students simple circle models as particle diagrams and ask them to **describe** how they are different (emphasising the word 'describe') – e.g. colour, size, shape, number of circles. Pairs compare answers with another group and make sure that they have only described what they saw. [O1]

Challenge and develop

- Ask the students 'What is the difference between 'describing' and 'explaining'?' Make sure the students understand that describing is purely observation and doesn't require an answer to the question 'why?'. Answers to explanation questions often begin 'because…'.
- Introduce the idea of a molecule explaining 'This is an atom because…', 'This is a molecule because…'. Show students representations of He, H_2 and HCl and ask them to **describe** *and* **explain** the differences, i.e. noting that some elements form molecules with themselves – they are mostly gases (not noble gases) and therefore non-metals: hydrogen, nitrogen, oxygen, fluorine, chlorine, bromine, iodine. [O1]
- **Group work** Use Worksheet 1.4.12. For the second and third sections, ask groups to **explain** what the diagrams might represent. Answers could be framed 'I/We think that this diagram represents… because…'. Choose one member from each group to **feed back** their ideas – one for each diagram. Other groups should identify the description/explanation and indicate whether or not the group has been successful. [O1, 2&3]

Explain

- **Pair talk** Show a building-brick model and remind the students about the work on symbols in the previous topic. Ask pairs to **summarise** what they can remember about the model – what the bricks represent, e.g. element, compound, ratio, formula. Explain the basic ideas from John Dalton's atomic theory (outlined in the

Student Book). Ask the students to compare this theory to the models that they have just summarised. Ask 'How could we use the circle model to represent elements, compounds and chemical reactions?'. [O1, 2&3]

- Explain that Dalton came up with this idea in 1803 (show Dalton's atoms) which pre-dates the first periodic table (1869) and was therefore produced before elements had letter symbols. Ask 'How do we know which are elements and which are compounds?', 'What do we know now that Dalton didn't in 1803?'. [O1&2]

Consolidate and apply

- Ask the students to represent elements and compounds using circle models, chemical names and symbols. They will need to demonstrate the abilty to **describe** and **explain**. [O1, 2&3]

  Circular coloured stickers or tiddlywinks are useful and novel for this – the students could also use modelling clay or draw around coins. It is important that the students acknowledge that atoms don't change size.

  Higher-attaining students may be able to appreciate that different atoms have different sizes (down a group atoms get bigger – GCSE concept) but that an atom of a particular substance does not change size.

Extend

- For students able to progress further, return to Dalton's atomic theory and the principle that 'Atoms cannot be made or destroyed'. Ask the students to **consider** what this means and **explain** what happens to atoms if they are never destroyed. Ask question such as 'Where did atoms come from in the first place?' In theory, they could contain atoms that made up Einstein or a dinosaur! [O2]

Plenary suggestions

What I did today Ask the students to **describe** something they have done today, **explain** something they have learned and draw a model to represent something they will remember from the lesson. Share these partners or as a round-robin within a group, with ideas being recorded on sheets of paper that circulated for comments and further ideas to be added.

Answers to Student Book questions

1. The atoms of each element are different.
2. An atom is one particle; a molecule has more than one atom joined together.
3. Two atoms that are joined/bonded together.
4. The particles should be represented using different colours: NaCl, one circle of one colour and one circle of another colour touching; CaO, one circle of one colour and one circle of another colour touching; HCl, one circle of one colour and one circle of another colour touching; $CaCl_2$, one circle of one colour and two circles of the same colour as each other but different from the first circle, all touching.
5. a) three diatomic molecules of an element b) one atom of an element c) two molecules of a compound containing two elements in the ratio 1 : 2 d) a molecule of an element containing eight atomsjoined in a ring
6. It is a molecule of a compound containing seven atoms; two hydrogen, one sulfur and four oxygen; ratio 2 : 1 : 4
7. Everything is made up of atoms;, they cannot be made or destroyed; all atoms in an element are the same; atoms are rearranged in chemical reactions.

Answers to Worksheet 1.4.12

1. a) 4 and 4 b) 2 and 2 c) 2 hydrogen and 1 oxygen

   d) An atom is a single particle; a molecule is two or more atoms joined together.
2. a) water b) helium atom c) oxygen molecule d) methane e) hydrogen chloride
3. a) A compound; two types of atoms are joined to form each molecule or unit of the compound.

   b) A mixture of a compound and an element; there are molecules made of two different types of atom joined; and separate atoms mixed but not joined.

   c) An element; a single type of atom.

   d) A mixture of two different compounds.

4.13 Understanding what happens when an element burns

Lesson overview

Learning objectives

- Make observations during chemical reactions.
- Write word equations to represent chemical changes.
- Explain chemical changes using a model.

Learning outcomes

- Identify risks and changes during a reaction and relate these to reactants and products. [O1]
- Make accurate observations and explain them using simple models and word equations. [O2]
- Explain observations using word equations and relate chemical symbols to a simple particle model using circle diagrams. [O3]

Skills development

- Thinking scientifically: evaluate risks
- Working scientifically: record evidence
- Learner development: collaborate effectively

Resources needed photos of melting and burning; equipment for practical demonstration of heating ice, burning paper, burning a candle in a jar; materials and equipment for a class practical as detailed in the Technician's notes; Worksheet 1.4.13; Practical sheet 1.4.13; Technician's notes 1.4.13

Common misconceptions When things burn they disappear and are destroyed forever. Heating and burning are the same.

Key vocabulary reaction, equation, reactant, product, atom

Teaching and learning

Engage

- Show the students a photo of melting – e.g. pouring molten metal; and a photo of burning, e.g. magnesium. Ask them to **describe** and **explain** what is happening. Students should **identify** melting and burning but may not be able to differentiate between them. They should **identify** that both need heat and some may identify both physical change and chemical change. [O2]

Challenge and develop

- Ask the students to **observe** and **record** accurate observations while you heat some ice and burn a small piece of paper. Emphasise the risks and safety precautions as well as good practice when using a Bunsen burner. Ask them to **identify** the difference between the two using leading questions such as 'Can the water be re-frozen?', 'Is it still water?', 'What about the paper?'. [O1, 2&3]
- Introduce the terms 'reversible' and 'irreversible' in relation to physical change and chemical change. Also introduce the terms 'reactants' (what we started with) and 'products'. Model using BEFORE/DURING/AFTER to describe a chemical reaction incorporating the students' observations of the paper. [O1, 2&3]

Explain

- Ask the students to **consider** the fact that if burning the paper was a chemical reaction, then what has it reacted with? They may **suggest** the flame, the heat, the air – and some may know the answer, oxygen. [O2]
- Demonstrate covering a burning candle with a jar, asking 'Why does it go out?'. Challenge the students to **develop an explanation**, linked to air and oxygen, and to **consider** whether oxygen is reactant or product. [O2]

- Return to the BEFORE/DURING/AFTER description, asking students to support the explanation of burning based on their observations. [O2]

Consolidate and apply

- The students should 'burn' copper powder, carbon powder and magnesium ribbon: see Technician's notes 1.4.13. Note the safety statement about light emitted as magnesium burns. Before commencing, the students should **identify** how they will work safely. Practical sheet 1.4.13 provides guidance and results tables. [O1]
- After completing the experiments, the students should **describe** and **explain** the reactions using the BEFORE /DURING/AFTER model. Task 1 of Worksheet 1.4.13 provides scaffolding to support this. [O1, 2&3]
- Model writing a word equation for the students: reactants → products. Emphasise the need for an arrow NOT an equals '=' sign, explaining that the substances are not 'equal' – new substances are produced in the reaction of the initial reactants. Students then construct equations for the reactions they have observed (task 2 of Worksheet 1.4.13) using circle models to help them as necessary. [O2&3]

  Higher-attaining students may be able to attempt the symbol equations. Balancing is not required at this stage, but the third section of the Student Book introduces the principle of balancing, for some students.

Extend

- Challenge students able to progress further to **consider** the flame and decide if it is part of the chemical reaction. Ask 'Would things burn without a flame?'. To help the discussion, demonstrate or show a video clip of phosphorus burning or potassium in water. Explain that the flame is needed to get the right temperature for the reaction to happen. Demonstrate burning ethanol and then vegetable oil to illustrate that ethanol is more flammable, so needs less heat to help it to burn. [O1, 2&3]

Plenary suggestions

What is burning? Use circle models, chemical symbols and names to explain what burning is. **Discuss** in groups to **identify** successes and the things that they need to improve (as a group). [O2&3]

Answers to Student Book questions

1. Chemical change is irreversible – new products are made, substances can look very different afterwards; physical change is reversible, same substance in different state (solid/liquid/gas).
2. It doesn't change its appearance, other than being liquid or solid, and you can repeat the process.
3. A chemical reaction that needs heat and oxygen; oxides are formed.
4. a) zinc + oxygen → zinc oxide b) sulfur + oxygen → sulfur dioxide
5. There are the same numbers of each type of atom on both sides of the equation.
6. a) potassium + oxygen → potassium oxide; circle model showing two circles of one colour and one circle of a different colour; separate, then all touching

   b) calcium + oxygen → calcium oxide; circle model showing one circle of one colour and one circle of another colour; separate, then touching

   c) hydrogen + oxygen → (di)hydrogen oxide (or water); circle model showing two circles of one colour and one circle of a different colour; separate then all touching

Answers to Worksheet 1.4.13

1. magnesium: *before*: grey metal; *during*: burns with an intense white flame; *after*: white ash
   copper: *before*: red-orange powder; *during*: glows dull red; *after*: surface turns brown-black
   carbon: *before*: black powder; *during*: glows a bit if heated strongly enough; *after*: black powder
2. magnesium + oxygen (*reactants*) → magnesium oxide (*product*)
   copper + oxygen (*reactants*) → copper oxide (*product*)
   carbon + oxygen (*reactants*) → carbon dioxide (*product*)
3. a) It has combined with oxygen from the air. b) It takes longer to start and is less reactive.
   c) It is more reactive than copper but less reactive than magnesium.

4.14 Observing how elements react in different ways

Lesson overview

Learning objectives

- Draw conclusions to explain observations.
- Use symbols and models to describe a chemical reaction.

Learning outcomes

- Make observations and identify reactants and products. [O1]
- Make accurate observations, identify differences and, with support, describe reactions using circle models or word equations. [O2]
- Suggest reasons for different observations, describe reactions using word equations and start to use symbols to model chemical reactions. [O3]

Skills development

- Thinking scientifically: use equations
- Working scientifically: develop explanations
- Learner development: act responsibly

Resources needed photos of different coloured fireworks; circle diagrams of simple molecules; photos of flame tests; Worksheet 1.4.14a; Worksheet 1.4.14b; Practical sheet 1.4.14; Technician's notes 1.4.14

Common misconceptions Things disappear or are destroyed when they burn.

Key vocabulary fuel, burning, acid, product, base

Teaching and learning

Engage

- Hand out the cards from Worksheet 1.4.14a and ask the students to match definitions of key terms from the 'prompt' cards (element symbol, molecule, formula of a compound, atom, reaction, reactants, products, metal, non-metal, metalloid, melting) with the 'answer' cards. [O1]

Challenge and develop

- Encourage the students to **explore** the names and formulas of chemicals – e.g. platinum, sodium chloride, carbon dioxide, krypton, water, methane, octasulfur/octathiocane (S_8). Ask 'How do we know whether they are elements or compounds?' [O3]
- Challenge the students to **suggest** how new compounds are formed, ensuring that melting and burning are differentiated. [O3]
- Ask the students to **explain** what happens when things burn, reminding them if necessary about the addition of oxygen. Follow up with further questions – e.g. 'What will the compound be called if calcium is burned in air?', 'What needs to be burned to produce zinc oxide?' [O2]

Explain

- Students should make and **record** accurate observations and write equations to describe chemical reactions. First demonstrate burning sulfur in oxygen (exercising caution, especially with asthmatics: see Technician's notes 1.4.14). Ask the students to write descriptions of the reactants before the reaction and afterwards. Worksheet 1.4.14b provides a writing frame (appearance before and after/equation/circle model). Add universal indicator and tell the students that red means an acid has been made (no detail required acids/indicators are not a focus here). Discuss and model the quality of observations made by the students so that they can make improvements next time. [O1, 2&3]

Consolidate and apply

- Students should then observe demonstrations of burning calcium, magnesium and carbon in oxygen, making and **recording** accurate observations. Worksheet 1.4.14b can again be used. The students must show attention to detail and spot the differences between the reactions in order to **identify** that metals and non-metals behave differently – highlight acidic gases (non-metals), solid bases (metals) and ensure that students recognise that the two types of oxides are chemical opposites (red and blue colour from indicator). [O1, 2&3]
- Students should then be supported by example, question and feedback to represent the reactions they have observed using symbols. This is an early opportunity but could work well given the exposure to the concept of the Periodic Table and the experience of seeing the reactions. [O2]
- Demonstrate a flame test (see Technician's notes 1.4.14) and then, if you think it appropriate, ask five students in sequence to demonstrate a flame test of another substance to the class. The remaining students **record** the element and the flame colour. Practical sheet 1.4.14 may be used. [O1&3]

Extend

- Ask students able to progress further to **identify the elements** needed for the fireworks in a given photo. [O1]

Plenary suggestions

What am I? Show the students a series of photos and ask them to use key words to describe the substance or to **identify** it – e.g. molecule of sulfur dioxide; molecule of oxygen; atom of calcium, flame test showing green flame (copper), burning magnesium. [O2]

Answers to Student Book questions

1. It contains copper or barium or both.
2. sulfur and oxygen
3. sodium and oxygen
4. Sodium would burn with a yellow flame and produce a solid/powder/white oxide that dissolves in water and is a base (blue UI); sulfur would produce a gas that is soluble in water and an acid (red UI).
5. carbon and sulfur = fuel; metals = coloured flames; iron = sparks
6. change of colour; produces smoke/gas; produces heat/gets hot/temperature goes up
7. *Melting* is a physical change – it happens at the melting point; the atoms are not reacting with anything.
   Burning is a chemical reaction with oxygen molecules – the atoms of the reactants, iron and oxygen, chemically join/bond to make a new product/compound called iron oxide.
8. iron + oxygen → iron oxide
9. Magnesium produces a spectacular effect; but the light can damage your eyes.
10. zinc + oxygen → zinc oxide
    magnesium + oxygen → magnesium oxide
    The circle models should be similar to that in Figure 1.4.13d of the Student Book.

Answers to Worksheet 1.4.14a

Prompt	1	2	3	4	5	6	7	8	9	10	11
Answer	D	K	J	B	E	I	G	A	F	C	H

Answers to Worksheet 1.4.14b

1. a) It is a reaction with oxygen which releases energy as heat/light.
   b) In the examples, the products from burning metals are solid bases. Non-metals produce acidic gases.
2. sulfur + oxygen → sulfur dioxide; calcium + oxygen → calcium oxide; magnesium + oxygen → magnesium oxide; carbon + oxygen → carbon dioxide
3. Circle models should show two oxygen atoms to each sulfur atom, and two oxygen atoms to each carbon atom. The metals both combine with oxygen 1 : 1. At this stage there is no need to consider compounds such as sulfur trioxide and carbon monoxide unless brought up.

4.15 Identifying the special features of carbon

Lesson overview

Learning objectives

- Explain the importance of carbon in our lives.
- Identify and explain the differences between an element and its compounds.

Learning outcomes

- Recognise where carbon and its compounds are used. [O1]
- Explain and identify different carbon compounds and their importance. [O2]
- Explain, using the correct terms, where carbon is found and why it is so useful. [O3]

Skills development

- Thinking scientifically: use equations (formulas)
- Working scientifically: interpret evidence
- Learner development: communicate effectively

Resources needed ten photos of objects/substances containing carbon; diagrams to show the structures of graphite, diamond, organic rings; shells, marble, sugar; diagram of the carbon cycle; materials and equipment as detailed in the Technician's notes; Worksheet 1.4.3a; Worksheet 1.4.15; Practical sheet 1.4.15a; Practical sheet 1.4.15b; Technician's notes 1.4.15

Common misconceptions Pencils have lead in them. Note the general limited knowledge of carbon's chemical applications.

Key vocabulary carbonate, carbohydrate, organic compound, polymer

Teaching and learning

Engage

- Display photos of 10 items (e.g. coal, shell, sugar, marble, diamond, pencil, polyethene bag, bread/flour, petrol, plastic bottle). The students **recall** as many of the items as possible after, say, two minutes. Then challenge them to **identify** a common link between the items (they all contain carbon). [O1&2]

Challenge and develop

- Ask the students to **identify** carbon in the Periodic Table and to list its symbol, atomic mass, atomic number, and group number. Explain that being in Group 14 (Group 4) means that carbon can form four chemical bonds and build giant networks, chains and ring structures. Show the structures of graphite, diamond, organic ring structures and chains. Ask the students to **identify** the elements (the two allotropes) and compounds (hydrocarbons). [O3]
- Show objects or images such as shells and marble pieces to introduce carbonate compounds like calcium carbonate. Ask the students if it is organic, asking them to **explain** why not. Show sugar and its structure asking how is it similar to or different from the carbonate (they should know that it is organic but not a hydrocarbon – higher-attaining students may predict the name as 'carbohydrate'). [O2&3]

Explain

- Ask the students 'How do we prove that these substances contain carbon?'. Blow into limewater and explain the carbon dioxide test. Ask the students to **draw conclusions**. Explain that when carbon and its compounds burn, they produce carbon dioxide (and carbon/soot if insufficient oxygen). [O1]
- Demonstrate the test for carbon dioxide using limewater and the test for water using blue cobalt chloride paper. Then burn some 'petrol' (hexane), collect the gas formed and test for water and for carbon dioxide

(see Technician's notes 1.4.15). The students can use Practical sheet 1.4.15a to guide their observations – support them in the analysis. [O1]

- Students should then **investigate** what happens when they burn bread (toast), sugar, powdered carbon and pass the gas(es) formed into limewater. They use similar apparatus to that used for the demonstration. They should **compare** their results – e.g. bread produces black soot, carbon produces cloudy limewater. They can use Practical sheet 1.4.15b. [O2&3]

Consolidate and apply

- Show the students the carbon cycle and ask them to link the photos/substances to the diagram – the message is that carbon compounds are everywhere. The students should use the cycle diagram to draw a spider diagram that **summarises** the different forms of carbon and its compounds. The information in the Student Book supports this, as does Worksheet 1.4.15. Students may find it useful to have access to other reference materials. [O1, 2&3]
- **Jigsaw activity** Run the activity with different group members **investigating** a group of compounds from polymers, carbohydrates, carbonates, proteins/fats and allotropes – alternatively they could tackle one aspect of the carbon cycle, e.g. photosynthesis, burning fuels. They regroup to collaborate and add to the group poster. Highlight the need for the use of accurate terms – e.g. inorganic/organic/element/compounds. [O1, 2&3]

Extend

For students able to progress further ask 'If we breathe out carbon dioxide, where does it come from?. Encourage students to **make links** between 'burning' carbon compounds and 'burning' food. [O2]

Plenary suggestions

Odd one out Present a series of three substances (photos/words/chemical structure/symbols) and ask the students to identify the odd one out and to **justify their choice**. [O1, 2&3]

Choose materials to highlight the key ideas in this topic – for example the sets of three might include: diamond, graphite, petrol; polyethene, petrol, shells; sugar, bread, marble; tree, person, oil.

Answers to Student Book questions

1. calcium, carbon, oxygen; found in shells, rocks like chalk, limestone and marble
2. *Carbonates* are made up of carbon and oxygen; *carbohydrates* also include hydrogen.
3. a) a carbohydrate b) a carbonate
4. compounds containing hydrogen and carbon only; commonly used as fuels
5. carbon dioxide (a cause of global warming); soot (black smoke, dirty, pollution)
6. Polyethene is a polymer/long chain of carbon and hydrogen atoms; used to make plastic packaging, bags and bottles.
7. Diamond is hard, crystalline and has all the carbon atoms locked in place; graphite is soft, conducts electricity and is formed of layers that can slide over each other. Both have very high melting points.
8. Diagram with appropriate demonstration of the differences between the element allotropes (diamond, graphite, graphene, carbon fibre, fullerene) and the compounds of carbon (carbonate, carbohydrate, organic, hydrocarbon, fuels, polymers).
9. lighter; more flexible; stronger than metals (accept cheaper, better insulator)

Answers to Worksheet 1.4.15

1. a) graphite; it is soft and marks paper; diamond; cutting other hard substances; honeycomb

   b) It is extremely light and strong, but it could crack more easily than metals like steel and is more expensive.
2. a) Bubble the unknown gas through limewater.

   b) It makes the limewater go cloudy/milky (then it turns clear again if more CO_2 is available).

   c) Test if the unknown gas allows things to burn. However, oxygen is present in the air so this could easily become mixed with the unknown gas and confuse the outcome.
3. a) It can form long chains and rings. b) from food (carbohydrates)

   c) in compounds such as proteins, fats, carbohydrates d) decompose and release CO_2; some may form fossil fuels

4.16 Understanding oxidation

Lesson overview

Learning objectives

- Describe oxidation.
- Recognise the effects of oxidation.
- Use data to support conclusions.

Learning outcomes

- Describe evidence of oxidation reactions. [O1]
- Explain why oxidation is a chemical reaction. [O2]
- Use a simple model/word equation to explain changes during oxidation reactions. [O3]

Skills development

- Thinking scientifically: use equations
- Working scientifically: develop explanations
- Learner development: communicate effectively

Resources needed photos of visible effects of oxidation; materials and equipment as detailed in the Technician's notes; Worksheet 1.4.16; Practical sheet 1.4.16a; Practical sheet 1.4.16b; Technician's notes 1.4.16

Common misconceptions Oxidation only happens when things burn. Burning always causes loss of mass.

Key vocabulary oxidation

Teaching and learning

Engage

- Show the students a series of photos demonstrating visible effects of oxidation – e.g. rusting gate/bridge, browning apple, tarnished silver, burning wood – and ask them to find the link between them. If the students are having difficulty, give them a clue by telling them that they all involve the same substance/reaction with the same substance (oxygen). Ask 'Which reaction might be the odd one out?'. (Fire is a fast reaction.) [O1]

Challenge and develop

- Introduce oxidation as a chemical reaction – it is not reversible and a new substance is formed. [O1&2]
- The students should carry out an experiment to heat a folded piece of copper metal. Encourage them to **explain precautions** that should be taken to reduce risks when heating the metal – e.g. using tongs to hold the copper, wearing eye protection to prevent hot materials getting into the eyes. On cooling, they should open out the copper and **make observations** (the outside of the heated metal goes black and the inside remains shiny). They can use Practical sheet 1.4.16a. [O1&2]
- Ask the students to **compare** the heating of copper with the heating of magnesium done in an earlier lesson – copper remains the same size, it just changes colour (may get green colouration in flame); magnesium reacts much more quickly/violently, burning with a bright white flame and leaving a white powder/ash. [O1&2]
- Discuss how the results provide evidence of a chemical change – there are permanent changes of colour and texture/properties, a new substance is formed, you cannot get the copper back (note that some students may think the black colour is soot and that the copper remains unchanged). [O1&2]

Explain

- Demonstrate the oxidation of copper in gas syringes (see Technician's notes 1.4.16) in order to show the removal of something (oxygen) from the air during the reaction. [O1]

- **Pair talk** The students should **observe** the reaction closely and **record their observations** following the prompts on Practical sheet 1.4.16b. They should **discuss** in pairs questions such as 'What changed?', 'Why do you think these changes have occurred?'. [O2]
- Ask the students to answer the questions on Practical sheet 1.4.16b. [O1, 2&3]

  Higher-attaining students should be encouraged to calculate the volume of air before and after the experiment (100 cm^3 to 80 cm^3) and **justify** the volume difference – this is the volume of oxygen in 100 cm^3 of air.

Consolidate and apply

- The students should **complete** tasks 1 and 2 on Worksheet 1.4.16. [O1, 2&3]
- Ask the students to **analyse the evidence** in Table 1.4.16b in the Student Book of the burning of magnesium, to write a word equation and draw a circle diagram to explain the data (questions 9 and 10). [O3]

Extend

- Ask students able to progress further to complete task 3 of Worksheet 1.4.16. This asks them to write symbol equations. Note that balancing equations is not required at this stage. The worksheet task also asks students to represent other reactions as circle models, enabling them to demonstrate a clear understanding of 'atom'/'element' and 'compound'. [O3]

  Higher-attaining students may be capable of balancing symbol equations.

Plenary suggestions

Equation quiz Ask the students to **complete** or write word equations for a series of oxidation reactions – e.g. carbon to carbon dioxide; sulfur + oxygen → sulfur dioxide; making lead oxide etc. (mini-whiteboards could be used). [O2&3]

Answers to Student Book questions

1. It is the name given to a reaction when oxygen is added to/reacts with a substance.
2. burning a fuel; browning an apple; rusting of iron 3. The copper goes black/changes colour.
4. Oxygen is used up in the reaction; it is added to the metal; it makes an oxide. 5. All the oxygen is used up.
6. The copper changes colour/goes from orange/brown to black; the copper reacts with oxygen in the air to form black copper oxide.
7. Oxygen is added to the copper; the copper oxide has more mass than the original copper.
8. The silver metal changes to white ash; the magnesium metal reacted with oxygen to form white magnesium oxide.
9. magnesium + oxygen → magnesium oxide
10. *Start*: two unjoined same-colour circles for two Mg atoms; two touching same colour circles(different to Mg colour) for an oxygen molecule O_2. *End*: two separate pairs of joined different-colour paired circles for MgO.

Answers to Worksheet 1.4.16

1. a) There will be at least one of: permanent colour change; change in texture; generates light/heat; new substance formed; cannot get the original substance back b) oxides
2. a) check circle diagrams b) i) copper + oxygen (reactants) → copper oxide (product)

   ii) magnesium + oxygen (reactants) → magnesium oxide (product)
3. a) i) $Cu + O_2 \rightarrow CuO$ ii) $Mg + O_2 \rightarrow MgO$ [balancing not required] b) Check circle diagrams

   c) i) $Zn + O_2 \rightarrow ZnO$ ii) $Ca + O_2 \rightarrow CaO$ [balancing not required]

   d) Magnesium is a solid and oxygen is a gas. Magnesium reacts with the oxygen to form a compound called magnesium oxide. During the reaction the atoms (particles) of magnesium and oxygen combine together. Magnesium oxide is a solid. Because the oxygen has combined with the magnesium, it is heavier than magnesium on its own.

Answers to Practical sheet 1.4.16b

1. To prevent the copper turnings entering the syringe.
2. Gases expand when heated; allowing the apparatus to cool to the original temperature gives a valid reading.
3. To ensure that all the oygen has reacted with the copper.
4. copper + oxygen (reactants) → copper oxide (product) 5. difference between start and end volumes

4.17 Investigating carbonates

Lesson overview

Learning objectives

- Describe the composition and uses of carbonate compounds.
- Recognise and explain thermal decomposition reactions.
- Identify carbon dioxide.

Learning outcomes

- Identify sources of calcium carbonate. [O1]
- Describe what is meant by a thermal decomposition reaction. [O2]
- Use a word equation to explain what happens during the thermal decomposition of carbonates. [O3]

Skills development

- Thinking scientifically: use equations
- Working scientifically: develop explanations
- Learner development: communicate effectively

Resources needed objects or photos of objects that contain calcium carbonate; materials and equipment as detailed in the Technician's notes; Worksheet 1.4.17; Practical sheet 1.4.17a; Practical sheet 1.4.17b; Technician's notes 1.4.17

Common misconceptions Heating things causes burning/oxidation.

Key vocabulary carbonate, stable, thermal decomposition, limewater

Teaching and learning

Engage

- **Pair talk** Give the students the name and formula of calcium carbonate ($CaCO_3$) and ask them to **interpret** these by naming all the elements, counting the numbers of atoms of each element, working out the ratio of the different atoms.
- Show the students a series of photos/objects that contain calcium carbonate to illustrate its importance – e.g. marble, sea shells, toothpaste, cement/concrete, chalk, indigestion tablets. This exercise relates to the introduction and 'Not just a rock' section in the Student Book. [O1]
- Explain that all carbonates have similar properties. Introduce copper carbonate ($CuCO_3$) and ask the students to **suggest** a formula. [O1]

  Higher-attaining students may be able to **calculate the mass** of one 'unit' of the compound $CuCO_3$ (referring back to work with the Periodic Table in Topic 4.3) and should be expected to use the terms 'molecule' and 'atom' correctly.

Challenge and develop

- Ask the students to complete tasks 1 and 2 on Worksheet 1.4.17. [O1, 2&3]
- Demonstrate the setting-up of equipment for the thermal decomposition of copper carbonate (see Technician's notes 1.4.17) and ask the students to name the different pieces of apparatus. Make a point of indicating the tight seal and emphasising the importance of avoiding overheating, which can result in powder leaving the boiling tube. [O2]
- Pairs of students should perform the decomposition of copper carbonate, following the procedures and safety precautions agreed beforehand. They can use Practical sheet 1.4.17a. They should **record** the starting mass, observations made during the experiment and after cooling, and the final mass of solid remaining. [O2]

Explain

- Demonstrate blowing gently into limewater and ask the students to **suggest** what causes the limewater to become cloudy (carbon dioxide). Ask for its formula and the link to their experiment.
- **Pair talk** Students should name and describe the starting materials (solid green copper carbonate, $CuCO_3$) and products (carbon dioxide gas, CO_2 and black powder). After their initial **discussion**, name the symbols to enable the students to **identify** the black powder (copper oxide, CuO). [O3]
- Ask the students to **explain** why they think the reaction is called 'thermal decomposition' – i.e. heat + breakdown. [O2&3]

Consolidate and apply

- Ask the students to read the section 'Heating carbonates' in the Student Book and to answer questions 4 to 8. State symbols are introduced here for the solids and gases; this will link with students' observations – black powder = solid, bubbles = gas. [O2]

Extend

- Ask students able to progress further to make some limewater following the guidelines on Practical sheet 1.4.17b. Alternatively they can **describe** and **explain** how it is made and how it identifies carbon dioxide, following reading the 'Making limewater' section in the Student Book. They can also answer task 3 of Worksheet 1.4.17. [O2&3]

Plenary suggestions

Summing up Students write, or are supported to write, an equation for the decomposition reaction – using words /symbols as appropriate. Ask the students to **predict/explain/justify** the mass change (decrease) using the equation – a gas is made; it escapes; causing a decrease in mass. [O2&3]

Answers to Student Book questions

1. a) one of: shellfish/oysters; snail shell; egg shell
   b) one of: chalk; marble; limestone; travertine
2. calcium oxide; heating calcium carbonate
3. *calcium carbonate:* indigestion remedy; purifying iron; *lime*: added to soils/water
4. Any reasonable safety precautions: clamp tightly but do not break glass; do not touch hot glass; bung/delivery tube should be secure; do not overheat one place on the test tube; point away from faces; use goggles to protect eyes; take care not to break delivery tube.
5. Green powder/solid/copper carbonate turns black; colourless limewater turns cloudy
6. Thermal = heat; decomposition = breakdown; nothing else is added
7. *s* = solid; *g* = gas
8. Carbon dioxide gas escaped out of the delivery tube.
9. calcium oxide + water → calcium hydroxide
10. Three different-colour circles to represent each element in $CaCO_3$; one for Ca, one for C, and three for O. Using the same colours; separate diagrams for CaO and CO_2.

Answers to Worksheet 1.4.17

1. a) egg shells, snail shells or shellfish shells b) chalk, marble, travertine or limestone
   c) calcium oxide d) by heating calcium carbonate e) carbon and oxygen f) $CuCO_3$
2. a) i) calcium oxide and carbon dioxide ii) magnesium oxide and carbon dioxide
   b) i) calcium carbonate → calcium oxide + carbon dioxide
   ii) magnesium carbonate → magnesium oxide + carbon dioxide
   d) purifying iron; making lime (to make cement and glass; added to soils; added to water to reduce acidity); used in toothpaste, chalk, indigestion tablets
3. a) i) $CuCO_3$ ii) CO_2 iii) CuO and CO_2 iv) $CuCO_3 \rightarrow CuO + CO_2$
   b) Calcium carbonate is heated in air to make calcium oxide. This is dissolved in water to make calcium hydroxide (limewater).
   c) Forms calcium carbonate; this is not very soluble so the limewater turns cloudy.

4.18 Explaining changes

Lesson overview

Learning objectives

- Observe and explain mass changes.
- Use scientific terms and simple models to explain chemical processes.

Learning outcomes

- Identify oxidation and decomposition reactions. [O1]
- Explain the differences between oxidation and thermal decomposition reactions. [O2]
- Use simple models and equations to explain the mass changes during oxidation and thermal decomposition reactions. [O3]

Skills development

- Thinking scientifically: use equations/use units and nomenclature
- Working scientifically: present evidence, develop explanations
- Learner development: collaborate effectively

Resources needed balance; balloon; dilute acid; carbonate; tiddlywinks/plasticine/molymods/bricks; Worksheet 1.4.18

Common misconceptions Heating always causes the same reaction. Note the general confusion between 'atom', 'molecule', 'element' and 'compound'.

Key vocabulary oxidation, thermal decomposition, reactants, products

Teaching and learning

Engage

- Show the students a series of the chemical formulas met in the Student Book and ask them to name the substances – e.g. Cu, O_2, CO_2, Mg, $CaCO_3$, MgO, $CuCO_3$. Ask them to **classify the substances** as elements/compounds or containing atoms/molecules.
- The students should draw a circle model diagram to represent a mixture of CuO, O_2 and Mg.

  Higher-attaining students could be asked to write the formula given the names, or formula/names from a circle model diagram/particle diagram.

Challenge and develop

- **Pair work** Ask the students to read the section 'Chemical reactions' in the Student Book, and then complete task 1 of Worksheet 1.4.18, which asks them to define oxidation and thermal decomposition and write general word equations. [O1]
- Although the use of state symbols – solid (s), gas (g) – is not formally required at KS3 it may be helpful to refer to them. Ask the students to **apply** these to the two reactions in the Student Book in this section:

  metal (s) + oxygen (g) → metal oxide (s); and metal carbonate (s) → metal oxide (s) + carbon dioxide (g)

Explain

- **Pair talk** The students use the general equations to **identify** similarities and differences between oxidation and thermal decomposition reactions – e.g. oxygen is added in oxidation but nothing is added in thermal decomposition; a gas is added in oxidation but a gas is produced in thermal decomposition; both produce oxides, both require heating (in these examples – but not always, for example sodium oxidises at room temperature). [O2&3]

- After a full class discussion, summarise the ideas provided by the students, give feedback and emphasise that the addition of oxygen (in oxidation) leads to a mass increase, and that producing a gas (in thermal decomposition) leads to a mass decrease. This is explained in the 'Mass changes' section in the Student Book. [O2&3]
- Ask the students to **complete** task 2 of Worksheet 1.4.18. [O2]

Consolidate and apply

- Introduce the Law of Conservation of Mass – the idea that mass cannot be created or destroyed, but can take new forms. That is, in chemical reactions we rearrange atoms (and hence mass) but the total mass/number of atoms does not change (this is covered in the Student Book). [O3]
- **Group work** Students produce a poster or models (circle models or using tiddlywinks, plasticine, molymod etc.) to explain how oxidation, thermal decomposition and dissolving demonstrate the conservation of mass (task 3 of Worksheet 1.4.18). [O1, 2&3]

Extend

Ask students able to progress further to **link** the loss of gas and the Law of Conservation of Mass by:

- demonstrating the reaction of an acid and a carbonate in a container on a balance with and then without a balloon (shown in Figure 1.4.18d in the Student Book)
- asking them to **calculate** the masses of reactants and products. [O3]

Plenary suggestions

Reaction rating Give the students a reaction and ask them to **identify** and **explain** whether it is oxidation or thermal decomposition or dissolving, and whether there is mass increase or loss of mass or no change in mass. Mini-whiteboards could be used or via pair talk – give pairs the opportunity to talk and decide before asking for feedback from one group. [O1, 2&3]

Answers to Student Book questions

1. an oxide 2. The compound breaks down when heated.
3. During oxidation, oxygen is added so the mass goes up/increases. During thermal decomposition, nothing is added so the mass does not increase; the mass goes down because a gas/carbon dioxide is produced that escapes.
4. no mass change in dissolving, mass increase in oxidation; oxidation is chemical change, dissolving is physical change
5. The numbers of each coloured circle are the same on both sides. 6. a) 40 g b) 64 g
7. a) The mass of the products is the same as that of the reactants; reactants = 100 g; products = 56 + 44 = 100 g so no mass is lost or gained

   b) start mass 100 g; end mass 56 g

   c) The symbol equation shows that the same amounts of each element are present before and after the reaction.

Answers to Worksheet 1.4.18

1. a) Oxygen is added to another element. b) element + oxygen (reactants) → element oxide (product)

   c) The breakdown of a substance when it is heated, to form a new substance.

   d) element carbonate (reactant) → element oxide + carbon dioxide (products)
2. a)

	Oxidation	Thermal decomposition	Dissolving sugar
What is added?	oxygen	heat	water
What is produced?	solid	solid and gas	liquid
Product made	element oxide	element oxide and carbon dioxide	sugar solution
Is heat needed?	not always	yes	no

   b) Oxygen is added in oxidation; carbon dioxide is released in thermal decomposition.

   c) Two of: Oxidation results in a solid; dissolving results in a solution. Oxidation is a chemical reaction (a permanent change); dissolving is not a chemical reaction (a reversible change). A new substance/oxide is made in oxidation. Oxygen is needed for oxidation but not for dissolving.

4.19 Checking students' progress

The 'Checking your progress' section in the Student Book indicates the key ideas developed in this chapter and shows how students progress to more complex levels. It is provided to support students in:

- identifying those ideas
- developing a sense of their current level of understanding
- developing a sense what the next steps in their learning will be.

It is designed either to be used at the end of a chapter to support an overall view of the progress, or alternatively during the teaching of the chapter students can self assess or peer assess using this topic as a basis.

It would be helpful if students can be encouraged to provide evidence from their understanding or their notes to support their judgements. In some cases it may be useful to explore the difference in the descriptors for a particular idea so that students can see what makes for a 'higher outcome'.

It may be useful with some descriptors to provide examples from the specific work done, such as an experiment undertaken or an explanation developed and recorded. If marking and feedback uses similar ideas and phrases this will enable students to relate specific marking to a more general sense of progress.

To make good progress in understanding science students need to focus on these ideas and skills:

Students who are making modest progress will be able to:	**Students who are making good progress will be able to:**	**Students who are making excellent progress will be able to:**
Give some examples of elements, locate them in the Periodic Table and use the table to identify metals and non-metals.	Give examples of elements and explain how they are organised in the Periodic Table.	Define elements, use symbols, link the organisation of the Periodic Table to element features and explain how scientists organised the Periodic Table.
Describe where some elements are found on Earth and identify some of the oldest known elements.	Explain why different elements are found in different places and why they were discovered at different times.	Use ideas and evidence to explain where and why elements and compounds were found.
Identify some common properties of metal elements and non-metal elements and their uses.	Classify metals and non-metals using their properties.	Identify similarities and differences between metals and how these relate to their uses; compare and contrast properties of metals and non-metals.
Identify metals and non-metals using data and suggest a reason for particular applications.	Explain the properties of elements using data and why they are used for different applications.	Select and justify the use of elements for different purposes, based on their properties.
Describe an example of a compound and represent a chemical reaction using a simple model.	Explain how compounds can be formed and explain a chemical reaction using simple models.	Make links between simple models of compounds and chemical symbols.
Identify changes during a reaction, relate these to reactants and products, and identify a difference between melting and burning.	Make accurate observations, explain them using a simple model and a word equation and explain differences between chemical and physical changes in terms of atoms.	Explain observations using word equations, relate chemical symbols to a simple circle model and use the correct terms and simple models to explain the differences between chemical and physical changes.
Make observations and identify reactants and products.	Make accurate observations, identify differences, and with support, describe reactions using simple models or word equations.	Suggest reasons for different observations, describe reactions using word equations and start to use symbols to model chemical reactions.
Recognise where carbon and its compounds are used.	Explain different ways in which carbon is important.	Explain, using the correct terms, where carbon is found and why it is useful.
Identify oxidation and decomposition reactions.	Explain why oxidation is a reaction; explain the differences between oxidation and thermal decomposition.	Use models and word equations to explain changes during oxidation and thermal decomposition reactions.

4.20 Answers to Student Book Questions

This table provides answers to the *Questions* section at the end of Chapter 4 of Student Book 1. It also shows how different questions assess attainment in terms of the focus and style of a question as well as the context. Question-level analysis can indicate students' proficiency in approaching different aspects of scientific understanding and different types of answer.

Q	Answer		Focus			Style			Context			
		Marks available	Knowledge and understanding	Application	Evaluation of evidence	Objective test question	Short written answer	Longer written answer	Symbols, particles and the Periodic Table	Properties of materials	Applications of materials	Chemical reactions
1	c	1	x			x						x
2	c	1	x			x			x			
3	c	1	x			x				x		
4	b	1	x			x			x			
5	Most metals are found as compounds in ores. It's the metal element that has the properties you want to use	2	x				x			x		
6	Any two from: • shiny v dull • strong v not as strong • ductile v non-ductile • malleable v non-malleable • sonorous v non-sonorous • conductor of heat v insulator • conductor of electricity v insulator	2	x				x			x		
7	Chemical change is irreversible	1	x					x				x
	Reasonable example, such as burning toast, frying egg	1		x				x				x
	Physical change is reversible, often involving a change of state	1	x					x				x
	Reasonable example, such as change of state	1		x				x				x
8	d	1		x		x					x	
9	d	1		x		x						x
10	b	1		x		x			x			
11	d	1		x		x						x

Q	Answer	Marks available	Focus: Knowledge and understanding	Focus: Application	Focus: Evaluation of evidence	Style: Objective test question	Style: Short written answer	Style: Longer written answer	Context: Symbols, particles and the Periodic Table	Context: Properties of materials	Context: Applications of materials	Context: Chemical reactions
12	Oxygen: two identical circles in contact	1		x			x		x			
	Carbon dioxide: three circles; the outer two should be the same as each other;and the same as in the molecule of oxygen, with the central one clearly different	1		x			x		x			
13	Any two from: won't rust, lasts longer, looks nicer, won't taint food taste, easier to clean	2		x			x				x	
14	Metal; strong, waterproof, malleable	2		x				x			x	
	Plastic; cheap, light, can be moulded, can be coloured	2		x				x			x	
15	Iron: a single circle *Sulfur*: single circle, shaded differently from the one for iron *Mixture of iron and sulfur*: a number of circles, not in contact nor in a regular pattern, some shaded the same as iron and some the same as sulfur *Iron sulfide*: several pairs of touching circles: one of each pair should be shaded the same as iron and the other the same as sulfur Allocate 2 marks for a completely correct answer; subtract 1 for a single error	2			x		x		x			
16	• good conductor	1			x			x			x	
	• sonorous	1			x			x			x	
	• low melting point	1			x			x			x	
	• shiny – doesn't easily react with oxygen/air	1			x			x			x	
	Total possible	**30**	**10**	**14**	**6**	**8**	**10**	**12**	**7**	**5**	**12**	**7**

5.1 Introduction

When and how to use these pages

The Introduction in the Student Book indicates some of the ideas and skills in this topic area that students will already have met from KS2 or from previous KS3 work, and provides an indication of what they will be studying in this chapter. *Ideas you have met before* is not intended to be a comprehensive summary of all the prior ideas, but rather to point out a few of the key ones and to support the view that scientific understanding is progressive. Even though we might be meeting contexts that are new to us, we can often use existing ideas to start to make sense of them.

In this chapter you will find out indicates some of the new ideas that the chapter will introduce. Again, it isn't a detailed summary of content. Its purpose is more to act as a 'trailer' and generate some interest.

The outcomes, then, will be recognition of prior learning that can be built on and interest in finding out more.

There are a number of ways this can be used. You might, for example:

- Use *Ideas you have met before* as the basis for a revision lesson as you start the first new topic.
- Use *Ideas you have met before* as the centre of spider diagrams, to which students can add examples, experiments they might have done previously or what they found interesting.
- Make a note of any unfamiliar/difficult terms and return to these in the relevant lessons.
- Use ideas from *In this chapter you will find out* to ask students questions such as:
  - Why is this important?
  - How could it be used?
  - What might we be doing in this topic?

Overview of the chapter

In this chapter, students will learn about ideas of forces, friction, movement and speed. They will learn how to represent the location, size and direction of forces using arrows. They will meet situations in which forces are balanced and others in which they are unbalanced. They will also learn to identify reaction forces.

The students will consider the effects that forces have – stretching, compressing, turning around a fulcrum, causing changes in speed or direction. They will learn that movement continues at the same speed and in the same direction unless a force acts. In analysing the force of friction they will consider where it is desirable, where it is unwanted and how it can be increased or reduced. They will have the opportunity to investigate the effect of streamlining in order to develop their understanding of water and air resistance.

The concept of speed will be explored and students will learn and practise the method for calculating it.

This chapter offers a number of opportunities for students to relate hands-on experience to slightly more abstract ideas. They will use a range of thinking and personal skills to help their learning and support their peers.

Obstacles to learning

The students may need extra guidance with the following terms and misconceptions:

- **Forces** Students may think that moving objects always have forces acting on them. Their experience makes it hard to accept the idea that an object which is moving will continue with the same speed and direction unless a force acts (Newton's First Law), because on Earth the forces of friction and gravity are always present.
- **Weight and mass** Students need to grasp the idea that weight is a force with the unit newton, yet when people talk about weight they often mean mass.
- **Elasticity** Students may think that elastic simply means stretchy; elasticity means an object or material returns to its original shape.

- **Free fall** On film, free-fall parachutists can appear to fly upwards when they open their parachute. Students may need help to realise that this is only a dramatic slowing in relation to the camera (which is still in free fall). At terminal velocity all forces are in balance so the object won't get faster.

	Topic title	**Overarching objective**
2	Discovering forces	Forces as pushes or pulls arising from the interaction between two objects Using force arrows in diagrams
3	Measuring forces	Forces measured in newtons
4	Understanding weight on other planets	Gravity forces acting at a distance on Earth and in space
5	Exploring the effects of forces	Forces being needed to cause objects to stop or start moving, or to change their speed or direction of motion
6	Understanding stretch and compression	Forces associated with deforming objects Measurements of stretch or compression as force is changed
7	Investigating Hooke's Law	Forces associated with deforming objects; stretching and squashing – springs Measurements of stretch or compression as force is changed Force–extension linear relation; Hooke's Law as a special case
8	Understanding friction	Rubbing and friction forces between surfaces
9	Exploring the benefits of friction	
10	Understanding air and water resistance	Forces: pushing things out of the way; resistance to motion of air and water
11	Discovering streamlining	
13	Exploring forces and motion	Forces being needed to cause objects to stop or start moving, or to change their speed or direction Balanced and unbalanced forces
14	Exploring how forces affect speed and direction	Change depending on direction of force and its size
15	Understanding speed calculations	Change depending on direction of force and its size Speed and the quantitative relationship between average speed, distance and time (speed = distance ÷ time)
16	Understanding turning forces	Moment as the turning effect of a force
17	Discovering moments	
18	Understanding the application of moments	

5.2 Discovering forces

Lesson overview

Learning objectives

- Recognise different examples of forces.
- List the main types of force.
- Represent forces using arrows.

Learning outcomes

- List some types of force and label diagrams to show the direction of forces. [O1]
- State the main types of force and draw force diagrams to show the size and direction of forces. [O2]
- Describe the main types of force and accurately draw force diagrams to explain the relative size and direction of applied forces and their effects. [O3]

Skills development

- Thinking scientifically: understand how theories develop
- Working scientifically: develop explanations
- Learner development: collaborate effectively

Resources needed pictures of e.g. tennis player, plane or bird taking off, roller coaster, vehicle on tow; suction jumper; wind-up mechanical toy; ball floating in a bowl of water; pendulum, large mass; air track and glider; toy car on a ramp; Worksheet 1.5.2

Common misconceptions When an object is stationary, no forces are acting on it. When an object is moving there must be a force acting on it.

Key vocabulary pushing force, pulling force, turning force

Teaching and learning

Engage

- Identify the students' experience of forces from KS2 by displaying a range of images that show different situations in which forces are in action. They have two minutes to **identify** some of the forces. Collect feedback, drawing out a range of descriptions and key words. Make a note of some ideas (incorrect and incomplete as well as correct), so that they can be displayed and revisited later. [O1]

Challenge and develop

- Explain how to represent forces using arrows (see the Student Book for examples). The direction of an arrow shows the direction that the force is acting. Force arrows should be labelled so they are not confused with any arrows showing direction of movement. The length of the arrow can represent how big the force is. [O1&2]

  Higher-attaining students may be able to draw force arrows to scale.

- Challenge the students, by examining a range of objects and equipment (see *Resources needed*), to **draw force diagrams** with arrows showing the direction, location and size of forces. [O1, O2]
- Ask the students to **consider** these three questions:
  - Are forces always present?
  - Can you have movement without forces?
  - Can forces be present even when there is no movement?

  Encourage students to present tentative ideas as well as those they are sure about. [O3]

- Students **discuss** the forces that they have identified. Encourage them to **identify** evidence and observations that support or contradict their answers to the questions. Feedback should give the opportunity to highlight where new ideas or evidence can lead to scientists modifying their views, and should ensure that all students have drawn the force arrows correctly. [O1, 2&3]

Explain

- **Pair talk** The students produce verbal or written **explanations** in relation to the three questions in *Challenge and develop*. Appropriate answers include:
  - Forces are present in most/all examples; gravity is exerting a pulling force in most cases.
  - Once an object is moving it will keep going even if no forces are acting (e.g. a spacecraft in outer space).
  - When forces are in balance there is no change in movement.
- The students can then complete the first two tasks of Worksheet 1.5.2. [O1, 2&3]

Consolidate and apply

- **Listening triads** Working in groups of three, the students revisit the images and ideas in the starter activity. Each student takes on a role – talker, questioner or recorder. The talker **explains** something; the questioner **asks for clarification**; the recorder **makes notes and gives a report** at the end of the conversation. Then the roles can be changed. [O1, 2&3]

Extend

- Students who are able to progress further can complete the third task on Worksheet 1.5.2. [O3]

Plenary suggestions

Learning triangle Students draw a large triangle with a smaller inverted triangle inside it. In the three outer triangles they write something they have seen, something they've done and something they've discussed. Then they add in the central triangle something they have learned.

Answers to Student Book questions

1. pulling force 2. gravity 3. pushing force from the engines; lift force from the wings
4. The downward pulling force of gravity; air resistance causing drag against forward motion.
5. The pushing force from the engines.
6. The increased team would produce a bigger force. The forces from each team would no longer be balanced, and there would be movement in the direction of the larger force – the stronger team would pull the weaker team forwards.
7. The forward pushing force should be bigger than any other forces; and should be in the direction that the car will move.
8. In each situation the students should show at least two forces – e.g. for the sailing boat they could show the pushing force of the wind and the resistance of the water. Challenge the students to think about the relative sizes of the forces.

Answers to Worksheet 1.5.2

1. a) i) two arrows acting along the rope, pointing outwards, equal in size and opposite in direction; no movement

   ii) right-hand force arrow larger than left-hand force arrow; movement arrow to the right

   iii) left-hand force arrow larger than right-hand force arrow; movement arrow to the left

   b) The first diagram is drawn as for (a)(iii). The second diagram has the left-hand force arrow unchanged, the right-hand force arrow larger, and the movement arrow to the right.

   c) i) There is no movement (or, if already moving, movement continues at the same speed and in the same direction).

   ii) The teams move in the direction of the larger force (or resultant force).
2. a) It will continue at the same speed and in the same direction unless another (unbalanced) force acts.

   b) air resistance; weight/gravity c) weight of the ball (gravity); upwards supporting force from ground
3. The burning produces a pushing force (due to the expansion of gases) that propels the firework upwards into the air. The pushing force is larger than the weight/gravity force. Air resistance acts to slow the rocket down. When the burning stops, the force of weight/gravity pulls the rocket back to Earth.

5.3 Measuring forces

Lesson overview

Learning objectives

- Measure forces using newtonmeters.
- Use the correct unit for force.
- Explain the difference between mass and weight.

Learning outcomes

- Recognise that a newtonmeter can be used to measure a force, and know that mass and weight are not the same. [O1]
- Use newtonmeters, have a basic understanding of mass and explain simply how gravitational force affects weight. [O2]
- Use newtonmeters with skill to measure a range of everyday forces, and correctly use scientific concepts to explain effectively the difference between mass and weight. [O3]

Skills development

- Thinking scientifically: use units and nomenclature
- Working scientifically: record evidence
- Learner development: communicate effectively

Resources needed newtonmeters with different ranges and scales; a variety of objects to weigh and drag, including a sports shoe for each group; Worksheet 1.5.3; Practical sheet 1.5.3

Common misconceptions Mass and weight have the same meaning.

Key vocabulary newton, newtonmeter, precision, weight, gravity, mass

Teaching and learning

Engage

- Identify the students' ideas about measuring force by demonstrating opening a door against the force from the closure mechanism. Ask how we could compare the force needed to open different doors. Follow this up by demonstrating using a newtonmeter to pull the door open steadily. [O1, 2&3]

Challenge and develop

- Show the students the newtonmeters (many may already have used them at KS2) and check that they know that they are used to measure force and that the unit is the newton (N). [O1]
- Give the students practice at using the newtonmeters to **measure** and **record** different forces. This should include the weights of objects as well as actions such as dragging objects and opening doors. They should **record** their evidence on Practical sheet 1.5.3. [O1&2]
- Ask the students to **explain** why they think the choice of newtonmeter is important. They should mention the need for an appropriate range and how finer divisions on the scale allow greater precision. [O1&2]
- Explain the definitions of mass and weight to the students: [O3]
  - mass – the amount of material (number and type of particles); the unit is the kilogram (kg) or the gram (g).
  - weight – a force due to the pull of gravity; the unit is the newton (N). The larger the mass of an object, the bigger the force of gravity acting on it.
- Discuss the confusion that exists with measuring mass and weight. When a person stands on some bathroom scales, they are measuring weight – the force with which gravity is pulling them down. However, the scales are calibrated in kg rather than N, which is technically incorrect. When they are manufactured, the

scales are calibrated for use on Earth to display mass. This works because the Earth's force of gravity per unit mass is (fairly) constant from place to place. [O3]

Higher-attaining students may be able to **explain** objects with the same size but with different masses, using the particle model.

Explain

- **Pairs to fours** The students **discuss** and note down their ideas in answer to Student Book questions 6, 7 and 8. They then join with another pair and **communicate their ideas**. Encourage the pairs to question each other and to modify their own ideas if necessary. During the activity, circulate and gather examples of the best explanations and any enduring misconceptions, so that whole-class feedback can be given. [O3]

Students not progressing to O3 can produce an A4 guide with a diagram and an **explanation** of how to choose and use a newtonmeter.

Consolidate and apply

- Ask selected students to **present** their explanations from the 'pairs to fours' discussions to the rest of the class. [O3]

Extend

- Ask students who are able to progress further to try weighing a mass in air and then in water and then to speculate why the readings are not the same. They can do an internet search for 'upthrust in water' for ideas to help. [O3]

Plenary suggestions

Quick quiz Use mini-whiteboards, or similar, to quickly check the students' **recall** of the key learning – the equipment for measuring mass and weight; the units for mass and weight; matching mass and weight to definitions provided. Alternatively, Worksheet 1.5.3 can be used. [O1&2]

Answers to Student Book questions

1. newton
2. N
3. newtonmeter (or forcemeter)
4. left-hand meter: 1.0 N; right-hand meter: 10 N
5. The left-hand meter; because its scale divisions are of smaller value.
6. Ideas such as: people do not understand the scientific use of the terms; we say 'weigh' something when we mean measure its mass; when we weigh ourselves on bathroom scales the unit is kg, but it should be N.
7. The mass would be the same on both; because the number and type of particles do not change. The weight would be bigger on the bigger planet; because the force of gravity would be greater.
8. Damage is caused by the impact between the two cars. The mass of the two cars is the same on the Moon as on the Earth. Only the weight differs and this is a force acting downwards, which is not relevant in the impact.

Answers to Worksheet 1.5.3

1. a) 5000 N b) 100 N c) 2000 N d) 20 N e) 5 N
2. a) true b) partly true; the unit of force is the newton (N) c) false; weight (or force) is measured with a newtonmeter

   d) partly true; a door needs a pushing force or a pulling force to open it

   e) false; if no forces are acting on a stationary object it will not move, and if no forces are acting on a moving object it continues at the same speed in the same direction
3. a) A newtonmeter with a small range is suitable for a relatively light object, such as a pencil case. A relatively heavy object, such as a bag of books, would need a newtonmeter with a larger range.

   b) The fine divisions on a newtonmeter with a small range allow a reading to be more precise. The reading on the newtonmeter with the large range would be less precise because the value of each division is larger.

5.4 Understanding weight on other planets

Lesson overview

Learning objectives

- Explain the meaning of 'weightless'.
- Investigate weight on the Moon and on different planets.
- Identify the link between weight and gravitational attraction.

Learning outcomes

- Know that objects have different weights on different planets and that in deep space objects are weightless. [O1]
- Explain the term 'weightless' and apply understanding to explain why weight changes on different planets. [O2]
- Explain weight in terms of gravitational attraction and apply this to deep space and different planets. [O3]

Skills development

- Thinking scientifically: analyse data
- Working scientifically: interpret evidence
- Learner development: develop resilience

Resources needed newtonmeter (0 to 10 N); 100 g masses on hangers; Worksheet 1.5.4

Common misconceptions Gravity is a downwards force only on Earth – there is no gravity in space.

Key vocabulary gravity, weightless

Teaching and learning

Engage

- Explore the students' thoughts about gravity. Ask them if they have seen a video of astronauts experiencing conditions in a space station. (Show one if possible.) Suggest that in such situations the senses cannot always be trusted; this looks and feels like weightlessness, but in fact gravity is still acting. [O1&2]
- Ask the students to what extent they agree with the statement 'Gravity pulls you down.' Extend their thinking by asking them what force they would experience in space; close to another planet; and far away from planets. [O1&2]

  Higher-attaining students may engage with the idea that gravity is an attraction between massive objects.

Challenge and develop

- Ask the students to **interpret the data** in Table 1.5.4 in the Student Book and produce a set of statements that **describe** the relationships in the table. [O1, 2&3]
- Students **read the scale** of a newtonmeter with a 100 g mass suspended from it. Explain that, on Earth, gravity pulls every kilogram of mass down with a force of 10 newtons. [O3]
- **Pair talk** The students **predict** what the newtonmeter would read if it and the mass were in different locations – above Earth; inside the Earth; on other planets; in outer space. [O2&3]
- Students **share ideas** about other situations, for example:
  - why gravity on the gas planet Saturn is less than that on Earth even though it is more than ten times the diameter (Saturn is less dense and has a lower mass than Earth)
  - why when comparing gravity of different planets we must specify the location, usually the surface (gravity decreases the further away you are from a planet.) [O2&3]

Explain

- Explain why weight is different in different locations, depending on mass and distance. Students need to show resilience in accepting changes to their ideas. They individually produce a short piece of writing to **explain the differences**. They then swap explanations a few times so that they can develop their ideas. [O3]
- Teacher–student feedback should draw out the key ideas and words in good explanations, so that students can **improve** their own. [O3]

Consolidate and apply

- Students answer Student Book questions 6, 7 and 8. [O2&3]
- Students answer the questions on Worksheet 1.5.4. [O1&2]
- Students **draw graphs** to display some relationships from Table 1.5.4 in the Student Book, for example surface gravity against how much you can lift. [O1, 2&3]

Extend

- Ask students able to progress further to **investigate** gravity due to black holes and why this is so strong. [O3]

Plenary suggestions

True or false? Display some true and false statements based on learning from the lesson. All students stand up. Display each statement in turn. After each, students indicate if they think it is true. All the students who respond incorrectly sit down. [O1, 2&3]

Answers to Student Book questions

1. The further away you are from any planet or star, the weaker the gravity.
2. Gravity from the Earth would gradually weaken as the spacecraft got further away. At a point in between the Earth and the Moon, the pull of gravity from each would balance – this point is closer to the Moon than the Earth. As the spacecraft travelled further, the pull of gravity towards the Moon would become bigger than the pull of the Earth.
3. Food would not stay on a plate, you could not drink from a cup, and so on.
4. on Earth
5. Moon, Mercury/Mars, Venus, Earth
6 The amount of material in an object does not change.
7. a) A force pulling you towards the Earth.
   b) You would start moving towards the Earth; and would fall faster and faster.
8. a) no weight b) reduced weight c) weight a fraction of that on the Earth's surface

Answers to Worksheet 1.5.4

1. a) Gravity arrow is the same in each diagram; no force from the hand once the ball has left the hand, because there is no longer contact; air resistance arrows are optional at this stage but should be in the opposite direction to travel and be larger when the speed is faster, e.g when the ball has just left the hand and when the ball has accerated due to gravity and almost reached the Earth.
   b) downwards; towards the Earth
2. a) pushing force b) the force of gravity c) deep space (accept a range of answers which convey correct meaning)
   d) no forces are acting so the rocket continues to travel in the same direction at the same speed
   e) be pulled towards the planet by its gravity
3. Scientific theories can be tested in different conditions, e.g. Newton's laws, medical understanding. Evidence of positive benefits, e.g. space industries can lead to new discoveries and technologies; they employ many people. Negatives: money could be spent on things of more direct benefit, e.g better health care.

5.5 Exploring the effects of forces

Lesson overview

Learning objectives

- Identify and describe the effects of forces of different sizes and directions.
- Predict and explain the changes caused by forces.
- Explain the concept of force pairs (action and reaction).

Learning outcomes

- State that forces are needed to change the motion of an object, and draw force arrows in diagrams. [O1]
- Correctly use force diagrams to explain the effects of forces and changes in motion; identify force pairs. [O2]
- Explain the effects of a range of forces and accurately illustrate these using diagrams, and explain effectively different examples of action and reaction. [O3]

Skills development

- Thinking scientifically: understand how theories develop
- Working scientifically: make predictions
- Learner development: ask questions

Resources needed marble; air track and glider; equipment for each group as detailed in the Technician's notes; graph paper; Worksheet 1.5.5; Practical sheet 1.5.5; Technician's notes 1.5.5

Common misconceptions Something stops moving because the force has run out.

Key vocabulary prediction, action force, reaction force

Teaching and learning

Engage

- Challenge the students' thinking by setting up, but not carrying out, some demonstrations.
  - 1: a marble on a smooth surface; ask students to **predict** what will happen if it is gently nudged.
  - 2: an air track and a glider; ask students to **predict** what will happen if the glider is gently nudged.

  Students should **give reasons** for their predictions of outcomes; these will be revisited later. [O1&2]

Challenge and develop

- Set up a trolley, string, pulley and masses at the edge of a bench. The pulley will need to be clamped rigidly to the edge of the bench. The bench and string need to be long enough for the trolley to be able to travel at least 1 metre across the surface by the masses dangling round the pulley over the edge of the bench. Ask the students to **predict** the effect on the trolley of increasing the mass on the hanger. [O1]
- Working in pairs, the students set up similar equipment to **investigate** the effect of at least five different masses on the time the trolley takes to travel a set distance. Practical sheet 1.5.5 gives details of the experiment. Students should state the effect that a bigger force has on the motion of the trolley. Students can **plot a graph** using the data from their investigation or from task 1 of Worksheet 1.5.5. [O1]
- The students should **draw diagrams** (see Worksheet 1.5.5):
  - to illustrate the main forces in action, including the pulling force along the rope and the friction force in the opposite direction
  - to show the forces involved once the string goes slack, but the trolley is still moving (no pulling force but friction still present). [O2]

  Higher-attaining students may draw diagrams showing different masses producing different forces, with the size of the force arrows showing the relative size of the forces.

- **Discuss** where pairs of equal and opposite forces exist in this situation – for example the trolley pushing down on the bench and the bench pushing up on the trolley. [O2&3]

Explain

- Show a video clip of a gun recoil. **Discuss** what is happening and support the students in **explaining** the forces involved, including action and reaction. [O2,3]

  Higher-attaining students may be able to **compare** different recoils, e.g. from a hand gun and a cannon.

Consolidate and apply

- Ask the students to **review** their **predictions** and **explanations** from the starter activity, and to make changes and additions. [O1, 2&3]
- They **share** examples of how they changed or added to their predictions or explanations, and why. [O1, 2&3]
- They indicate what led to new thinking. Help them to see the link between new observations and the development of new ideas. [O1, 2&3]

Extend

- Ask students able to progress further to **consider** how in rocket motion a force is produced to push the rocket forward, despite no atmosphere to provide a reaction force. (Exhaust gases provide the reaction force.) [O3]

Plenary suggestions

The big ideas The students compose three sentences, each using an idea and one of the lesson key words. [O1, 2&3]

'I want to know more about' The students ask one question about what they would like to find out about next.

Answers to Student Book questions

1. downward pull of gravity (weight)
2. a) gravity pulling downwards and the upward force from the bench
   b) forces as in (a) and also a forward force from the weighted string (and a force of friction opposing the motion)
   c) forces as in (a) (plus force of friction opposing the motion); no forward force
3. a) The larger the mass hanging on the pulley, the faster the trolley will go / the shorter the time it will take to travel the distance along the bench.
   b) The larger the mass, the greater the force on the trolley, so the faster it will go (the higher the acceleration).
4. The trolley would be slower (note that at this stage a quantitative response is not expected).
5. a) *action force*: bat on ball; *reaction force*: ball on bat b) *action force*: ball on hand; *reaction force*: hand on ball
   c) *action force*: hand pulling on handle; *reaction force*: handle pulling on hand
6. Each diagram should show equal and opposite force arrows; acting on different objects (action and reaction).

Answers to Worksheet 1.5.5

1. a) 16, 8, 6, 4, 3 b) Ensure that the curve is smooth and is not extrapolated.
   c) *The greater the mass on the pulley*, the larger the force of gravity/weight. This produces a bigger pulling force on the trolley and so the trolley moves faster.
   d) i) pulling force along the rope; downward-acting force of weight of the trolley; upward reaction force of bench (and force of friction opposing movement) ii) as for (i) except no pulling force along the rope (ignore weight of the cord)
2. Ensure that force arrows are drawn at the point of action; in the correct direction; and to the correct scale.
   a) only gravity acting downwards; and the table balancing this with an equal and opposite force
   b) additional forces to (a): pulling force along the rope; air resistance and friction opposing movement; but smaller than the pulling force c) similar to (b) but no pulling force along the rope
3. *Prediction*: say what we think will happen, based on prior knowledge or ideas *Action force*: one half of a pair of forces
   Reaction force: a force equal and opposite to an action force

5.6 Understanding stretch and compression

Lesson overview

Learning objectives

- Explain the relationship between an applied force and the change of shape of an object.
- Investigate forces involved in compressing and stretching materials.
- Identify applications for compressible and stretchable materials.

Learning outcomes

- State that applying a force can compress or stretch an object, and state that the bigger the force the larger the deformation. [O1]
- Use the understanding of forces changing an object's shape to consider the quality of evidence when investigating change in shape. [O2]
- Explain how forces can cause an object to deform, link the deformation to the size of the force, and recognise that for a range of forces the amount of deformation is linear and that this can be used to design machines for measuring forces. [O3]

Skills development

- Thinking scientifically: consider the quality of evidence
- Working scientifically: interpret evidence
- Learner development: ask questions

Resources needed materials and equipment as detailed in the Technician's notes; graph paper; Worksheet 1.5.6; Practical sheet 1.5.6; Technician's notes 1.5.6

Common misconceptions Elastic behaviour refers to only stretching and does not include compressing or returning to the original shape.

Key vocabulary compress, stretch, elastic behaviour, elastic limit, brittle

Teaching and learning

Engage

- Perform some demonstrations (see Technician's notes 1.5.6 for details including safety precautions) that allow the students to **compare** and **contrast** the behaviour of an elastic material, a ductile material and a brittle material when a force is applied. If possible, show students a video of testing elastic behaviour. [O1]

Challenge and develop

- The students **consider** the choice of foam for soft furniture and **identify questions** they would need to know the answer to in order to choose an appropriate foam. [O1]
- They **investigate** how the size of the force applied affects the compression of foam. A board is placed on top of a piece of foam to distribute force evenly, and masses are placed on top. Practical sheet 1.5.6 can be used to guide students' practical work and analysis of results. The students state the relationship between the force applied and the amount of compression. Worksheet 1.5.6 reinforces the data-handling or can be used with the students' own data. [O1, 2&3]

  Higher-attaining students might independently see the need for repeats and take steps to avoid problems relating to the foam compressing unevenly.

- The students can **compare** how by much different types of foam compress. They should add masses until the foam is fully compressed to illustrate the importance of density. [O1, 2&3]
- Ask the students to **evaluate** the quality of their data and **suggest** how it could be improved (e.g. carrying out repeats, using a more accurate method for measuring thickness). [O2]

Explain

- **Group talk** The students should **link** the concept of balanced forces to stretching and compression. At equilibrium, the forces of weight and restoring elastic force are balanced. When more force is added, the foam compresses more and the restoring force increases until it balances. [O1&3]
- The students **explain** the application to weighing machines and share explanations with other groups. [O3]

Consolidate and apply

- The students **plot** and **analyse** a line graph (see Student Book questions 5 and 6 or Worksheet 1.5.6). [O1&3]
- The students **apply** the findings from their investigation to the choice of foam in furniture (too rigid – it does not adjust its shape to the person; too soft – it fully compresses, and so gives little additional comfort). [O3]

  Higher-attaining students could **explain** the effects as the foam approaches full compression and how this affects comfort.

Extend

- Students able to progress further can use the results to **suggest** how a cushion on the base of a settee could be constructed for people of a wide range of body weights to be supported in comfort. (Use a greater thickness of foam; use two or more foams of different compressibility.) [O3]

Plenary suggestions

The big ideas Ask the students to write down three things they have learned during the lesson. Then ask them to share their facts in a group and to compile a master list of facts, with the most important at the top. Ask for ideas to be shared to find out whether groups agree or not. [O1, 2&3]

Answers to Student Book questions

1. foam, metal springs, carbon fibre, climbing ropes, rubber balls, gases
2. liquids, sand, dough 3. glass, china, some plastics
4. Scales labelled including units; scales chosen so that the data fills at least half the available space; points marked accurately in fine pencil; smooth line/curve through points (or line of best fit); title
5. Line graph correctly plotted; the greater the force applied to the spring, the more it is compressed; each additional 10 N gives 3.1 cm of additional compression; except for the last reading.
6. a) Up to 50 N the spring compresses by 3.1 cm for every 10 N added; with 60 N it only compresses a little extra (0.6 cm).

   b) The spring has become fully compressed.
7. a) It might compress fully with the applied force and so would offer little comfort or support.

   b) The applied force might not compress it at all and so it would be little more comfortable than the wood or other hard material of the chair.
8. Springs stretch or compress in uniform amounts; whenever a certain weight is added (idea of proportionality).
9. The sudden shock of being stopped by a rope with no stretch could injure the climber or snap the rope.

Answers to Worksheet 1.5.6

1. a) Use of a fine pencil; accurate marking of points; labelled axes with units; smooth curve drawn through the points.

   b) Suitable rules based on (a).
2. a) The greater the force applied, the thinner the foam becomes. Beyond a force of a certain size the cushion does not become any thinner.

   b) 1000 N (or slightly less)

   c) i) It would be suitable for the base of a chair for all but the largest of adults; because it would not be fully compressed by their weight.

   ii) It would be suitable for the back of a chair; because it compresses only a few cm when smaller forces are applied.
3. The progressive crumpling of a bumper allows the car and passengers to slow down over a finite distance; rather coming to a sudden halt that would result in more injuries.

5.7 Investigating Hooke's Law

Lesson overview

Learning objectives

- Investigate the effects of applied forces on springs.
- Generate data to produce a graph and analyse outcomes.

Learning outcomes

- Carry out an investigation into springs and gather data to show simply the relationship between load and extension. [O1]
- Use their own data to state Hooke's Law and explain the elastic limit of a material. [O2]
- Obtain a precise set of data by investigation, produce accurately drawn graphs to illustrate Hooke's Law, and explain the behaviour of a material at the elastic limit. [O3]

Skills development

- Thinking scientifically: analyse data
- Working scientifically: present evidence
- Learner development: collaborate effectively

Resources needed equipment as detailed in the Technician's notes; Worksheet 1.5.7; Practical sheet 1.5.7; Technician's notes 1.5.7

Key vocabulary extension, Hooke's Law, elastic limit

Teaching and learning

Engage

- Raise the students' curiosity by having three stands and clamps, each supporting a spring and a different hanging mass. Give the students a minute to **make observations** and **consider questions** they could investigate. [O1]
- Identify the three main questions this lesson will investigate:
  - Does a spring stretch by regular amounts as more load is suspended from it?
  - What is the elastic limit for a spring?
  - What happens to a spring when its limit is reached? [O2&3]
- Ask the students to **recall** from the previous lesson what is meant by 'elastic behaviour'. [O1, 2&3]

Challenge and develop

- Demonstrate the apparatus and procedure for investigating the extension of a spring when masses are hung from it. For ease and accuracy, clamp the metre rule alongside the spring with the zero mark aligned with the pointer label (see Practical sheet 1.5.7). Instruct the students to remove the hanging weight before increasing the load to check that the spring is undamaged and still shows elastic behaviour. [O1, 2&3]
- The students **record their observations** on Practical sheet 1.5.7 from their own experiment, or from the teacher demonstration, of the outcome of adding masses until the spring is permanently deformed. [O2&3]
- They **present their data** in the form of a line graph. [O1, 2&3]

  Higher-attaining students may realise earlier, through careful observation, when the elastic limit is reached.

Explain

- The students state and **explain** the relationship between the load on the spring and its extension. [O2]
- They work in their practical groups to **explain** how they can tell when the elastic limit is exceeded. [O2&3]

Higher-attaining students may be able to **quantify** the relationship between force and extension.

Consolidate and apply

- Select some students to **present** their statements and explanations of Hooke's Law. [O2&3]
- Students can complete Worksheet 1.5.7 to reinforce ideas about elastic limit, relative size of forces and Hooke's Law. [O2&3]
- **Pair talk/pairs to fours** The students **suggest** two good features of the statement/explanation that was presented and one for improvement, i.e. two WWWs (What Went Well…) and one EBI (Even Better If…). [O2&3]
- Ask the students to **identify** the key features of a good graph – they may have listed these in tackling question 4 of the previous lesson. [O3]

Extend

For students able to progress further:

- Ask them to **consider the reliability** of the data they have collected – how they could judge its reliability, and how they might improve its reliability. (They should carry out repeats – when results are reliable, repeated observations are the same or close to the original readings.) [O3]
- Introduce the vocabulary for describing a relationship when a graph is a straight line through the origin, i.e. *directly proportional*. Note: materials may stop deforming proportionally before the elastic limit. [O2&3]

Plenary suggestions

Exit slips Each student **describes** one situation in which knowing about elastic limits is important and writes it on an 'exit slip', which they have to hand in before leaving. These could be reviewed at the start of the next lesson, depending on how well the concept has been understood. [O1, 2&3]

Answers to Student Book

1. newtonmeter (forcemeter), car or bike suspension, mechanical toys, bathroom scales, curly electrical lead, door closer
2. The elastic material will return to its original shape after a force has deformed it; it easy to manufacture into the required shape; does not break easily; does not corrode
3. a) 6 cm b) 21 cm c) 0.6 cm
4. Words to the effect of 'the extension of a spring is directly proportional to the force applied to it'.
5. As the force increases, the spring extends more. The extension increases by regular amounts (there is a directly proportional relationship) until a certain force is exceeded. Then the spring extends much more with an increase of force, until it breaks.
6. a) 5 N b) 5 cm
7. a) between about 8 N and 8.5 N (The elastic limit may be slightly beyond the linear region.)
   b) You can only tell by checking if the spring returns to its original length.

Answers to Worksheet 1.5.7

1. a) i) As the spring unwinds it makes the toy move; it can be used again and again.
   ii) The rope absorbs more of the shock of a fall than a non-elastic rope would.
   iii) It makes the costume tight-fitting but still allows the person to move.
   b) i) The spring would break (or stretch) meaning that the toy would not work (so well).
   ii) The rope could be weakened and may snap more easily in future.
   iii) The material could rip or be left permanently stretched.
2. a) Suggested order: vii); v); i); viii); vi); iii); ii); iv)
3. Elastic behaviour, so can be used many times; predictable, linear extension or compression makes calibration and reading straightforward.

5.8 Understanding friction

Lesson overview

Learning objectives

- Identify the force of friction between two objects.
- Describe the effects of friction.
- Understand that friction acts in the opposite direction to the direction of movement.

Learning outcomes

- State that friction slows an object down or stops it from moving. [O1]
- Explain friction in terms of contact forces opposing the movement. [O2]
- Provide a detailed explanation in terms of contact forces between two surfaces and understand that friction always opposes the direction of movement. [O3]

Skills development

- Thinking scientifically: ask questions
- Working scientifically: develop explanations
- Learner development: respect others

Resources needed ramp and trolley; range of photographs to show situations where friction is occurring; examples of real-life devices so that students can experience friction – for example mechanical toys, stiff hinges, scissors; large sheets of paper; Worksheet 1.5.8

Common misconceptions A force arrow is the same as an arrow indicating movement.

Key vocabulary friction, contact force, lubricant

Teaching and learning

Engage

- Revisit the 'exit slips' from the previous lesson to highlight learning or correct misconceptions. [O1, 2&3]
- Elicit prior knowledge of friction (Worksheet 1.5.8 question 1). Then the students **compose questions** designed to:
  - find out what others know about friction
  - improve their own knowledge and understanding. [O1, 2&3]
- The students share their questions with the class – display the questions prominently so that they can be reviewed later. The aim is for students to be able to answer as many as possible by the end of the lesson. [O1, 2&3]
- Put a dynamics trolley on a ramp, initially flat on the bench. The students **explain** why the trolley is not moving (no horizontal force). Raise the ramp slightly, but not enough to make the trolley move. Again they **explain** why it does not move. (All forces in balance.) Now raise the ramp so that the trolley accelerates down the ramp. (The weight of the trolley overcomes friction.) Finally lower the ramp to a predetermined level at which the trolley, once moving, continues down the ramp at a steady speed. The students **identify** why the trolley does not accelerate. (The forces due to friction and weight are balancing each other.) [O1]

Challenge and develop

- The students **suggest** more precisely what they think friction is and where it is located (in the demonstration, friction is occurring between the trolley wheels and the surface of the ramp). [O2]

  Higher-attaining students may **identify** other sources of friction, e.g. between the wheels and the axle.

- Ask the students to **examine** a range of objects or pictures distributed around the room and **identify** where friction might be occurring in each situation (task 2 on Worksheet 1.5.8). [O2&3]

  Higher-attaining students may be able to **identify** additional sources of friction independently.

- The students **suggest** ways in which friction could be reduced in the situations and devices they have looked at. [O1&2]

Explain

- Students **draw annotated force diagrams** to show and **explain** that the friction force arrow always acts in the opposite direction to the movement. They should draw and label in a way that makes the force arrow distinct from any arrows indicating movement. [O2&3]

Consolidate and apply

- **Envoys** The students work in groups and draw an outline of a car in the centre of a large sheet of paper. Around the outside they put labels to **identify** all the locations where friction occurs. They may add a few essential details to the diagram to make their descriptions clear. An envoy takes the piece of paper and visits another group to **explain their ideas**. The groups gather ideas from each envoy visiting them and when their own envoy returns they add to their explanations and descriptions. As well as adding to the students' understanding, this activity develops their respect for others and their communication skills. [O1, 2&3]

Extend

- Ask students able to progress further to use the idea that friction is a contact force and that it acts in the opposite direction to movement to try to **explain** how friction occurs. It will help them to visualise this if they draw what rough surfaces would look like if very highly magnified. [O3]

Plenary suggestions

Traffic lights Revisit the questions displayed at the start of the lesson. The students indicate their confidence in being able to answer each question by red, amber and green. Use probing questions to check those students expressing confidence and to explore the doubts in students expressing lack of confidence. [O1, 2&3]

Answers to Student Book questions

1. It is steep, so the weight of the person helps to overcome the force of friction. The surface of the slide is smooth and the water makes the surface more slippery.
2. For example, a wheeled vehicle rolling along, a ball rolling along, a supermarket trolley being pushed across a car park, the brakes on a bicycle.
3. in the opposite direction to any movement
4. The object in the middle diagram will move to the left ; the pushing force is bigger than the friction.
5. The diagram should show bumpy surfaces and have explanatory labels.
6. There would be friction, for example: between tyres and road surface; between brake pads and wheels; between wiper blades and windscreen; in door hinges; in moving parts of engine; between driver's hands and steering wheel.
7. A bigger force (and so more energy) would be needed to make things work/move; there would be wear on moving parts; unwanted heat would be produced.

Answers to Worksheet 1.5.8

1, 2. Encourage students to be as precise as possible in the language they use and in their descriptions of the location and effects of friction. Students should comment on friction resisting movement and may also mention friction helping to provide grip in some situations.

3. a) The force of gravity/weight pulling the trolley down the ramp is balanced by the force of friction acting against the movement.

   b) Arrow parallel to ramp pointing down due to weight/gravity; equal and opposite arrow representing friction, downward force of weight and reaction force of the ramp acting upwards. (Avoid getting into resolution of and resultant forces at this stage.)

   c) Oil the wheels; make the surface smoother; add weight to the trolley; make the ramp steeper.

5.9 Exploring the benefits of friction

Lesson overview

Learning objectives

- Describe applications that make use of friction.
- Design procedures for investigating the force of friction.

Learning outcomes

- List examples of situations that need friction. [O1]
- Explain why friction is beneficial in a range of situations. [O2]
- Include the essential features in a plan to investigate the force of friction. [O3]

Skills development

- Thinking scientifically: evaluate risk
- Working scientifically: design investigations
- Learner development: plan progress

Resources needed two large softback books such as phone directories; apparatus for students to look at to enable them to plan (not carry out) an investigation into friction: newtonmeters; masses; buckles on straps of different materials; ramp; small sheets of different types of rubber/plastic; scissors; glue; Worksheet 1.5.9

Key vocabulary independent variable, dependent variable, control variable, reliable, safety

Teaching and learning

Engage

- Demonstrate what a big force friction can be using two softback books with alternate pages from each book interleaved. Trying to separate the two books by pulling the spines in opposite directions is extremely hard. [O1&2]

  Higher-attaining students should be able to **explain** the cumulative effect of adding many small frictional forces together.

- Explore the idea of friction being useful by showing the students a brief video clip of motor racing (cars or motorbikes). They **identify** areas where friction is useful (between the track and tyres; between the surfaces of the brake discs and pads). [O1&2]

Challenge and develop

- Ask the students to **explain** why friction is useful in a range of situations. They can use Worksheet 1.5.9. [O2]
- Students **design an investigation** (but not necessarily carry it out) to test the size of frictional forces in a scenario. For example:
  - Which material is best for a strap with a buckle?
  - Which type of rubber gives most grip for a trainer or a tyre?
  - Which substances could reduce grip?

  Aspects for students to **consider** include the method for measuring the force (newtonmeter, with hanging masses or masses sliding on a slope); variables to change, and those to control and measure; reliability. The students should also **evaluate risk** in their procedure (e.g. from falling weights, snapping or slipping straps, spillage of substances). [O3]

Explain

- In planning the investigation, the students **explain their reasons** for the processes and steps they have selected. [O3]

Higher-attaining students should **explain** why they should carry out repeat tests independently.

Consolidate and apply

- **Pair talk** The students work in pairs to **describe their plan** to another student who has been working separately. To help to plan progress, they **identify** three good features of their plans and one or two points for improvement. [O3]

Extend

- Ask students able to progress further to **consider** the use of oil as a lubricant and how some applications require relatively thin oils (e.g. sewing machines, hair clippers, fishing reels) while others require thicker oils (e.g. heavy machinery). [O2&3]
  - What issues could be caused by using oil of the wrong runniness (viscosity)?
  - How could the viscosity of oil be quantified? (drip or flow tests)

Plenary suggestions

Jumbled words Display a list of words jumbled up for students to rearrange into a clear summary description of friction. Suggested description: 'Friction is a contact force that prevents objects moving or slows them down. Friction always acts in the direction opposite to the movement of an object. Friction can be useful or unwanted depending on the situation.'

Answers to Student Book questions

1. Your hand would not be able to grip the handle; your feet would slide on the floor.
2. a) unwanted (but you would have no control) b) useful c) useful d) useful
3. Diagrams should show the force of friction in directions that prevent sliding/slipping.
4. The strap is bent back on itself; so there is friction between different parts of the webbing. As you pull harder, the webbing tightens on itself; increasing friction further.
5. Racing cars drive as fast as possible; so the carbon ceramic brakes get hot enough to work properly. In a family road car the braking is much more gentle; and the weather is very variable so the brakes may not get hot enough for carbon ceramic brakes to work.
6. a) *independent variable*: the material of the surface; *dependent variable*: the slope of the ramp when the object starts to slide; *variables to control*: weight and material of the object

   b) The tests would need to be repeated. If the results are reliable, the ramp angle at which the object starts to slide will be similar or the same for the same material in each test.

   c) The ramp should be secured so that it cannot fall; the bottom of the ramp should be positioned so that a sliding object cannot cause damage; the investigation should be carried out away from where others are working or walking.

Answers to Worksheet 1.5.9

1. a) *useful friction*: hand gripping a racket, clothes peg, climber on a rock face, a strap buckle; *unwanted friction*: skier (ignoring control, belts and buckles); *both useful and unwanted*: bicycle (useful on tyres and brakes, unwanted on moving parts), sprinter (useful on shoes, unwanted air resistance)
2. a) Tyre B (disadvantage is higher cost) or tyre C (disadvantage is less grip so poorer safety)

   b) Tyre A (problem in wet weather, different tyres would be needed) – students may suggest tyre B, in which case the problem would be that cars with tyre A would out-compete them in dry conditions)

   c) Tyre B (best safety, cost is worth it)

   d) Quantitative information is required as opposed to descriptive information, e.g. stopping distance in different conditions, purchase price, expected mileage.
3. The skis have special 'skins' on their bases: tiny hairs that lie flat when they move across the snow in one direction and stand up when they move the opposite way. Analogy: stroking a cat head to tail and tail to head.

5.10 Understanding air and water resistance

Lesson overview

Learning objectives

- Link frictional forces between surfaces to 'drag' between objects in a fluid.
- Discuss examples of frictional drag in air and in water.
- Consider the effects of friction on sky divers.

Learning outcomes

- Know that objects are slowed down by drag forces. [O1]
- Explain air and water resistance in terms of frictional drag, and recognise this as a contact force. [O2]
- Understand that frictional drag is a contact force, and explain the motion of a sky diver in relation to the effects of frictional forces. [O3]

Skills development

- Thinking scientifically: understand how theories develop
- Working scientifically: develop explanations
- Learner development: communicate effectively

Resources needed electric fan; Worksheet 1.5.10

Common misconceptions As something falls to Earth it continues to get faster and faster. When a parachutist deploys the parachute he/she will suddenly shoot upwards.

Key vocabulary air resistance, water resistance, terminal velocity, particle, collide

Teaching and learning

Engage

- Explore the students' current understanding by showing them a video clip of a parachutist in free fall. Students say/write questions that explore the events in the video. Note down all the questions so that they can be revisited. [O1]

Challenge and develop

- Set up a fan at the front of the class and ask the students in front of the fan to **describe** what they feel. Ask whether there would be any difference between this and what they would feel if they were riding a bike in the open air. [O1, 2&3]
- Discuss what the air feels like, and the reasons for this, as it moves past you or you move through it (there is no difference between the two situations). Help the students to make the link between the fact that air is made of particles and these particles colliding with the surface of any objects moving through the air. [O2&3]
- To help students **consider how theories develop**, ask them to review the statements in task 1 of Worksheet 1.5.10 and to state to what extent they support the theory that air resistance and water resistance are types of friction. [O2&3]
- The students **consider** the concept of terminal velocity for a falling object such as a sky diver. Refer to the second section in the Student Book. [O1, 2&3]
- Explain to the students that the reason that a parachute slows a falling person is that it has a large surface area, so it collides with more particles and thus increases friction. [O1, 2&3]

  Higher-attaining students could **identify** other factors that affect the speed of the skydiver (body position, clothing).

Explain

- The students use the idea of the forces caused by weight and by frictional drag to **explain** and **communicate** effectively the movement and speed of a sky diver on stepping from the plane. (The sky diver gets faster and faster until terminal velocity is reached; then slows down dramatically when the parachute opens and descends at a slower steady speed.) [O3]

Consolidate and apply

- The students **draw force diagrams** to illustrate the relative forces at different points in a sky dive. [O1, 2&3]
- **Small group discussion** Show the students a video clip of a sky diver who appears to go upwards when the parachute is opened. Students **suggest** what is really happening. (Before the parachute is opened the subject and the photographer are falling at the same rate. When the parachute opens, the subject slows dramatically but the photographer continues to fall at terminal velocity. The *relative* movement gives the impression that the parachutist has shot upwards.) [O3]

Extend

- Ask students able to progress further to look on the internet for pictures of speed skaters. They should **observe** features of the helmet and clothing and **suggest** how the design has reduced drag. [O3]

Plenary suggestions

Team challenge Working in groups of four and referring to an image or video of Olympic cyclists, the students complete as many sentences as possible from provided stems in as short a time as possible. [O1, 2&3]

Suggested sentence stems:

- Drag is …
- Two reasons why it is important to think of air resistance are ... (increases speed, reduces the energy needed)
- Three ways that Olympic cyclists reduce drag are … (crouched riding position, skin-tight clothes, streamlined helmet)

Answers to Student Book questions

1. friction
2. opposite to the direction of movement
3. It balances the pushing force from the engine.
4. Water resistance is bigger because water is denser.
5. When terminal velocity is reached in free fall; when lower terminal velocity is reached with a parachute deployed.
6. In the early part of the free fall; up to the point when terminal velocity is reached.
7. a) When the parachute opens b) Upwards friction arrow must be longer than downwards force of weight.
8. Each particle has tiny mass so has a tiny impact.
9. Water is denser than air so the particles are closer together. This means there are more collisions when we move through water and so there is higher resistance.

Answers to Worksheet 1.5.10

1. a) Supports; you can feel the between the air particles and your skin.

   b) Supports; you collide with more air particles when you head into the wind as opposed to downwind.

   c) Does not support without having data to compare different shapes.

   d) Supports; in space there is no air to resist the movement.

   e) Partially supports; factors other than air resistance could also influence top speed, e.g power of engine, friction of tyres on the road.
2. Students need a method for measuring the speed of the water (e.g. a flow meter or a distance/time calculation) and a method for measuring the force of the flow (e.g. a newtonmeter attached to a disk at 90° to the water flow).
3. The speed of the current and the water resistance resulted in large forces on the fences, equipment and cars; so the force of friction with the ground was overcome.

5.11 Discovering streamlining

Lesson overview

Learning objectives

- Recognise natural and man-made examples of streamlining.
- Link streamlining to fuel efficiency in vehicles.
- Evaluate the use of data collected from investigations of drag.

Learning outcomes

- Recognise streamlined shapes and know that this helps them to move through air or water. [O1]
- Investigate streamlining and use scientific vocabulary to explain how streamlining reduces the forces of friction on an object moving through a fluid. [O2]
- Evaluate data from an investigation into streamlining and explain the findings in terms of frictional drag. [O3]

Skills development

- Thinking scientifically: consider quality of evidence
- Working scientifically: evaluate data
- Learner development: collaborate effectively

Resources needed materials and equipment detailed in the Technician's notes; reference books; Worksheet 1.5.11; Practical sheet 1.5.11; Technician's notes 1.5.11

Common misconceptions Drag is only affected by the front and side of an object, not by the way air or water flows from the back of the object.

Key vocabulary streamlined, evaluate, turbulence

Teaching and learning

Engage

- Show the students pairs of images (streamlined and not streamlined). The students **compare** and **contrast** to answer the question 'What features make a streamlined shape?' [O1]

Challenge and develop

- The students **collaborate** in groups to **investigate** the effect of shape on streamlining. Provide each group with several pieces of clay with equal masses. They mould them into a range of streamlined and non-streamlined shapes (see the Student Book), and then test each by timing how long it takes to fall through a certain depth of wallpaper paste (be mindful of the irritation hazard according to the information on the paste packet). Students can use Practical sheet 1.5.11 to guide them in their investigation and the analysis of the results. [O2]
- Students **evaluate** their procedure and **consider the quality of evidence** from their first set of data. [O3]
  Ideas for students to consider:
  - Should the tests be repeated and why? How many repeats are needed?
  - What errors could occur in timing?
  - Did the shape touch or come close to the side of the container? What effect could this have?
  - Is the wallpaper paste of even thickness throughout?
- Discuss the wind tunnel image in the Student Book, so that they can deduce how streamlining affects the movement of an object through a fluid. They **consider the quality of this evidence** in relation to how it helps them to understand the findings from their own investigation. (Smooth flow reduces drag and indicates good streamlining. Turbulent, broken flow increases drag and indicates poor streamlining.) [O2&3]
  Higher-attaining students may be able to understand the importance of front surface area as well as shape.

Explain

- The students **explain** with the aid of diagrams why the various shapes they tried were well or badly streamlined and **link** it to their results (e.g. comparing rounded/pointed fronts, rounded/tapered rear, stable shapes that do not rotate). Break this activity into two, so that they have an opportunity to collaborate with others in **comparing** ideas, before completing their own explanations. [O2&3]

Consolidate and apply

- The students **explain the benefits** of streamlining in nature and vehicles (higher speed, less energy). [O1&2]
- They use Worksheet 1.5.11 to **consider features** that contribute to streamlining and also the reliability of data. [O2&3]
- To reinforce ideas about streamlining, the students draw their own mythical creature or fantasy car, which is highly streamlined, and annotate their drawing using words such as 'streamlined', 'friction', 'turbulence' to **explain** how the design works. [O1, 2&3]

Higher-attaining students could **compare** modern and old car designs and also possibly **suggest** why Formula One cars do not appear to be particularly streamlined. (There is a trade-off between streamlining and generating the downforce that improves the grip of the tyres on the track.)

Extend

- Ask students able to progress further to **find out about** the space shuttle, in particular:
  - the speed it travelled at different points on its journey back to Earth
  - how air resistance affected it (especially the heating effect of entering the Earth's atmosphere)
  - how its design helped it to deal with air resistance and its effects. [O1&2]

Plenary suggestions

Hot seat Ask each student to **think up a question** about streamlining and drag. Select someone to sit in the 'hot seat'. Students ask their question and say whether the answer given is correct or incorrect. [O1, 2&3]

Answers to Student Book questions

1. more pointed; no sharp corners 2. Two of: less energy wasted; less force needed; saves fuel; faster top speed
3. Streamlining reduces friction between an object and air/water moving past it. 4. The sphere; sinks in the shortest time.
5. a) Not very reliable; there is quite a difference between the trials.
   b) For example: the variables may not have been properly controlled, such as masses of shapes or thickness of paste; the shapes could have touched the container as they sank; the shapes may have sunk in a random path.
6. Two of: smaller frontal area; pointed but smooth shape meeting the air flow; smooth tapered shape at the rear
7. If the rear of the shape is has sharp edges they will cause turbulence; which increases drag.
8. They can test more designs; can use models instead of real cars; can test in a controlled environment.

Answers to Worksheet 1.5.11

1. a) *Helps*: angled windscreen, smooth underside, flush-fitting glass; *Hinders*: large frontal area, towing a trailer, opening the windows, radio aerial on the roof, wing mirrors; *No effect*: carrying more people, tyre pressure too high
   b) Anything that is in the airflow adds air resistance. Having small, smooth designs helps the air to flow past easily. Weight or items inside the car have no effect because they do not affect the airflow.
2. a) Students should show understanding that smooth curved surfaces and more pointed leading surfaces make a shape more streamlined. Stability of the shape also is a factor (tumbling is worse than a smooth, straight path). Suggested order: A = sphere; B = cube; C = pyramid; D = torpedo; but accept a different order which is consistent with their reasoning.
   b) Overall order in each set of data is the same; B and C agree in both trials; A and D are quite different; overall the data not very reliable.
   c) Carry out more trials; use electronic time gates; check all variables are controlled.
   d) Human errors in timing are much bigger. The differences between the objects are of a much larger scale. Students should round the times to the nearest second or half second.
3. The barbel is best suited to fast-flowing water; it has a torpedo shape as opposed to a deeper, flatter-sided body; it has a powerful tail to swim against the flow; its fins allow it to control its body in a fast current.

5.12 Applying key ideas

Adventure sport

Objectives

- Identify and represent forces in a range of situations, including less familiar ones.
- Apply ideas about elastic behaviour.
- Use ideas about forces and air resistance in an unfamiliar context to analyse problems.

Outcome

- Making clear and effective responses to questions, indicating understanding and the next steps in learning.

The purpose of this activity is to provide an opportunity to see how successfully the students are grasping the key ideas so far. It isn't designed to be used as a formal test – it might be that students work on the tasks collectively. It provides an opportunity for you to look at written work, engage students in discussions and form ideas about progress being made.

The tasks are progressive. Lower-attaining students should be able to tackle the first two or three tasks, while higher-attaining students will find the later tasks more challenging.

Resources needed picture of a sailing yacht in motion

Teaching & learning

Engage

- Display a picture of a yacht to give an example of a less familiar situation – one that the students have not encountered in this topic involving forces. They work in pairs to **identify** as many forces as possible that are in action. Collect initial feedback by asking groups to declare the number of forces. Complete the activity by asking individual students to add force arrows to the display picture.

Challenge and develop

- Ask the students to think about the forces involved in sporting and adventure activities. Help them to gather the information by compiling a table:

Activity	Forces involved

Explain

- The students **describe** and **explain** the forces they identified in the previous activity.

Consolidate and apply

- Now ask them to read the text in the Student Book about paragliding and to attempt the tasks. They might do this individually or collaboratively. In either case, encourage them to **identify** and **record** their ideas. Ask them to present their responses to various tasks, either orally or by displaying their work.

Extend

- For some students the later tasks give opportunities for extension work.

Plenary

The big ideas Ask the students to each pick out one key bit of learning from the tasks. Provide the class with some overall feedback, indicating ideas that they have grasped effectively and those that may need developing further.

Likely responses and next steps in learning

1. The force of weight or gravity pulls downwards. Friction in the form of air resistance or drag acts in the direction opposite to movement. The forces are balanced if the speed and direction are not changing.
2. The force arrow for weight should point vertically downwards from the glider. The force arrow for drag should point from the glider in the opposite direction to the glide path. Drawing the arrows to a precise scale is beyond what is expected. As additional information – by using a parallelogram, the pulling force of the wing (known as lift, which acts at right angles to the airflow) can be broken down into a force acting vertically upwards and the force of drag.
3. Useful friction examples: the straps on the harness.

   Unwanted friction: air resistance against the glider, pilot, harness and lines as they move through the air.
4. If the padding is too hard it could give the pilot a sudden and hard landing. If too soft, the pilot could fully compress the padding and be stopped suddenly by the hard ground underneath. If the padding is too bouncy the pilot could bounce up and have another heavy landing, which could make injury more likely.
5. To reduce drag, there should be a streamlined harness, thinner lines, smoother surface materials and a more reclined pilot position. The wing produces a lift force and can be redesigned to produce more lift.
6. Encourage the students to include force diagrams with their explanation. The additional force is the pushing force from the engine. The weight force will increase due to weight of the engine, but still act vertically downwards. The push from the engine causes the pilot to swing forwards slightly so that the wing tilts more upwards – the flight path becomes horizontal or inclined upwards. The bigger the pushing force from the engine, the more the whole system points upwards, including the pushing force from the engine. The pulling force from the wing moves correspondingly, because it is always at right angles to the flight path. The drag is in the opposite direction to flight. When the glider is flying steadily, all these forces are balanced.

5.13 Exploring forces and motion

Lesson overview

Learning objectives

- Recognise that for an object to start moving there must be a force applied.
- Describe the effects of balanced and unbalanced forces.
- Explain the significance of balanced and unbalanced forces on a moving object.

Learning outcomes

- Describe the effects of balanced and unbalanced forces, and know that an unbalanced force is needed for a change to take place. [O1]
- Identify and record suitable evidence in exploring the forces on a model glider; identify examples of balanced and unbalanced forces and explain the effect on motion. [O2]
- Explain examples of balanced and unbalanced forces and correctly predict the relative motion produced by unbalanced forces; explain the concept of a reaction force using simple examples. [O3]

Skills development

- Thinking scientifically: consider the quality of evidence
- Working scientifically: record evidence
- Learner development: develop resilience

Resources needed A4 sheets of paper suitable for making paper aeroplanes; 10 m measuring tapes; Worksheet 1.5.13; Practical sheet 1.5.13

Common misconceptions Objects will stop moving if a force acts.

Key vocabulary balanced (forces), unbalanced (forces), reaction force

Teaching and learning

Engage

- Identify the students' strengths and weaknesses in thinking about forces by giving them a 'true/false' quiz. Do not mark or give any feedback at this stage. The students should keep a note of their responses to revisit later in the lesson. [O1, 2&3]
- Warn the students that the lesson may challenge them in a variety of ways and that they will need to **show resilience** in overcoming difficulties in gathering data in the paper aeroplane investigation.

Challenge and develop

- Challenge the students to **design and make** a paper plane that will travel furthest in the class. Provide a few alternative designs (freely available from the internet if you search for 'paper gliders') and ask students to select one. Allow some initial testing and then, before any competition, **discuss** what data should be collected and how to get good quality data. Some hints about controlling variables are given on Practical sheet 1.5.13. [O2]

  Other ideas the students can **consider**:

  - How many attempts?
  - Should the result be a mean distance or the best distance?
  - Under what circumstances, if any, should another try be allowed?

  Higher-attaining students could **consider** if unusual results should be disregarded or not.

- The students **carry out** their investigation and **record** their results. They can use Practical sheet 1.5.13. [O2]
- Discuss the forces acting on a glider as it is thrown and settled in steady flight (Student Book. [O1&2]

Explain

- The students **explain** what force causes a glider to slow down in flight (air resistance/drag). [O1]
- They **explain** how forces can result in a gliding flight that does not change speed or direction. (All the forces in action must balance one another.) [O2]
- The students **predict** and try to **explain** what happens to the forces on a real glider if the pilot points the nose downwards. They draw force diagrams to help show their ideas. (Even in level flight, the pulling force from the wings acts in an upwards and forwards direction. The more the wings are angled downwards, the more the pulling force from them is angled forwards. Because this force has changed direction it no longer balances the other forces. This causes the glider's speed to increase. As speed increases, so does drag and eventually the forces balance again with the glider travelling at a new higher speed and steeper glide angle.) [O3]

Consolidate and apply

- Ask the students to answer Student Book questions 5, 6 and 7. [O3]

  Higher-attaining students could draw the bridge flexed and comment on movement and forces involved.
- The students **identify the forces** acting on a glider using Worksheet 1.5.13, and **compare the forces** on gliders of different designs, which travel at different speeds and angles. [O2&3]
- They **summarise key points** for collecting good quality data (what to measure and how, repeats, when to take additional repeats, how to treat anomalous results). [O2]

Extend

- Students able to progress further could **find out about** human-powered flight and **identify** all the forces involved. [O3]

Plenary suggestions

True or false? Revisit the true/false statements from the starter activity to check progress. [O1, 2&3]

Whole class discussion The students identify one or two areas they had difficulty with in the lesson and explain how they overcame them.

Answers to Student Book questions

1. weight, drag, the upward pulling force from the wings 2. long wings, streamlined shape to reduce drag
3. In both situations the forces are balanced; neither speed nor direction is changing. In (b) there is the additional force of friction being balanced by the car's weight, therefore speed does not change.
4. At the start there is a pushing force; which moves the car forwards against the force of friction. Once it is released only friction remains; which slows the car until it stops.
5. Should show downwards force arrow(s) due to the weight of the bridge; balanced in size and direction by upward reaction force arrow(s) from the ground. 6. As for question 5 with a lorry; all the force arrows larger; still in balance.
7. There would be an additional horizontal pushing force on the bridge support(s) caused by the water; and an equal and opposite reaction force.

Answers to Worksheet 1.5.13

1. a) If you make more than one change at a time you will not know which has made a difference.

   b) To check if the data can be relied on; gives greater confidence when drawing conclusions.
2. a) weight/gravity force acting vertically downwards; drag acting in the direction opposite to flight

   b) To travel further a plane needs to be more streamlined; and/or the wings need to produce a larger lift force.

   c) The plane's forward speed is balanced by the wind blowing against it; it sinks downwards due to gravity.

   d) Flap wings faster to produce more forward pushing force; pull wings in slightly to reduce drag and increase forward speed; fly through sheltered areas where there is less wind.
3. a) Main forces: weight, drag, lift. Students may also find out about forces called 'heal' and 'drive'. The flow of air over the sail produces a pulling force, in a similar way to how an aircraft's wings work.

   b) Air accelerates over sail; producing larger pulling force.

   c) Hold the sail at an angle to the wind; they zigzag upwind.

5.14 Exploring how forces affect speed and direction

Lesson overview

Learning objectives

- Recognise that the size of a force determines its effect.
- Recognise that the direction of a force determines its effect.
- Provide examples to illustrate where a force of precise strength and direction is needed.

Learning outcomes

- Predict relative motion produced by different forces on an object. [O1]
- Apply an understanding of forces to explain simply the changes caused by forces of different magnitudes and directions. [O2]
- Apply an understanding of forces to explain, using accurately drawn force diagrams, the changes caused by forces of different magnitudes and directions. [O3]

Skills development

- Thinking scientifically: ask questions
- Working scientifically: make predictions
- Learner development: plan progress

Resources needed water bottle rocket, available in kit form or home-made using instructions from the internet (search for 'water powered rocket'); access to a large outside space such as an empty playing field; target; video camera; Newton's cradle; Worksheet 1.5.14

Common misconceptions A force arrow is the same as an arrow indicating movement.

Key vocabulary horizontally, vertically

Teaching and learning

Engage

- Show the students a water bottle rocket and explain how it works. Demonstrate the rocket in a safe outside space, initially by firing it straight upwards. Alternatively, show a video clip of one being fired. Ask the students what questions they would need the answer to in order to plan to make the rocket hit a target. [O1]

Challenge and develop

- **Pairs to fours** Focusing on the size of the force and the direction of the force, ask the students to **make predictions** about what will affect where the rocket will land (initial force, direction of firing, mass, shape). Discuss their ideas. [O1, 2&3]
- If possible, test some of the students' predictions by firing the rocket towards a target, in the safe outside space. During the tests, ask students to video the flight from a distance, so that the full motion from launch to landing can be recorded. [O1, 2&3]

  Higher-attaining students could **predict** the effect of head winds of different strengths on the flight path.

Explain

- **Group work** Using the videos of the rocket testing, students draw the path of the rocket and **analyse** the forces on it to explain the motion. [O1&2]
- Guide the students in **describing** the motion of the rocket separately in horizontal and vertical directions: Refer to Worksheet 1.5.14. [O1, 2&3]
  - *Horizontally*: the rocket continues to travel horizontally, although the speed decreases because of the frictional force of air resistance.

- *Vertically*: the rocket travels upwards, but with an ever-decreasing vertical speed; it is momentarily stationary in a vertical direction (stays at the same height, while still continuing horizontally); then it accelerates downwards.

Higher-attaining students could add additional trajectories to their diagrams to show what happens when the launch force is increased and what happens when the direction of the launch force is altered. (Increasing force has a diminishing return because air resistance increases at a greater rate than speed. In no wind, the launch angle for maximum range is 45°.)

Consolidate and apply

- The students **draw two force diagrams** to show the directions and sizes of the forces during the launch and the flight of the rocket. (Once the pressure has equalised in the rocket, it no longer has any propelling force, so only gravity and drag are acting.) [O2&3]
- Use task 3 of Worksheet 1.5.14 to ask the students to **explain** how and why the forces would be different on the Moon and how the path of the rocket would be different. (No air resistance, so horizontal speed does not decrease. Weaker gravitational attraction, so it would fall to the ground more slowly. The rocket would go higher and further.) [O1, 2&3]

Extend

- Present Newton's cradle and ask students able to progress further to **explain** what happens when:
  - one ball is made to hit the others gently
  - one ball hits the others hard
  - two balls simultaneously hit the others. [O3]

Plenary suggestions

Learning triangle The students draw a large triangle with a smaller inverted triangle inside it. In the three outer triangles they write something they've done, something they've learned, and something that surprised them. Then they add in the central triangle something else they want to know. [O1, 2&3]

Answers to Student Book questions

1. Maximum force might be used for a goal kick so the ball travels as far as possible; smaller force for a pass because a team mate needs to control the ball; a longer pass needs more force for the ball to reach team mate.
2. For example: they could crash, by veering off the road or hitting another vehicle.
3. It will make the arrow's path curve downwards. 4. It will slow it down; but only a little because it is so streamlined.
5. It goes straight up; gradually slows until it momentarily stops; then fall back to Earth getting faster and faster. The main force is the weight of the arrow (gravity).
6. The further the string is pulled back, the greater the force on the arrow when the string is released.
7. (For the same direction of launch) an arrow would go further and higher because the propulsion force and the launch speed would be higher; the smaller drag would also increase its range; they would both be affected equally by gravity, taking a downward-curving path. The arrow and ball would fall at the same rate but the arrow's higher horizontal speed would means that the downward curve is extended over a greater distance. A heavier ball would not go so high because its higher weight is pulling it down.

Answers to Worksheet 1.5.14

1. a) Arrows 1 and 2: both curved (parabolic); one half the size of the other; arrows 3 and 4: both straight up and down, one half the size of the other, heights corresponding to previous two; arrows 5 and 6: both downwards curving paths, one travels twice as far as the other

   b) downwards pull of gravity/weight acting at all times; air resistance acting against the direction of movement (the higher the speed, the bigger the air resistance)
2. a) No upward force; gravity/weight acts downwards; reduces the speed. b) Force due to gravity/weight has stopped it going any higher. c) Vertical speed downwards increases; until terminal velocity reached (if tower tall enough).

   d) It is slowed by air resistance; which is a smaller force than gravity/weight in this situation.
3. If the launch force was the same, the upward vertical speed would be similar at first; but it would reduce at a slower rate. As it started to fall, its speed would increase; but more slowly than on Earth. The differences are due to the weaker gravity of the Moon; meaning the rocket weighs less. The horizontal speed would remain the same because there is no atmosphere (so no air resistance).

5.15 Understanding speed calculations

Lesson overview

Learning objectives

- List the factors involved in defining speed.
- Explain a simple method to measure speed.
- Use the speed formula.

Learning outcomes

- Describe a method in simple terms to find the speed of an object. [O1]
- Explain the concept of speed and demonstrate how the speed equation is derived using their understanding of speed. [O2]
- Provide an effective explanation of the concept of speed and independently derive the equation for speed; link their understanding of the speed equation to explain the operation of speed cameras. [O3]

Skills development

- Thinking scientifically: use equations
- Working scientifically: develop explanations
- Learner development: act responsibly

Resources needed 10 m measuring tape; stopwatches; mini-whiteboards; marker pens; calculators; video camera; Worksheet 1.5.15; Practical sheet 1.5.15

Key vocabulary distance, speed, unit, formula, average

Teaching and learning

Engage

- Ask the students to **recall** a car journey they have made and ask them what the speed limit was on the roads they were travelling on. Ask them to state the units. They write a few examples of the speeds with units (miles per hour, mph). Ask them to **suggest** other units speed may be measured in. [O1, 2&3]
- Guide the students in deconstructing the units and stating what quantity each of them measures (distance and time). This leads them to see that speed is how far is travelled in a certain time. [O1, 2&3]

Challenge and develop

- Use a few very simple examples to illustrate the principle of speed measurement and calculation:
  - a person travels 10 km in 1 hour, so their speed is 10 km per hour (10 km/h)
  - someone else travels the same distance but it takes 2 hours, so they only travel 5 km in an hour and their speed is 5 km/h.

  After a few more simple examples, help students to identify the process – they are dividing the distance travelled by the time it takes. Establish that speed = distance travelled divided by time taken. [O2]
- Working outside or in a sports hall and using Practical sheet 1.5.15, the students mark out a 10 m distance and then **collect data** by timing how long it takes to walk, jog, run and hop the 10 m distance. They can **record data** on mini-whiteboards. Prior to the activity ask them to compose a short list of suggestions that would constitute acting responsibly during the activity. [O1]
- For ease of calculation during this part of the learning, ask the students to round each measured time to the nearest second. Students then **calculate the speed** in metres per second. [O1, 2&3]

  Higher-attaining students may be able to **suggest** how a car's speed is indicated (circumference of tyres and number of turns of the wheel measures distance, or satnav tracks distance covered when the car moves).

Explain

- **Group task** The students **plan a presentation** of how to calculate speed, showing the reasoning behind the method – they could film themselves giving their explanation. [O1, 2&3]

Consolidate and apply

- Students use Worksheet 1.5.15 to do further speed calculations with less convenient numbers. They should **estimate** their answers as a method of checking the calculation. [O1&2]

  Higher-attaining students may be able to **predict** the effect of changing the diameter of a car's wheels on the speedometer reading (bigger diameter wheels make the speedometer under-read).

Extend

- Using the example of averaging speed cameras, ask students able to progress further to **calculate speed** when told the distance between the cameras and the time at which a car passes each of the two cameras. [O3]

Plenary suggestions

Quick quiz Set some quiz questions, such as:

- Speed is measured in ...
- What equipment do you need for taking measurements to calculate speed?
- The method for calculating speed is ... [O1, 2&3]

Answers to Student Book questions

1. The distance covered in a certain time.
2. The distance covered and the time taken.
3. B
4. C
5. speed = distance ÷ time; speed = 15 ÷ 1.5 = 10 km/h
6. 0.5 m/s
7. Calculation of average speed uses the whole distance and the total time for the journey. During a journey you need to slow down and speed up at appropriate times.
8. Drivers could slow down briefly for a camera measuring at one spot but exceed the speed limit the rest of the time. Cameras that work out the average speed over a long stretch of road will be able to tell if drivers do this.

Answers to Worksheet 1.5.15

1. a) speed = distance travelled ÷ time taken
   b) kilometres per hour (km/h); metres per second (m/s); miles per hour (mph)
2. a) 50 km/h b) 12 km/h c) 19 km/h d) 24 km/h e) 40 m/s f) 70 km/h
3. a) 7.5 km/h
   b) The car's speed is a lot slower than the top speed for much of the journey; this decreases the average.
   c) Victoria: 10 km/h; Laura: 17.6 km/h
   d) Laura may have been able to continue without stopping at junctions; or she may be fitter than Victoria

5.16 Understanding turning forces

Lesson overview

Learning objectives

- Describe the forces acting on a see-saw.
- Understand that the forces turn about the fulcrum.
- Explain how to balance different weights on a see-saw.

Learning outcomes

- Describe simply the motion of a see-saw when loads are applied. [O1]
- Explain how a fulcrum produces a turning effect from a vertically applied force; explain the effect of changing the size of the force and its distance from the fulcrum. [O2]
- Explain the effect of turning forces in terms of a changing the size of the force and its distance from the fulcrum, and draw and fully label diagrams using correct scientific vocabulary and force arrows. [O3]

Skills development

- Thinking scientifically: use units and nomenclature
- Working scientifically: interpret evidence
- Learner development: communicate effectively

Resources needed *for initial demonstration*: large mass, e.g.10 kg; long plank of wood, e.g. 2 m; something to use as a fulcrum, e.g. a log; *for each group of students*: 10 g slotted masses; balance beam; fulcrum (e.g. a pencil or triangular section of wood); Worksheet 1.5.16; Practical sheet 1.5.16; Technician's notes 1.5.16

Key vocabulary turning force, pivot, fulcrum

Teaching and learning

Engage

- Explore the students' ideas by using the plank as a see-saw/lever to lift the large mass, by pressing down with one finger. Students **compare** the force needed with the fulcrum in different positions. [O1]
- Stimulate discussion by using two student volunteers. Ask the smaller student to push open a door, while the larger one tries to prevent it. The stronger student should push the door at a point very close to the hinge, while the other student pushes at or near the handle. [O1]
- Introduce the terms 'turning force' and 'fulcrum'. The fulcrum, or pivot, changes the pushing force into a turning force. [O2]

Challenge and develop

- Working in threes using balance beams, fulcrums and masses, the students **explore** the question 'What effect does the distance of the force from the fulcrum have on the turning effect?'. Use the first section of the Student Book to help them prepare for the practical activity. Encourage students to be systematic in their data gathering. They may refer to Practical sheet 1.5.16 for guidance. They **record their evidence**, using the correct units. [O1, 2&3]
- Each group of students composes a statement that **interprets the evidence** they have collected in relation to the question above. For example, 'the further away a force is from a fulcrum, the bigger the turning effect it produces'. [O1, 2&3]
- The students **explore** a further question: 'What effect does the size of vertical force have on a turning effect?' [O1, 2&3]

Explain

- **Pair talk** The students work with a partner to **produce an explanation** of how the distance of a force from a fulcrum affects the size of the turning effect. Emphasise that this requires them to communicate effectively verbally and in writing. Firstly they **discuss** the ideas to be included in an explanation; they then draft individually; then give feedback on each other's explanations (e.g. two WWWs (What Went Well ...) and one EBI (Even Better If ...)); finally they rewrite their explanations individually. [O2&3]

  Higher-attaining students should give detailed and constructive feedback to others.

Consolidate and apply

- Ask the students to **draw force diagrams** to show see-saws in the following situations: [O2&3]
  - balanced with equal weight on both sides (weights must be equal distance from fulcrum)
  - balanced but with more weight on the right side than on the left side (larger weight must be closer to the fulcrum)
  - unbalanced with equal weights on each side (weights should be different distances from the fulcrum).
- The students can complete Worksheet 1.5.16 to reinforce their learning and **explain** their thinking. [O1, 2&3]

  Higher-attaining students could **consider** what would happen to a see-saw if the fulcrum was not central.

Extend

- Ask students able to progress further to **write an explanation** to accompany each of the force diagrams in the first 'Consolidate and apply' activity. [O3]

Plenary suggestions

Evaluation The students **identify** what helped them communicate effectively in helping each other to develop their explanations (e.g. use of diagrams with labels, using positive, constructive language when giving feedback). [O1, 2&3]

Answers to Student Book questions

1. vertically down towards the (centre of the) Earth
2. A fulcrum is present, which acts as a point around which the pushing or pulling force causes turning.
3. the shaft at the centre of the blades
4. The small child would move downwards. This is because when the big child moves closer to the fulcrum, the turning force on their side gets smaller and the small child's turning force gets bigger; the see-saw is no longer balanced.
5. They need to sit on opposite sides of the see-saw; at equal distances from the fulcrum.
6. Diagrams should show straight arrows for the push of the person; and the pull of the spring; acting in opposite directions. The pulling force from the spring is closer to the fulcrum than the pushing force from the person.
7. The push from the person can be less than the pull of the spring because the turning force is bigger; due to the person's pushing force being further away from the fulcrum.
8. For example opening a cupboard, tightening a clamp, turning on a gas tap.

Answers to Worksheet 1.5.16

1. R; equal; L
2. a) L; equal; R

   b) The bigger the force and the further away it is from the fulcrum, the bigger the turning force.
3. a) A fulcrum stops the object being pushed along by the force; the object turns around the fulcrum.

   b) The weight of the 50 g mass would need to be acting in the opposite direction to that of the 100 g mass; and be twice as far from the fulcrum.

   c) It is worse to have the fingers close to the hinge because they can only produce a small turning force to resist the door. When the fingers are further away they produce a larger turning force to resist the door.

5.17 Discovering moments

Lesson overview

Learning objectives

- State and use the law of moments.
- Describe how turning forces can be increased.
- List some examples of levers used as force multipliers.

Learning outcomes

- Provide a simple description of the effect of increasing the length of a lever. [O1]
- Use the moments equation (moment = $F \times d$) and explain how to apply this to simple machines. [O2]
- Explain how moments apply to simple machines and explain how forces are multiplied by these devices. [O3]

Skills development

- Thinking scientifically: ask questions
- Working scientifically: record evidence
- Learner development: collaborate effectively

Resources needed *for initial demonstration*: large mass, e.g.10 kg; another large mass twice the size of the first; long plank of wood, e.g. 2 m; *something to use as a fulcrum*, e.g. a log; *a range of devices that use levers*: e.g. garlic crusher or nutcracker (scissor-type), secateurs, long-handled garden cutters, spanner, tin snips; *for each group of students*: 10 g slotted masses; balance beam; fulcrum; Worksheet 1.5.17; Practical sheet 1.5.17; Technician's notes 1.5.17

Key vocabulary moment, lever, load, effort, force multiplier

Teaching and learning

Engage

- Challenge the students' understanding of the previous lesson by setting up a demonstration where a large weight is balanced on a see-saw by a weight half the size. Ask the students to **explain** why it balances and then get them to focus more closely on the distance that each of the loads is from the fulcrum. [O1]
- Tell them that they are trying to discover the law of physics that concerns turning forces. Students **pose questions** or **suggest a hypothesis** to investigate, based on the demonstration. [O1].

Challenge and develop

- Working in groups of three, the students **investigate** how the size of the force and its distance from the fulcrum affect the size of the turning force. Get them to keep a constant weight and distance on one side and find different combinations on the other side that achieve balance. They should **collect** and **record** sufficient evidence to be able to answer the question posed. They can use Practical sheet 1.5.17. [O1, 2&3]
- With reference to the Student Book and the results the students gained from their investigation, establish the following:
    - moment is the term for a turning force
    - moment = force × distance of the force from the fulcrum
    - for a balanced see-saw, anticlockwise moment = clockwise moment (the law of moments). [O2&3]

Explain

- Bring into the classroom some devices that work by lever action – such as a spanner, a nutcracker, secateurs. Giving adequate safety advice, allow students to **investigate** how they work. [O1]

- Pick one or more examples of a *simple* lever in action (a crowbar, secateurs or scissors) and ask the students to **explain** how the lever works and how it helps a task to be performed. Note that a nutcracker and a garlic press are rather more complex because the fulcrum is at one end. [O1, 2&3]
- Encourage the students to **explain** how the effort and the load distances from the fulcrum are crucial for a simple lever to act as a force multiplier. [O3]
- Students who have a particularly effective explanation **present** it to the rest of the class. [O2&3]
- Ensure the students realise that a lever allows a small force to exert a much bigger one on the other side of a fulcrum. For example, with a pair of scissors the fingers are further away from the fulcrum than the blades and so produce a big moment. The blades are closer to the fulcrum so the force there is larger. [O2&3]

Consolidate and apply

- Use the Student Book text, diagrams and questions to consolidate the students' ideas about moments and levers. [O1, 2&3]
- The students can reinforce their ideas about moments further using Worksheet 1.5.17. [O1,2&3]

  Higher-attaining students could **consider** the difference between the biceps and the human elbow joint and the levers studied so far. The muscle acts on the same side of the fulcrum as the force it is opposing (e.g. when lifting a heavy object held in the hand).

Extend

- Students able to progress further can **consider** how moments are a vital factor in the stability of structures and vehicles. For example, they could **compare** what angle a double-decker bus could lean at, compared with a racing car. [O3]

Plenary suggestions

The big ideas The students work in small groups to **summarise** how a lever works, using a large sheet of paper, drawing a diagram and writing no more than ten words. [O1, 2&3]

Evaluation The students identify how effectively they **collaborated** when carrying out the investigation and producing explanations.

Answers to Student Book questions

1. the turning effect of a force about a pivot/fulcrum 2. the size of the force; the distance from the fulcrum
3. You can produce a larger moment using a long spanner compared to a short one; because the distance to the fulcrum is longer.
4. 40 N m 5. a) 20 N m b) 20 N m or greater c) at least 10 N
6. It allows a bigger force to be produced; for example, a large load can be moved using a small effort.
7. A small force at the end of the handle produces a large force on the other side of the pivot; to cut through the twig.
8. The pivot is at one end of the device; the small force at the end of the handle produces a larger force nearer to the pivot.

Answers to Worksheet 1.5.17

1. a) … a fulcrum stops an object from being pushed along. The fulcrum and the force are in different positions.
   b) … small moment or turning force c) … large moment or turning force
   d) … having the small force further away from the fulcrum and acting in the opposite direction
   e) … the see-saw balances
2. a) 1 m to the right of the fulcrum b) on the left, 0.32 m from the fulcrum
   c) The see-saw would rotate clockwise because the clockwise moment is bigger (1.98 N m compared to 1.75 N m).
3. a) The moment is larger when a person has long forearms compared to short forearms, provided the force/weight is the same.This is because, even though the muscle moves the same distance in each case, the end of a longer arm would move further than the end of a shorter arm. Diagrams help students to provide clear explanations.
   b) In sports requiring strength, people with shorter forearms could withstand or produce larger turning forces (all other things being equal).

5.18 Understanding the application of moments

Lesson overview

Learning objectives

- Link the law of moments to the design of cranes.
- Explain why counterweights are needed by cranes.
- Investigate the lifting capacity of a crane.

Learning outcomes

- Recognise, through safely conducted practical experience, the need for a counterweight. [O1]
- Apply an understanding of the law of moments to real-life design problems and explain the operation of simple cranes. [O2]
- Explain the design principles of simple cranes effectively; recognise limiting factors for large cranes when lifting loads and demonstrate these using model cranes. [O3]

Skills development

- Thinking scientifically: evaluate risks
- Working scientifically: make predictions
- Learner development: act responsibly

Resources needed *equipment to make model cranes*: kits are available but standard lab equipment can be used (see the Technician's notes); metre ruler; range of masses on hangers; string; *optional for plenary*: car jack; Worksheet 1.5.18; Practical sheet 1.5.18; Technician's notes 1.5.18

Key vocabulary counterweight

Teaching and learning

Engage

- Explore the students' understanding about moments so far by demonstrating a small weight hanging from a model crane. Students **suggest** factors that could determine the maximum load that the crane could support. (Too much weight could make the crane topple.) [O2]
- Show the students pictures of a tower crane and point out that they are used in the construction of tall buildings and have to be able to lift huge weights. Draw the students' attention to the counterweight. [O1]

Challenge and develop

- Working in pairs, students set up their own model cranes using Practical sheet 1.5.18 for guidance. The cranes should be used on the floor rather than on benches where they could topple from higher. [O1]
- Using their knowledge of moments, the students first **predict** the stability of the crane at a number of different load and counterweight positions on the jib. [O2&3]

  Higher-attaining students may be able to make quantitative predictions by using moment calculations.
- The students **test their predictions** of the stability of the crane. Prior to starting work, they should **evaluate the risks** posed by this practical activity and **identify** what steps they should take to minimise the risks. [O1, 2&3]
- Students **make further predictions** and do further tests of how the counterweight will need to be moved to different positions for the crane to be made stable with different load sizes and load positions. (Note that on a crane, the simplest way to maintain balance is by moving the counterweight rather than adding to or taking from it.) [O2&3]

Explain

- The students use a written account and moment calculations to **explain** how a crane's balance can be maintained for different sizes and positions of loads, without changing the size of the counterweight. [O2&3]

Consolidate and apply

- The students **examine** pictures of other types of crane and **suggest** how stability is achieved (e.g. a broader base to move the fulcrum point and counterweight). [O1, 2&3]
- Ask the students to complete Worksheet 1.5.18 to consolidate ideas about moments. [O1, 2&3]

Extend

- Ask students able to progress further to look at diagrams of jointed bones and muscles to **deduce** where the load, effort and fulcrum are positioned, and to draw labelled diagrams. [O3]

Plenary suggestions

Evaluation Students **evaluate** how well they assessed and managed risk during the practical activity and what improvements could have been made. [O1]

Application Demonstrate a car jack. The students work in pairs to think of a statement to **explain** how the device uses moments. (The long handle allows a small force from the person to produce a big force because the car is much closer to the fulcrum.) [O1, 2&3]

Answers to Student Book questions

1. The load picked up causes a moment or turning force.
2. a counterweight; a broad base
3. It needs to balance the moment of the load exactly.
4. It needs to provide moments that can balance different load sizes and positions.
5. along the jib; away from the tower fulcrum
6. move the counterweight in towards the tower fulcrum
7. The load that the crane is lifting.
8. a) 20 000 N m b) 500 N
9. The strength of the jib, the tower, the foundations and the lifting cables; the weather (a strong wind could make the load swing).

Answers to Worksheet 1.5.18

1. a) clockwise b) clockwise c) balanced d) anticlockwise
2. Check for a wide range of ideas with precise use of language, including scientific terms.
3. a) A is stable because there is no turning force. B has a clockwise moment so returns to upright. C has an anticlockwise moment and will tip onto its side.

   b) Ideas about broad bases making objects more stable; weight acting within the area of the base of the object; how far/to what angle an object can be tipped before the moment ceases to be a restoring force. (Centre of gravity not needed at this stage.)

5.19 Checking students' progress

The *Checking your progress* section in the Student Book indicates the key ideas developed in this chapter and shows how students progress to more complex levels. It is provided to support students in:

- identifying the key ideas
- developing a sense of their current level of understanding
- developing a sense of what the next steps in their learning are.

It is designed either to be used at the end of a chapter to support an overall view of progress, or alternatively during the teaching of the chapter. Students can self-assess or peer-assess using this as a basis.

It would be helpful if students can be encouraged to provide evidence from their understanding or their notes to support their judgments. In some cases it may be useful to explore the difference in the descriptors for a particular idea so that students can see what makes for a 'higher outcome'.

It may be useful with some descriptors to provide examples from the specific work done, such as an experiment undertaken or an explanation developed and recorded. If marking and feedback use similar ideas and phrases this will enable students to relate specific marking to a more general sense of progress.

To make good progress in understanding science students need to focus on these ideas and skills:

Students who are making modest progress will be able to:	**Students who are making good progress will be able to:**	**Students who are making excellent progress will be able to:**
List types of force and represent forces using force diagrams; use newtonmeters.	Describe the size and direction of forces using force diagrams.	Explain the how the size and direction of forces determines their effects.
Identify gravity as a pulling force and distinguish between mass and weight.	Describe what is meant by mass, explain how gravity forces affect weight, explain why weight varies from planet to planet and explain the term 'weightless'.	Explain weight as a gravitational attraction between masses which decreases with distance; use scientific concepts to explain the difference between mass and weight.
Know that forces can lead to changes in shape and investigate the change of shape of a spring.	Explain the relationship between the amount of change in shape and the size of the force, and use data to state Hooke's Law.	Collect accurate data about forces changing the shape of an object, recognise when shape changes regularly with force size, and explain behaviour when the elastic limit is exceeded.
Identify some situations where forces are balanced and recognise that unbalanced forces are needed for a change to take place.	Identify forces acting in pairs, and apply an understanding of forces to explain how a force can cause a change in speed and direction.	Identify different examples of forces and reaction forces, and predict the changes of speed and direction that different forces can cause.
Recognise that friction is a force that slows objects down or stops them from moving.	Explain that friction is a contact force opposing the direction of movement.	Provide a detailed explanation of friction between surfaces.
List examples where friction is useful and when it is unwanted, recognise that drag forces slow things down, and recognise that streamlining helps objects move through air or water.	Compare contrasting situations involving friction, explain how friction can be increased or reduced, explain air and water resistance, and explain how streamlining reduces such resistance.	Explain air and water resistance in terms of frictional drag, explain the forces on flying or falling objects, and explain streamlining using scientific vocabulary.
Explain how to find the speed of an object.	Explain the concept of speed and use understanding of speed to explain how the equation for speed is derived.	Independently derive the equation for speed and use understanding of the speed equation to explain how speed cameras work.
Describe the balancing of a see-saw with different loads, recognise situations where balance is important, and describe the effect of increasing the length of a lever.	Explain how a fulcrum allows a turning motion, explain the effect of changing the size of a force or its distance from the fulcrum, and use and apply the law of moments.	Explain moments using force diagrams and the law of moments, explain how levers can act as force multipliers, and explain and demonstrate the design principles of a crane.

5.20 Answers to Student Book Questions

This table provides answers to the Questions section at the end of Chapter 5 of the Student Book. It also shows how different questions assess attainment in terms of the focus and style of a question as well as the context. Question level analysis can indicate students' proficiency in approaching different aspects of scientific understanding and different types of answer.

Q	**Answer**		**Focus**			**Style**			**Context**			
		Marks available	Knowledge & understanding	Application	Evaluation of evidence	Objective test question	Short written answer	Longer written answer	Forces and gravity	Friction	Turning forces	Speed
1	b	1	x			x			x			
2	c	1	x			x						x
3	c	1	x			x			x			
4	d	1	x			x			x			
5	Gravity (or weight) pulling downwards	1	x				x		x			
	Friction (and air resistance) resisting movement	1	x				x		x			
6	It gives it a higher top speed	1	x				x			x		
	It reduces the amount of fuel (or energy) needed	1	x				x			x		
7	Gravity (or weight) produces downward forces	1	x					x			x	
	The fulcrum causes the downward forces to act as turning forces	1	x					x			x	
	One person creates an anticlockwise turning effect, the other a clockwise turning effect	1	x					x			x	
	For balance, the larger force (weight) needs to be closer to the fulcrum than the smaller one, so that the turning effects (moments)are equal	1	x					x			x	
8	a	1		x		x					x	
9	d	1		x		x			x			
10	c	1		x		x						x
11	d	1		x		x			x			

Chapter 5: Forces and their Effects

Q	Answer	Marks available	Focus: Knowledge & understanding	Focus: Application	Focus: Evaluation of evidence	Style: Objective test question	Style: Short written answer	Style: Longer written answer	Context: Forces and gravity	Context: Friction	Context: Turning forces	Context: Speed
12	Downward-pointing force arrow from the object, labelled 'weight' Smaller upward arrow on the object labelled 'drag' or 'air resistance' (Arrows correct, not correct labels: 1 mark)	2		x			x		x			
13	Downward weight arrow equal and opposite to upward air resistance arrow	1		x			x		x			
	Statement that forces of weight and air resistance are balanced so speed does not change	1		x			x			x		
14	Elastic means that an object returns to its original shape when a force which deformed it is removed	1		x				x	x			
	The soles do not become permanently compressed	1		x				x	x			
	so they can continue to cushon the feet	1		x				x	x			
	Shoe can bend, straighten and be undamaged	1		x				x	x			
15	May be true depending on:											
	• the leverage (position of fulcrum, length of lever)	1			x		x				x	
	• the strength of the components	1			x		x				x	
16	Padding A compresses progressively but at higher forces (or higher impact speeds) becomes 'solid' and so stops cushioning	1			x			x	x			
	Padding B compresses progressively, even with large forces	1			x			x	x			
	Padding C is fully compressed by small forces so only protects at low forces (impacts at low speeds)	1			x			x	x			
	Padding B is best because it works for the widest range of forces (or impacts at the widest range of speeds)	1			x			x	x			
	Total possible:	**30**	**12**	**12**	**6**	**8**	**10**	**12**	**18**	**3**	**7**	**2**

6.1 Introduction

When and how to use these pages

The Introduction in the Student Book indicates some of the ideas and skills in this topic area that students will already have met from KS2 or from previous KS3 work, and provides an indication of what they will be studying in this chapter. *Ideas you have met before* is not intended to be a comprehensive summary of all the prior ideas, but rather to point out a few of the key ones and to support the view that scientific understanding is progressive. Even though we might be meeting contexts that are new to us, we can often use existing ideas to start to make sense of them.

In this chapter you will find out indicates some of the new ideas that the chapter will introduce. Again, it isn't a detailed summary of content or even an index page. Its purpose is more to act as a 'trailer' and generate some interest.

The outcomes, then, will be recognition of prior learning that can be built on and interest in finding out more. There are a number of ways this can be used. You might, for example:

- Use *Ideas you have met before* as the basis for a revision lesson as you start the first new topic.
- Use *Ideas you have met before* as the centre of spider diagrams to which students can add examples, experiments they might have done previously or what they found interesting
- Make a note of any unfamiliar/difficult terms and return to these in the relevant lessons.
- Use *In this chapter you will find out* to ask students questions such as:
  - Why is this important?
  - How could it be used?
  - What might we be doing in this topic?

Overview of the chapter

In this chapter, the students will learn about ways in which energy can be transferred, and that energy is conserved. They should become aware that the concept of energy transfer is relevant in all areas of science. They will learn to represent different changes in energy transfer diagrams, including Sankey diagrams. Potential energy in the forms of gravitational, elastic and chemical energy will explored. Students will investigate how work is done in different contexts. They will learn the connection between heat and temperature, and relate this to energy transfer when fuels are burnt. Finally, a large part of the chapter is on sound energy – how sounds are made, how sound energy is transferred by waves, how we hear sounds, and applications including ultrasound and infrasound.

This chapter offers the opportunity for students to plan investigations of energy changes in the context of elastic potential energy and the energy of different fuels. They learn to interpret wave diagrams in terms of frequency and amplitude, and make use of simple models and analogies.

It is important to establish the use of either the 'transfer' model or the 'transformation' model to discuss energy changes, and stick to the terminology consistently. The Student Book uses the 'transfer' model – this is a stronger foundation for progression to ideas at Key Stage 4 and is used in the Programme of Study.

Obstacles to learning

Students may need extra guidance with the following common misconceptions:

- **Energy** Students' misconceptions include: energy is 'used up'; we can run out of energy; all energy transfers are useful; energy is a kind of 'stuff', a material object; energy and force are the same thing.
- **Potential energy** Students may think that height can have nothing to do with energy; all fuels have the same energy; all fuels are called petrol.
- **Heat and temperature** Heat and temperature may be confused; students think there can be a quantity of 'cold'.

- **Sound** Students may think that sounds are only made in the air; you don't need materials to make sounds; pitch and loudness are the same; sounds waves travel instantaneously; sounds can be heard in space; the ear only consists of the part we can see; loud sounds cannot harm the ear; ultrasounds are very loud sounds.

	Topic title	**Overarching objectives**
2	Exploring energy transfers	Other processes that involve energy transfer: changing motion, dropping an object, completing an electrical circuit, burning fuels Energy as a quantity that can be quantified and calculated; the total energy has the same value before and after a change.
3	Understanding potential energy and kinetic energy	Other processes that involve energy transfer: changing motion, dropping an object
4	Doing work	Work done; simple machines give bigger force but at the expense of smaller movement (and vice versa): product of force and displacement unchanged
5	Looking at dynamos	Other processes that involve energy transfer: changing motion, completing an electrical circuit
6	Understanding elastic potential energy	Other processes that involve energy transfer: stretching a spring. Work done and energy changes on deformation. Comparing the starting with the final conditions of a system and describing increases and decreases in the amounts of energy in elastic distortions
7	Knowing the difference between heat and temperature	Heating and thermal equilibrium: temperature difference between two objects leading to energy transfer from the hotter to the cooler one Comparing the starting with the final conditions of a system and describing increases and decreases in the amounts of energy associated with temperatures
8	Thinking about fuels	Fuels and energy resources; other processes that involve energy transfer: burning fuels, metabolism of food
9	Investigating fuels	Fuels and energy resources; other processes that involve energy transfer: burning fuels Comparing the starting with the final conditions of a system and describing increases and decreases in the amounts of energy in chemical compositions
11	Exploring sound	Sound produced by vibrations of objects; sound waves are longitudinal
12	Describing sound	Sound produced by vibrations of objects, in loudspeakers; detected by their effect on microphone diaphragm and the ear drum Frequencies of sound waves, measured in hertz (Hz)
13	Measuring the speed of sound	Echoes; the speed of sound in air
14	Understanding how sound travels through materials	Sound needs a medium to travel; the speed of sound in air, in water, in solids
15	Learning about the reflection and absorption of sound	Echoes, reflection and absorption of sound
16	Hearing sounds	Sound produced by vibrations of objects, detected by their effects on microphone diaphragm and the ear drum Waves transferring information for conversion to electrical signals by microphone
17	Understanding factors affecting hearing	Auditory range of humans and animals
18	Finding out about sounds we cannot hear	Auditory range of humans and animals Pressure waves transferring energy; use for cleaning and physiotherapy by ultrasound

6.2 Exploring energy transfers

Lesson overview

Learning objectives

- Recognise what energy is and its unit.
- Describe a range of energy transfers using simple diagrams.
- Use a Sankey diagram as a model to represent simple energy changes.

Learning outcomes

- Define the unit of energy and describe some simple energy transfers. [O1]
- Interpret and draw energy transfer diagrams. [O2]
- Use Sankey diagrams to explain a range of energy changes and demonstrate that all energy is accounted for. [O3]

Skills development

- Thinking scientifically: ask questions
- Working scientifically: present evidence
- Learner development: collaborate effectively

Resources needed range of items for demonstrating energy transfers – such as a simple electrical circuit switching on a bulb or a buzzer, a kettle, a candle burning, an iPod; circus or images of energy transfers for students to explore – e.g. torch, solar calculator, hand warmer, wind chime, solar panel, hairdryer, electric heater, pictures of a log fire, wind turbine, car, cake; squared paper; Worksheet 1.6.2

Common misconceptions Energy is used up/created. Energy is a kind of stuff. Fuels are energy.

Key vocabulary joule, energy transfer diagram, Sankey diagram

Teaching and learning

Engage

- Write the word 'ENERGY' on the board and ask the students to provide as many words as they can which they associate with it. Turn this into a mind map. [O1]

Challenge and develop

- Demonstrate a range of energy transfers. This could include a simple electrical circuit switching on a bulb or a buzzer, a kettle, a candle burning or someone running on the spot. Tell the students that all these changes involve energy. [O1]
- Explore the meaning of the term 'energy' during these demonstrations. Introduce the unit for energy, the joule (J). Ensure that the students understand that energy is transferred in a number of ways, including by electricity, heat, movement, sound and light. You could mention the term 'kinetic energy' for energy transferred by movement. [O1]
- Discuss the energy transfers in each of the demonstration scenarios and model how to draw simple energy transfer diagrams, and also, for higher-attaining students, Sankey diagrams to represent them (see the Student Book).

  Emphasise the fact that all energy is always accounted for – it cannot be created or destroyed, only transferred by different processes. Students can attempt the tasks on Worksheet 1.6.2. [O1, 2&3]

  Task 3 on Worksheet 1.6.2 asks higher-attaining students to **draw Sankey diagrams** using the given values.

Explain

- Group the students in ability groups of four. Provide them with a differentiated circus of activities or images for them to **investigate**. Ask them to sketch their **predictions** using simple energy transfer diagrams or Sankey diagrams as appropriate. [O2&3]

  Lower-attaining students could be given, for example, a torch, a solar calculator, a hand warmer, a wind chime.

  Middle-attaining students could be given a hairdryer, a pictures of a log fire and an electric heater.

  Higher-attaining students could be given pictures of a wind turbine, a car, a cake.

- Review the students' answers. Discuss the idea of some energy transfers being useful and some not. [O2&3]

Consolidate and apply

- Sketch on the board some example Sankey diagrams, which include non-useful energy transfer(s). Working in ability pairs, the students **write an explanation** of what the diagrams show. Ask them to **identify** the useful and useless energy transfers. See if they can **predict** the appliance(s) transferring the energy. [O2&3]

Extend

For students able to progress further:

- Introduce the idea of *energy efficiency*. For Sankey diagrams they have come across (such as that drawn using the data in question 6 of the Student Book), ask the students to **calculate** the efficiency of the energy transfer – (useful energy transferred/total energy transferred) × 100%. [O3]
- Ask them to **consider** what could be done to make the transfers more efficient (question 7 in the Student Book). [O3]

Plenary suggestions

What have I learned? Return to the mind map from the beginning of the lesson and ask the students to amend their earlier ideas in light of their learning. [O1, 2&3]

Answers to Student Book questions

1. the lit candle and the light bulb
2. a) The candle on the left is transferring energy to the surroundings by light and heat.

   b) The right-hand candle is not lit, so it is not possible to transfer energy.
3. Energy is transferred to a bulb by electricity; then energy is transferred from the bulb by light and heat to the surroundings.
4. a) electrical energy → energy by heat + energy by sound

   b) electrical energy → energy by heat + energy by light

   c) chemical energy → energy by heat + energy by sound + energy by light
5. a) *useful*: heat; *unwanted*: sound b) *useful*: heat; *unwanted*: light c) *useful*: heat; *unwanted*: sound
6. Check the proportions on the diagrams; that the useful movement energy transferred points to the right; that the heat and sound transferred point downwards.
7. Suggestions such as reduce friction in the motor.

Answers to Worksheet 1.6.2

1. torch: electrical energy → energy by light (+ energy by heat); solar panel: energy by light → electrical energy; wind chime: kinetic energy → energy by sound
2. a) A: 6 J by heat; B 7 J by heat; C 65 J by heat and sound; D 5 J by sound; E 6 J by heat and sound; F 30 J by heat and sound

   b) Check the grids are shaded correctly with the right number of squares for energy transferred usefully and energy wasted.
3. Check the proportions on the diagrams; and that the useful energy transferred points to the right and the non-useful energy transferred point downwards.

6.3 Understanding potential energy and kinetic energy

Lesson overview

Learning objectives

- Recognise energy transfers due to falling objects.
- Describe factors affecting energy transfers related to falling objects.
- Explain how energy is conserved when objects fall.

Learning outcomes

- Describe examples of energy transfer that include gravitational potential energy. [O1]
- Describe how changing height and gravity affect gravitational potential energy. [O2]
- Analyse different situations explaining how gravitational potential energy is transferred and how energy is conserved. [O3]

Skills development

- Thinking scientifically: ask questions
- Working scientifically: design investigations
- Learner development: act responsibly

Resources needed bouncy ball; *per student group*: three water balloons; bucket; paper towels, metre rule; Worksheet 1.6.3

Common misconceptions Only objects that are moving can have energy.

Key vocabulary gravity, gravitational potential energy, kinetic energy

Teaching and learning

Engage

- Refer to the Student Book. Discuss the 'teaser' photo of the vertical drop ride and what is happening in terms of energy transfer. Introduce the idea of *gravitational potential energy* (GPE) and its link to height. [O1]
- Alternatively, demonstrate a bouncy ball being dropped from different heights. Ask the students to **make observations** about the height of rebound. Question them about why the ball behaves in this way and encourage them to use ideas about GPE and energy transfer. [O1]
- Working in pairs, the students **discuss** a range of different situations where GPE is involved and the energy transfers that take place. Take feedback and list their ideas on the board. [O1]

Challenge and develop

- Show a video of Olympic-standard divers in action. Discuss the energy transfers from diving boards of different heights. Question the students about the energy transfers taking place at certain points of a dive and explore the differences for different heights. [O1&2]
- Introduce the factors that affect gravitational potential energy, using the second section in the Student Book. Discuss how GPE is dependent on the force of gravity as well as the height of the object. Discuss the transfer between GPE and kinetic energy (KE), reminding the students that the total energy after a change is the same as the total energy before – energy is 'conserved'. [O2&3]
- Establish the link between kinetic energy and speed – the more KE there is, the faster the object moves. [O2]
- With the students working in mixed ability groups of four, provide each group with Worksheet 1.6.3, three identical water balloons, a bucket, paper towels and a metre rule. Ask them to **plan an investigation** to find the minimum height of drop to burst a water balloon. [O2]

- Select one or two groups to present their plans. Ask the class to comment on the quality of the plans and **identify any areas for improvement**.
- Ask the groups to **discuss** how to safely carry out the investigation. Take feedback from their ideas. Discuss how to record the results. [O2]
- After a discussion about acting sensibly and responsibly, allow groups to **carry out** their investigation in a suitable place and to **record their results**. Ensure that all water is mopped up afterwards. [O2]

Explain

- Ask groups to **explain their results** using ideas about energy transfer. An energy transfer diagram should accompany each explanation. [O2&3]

  Higher-attaining students should be able to account for all the energy transferred at the point of the balloon bursting, and at other heights of the drop. They should **identify** all the useful and useless energy transfers involved.
- Students should answer questions 3–6 in the Student Book to reinforce their understanding of how height and gravity affect GPE and to **analyse** further situations using GPE. [O2&3]

Consolidate and apply

- Introduce the principle of a hydroelectric dam. Try to show a video of one working. [O1, 2&3]
- In pairs, the students should **explain** how this is a useful example of transferring gravitational potential energy. They should draw an energy transfer diagram to show all the changes. They should **explain** how energy is conserved. [O1, 2&3]

Extend

For students able to progress further:

- Ask them to **carry out some research** and produce their own Sankey diagram for the Three Gorges plant ('Did you know' feature in the Student Book) identifying all the possible causes of wasted energy. [O1, 2&3]
- They could **find out** how to improve the efficiency of hydroelectric plants. [O3]

Plenary suggestions

What do I know? Ask the students to **reflect on** one thing from the lesson they are sure about, one thing they are not sure about and one think they need to find out more information on. Ask them to work in groups of five to six to agree on group lists, and ask each group to say what they decided. Then agree as a class about what they are confident about, what they are less sure of and what things they want to know more about. [O1, 2&3]

Answers to Student Book questions

1. joule, J 2. gravity 3. 10 m high 4. Saturn 5. a) A b) C c) A d) C
6. The graph(s) should show a decreasing line for GPE and an increasing line for KE.

Answers to Worksheet 1.6.3

1. a) height c) balloon bursts or not e) amount of water in the balloon; type of balloon; surface of the floor; the height from the same place g) slipping on wet floors; people getting wet h) mop up spillages; use screen to avoid splashes
2. a) If the balloon bursts at one height but not 10 cm below, carry out the investigations at intermediate heights to get an accurate value for height. Use a ruler with a millimetre scale.

   b) Repeat the investigation until three similar readings are obtained; omit anomalous results in mean value calculation.
3. a) Compare results with those of another group. b) See if repeat readings are close in value.

   c) e.g. use an accurate digital height-measuring device to measure the height from which the ballon is dropped.

6.4 Doing work

Lesson overview

Learning objectives

- Recognise situations where work is done.
- Describe the relationship work done = force × distance.
- Apply the equation for work done to different situations.

Learning outcomes

- State different situations where work is done. [O1]
- Make connections between energy transferred, work done and force in different situations. [O2]
- Explain how simple machines make work easier by changing the force and distance moved. [O3]

Skills development

- Thinking scientifically: use equations
- Working scientifically: interpret evidence
- Learner development: ask questions

Resources needed heavy object with a rope attached, or shopping bag filled with items; long plank; wooden block; sticky notes; *for a circus*: screwdriver to open tin lid, wheelbarrow and load to lift, box to drag; metre rules; newtonmeters; Worksheet 1.6.4.

Common misconceptions Energy and force are the same thing. The distance for calculating work done by a lever is the distance from the fulcrum.

Key vocabulary work done .

Teaching and learning

Engage

- Demonstrate dragging a heavy object along a surface by a rope. (Alternatively use a heavy shopping bag loaded with items that needs to be lifted.) Select volunteers and ask the students to see how far they can move the object. Question them about how they feel, and if they think any energy has been transferred in moving the object. Introduce the idea of work done and how it applies to situations in which forces are used. Ask the students what they notice when they have to move it a longer distance. Discuss the link between work done and distance. [O1, O2]

Challenge and develop

- Set up a circus of different activities for pairs of students to try out, such as a heavy box to drag, push or lift, a door to open, a 1 kg weight to lift through a distance of 1 m, a stool to step on. Provide metre rules and newtonmeters. Ask the pairs to **discuss** each situation and **identify the forces** in each case. Introduce the terms 'effort' for the force applied and 'load' for the weight to be moved. Ask the students to identify where each of these are, and select volunteers to mark them with arrows labelled 'E' and 'L' using sticky notes. [O1]
- Use the activities, a newtonmeter and a metre rule to introduce the relationship work done = force × distance. Discuss the units used in this relationship and the need to change cm into m. The distance here is the displacement, in the direction of the force, through which the force moves. [O2]
- Show the students the heavy object again – discuss ways to lift it. Select volunteers and ask them to try to lift it with their hands. Now demonstrate lifting it using a long plank as a lever with a wooden block as a fulcrum. Explore reasons why this is much easier. Talk about the effort required – establish that the work done in lifting the load though a certain height is the same, with or without the lever, because it is load × distance moved by load. Also emphasise that energy is conserved – the work done on the load by the lever is equal to

the work done by the effort (by the person). The reason why the lever makes the job easier is because the lever reduces the effort needed, because the distance through which the effort moves is larger. [O2&3].

load × distance moved by load = effort [small] × distance moved by effort [large]

- The students can answer the questions on Worksheet 1.6.4.

Explain

- Ask the students to produce a poster to **explain** what is meant by 'work done' in at least three different situations. [O1&2]

Consolidate and apply

- Ask the students to answer the Student Book questions. [O1, 2&3]
- They should complete Worksheet 1.6.4 to consolidate their understanding of where work is done in everyday situations, and to reinforce their understanding of the relationship between work and force. [O1&2]
- Working in pairs, the students could make a tour of the room and **identify** as many different levers, or other machines, that make work easier. Ask them to select one such item and be prepared to **explain** how it works. [O1&2]

Extend

- Ask students able to progress further to **research** how gears reduce the effort force that needs to be applied. They should be prepared to **make a presentation** of their findings. [O2&3]

Plenary suggestions

Summarising Ask the students to **summarise** in three sentences what they have learned about work done. Then ask them to reduce this to ten words. [O1, 2&3]

Answers to Student Book questions

1. The strongman pulling the truck.
2. *Strongman*: chemical energy from muscles → energy by movement to the truck + energy by heating
   Fairground striker: chemical energy from muscles → energy by movement to the hammer → energy by movement to the puck → gravitational potential energy
3. a) 50 N × 1 m = 50 J b) 100 N × 6 m = 600 J
4. 20 000 N × 1000 m = 20 000 000 J
5. a) 100 N × 1 m = 100 J b) 100 J c) 200 N × height = 100 J; so height = 0.5 m

Answers to Worksheet 1.6.4

1. Work is done in a, b and e.
   a) force in the direction the ball is being hit by the bat; arrow between where the ball first came into contact with bat and where the ball left the bat
   b) force in the direction the car is being pushed; arrow between where the car started and where it stopped

   e) force in the direction the book is being lifted; arrow between where the book started and the height of the shelf
2. a) 35 × 2 = 70 J b) 25 × 5 = 125 J c) 2 × 0.1 = 0.2 J
3. a) 10 × 0.1 = 1 J b) $F_1d_1 = F_2d_2$; 1 = F_2 × 0.02; F_2 = 1 ÷ 0.02 = 50 N
   c) It will be easier to open the lid; the work needed to be done by the screwdriver to open the lid is the same, but the screwdriver handle will move further; so the force needed to be applied to the screwdriver handle will be lower

6.5 Looking at dynamos

Lesson overview

Learning objectives

- Describe the energy changes in a dynamo.
- Explain how a dynamo works.

Learning outcomes

- Describe different applications for dynamos. [O1]
- Describe the energy transfers in a dynamo. [O2]
- Explain the advantages and disadvantages of using dynamos. [O3]

Skills development

- Thinking scientifically: ask questions
- Working scientifically: interpret evidence
- Learner development: collaborate effectively

Resources needed equipment and materials for demonstration as detailed in the Technician's notes; dynamo kit (optional); devices using a dynamo e.g. wind-up radio / torch / lantern / mobile phone charger; poster paper; access to the internet; Worksheet 1.6.5; Technician's notes 1.6.5

Key vocabulary dynamo, kinetic energy, magnetism, electrical energy

Teaching and learning

Engage

- Ask the students to **imagine** a situation in which they are camping. Question them about what types of energy they might have available. Discuss what sources of electrical energy they have. Introduce the term 'dynamo' and explain what a dynamo is – a conductor and a magnet moving relative to one another to generate an electric current. [O1]
- Ask them to **consider** the images in the Student Book of devices that use dynamos. Ask them to **suggest** further examples of uses. [O1]

Challenge and develop

- Demonstrate moving a single copper wire, connected to a very sensitive ammeter, in and out of the magnetic field of a horseshoe magnet. Ask the students to **make observations** of what happens. Now show the effect of relative motion between a coil of wire and a magnet – see Technician's notes 1.6.5. What do the students now **observe** that is different? Relate this to a dynamo and demonstrate a dynamo kit, if available. Ask them to state the energy transfers taking place. [O2]
- Ask the students to **discuss** in pairs how they could **investigate** how the spin speed in a dynamo would affect the current produced (task 1 of Worksheet 1.6.5). Collect feedback from selected pairs, posing some key questions. [O2]

  Possible questions:
  - What is the independent variable? (spin speed)
  - What is the dependent variable? How will you measure it? (current sensitive ammeter)
  - Which variables would need to be controlled? (number of turns on coil; strength of magnet)
  - What do you predict? Why do you think this?
  - Do you think there is a limit to how much electrical energy can be transferred? If so, what decides the limit?

  Higher-attaining students could **consider** if there is useless energy transfer in a dynamo system and what could be done to minimise energy losses.

- If possible, show the students a range of different dynamo applications. If not, show images of some. Ask them to **write an explanation** for how the device works in each application. [O2]
- **Group work** Ask the students to **carry out their own research** on dynamos and to prepare a poster about their historical and current uses, and why they are not used as widely today. [O1, 2&3]

Explain

- Ask the students to **draw an energy transfer diagram** for a dynamo, showing the useful and useless energy transfers (task 2 of Worksheet 1.6.5). [O2]
- Ask them to look at one particular application of a dynamo as shown in task 3 of the worksheet. Ask them to **draw up a table/list of advantages and disadvantages** in using a dynamo to operate this device, as opposed to using batteries or generated-electricity from the mains (task 3 of Worksheet 1.6.5). [O3]

Consolidate and apply

- Working in pairs, the students imagine they are on a desert island. Ask them to **design** as many appliances as they can that could be run using dynamos. They should draw a diagram of their designs. [O1&2]
- **Pairs to fours** Ask each pair to join up with another pair to share and combine their ideas. They should **discuss** the advantages and disadvantages of using dynamos in each situation. Select different groups to **present** their ideas. [O2&3]

Extend

- Ask students able to progress further to **research** why the direct current (d.c.) produced by a dynamo was replaced with generated alternating current (a.c) (see 'Did you know?' in the Student Book). They should search for information on Nikola Tesla and the history of a.c. [O3]

Plenary suggestions

Learning triangle Ask the students to draw a large triangle with a smaller inverted triangle that just fits inside it. Ask them to think back over the lesson and in the outer three triangles write something they've seen, something they've done, and something they've discussed. Then ask them to add in the central triangle something they've learned.

Alternatively, ask them to complete the sentence: 'If I could, I would replace… with a dynamo. This is because…'.

Answers to Student Book questions

1. for example, mobile phone charger
2. There is no need to plug into an electricity supply; or use batteries (with consequent environmental advantages).
3. Energy is transferred by heat and sound.
4. Check that diagrams show kinetic energy being transferred to electrical energy; with a small amount of heat and sound.
5. Use stronger magnets; use more turns; or more coils; spin the coils faster.
6. Water flows 24 hours a day, as long as there are no climatic changes; this is a free source of energy.
7. Steam can be made to turn the coil much faster by increasing the steam pressure; you can also control the speed of coil rotation.

Answers to Worksheet 1.6.5

1. kinetic energy → electrical energy
2. chemical energy from muscles → kinetic energy of handle (useful) + heat energy (useless) → kinetic energy of coil (useful) + heat energy (useless)→ electrical energy (useful) + heat energy (useless)
3. *Advantages*: low cost; won't run out unless the component wears out; energy is always available

   Disadvantages: lighting is only provided when the handle is turned; limited amount of power produced, only suitable for low power applications; limited control of current – only one light level available

6.6 Understanding elastic potential energy

Lesson overview

Learning objectives

- Describe different situations that use the energy stored in compressing and stretching elastic materials.
- Describe how elastic potential energy in different materials can be compared.
- Explain how elastic potential energy is transferred.

Learning outcomes

- Recognise that work is done when energy is transferred by elastic potential energy. [O1]
- Investigate how different materials transfer energy by elastic potential energy. [O2]
- Use models to account for differences between different elastic materials. [O3]

Skills development

- Thinking scientifically: use models
- Working scientifically: develop explanations
- Learner development: ask questions

Resources needed toys that use elastic potential energy – e.g. dart gun, bow and arrow, wind-up toy; lengths of wool or string; equipment and materials for class practical as detailed in the Technician's notes; Worksheet 1.6.6; Practical sheet 1.6.6; Technician's notes 1.6.6

Common misconceptions Force and energy mean the same.

Key vocabulary elastic potential energy, work done

Teaching and learning

Engage

- Remind the students about work from Chapter 5 on elastic materials and Hooke's Law. Ask them to **recap** three things they remember. They could begin to fill in a KWL grid – 'what I Know; what I Want to know; what I have Learned'. [O1]
- Show a video of a bungee jump or a catapult being fired. Ask them, in pairs, to **discuss the energy transfers** taking place. [O1]
- Review the students' ideas about the energy transfers in the video, and introduce the term 'elastic potential energy' – refer to the Student Book. Discuss the relationship between energy transferred and work done. [O1]
- Demonstrate different toys that use elastic potential energy – e.g. a dart gun, a bow and arrow, wind-up toys. Discuss with students where the energy comes from. [O1]
- Students should draw up a list of other examples of applications of elastic potential energy. [O1]

Challenge and develop

- Provide the students with three different types of elastic bands. Ask them to **follow the instructions** on Practical sheet 1.6.6 and **investigate** which materials can store and transfer the most elastic potential energy. Discuss students' findings. [O1, 2&3].

  Ask higher-attaining students to **suggest** possible reasons for differences between materials.
- Explore with the students why elastic materials behave in the way that they do. Referring to Figure 1.6.6c in the Student Book, use lengths of wool or string as a model to represent the molecules in long chains, which straighten out when a force is applied to them. Apply the model to how elastic materials behave under force, and discuss how the stored elastic potential energy is released (when the elastic material returns to its original shape). [O3]

Explain

- Ask the students to complete task 1 of Worksheet 1.6.6, which asks them to **draw an energy transfer diagram** for a situation involving elastic potential energy, and to consider useless energy transfers and work done. [O1&2]
- Ask the students to **write an explanation** of the energy transfer in different elastic materials, using diagrams to show how the materials behave and transfer energy to do work. Task 2 of Worksheet 1.6.6 asks students to consider why elastic is able to stretch more easily than a stiff spring. [O2&3]

  Higher-attaining students should be able to **explain the behaviour** of different elastic materials using the particle model (task 3 of Worksheet 1.6.6). [O3]

Consolidate and apply

- Working in pairs, ask students to imagine they work for a bungee-jumping firm. Ask them to prepare a sales leaflet **explaining** how a bungee jump works, and how effective it is at transferring elastic potential energy. [O2&3]

Extend

- Ask students able to progress further to **compare** and **contrast** gravitational potential energy and elastic potential energy. They should **explain** how each is transferred, writing which is the most effective at storing and transferring energy and give examples of their applications. [O2&3]

Plenary suggestions

Review Return to the KWL grid, partly completed at the start of the lesson. Ask the students to complete the grid, reflecting on what they have learned. Ask them to **consider** if there are any more things they want to find out. [O1, 2&3]

Answers to Student Book questions

1. archery bow
2. Energy is stored in a spring when it is compressed; when the spring is released, the energy is transferred by movement; causing 'Jack' to bounce up.
3. a) They should stretch the elastic by the same distance; use an identical object to fire;, carry out the investigation at the same time; under the same wind conditions.

   b) They should measure how far the object travelled; this gives a measure of how much energy is transferred.
4. Stored energy is tranferred by chemical reactions in a person's muscles to energy by movement in the arm. This is transferred to energy by movement in the spring of the clock. The energy is stored as elastic potential energy in the spring until it is released. It is then transferred to energy by movement to make the clock cogs turn around . Then energy is transferred slowly over time, making the hands move.
5. No; most materials don't have a structure that allows the lengths of the moelcules to be altered.
6. Find the work done by each and compare the values.

Answers to Worksheet 1.6.6

1. a) Chemical energy from muscles → elastic potential energy in bow string (useful) + heat (useless) → kinetic energy of arrow (useful) + sound energy (useless) b) Force exerted on bow string; the amount of useless energy transferred.
2. a) The type of material and how easy or hard it is to stretch. If it is harder to pull back (i.e. a bigger force is required), then more elastic potential energy can be stored.

   b) It is hard to squash or stretch a stiff spring, so a lot of energy (transferred from movement) can be stored and then slowly released when the car is moving up and down. If an elastic rope was used it would release the energy quickly because it is easy to stretch and would not be suitable for this job.
3. A model showing particles moving closer together when the spring is squashed; some idea that a lot of force is needed to push the particles together compared to an elastic rope where the long strands of molecules are straightened when pulled.

6.7 Knowing the difference between heat and temperature

Lesson overview

Learning objectives

- Recognise what we mean by temperature.
- Describe how temperature differences lead to energy transfer.
- Explain the difference between heat and temperature.

Learning outcomes

- Use a thermometer to measure temperature. [O1]
- Make predictions about the direction of heat flow. [O2]
- Analyse different situations in terms of heat and temperature. [O3]

Skills development

- Thinking scientifically: use models
- Working scientifically: develop explanations
- Learner development: ask questions

Resources needed equipment and materials for demonstration and class practical as detailed in the Technician's notes; Worksheet 1.6.7; Practical sheet 1.6.7; Technician's notes 1.6.7

Common misconceptions Heat and temperature mean the same. There can be a quantity of 'cold'.

Key vocabulary temperature, degrees Celsius, heat

Teaching and learning

Engage

- Provide three bowls – one full of warm water at 40 °C, one with cold water with ice cubes in it at 10 °C, and one with lukewarm water at 20 °C. Select students to place their hands in each of the three bowls in turn and **describe** what they feel. Use the demonstration to explore the meaning of the word 'temperature'. [O1]
- Show the students pictures of a range of different objects and ask them to rank them in order of the highest temperature to the lowest temperature. [O1]
- Show them a range of different thermometers and demonstrate taking the temperature of different objects us. Discuss the advantages and disadvantages of each. [O1]

Challenge and develop

- Introduce the idea that all substances above absolute zero (−273 °C) and their particles have some kinetic energy, even if they are very cold. The higher the temperature, the more kinetic energy the particles have.
- Working in groups of four, students carry out the class practical using Practical sheet 1.6.7. They **investigate** the effect of temperature differences in two identical metal blocks. They may need practice with the use of callipers beforehand. The students should use the questions on the sheet to **consider their observations**. Collect feedback from the groups. [O2]
- Return to the demonstration with the three bowls of water and modify it – fill one bowl with hot water from the tap and another with cold water and add some ice. Mix hot and cold water in the third bowl so that the temperature is between the others. Now ask a volunteer to put one hand in the hot water and one in the cold water for about 30 seconds. At exactly the same time they take both hands out of the bowls of water and quickly put them together into the bowl of tepid water. Ask the volunteer 'How does each of your hands feel? Can you describe it to the class?'. Ask the students to **explain** what is happening in terms of heat flow between the hands and the water in the different bowls. [O2]
- Introduce the difference between the concepts of heat and temperature. Refer to the third section of the Student Book. Demonstrate (or refer to Figure 1.6.7c) a small container of very hot water and a large

container of lukewarm water. Ask which has the highest temperature. Relate the temperature to the movement energy of the particles in the water. Select students to **role-play** the two situations. Provide one or two students with '80' labels to represent the temperature of the water in the small container, and the rest of the class with '30' labels to represent the temperature of the water in the large container. Introduce the idea that the total heat energy in each depends on the number of particles and not *just* on their temperature. [O3]

Explain

- Ask the students to answer the questions on Worksheet 1.6.7 about temperature, heat and how heat is transferred. [O1, 2&3]

Consolidate and apply

- Working in pairs, ask the students to answer the Student Book questions. [O1, 2&3]
- Return to the pictures from the starter. Ask the students to rank the images in terms of the amount of heat each picture infers and to **explain their ideas**. [O3]

Extend

- Ask students able to progress further to **suggest** whether or not different materials will reach the same temperature if they are given the same amount of heat energy. (They don't; some materials 'hold' more heat.)

Plenary suggestions

What have I learned? Ask the students to **write definitions** of 'temperature' and 'heat' and to **explain** how they are different. Alternatively, students could draw a cartoon strip to **summarise** their learning.

Answers to Student Book questions

1. A; C; B; D 2. 1e; 2f; 3d; 4c; 5a; 6b
3. a) from surroundings to ice cube b) from ice cube to surroundings c) no (net) heat transfer
4. a) quickest b) slower because the temperature difference smaller c) no transfer because no temperature difference
5. In the freezer; there is a bigger temperature difference; so heat will be transferred from the water to the freezer faster; so the water will cool more quickly.
6. The gigantic iceberg has more energy; there are many more particles in an iceberg compared to those in the cup of water; when you add up the number of particles and the amount of energy each one has, there will be more energy overall in the iceberg. (Ensure students don't think that particles of ice at 0 °C have no movement energy.)
7. Particles in a hotter object have more kinetic energy; they move around, or vibrate, and pass on some of their energy in collisions; the particles in the cooler object gain energy while those in the hotter object lose energy.

Answers to Worksheet 1.6.7

1. a) 0 °C b) 100 °C c) below about 12 °C d) 40–50 °C e) 37 °C f) 5 °C g) 70 °C h) 15–20 °C i) 18–22 °C
2. a) The ice cube is at 0 °C; the room is at about 20 °C. Energy by heat will be transferred from the room to the ice cube; this will increase the energy of the particles in the ice cube; until the temperature of the ice cube reaches over 0 °C and melts.

   b) The ice cube is at 0 °C; the freezer is at about −15 °C; energy will be transferred by heat from the ice cube to the freezer; so the ice cube will become cooler than 0 °C; it will stay frozen.

   c) Objects put into the fridge are at room temperature (about 20 °C); the fridge is at about 5 °C; energy will be transferred by heat from the objects to the fridge; so they will become cooler; until they reach 5 °C.
3. a) *Temperature* is a measure of how fast particles are moving or vibrating – their individual kinetic energy. For example, the particles in a pan of boiling water (at about 100 °C) are moving much faster and have more kinetic energy than the particles in the hot bath water (about 40 °C).

   b) *Heat* is a measure of the total energy in something; which depends on how fast its particles are vibrating; and how many particles there are. A bath of hot water has more heat because it has a much higher mass and so there are many more particles with energy; compared to many fewer particles in the pan with higher energy.

6.8 Thinking about fuels

Lesson overview

Learning objectives

- Identify examples of fuels and their uses.
- Describe combustion of fuels and recognise that different fuels transfer different amounts of energy.
- Describe the advantages and disadvantages of using different fuels.

Learning outcomes

- Describe what is meant by a fuel and give examples. [O1]
- Explain how combustion is useful in terms of energy transfer and some of its drawbacks, and identify key variables to change, measure and control. [O2]
- Explain why different fuels have different properties, and explain how to plan to collect valid, accurate and reliable evidence. [O3]

Skills development

- Thinking scientifically: ask questions
- Working scientifically: design investigations
- Learner development: communicate effectively

Resources needed different coloured sticky notes; materials and equipment as detailed in the Technician's notes; Worksheet 1.6.8; Technician's notes 1.6.8

Common misconceptions Fuels are only liquid fuels, such as petrol for cars.

Key vocabulary chemical potential energy, oxygen, combustion, hydrocarbon, fossil fuel.

Teaching and learning

Engage

- The students work in groups of three. Select volunteers to **test** a range of different materials in front of the class, under careful supervision. They should first say which can be used as a fuel from water, cooking oil, candle, paper, wooden splint and metal. Collect feedback and discuss the meaning of the word 'fuel'. Introduce the idea that a fuel has chemical potential energy. [O1]
- Show a video of different fuels, or use examples from the Student Book, to discuss how fuels release energy. Ask the students to **draw an energy diagram** to show the energy transfer in a fuel. [O1&2]

Challenge and develop

- Demonstrate the set-up for burning foods – see Technician's notes 1.6.8. Discuss the independent, dependent and control variables in the investigation and how to collect accurate, valid and reliable evidence to test the energy given out by different foods. Provide the definitions for 'valid' and 'reliable' evidence, emphasising that for validity the investigation needs to be fair, and for reliability it should be repeatable. Ask the students to **make observations** when the food burns and to **discuss** the energy transfer. [O2&3]
- Discuss with students some of the problems with the products of burning fuels. [O2]
- Arrange the students in ability groups of four. Provide them with Worksheet 1.6.8 for guidance and ask them to **design an investigation** to answer one of the following questions: [O2&3]
  - lower and middle-attaining students – **A** Do solid fuels release more energy than liquid or gas fuels?
  - higher-attaining students – **B** Which alcohol releases the most energy?

  Discuss with higher-attaining students how fuels release energy, in terms of their reaction with oxygen, and why some fuels might release more energy than others. [O3]

Explain

- Ask the groups to **present** their investigation designs, stating all variables and how they would collect accurate, valid and reliable evidence. Discuss these and identify good features and areas for improvement. [O1, 2&3]

Consolidate and apply

- Groups could produce a leaflet on 'The advantages and disadvantages of using fuels'. [O2]
- Use the Student Book to consolidate ideas about fuels and how they release energy. Ask the students to complete the questions and **peer-review** the answers. [O1, 2&3]

Extend

- Ask students able to progress further to **research** hydrocarbon fuels and find out what factors affect how much energy is released. [O2&3]

Plenary suggestions

Quick on the draw Arrange the students in groups of four. Provide each group with one of five questions on different-coloured sticky notes. Each group tries to answer the question – then one person shares the group's response. If they get it right, they can attempt the next question. [O1, 2&3]

The following questions could be asked:

- Define what is meant by a fuel.
- Which gas do fuels react with?
- Give an example of a solid fuel, a liquid fuel and a gas fuel.
- Why don't all fuels release the same amount of energy?
- What are the main problems with using fuels?

Alternatively, the students could think about the materials they tested at the start of the lesson and use particular examples to **explain** what is meant by a fuel, and how and why fuels differ from each other. [O1, 2&3]

Answers to Student Book questions

1. Liquid fuels transfer energy more quickly; they can flow in pipes and so be transported easily.
2. Suggestions about possible effects – for example vehicle use.
3. *Useful*: chemical energy transferred by heat energy to surroundings; *useless*: energy transferred by light and sound to surroundings
4. For example, the convenience of their form; the amount of useful energy transferred; the pollution caused on burning
5. No carbon dioxide is made when it burns; so no contribution to global warming; no pollution.
6. All our vehicles are designed to run using them; it is difficult to change our systems to use alternative fuels; applications using alternative fuels are still being researched.

Answers to Worksheet 1.6.8

1. a) A: the state of the fuel – solid, liquid or gas; B: the type of alcohol

   b) A: a solid fuel, a liquid fuel and a gas fuel; B: different alcohols available

   c) How much energy is transferred when the fuel burns d) Measure the temperature increase of the heated waterl.

   e) The amount of water; the time the fuel burns for; the distance of the burning fuel from the water; the insulation of the beaker with water in it.

   f) For example, 20 cm^3 water; 1 minute; as close as possible; put a lid over the beaker.

   g) Burning fuels could set other things alight; beaker is hot after heating; spillage could cause slips;

   h) Remove all flammable materials from the vicinity of the burning fuel; keep hair tied back and away from flames; wear safty goggles; do not touch the beaker until it has cooled down; wear a heatproof glove; mop up all spillages.
2. a) Make accurate measurements with thermometer; use a 10 cm^3 measuring cylinder to measure the water.

   b) Repeat the investigation three times; ignoring any anomalous results when calculating an average.
3. a) Have two different groups carry this out in the same way; see if they obtain the same results.

   b) See if repeated readings are close together.

   c) Minimise heat losses by insulating the beaker as well as possible.

6.9 Investigating fuels

Lesson overview

Learning objectives

- Describe how to measure the energy of fuels.
- Collect evidence to investigate the energy of different fuels.
- Present data using appropriate graphs and evaluate the quality of evidence collected.

Learning outcomes

- Follow a procedure to collect evidence and present data with help. [O1]
- Control all variables and collect valid evidence; present data and interpret evidence independently. [O2]
- Present and compare data about the energy per gram to compare fuels; collect accurate, valid and reliable evidence. [O3]

Skills development

- Thinking scientifically: consider the quality of evidence
- Working scientifically: record and present evidence
- Learner development: plan progress

Resources needed graph paper; materials and equipment as detailed in the Technician's notes; Worksheet 1.6.9; Practical sheet 1.6.9; Technician's notes 1.6.8 and 1.6.9

Common misconceptions All fuels give out the same amount of energy.

Key vocabulary combustion

Teaching and learning

Engage

- Ask the students to develop an acrostic of the word FUEL.
- Demonstrate (or present scenarios of) the burning food investigation from the previous lesson (see Technician's notes 1.6.8) with a number of deliberate mistakes, relating to variables. For example, hold the food a long way from the flame and keep changing the distance during the burning; use different amounts of water / food in different set-ups; have one with a lid on the beaker and another with no lid; take the temperature reading while the thermometer is touching the bottom of the glass. Ask the students to **identify** and **correct** the mistakes. [O2]

Challenge and develop

- Explore how to measure the energy in fuels in order to collect accurate, reliable and valid evidence. Discuss the importance of reducing heat losses and ways of achieving this. [O1, 2&3]
- Put the students in the same groups as in the previous lesson. Ask them to make amendments to the plans they developed, as required. If needed they could refer to the procedure on Practical sheet 1.6.9. Discuss safety precautions. [O1, 2&3]
- Students should follow their checked procedures, or the procedure on Practical sheet 1.6.9, and **collect** and **record evidence** about the energy of different fuels. See Technician's notes 1.6.9. Reinforce safety issues before allowing students to start. [O1, 2&3]

  Provide higher-attaining students with some knowledge of the chemical nature of the fuels – for example the number of carbon atoms per molecule of the alcohols used. Ask them to make **links** between this and their results.

- The students should **draw bar graphs** of their results. [O1, 2&3]

- Ask selected students to **present** their graphs. Discuss the quality of data obtained, and discuss any areas of possible improvement. [O3]

Explain

- The students should **write an explanation** of their results, using ideas about the combustion of fuels and why different fuels transfer different amounts of energy. They could include ideas about how easy or hard different fuels were to ignite. [O2&3]

  Higher-attaining students should **evaluate** the quality of their data and **suggest** ideas for improvement. They could **compare** the values of fuel energy per gram obtained by experiment with those in Table 1.6.9 in the Student Book and try to account for the differences. [O3]

Consolidate and apply

- Present students with a graph of the energy per gram of different fuels, on Worksheet 1.6.9. Ask them to use the data to answer the questions in sections 1 and 2. They can then answer questions 6—8 in the Student Book. [O2&3]

Extend

- Ask students able to progress further to **compare** and **contrast** the 'bomb calorimeter' with their own experimental design, using section 3 of Worksheet 1.6.9. They should use ideas about energy transfers in their explanations.

Plenary suggestions

What I have learned Ask the students to complete these sentences:

- In this lesson I have found out…
- I have learned to improve my skills in…
- Next time I need to…

Answers to Student Book questions

1. gas; wood; coal; oil; petrol; diesel 2. increase the amount of fuel; change the type of fuel
3. wood 4. about 3 g 5. hydrogen; has the highest energy per gram
6. *Strengths* of bar graph: easy to see and compare lengths of bars; can take readings from the graph; large data sets can be represented; simple patterns can be identified and predictions made

   Weaknesses of bar graph: mathematical relationships are hard to identify

   Strengths of pie chart: visually clear

   Weaknesses of pie chart: hard to compare values; better for smaller data sets; can't take readings from the chart; or make predictions
7. Line graphs may be produced from continuous data, not discrete data.
8. Not really; except that fuels from fossil fuels have similar amounts of energy.

Answers to Worksheet 1.6.9

1. The more carbon atoms per molecule, the more energy stored in and transferred by the fuel.
2. a) There should be labels on the axes; units; names of fuels; a proper graph title; it would be better as a bar graph

   b) Should draw a bar graph; ensure they label axes fully; and include a descriptive title.
3. a) In a bomb calorimeter conditions are better controlled; heat losses to the surroundings are reduced to a minimum; so nearly all the energy from combustion is transferred to the water; which allows it to be measured accurately. The amount of oxygen can be controlled to ensure all the fuel is burnt.

   b) Reduce heat losses by insulating the equipment.

   c) There were higher heat losses to the surroundings in the laboratory equipment; so the temeprature of the water did not rise so high; and a lower figure for the heat transfer was obtained.

6.10 Applying key ideas

Energy changes – making electricity

Objectives

- Extract ideas about energy transfers and fuels from earlier sections of the chapter.
- Apply ideas about how energy is transferred to explain its application in making electricity.
- Use ideas and information about electricity generation to compare different energy transfers.

Outcome

- Making clear and effective responses to questions, indicating understanding and the next steps in learning.

The purpose of this activity is to provide an opportunity to see how successfully students are grasping the key ideas so far. It isn't designed to be used as a formal test; it might be that students work on the questions collectively. It provides an opportunity for you to look at written work, engage students in discussions and form ideas about progress being made.

The tasks are progressive. Lower-attaining students should be able to tackle the first two or three tasks, while higher-attaining students will find the later tasks more challenging.

Resources needed different types of dynamo if possible, or photographs; video of a bicycle dynamo in operation; video of a water wheel running a dynamo/generator; Worksheet 1.6.10

Teaching & learning

Engage

- Challenge the students to think back over the last few lessons and **identify** some of the key ideas they have met. Draw out some responses about these ideas and say that it's important as learners that we develop a sense of our own progress.
- Provide the students with some dynamos to look at, referring back to the learning from Topic 6.5. Recap how they work. Explain that dynamos can use different methods to transfer energy, and will therefore be a useful way of revising energy transfers in general.
- If possible, show the students a video of a bicycle dynamo in operation, and one of a water wheel running a dynamo.

Challenge and develop

- **Pair talk** Ask the students to **consider** the useful and useless energy changes in each of the dynamo systems. How could the useless energy be reduced?
- Show them a simple outline of the energy changes at a coal-fired electricity generating station. Ask them to **discuss** in their pairs how they would go about **comparing** the sources of energy for the different dynamos with the energy source for the power station. What features would they need to consider?

Explain

Ask the students to read the passage in the Student Book. Depending on their ability to assimilate text, you may need to adopt strategies such as:

- Have students working in pairs and hand out Worksheet 1.6.10 (a copy of the text) and highlighters. One student highlights key ideas and the other highlights (with a different colour) any words they don't understand.
- Using the text as a source of ideas, draw a spider chart with 'energy transfers' at its centre and write ideas and applications around it.
- Work with groups of students who have difficulty with reading to support them in decoding the text and accessing the ideas.

Consolidate and apply

Now ask the students to attempt the Student Book tasks. They might do this individually or collaboratively. In each case, encourage them to **identify** and **record** their ideas.

- Ask the students to present their responses to various tasks, either orally or by displaying their work.

- Check their answers and provide feedback to their responses, as a class.

Extend

- For students able to progress further, task 5 is an opportunity for extension work.

Plenary

How well did we do? Ask the students for responses to questions such as:

- 'How well did we approach the tasks?'
- 'Did we manage to present some high-quality responses?'
- 'Which tasks could we answer really well?'
- 'What did we not understand at all?'
- 'Are there some ideas that we need to strengthen in later lessons?' If there are, make a note.

Provide the class with some overall feedback, indicating ideas that they have grasped effectively and those they may need developing further.

Likely responses and next steps in learning

1. This gives the students an opportunity to recall aspects of gravitational potential energy and what happens in energy transfers involving it. They should be able to recall that gravity is a force, pulling the water down. This enables the transfer from gravitational potential to kinetic energy. Some may identify that heat is also transferred, caused by friction with the falling water particles. If students are struggling with this, remind them of more familiar contexts, such as trampolines and skydivers. Make comparisons between these and water falling. This task checks the ability of students to use the correct terms in describing energy transfers.
2. This involves some application of understanding, the ability to use the text and to draw energy transfer diagrams. The students should be able to identify the starting energy in all cases and how this is transferred in different ways. Example b) is rather harder than example a). The first can be modelled together if students are struggling, then they can try the next independently. This task checks the ability of students to recognise energy transfers and to draw them in a diagram. Higher-attaining students could be challenged to draw Sankey diagrams.
3. This increases the application of understanding by asking the students to think about transfers that have not been specified in the text. They have to make decisions about energy transfers that are useless, and where they come from. Use more concrete contexts first – for example the sound made by a hairdryer – to remind them of why some transfers are useless. In a bicycle dynamo, energy transferred by heat comes from friction in the wheel of the dynamo, and/or between the bicyle wheel and the cogs of the dynamo.
4. The students are required to apply their understanding of energy transfers to less familiar contexts. They are expected to identify key energy transfers, recognising that in one energy is transferred by combustion of fuels and in the other energy is transferred by gravitational potential energy. In their comparison, some mention of relative energy losses/efficiency is expected.
5. The final task draws different, abstract ideas together. A detailed explanation of how energy is transferred using a hand-crank dynamo is required, with effective use of terminology. Students should explain how chemical energy from food is transferred in our muscles, how elastic potential energy stored in the strands of expanding and contracting muscle transfers energy, and how energy is transferred by the dynamo. Useless energy transfers should be identified and predictions made about the relative quantity of energy that might be wasted in each transfer. Finally, students should be able to construct a Sankey diagram for the overall process, including all useless energy transfers.

6.11 Exploring sound

Lesson overview

Learning objectives

- Identify how sounds are made.
- Describe how sound waves transfer energy.
- Explain how loud and quiet sounds are made.

Learning outcomes

- Recognise the need for vibrations to make sound waves. [O1]
- Describe the features of a longitudinal sound wave. [O2]
- Use the slinky model to make connections between loudness and amplitude. [O3]

Skills development

- Thinking scientifically: use units and nomenclature
- Working scientifically: develop explanations
- Learner development: ask questions

Resources needed range of musical instruments – including string, wind and percussion; signal generator; loudspeaker with the cover off; rice; sound-producing items for a circus – e.g. triangle, whistle, bell, guitar, wind chimes; decibel meter; slinky spring; Worksheet 1.6.11; Practical sheet 1.6.11; Technician's notes 1.6.11

Common misconceptions Material objects are not needed to make sounds.

Key vocabulary vibrate, longitudinal wave, decibel (dB), amplitude

Teaching and learning

Engage

- Show the students video clips of inspiring sounds. Explore how we make sounds and why there are so many different sounds. [O1]
- Ask the students to make a sound and touch their voice box. What do they notice? Discuss what happens when they change the tone and loudness of their voice. [O1]
- Play some different musical instruments and ask the students to **observe** and **discuss** in pairs how different sounds are made. Question them about the need for vibrations. [O1]

  For example:

  - Where do the vibrations come from?
  - What do you think happens to the vibrations when the sound is loud, or quiet?
  - How do you think the vibrations change with higher- and lower-pitched sounds?

Challenge and develop

- Demonstrate a loudspeaker with the cover off, so the students can see the 'drum'. Put some rice grains on its surface and turn on the sound using a signal generator. If the frequency is low enough and the volume high enough, the students can observe the rice grains jumping. Ask them to **make observations** of what happens when the sound is made louder. Link this with the amount of energy transferred. You could introduce the decibel as the unit of loudness. [O1]
- Set up a circus with different sound-producing items. Ask the students to **investigate** how each item makes a sound, how a loud sound is made and how a quiet sound is made. They should **record** how the sound is produced and how it can be altered in loudness (Worksheet 1.6.11). If a decibel meter is available, students can **record** the values of the sounds made when they are hit/ plucked with a similar energy. They can use Practical sheet 1.6.11. [O1]

- Demonstrate a slinky spring, to show how sounds waves are produced and how longitudinal vibrations make the wave transfer energy. [O1&2]
- Challenge pairs of students to use the slinky to **model** how to make a sound louder and softer, explaining what they are doing and why. Ensure that they understand the relationship between the energy of the vibration and the loudness. [O1&2]
- Ask them to **identify** how the longitudinal slinky wave changes with greater energy input ('louder sound') – they should notice there is greater compression (coils more squashed together) and rarefaction (coils pulled further apart). Introduce the term *amplitude*, for the 'size' of the vibration. [O1, 2&3]

Explain

- Relate the movement of the coils of the slinky spring to the movement of air particles as a sound wave progresses. [O1&2]
- Ask the students to **describe** a particular sound and to **explain** how it is sent from the object to reach our ears. [O1&2]

  Higher-attaining students could **consider** how sound travels in the sea.

Consolidate and apply

- Play three sounds of different volume. Ask the students to draw and label a longitudinal wave to represent them. Ask them to **explain** what has changed in the wave in each case. [O2]
- Ask the students to answer the questions on Worksheet 1.6.11. [O1, 2&3]

Extend

- Students able to progress further can **research** how different animals on land and in the sea produce vibrations to make their sounds. They could present a one-minute talk. [O1]

Plenary suggestions

Definitions Ask the students to write or draw definitions to **explain** the meaning of 'vibration', 'longitudinal wave' and 'amplitude'. [O1]

Answers to Student Book questions

1. As the metal bell is hit by the clanger, it vibrates and passes the vibrations to the air particles.
2. The vibrations of the instruments/voices cause nearby air particles to vibrate. These air particles bump into others, transferring the vibrations through the air; until they reach the ears in the audience.
3. The particles vibrate to and fro about their rest position; resulting in some being squashed together and some being pulled apart.
4. It passes on from one 'layer' of particles to the next; away from the source of sound.
5. 1d; 2a; 3b; 4c
6. It decreases with distance from the source of sound; the energy has spread out.
7. Yes; there is a limit to how far the air particles can be compressed and pulled apart; and therefore how much energy can be transferred.

Answers to Worksheet 1.6.11

1. b) *Guitar*: strings are plucked; causing vibration of the strings; that transfers to the air particles; *drum*: drumskin is hit; causing the skin to vibrate; and pass the energy to the air particles; *recorder*: column of air in the recorder tube vibrates; and as it passes through the holes the vibrations are passed through the surounding air.
2. vibrates; strings; air; invisible; energy; waves; energy; amplitude
3. The following ideas should be included: how the vibration is made; the vibration causing air particles to be squashed together and others to move apart; the energy of the wave is passed on from layer to layer of air particles in a longitudinal wave; loud sounds transfer more energy than quiet sounds; because the amplitude of the longitudinal wave is greater.

6.12 Describing sound

Lesson overview

Learning objectives

- Describe how the pitch of a sound wave can be changed.
- Apply the terms frequency, wavelength and amplitude to different waveforms.

Learning outcomes

- State what is meant by the term 'frequency' and how it relates to the pitch of sound. [O1]
- Relate the terms 'frequency', 'wavelength' and 'amplitude' to different waves. [O2]
- Draw and interpret wave diagrams that represent different sounds. [O3]

Skills development

- Thinking scientifically: analyse data
- Working scientifically: interpret evidence
- Learner development: communicate effectively

Resources needed mini-whiteboards (optional); graph paper; equipment and materials as detailed in the Technician's notes; pieces of coloured wool; drinking glasses with different amounts of water in them; instrument such as a recorder; Worksheet 1.6.12; Technician's notes 1.6.12

Common misconceptions Pitch and loudness mean the same.

Key vocabulary frequency, waveform, wavelength, amplitude, microphone

Teaching and learning

Engage

- Recap ideas from the previous lesson. Hand out mini-whiteboards or paper. Play one note on an instrument such as a recorder. Play the note at four or five different levels of loudness. Ask the students to listen and draw one vertical line each time you play a note – the louder the note, the longer the line. Relate these lines to the amplitude of the note. [O2]
- Now play some different notes on the instrument. Ask the students to describe the differences between them. Introduce the term *pitch*. Ask the students to draw a horizontal line for each note – the lower the pitch, the longer the line. [O1]

Challenge and develop

- Set up a static sinusoidal trace on an oscilloscope connected to a signal generator (or use software); also connect a loudspeaker. Explain that the trace represents features of the sound wave. Use the Student Book diagrams to relate loudness and pitch to different parts of the wave. Make the sound louder and quieter so the students can **observe** what happens to the waveform (**L**oud note = **L**arge amplitude). Now change the pitch so they can see the change in wavelength (**L**ow note = **L**ong wavelength and **L**ow frequency). Avoid sustained loud, low frequencies and high frequencies because both can cause some individuals to experience unpleasant sensations. [O1, 2&3]
- Use the slinky model in conjunction with the oscilloscope. Ask the students to **compare** the two waveforms, **identifying** different parts of the wave in each. Ask them to **predict** how to change the slinky model to represent different pitched notes. If necessary attach different pieces of coloured wool to the slinky to help the students to see different parts of the wave more clearly. [O1, 2&3]
- Now connect a microphone to the oscilloscope, in place of the signal generator. Ask some students to play notes or sing into the microphone. The students should see that a real sound is not a pure note (not a single wave form), but more complex, combined waves that give the characteristic sound quality. [O3]
- Ask the students to answer questions 1 to 6 in the Student Book. [O1, 2&3]

Explain

- Demonstrate making sounds by running a finger over the rim of the glass. Use glasses holding different amounts of water (or show a video of this). Ask the students to work in pairs and **think of an explanation** for the change in pitch they can hear. [O1, 2&3]
- Ask them to **explain the differences** between the amplitude, frequency and wavelength, the pitch and the loudness of the sound waves produced, using words and wave diagrams in their explanations. [O1, 2&3]

Consolidate and apply

- **Group work** Ask the students to make up a short 'tune' by drawing different wave diagrams in succession. They should alter the pitch and the loudness of the sounds. They should then give these to another group and ask the group to either play or sing the notes. [O3]

  Higher-attaining students might be expected to think up a greater variety of and more complex notes.
- Ask the students to **complete** the tasks on Worksheet 1.6.12. Task 1 provides the students with an opportunity to **describe** and **demonstrate** an understanding of how technology can enable us to 'see' sounds. [O1, 2&3]

Extend

- Ask students able to progress further to do question 7 in the Student Book and then to **find out about** other applications of waveforms. [O3]

Plenary suggestions

Definitions Ask the students to add to their list of definitions from the previous lesson, including the terms frequency, pitch, wavelength, oscilloscope, signal generator, loudspeaker, microphone.

Answers to Student Book questions

1. any sensible answers
2. How high or low (pitched) the note is.
3. It is easier to see and measure the amplitude and wavelength.
4. a) increases in height (amplitude) b) decreases in wavelength
5. a) A and/or B b) D c) B; it has the biggest amplitude; and a higher frequency than A; so it transfers more energy per second.
6. *loud high-pitched*: large amplitude; high frequency (short wavelength); *quiet low pitched*: small amplitude, low frequency (long wavelength)
7. Initially a very large amplitude and quite high frequency; then it decreases in amplitude significantly; and decreases slightly in frequency.

Answers to Worksheet 1.6.12

1. The key elements are the use of the signal generator to generate different sounds and the oscilloscope to provide a visual representation.
2. *high frequency*: waveforms should be produced with small wavelengths and many waves

   low frequency: only a few waves in the box; same amplitude as the first diagram; but longer wavelength
3. a)–c) check diagrams d) sound gets quieter e) sound gets lower pitched

   f) The person whispering would generate a waveform of smaller amplitude than the person speaking.

6.13 Measuring the speed of sound

Lesson overview

Learning objectives

- Describe what an echo is.
- Describe how the speed of sound can be measured using echoes.
- Calculate distances using ideas about echoes.

Learning outcomes

- Recognise an echo as a reflection of sound; follow a procedure to measure the speed of sound. [O1]
- Describe how echoes can be used in different applications. [O2].
- Explain how echoes can be used to measure the speed of sound and the distance of objects in different applications. [O3]

Skills development

- Thinking scientifically: use equations
- Working scientifically: record evidence
- Learner development: collaborate effectively

Resources needed Worksheet 1.6.13; Practical sheet 1.6.13

Common misconceptions Sound travels instantaneously.

Key vocabulary reflection, echo, speed of sound, sonar

Teaching and learning

Engage

- Show the students a video clip of lightning and thunder. Tell them that these light and sound effects are produced at the same time. What can the students infer about the speed of light and of sound? [O1]
- Alternatively, show a video clip of a Concorde plane and ask 'What do we mean by the sound barrier?' and 'What happens when the barrier is broken?' (Show Concorde exceeding the speed of sound and emitting a sonic boom. [O1]
- Either demonstrate echoes outside in a suitable place, or show a video of echoes in a cave. Question the students about what an echo is and how it is made (by reflection of the sound wave from a hard surface). [O1]

Challenge and develop

- Arrange the students in groups of four and ask them to **follow the instructions** on Practical sheet 1.6.13 to measure the speed of sound. Allow them some time to **discuss** how to carry out the investigation so that they **collect data** as accurately and reliably as possible. Recap (from Topic 5.15) how to calculate the speed using their results. [O1]
- Ask the students to **compare** their values with calculated values for the speed of sound and to **discuss** differences. Ask questions about how the quality of the investigation data could be improved. [O2&3]
- Refer to the third section of the Student Book and discuss how echoes are used to measure distances that can't be easily measured directly. [O2]
- Model some example questions involving the speed of sound and then ask the students to **calculate** the answers to the Student Book questions 5–7, and the differentiated questions on Worksheet 1.6.13. [O2&3]

Explain

- **Pair talk** Working in pairs, ask the students to **discuss** and draw diagrams to **explain** the energy changes taking place when a sound wave is reflected as an echo. [O1]
- In their pairs, they should then **explain** to each other the method for measuring the speed of sound. [O3]

Consolidate and apply

- Ask the students to **complete** Worksheet 1.6.13, which will consolidate the learning from their practical work, and also introduce the topic of echo sounding. [O1, 2&3]
- Working in pairs, ask the students to **prepare a short presentation** for a group of fishermen, **explaining** to them how sonar works by using an echo to measure the distance to a shoal of fish. [O2&3]

Extend

- Ask students able to progress further to use ideas about particles to **explain** why sound might travel much more slowly through air than through water.

Plenary suggestions

What's the order? Muddle up the following statements about sonar and ask the students to put them in the correct order. You could display them on the board or issue them as a card sort.

- Pulses of sound are produced by the echo sounder of the sonar system.
- Each pulse travels to the sea bed.
- The pulses reflect off the sea bed.
- The pulses travel back to the sonar system. The sonar system calculates the distance to the sea bed.

Answers to Student Book questions

1. Sound waves bounce off a surface to make an echo.
2. Anywhere sound cannot bounce back – e.g. across an ocean, or where soft surfaces absorb much of the sound.
3. Use a solid barrier a known distance from where a sound is made; measure the time taken for the echo to reach the person making the sound; the speed of sound is double the distance divided by the time taken.
4. speed = (1500 × 2) ÷ 10 = 300 m/s
5. distance = speed × half recorded time = 330 × (3.5 ÷ 2) = 577.5 m
6. distance = speed × half recorded time = 1500 × (2 ÷ 2) = 1500 m
7. distance = speed × half recorded time = 1500 × (5 ÷ 2) = 3750 m

Answers to Worksheet 1.6.13

1. a) a reflection of sound
   b) The sound waves bounced off the steel sheet back to Peter.
   c) *accurate*: measure distance exactly using a metre ruler; *reliable*: repeat until three consistent results are obtained
   d) speed of sound = total distance travelled by the echo ÷ time taken = (600 × 2) ÷ 4 = 300 m/s
2. a) longer time; further to travel
   b) Any sensible answer: e.g. deep water is hard to se through because light is absorbed quickly; the surface has waves; it is hard to judge distances through water.
   c) The reflections come from the fish instead of the seabed; the fish swim above the seabed.
   d) The times would keep changing from long to short; depending on the positions of the shoals.
   e) Provide access to the internet, or books, for the students to carry out their own research.
3. a) distance travelled = speed of sound × time taken
   b) total distance travelled = 1500 × 0.1 = 150 m; distance to shoal = half the total distance travelled = 75 m
   c) time taken = total distance travelled ÷ speed
   d) time taken = (21 000 × 2) ÷ 1500 = 28 s

6.14 Understanding how sound travels through materials

Lesson overview

Learning objectives

- Recognise how the speed of sound changes in different substances.
- Use the particle model to explain why there are differences when sound travels through solids, liquids and gases.

Learning outcomes

- Describe the effects of different materials on the transmission of sound. [O1]
- Use the particle model to explain why sound cannot travel through a vacuum. [O2]
- Use the particle model to explain why the speed of sound is different in different materials. [O3]

Skills development

- Thinking scientifically: use models
- Working scientifically: develop explanations
- Learner development: communicate effectively

Resources needed graph paper; equipment as detailed in the Technician's notes; Worksheet 1.6.14; Practical sheet 1.6.14; Technician's notes 1.6.14

Common misconceptions Sound cannot travel through solids and liquids. Sound can pass through a vacuum.

Key vocabulary particle, vacuum, hypothesis

Teaching and learning

Engage

- Show the students a video of whales communicating under the sea. Discuss how this communication is possible. Students could imagine being in a swimming pool. Could they hear sounds under the water? If so, how is this possible? [O1]
- They should **share their ideas** about how sounds can be heard under water, and the method by which sound waves travel through liquids and solids. [O1]

Challenge and develop

- Demonstrate an electric bell in a bell jar attached to a vacuum pump as outlined in Technician's notes 1.6.14. Alternatively, show a video of this experiment. Explore what a vacuum is and why it is not possible to hear sounds through this medium. [O2]
- Set up the three experiments on Practical sheet 1.6.14. Working in pairs, the students try out each experiment in turn. These demonstrate that sounds travel best through solids, then liquids and then gases. [O1&3]
  - Experiment 1 involves making two versions of a 'string telephone' – one with string and one without. Ask the students to **compare** how well sound is transmitted through the air and through the string. [O1]
  - In Experiment 2, students put a battery-operated radio or buzzer under water in a polythene bag. They listen to sounds travelling under water, using a hydrophone. [O1]
  - In Experiment 3 one student taps a long metal rod gently at one end, while their partner listens with one ear close to the rod to try to hear the softest tap. This is repeated using a wooden rod. Students need to be careful to keep the source of sound as consistent as possible for meaningful results. [O1]
- Students should **record their observations** from each of the experiments. Take feedback and discuss what is happening in each case. [O1]

- Ask the students to **read** about the particle model of solids, liquids and gases in the third section of the Student Book and **relate these ideas** to their experiments. [O1, 2&3]

Explain

- Arrange the students in groups of six. They should use role play and/or draw particle diagrams to **explain** why there is a difference in the speed of sound in solids, liquids and gases – and why sound does not travel in a vacuum. [O1, 2&3]

  Higher-attaining students could **explain** how sound-proofing windows are designed, using ideas about particles. [O2&3]

Consolidate and apply

- Ask the students to answer the differentiated questions on Worksheet 1.6.14. [O1, 2&3]

Extend

- Students able to progress further can use the particle model to **explain** why the speed of sound in lead is so much lower than its speed in steel (see Table 1.6.14 in the Student Book). [O3]

Plenary suggestions

Challenge Pose questions linked to the lesson's work, such as 'Why can't we hear the Sun even though it is probably very noisy?' Or ask the students to explain the tag line in the film *Alien* – 'In space no one can hear you scream.'

True/false quiz Provide the students with ten statements about sound travel and ask them to say if the statements are true or false.

Answers to Student Book questions

1. There are no particles; so the energy from the vibrations cannot be passed on.
2. Solids contain particles that can vibrate; so the energy from the vibrations can be transferred.
3. a) diamond b) carbon dioxide c) fastest in solids
4. Ice; the particles are closely packed in fixed positions about which they can vibrate and pass on the vibrations to their neighbours. In liquid water the particles are randomly arranged and do not affect one another as strongly. (In reality the speed depends on the level of impurities.)
5. The particles may be closer together; may have stronger elastic forces; may have more vibrational energy.
6. The higher the temperature, the more energy the particles will have; so more frequent, more energetic collisions with their neighbours are likely to happen; so the faster the sound energy will pass.

Answers to Worksheet 1.6.14

1. a) bar graph drawn; material on *x*-axis, speed and units on *y*-axis, suitable scale, correct bars plotted, bars equally spaced

   b) a space with no particles

   c) Sound needs particles in order to carry the vibrational energy; if there are no particles there is no way for the energy to be transferred.
2. a) Sound travels fastest through solids, then liquids; and slowest through gases.

   b) In solids the particles are very close together and linked through elastic forces, and so can pass the sound on faster; in gases the particles are much further apart and collide much less frequently and it takes longer for the sound energy to be carried.
3. This is an opportunity to relate the particle model to real life. Look for clarity and accuracy in explanations and diagrams. Essentially the points to be made are as those in question 2b); the particles in the solid metal rail are packed closely together; and there are many collisions between neighbouring particles when they vibrate; this enables the energy from the vibration to be passed on very quickly. Tthe far more widely spaced air particles collide much less frequently; so carrying the sound of the train more slowly.

6.15 Learning about the reflection and absorption of sound

Lesson overview

Learning objectives

- Recognise which materials affect the quality of sound.
- Analyse the effect of different materials on sound waves.
- Use ideas about energy transfer to explain how soundproofing works.

Learning outcomes

- Name materials that reflect and absorb sound. [O1]
- Design an investigation and collect evidence about the ability of different materials to reflect and absorb sound. [O2]
- Explain why some materials are good at reflecting and absorbing sound. [O3]

Skills development

- Thinking scientifically: ask questions
- Working scientifically: design investigations
- Learner development: collaborate effectively

Resources needed equipment and materials as detailed in the Technician's notes; Worksheet 1.6.15; Practical sheet 1.6.15; Technician's notes 1.6.15

Common misconceptions All materials reflect sound equally.

Key vocabulary reflect, absorb, soundproofing

Teaching and learning

Engage

- Ask the students to imagine being in a room where there is a party going on. Ask:
  - Why is the sound we hear much quieter if we go into the room next door?
  - Where has the energy been transferred to?

  Establish that much of the sound in the party room is absorbed by the items in the room, and that some is reflected from the walls – only the remainder is transmitted through the wall to the room next door. [O1]
- Then ask 'What would the sound be like in the corridor if the door was open?', 'How does sound get round corners?'. Bring out ideas that sound travels in all directions, and some materials are good at reflecting the path of the sound waves. [O1]

Challenge and develop

- Group the students in fours and provide them with Practical sheet 1.6.15 and the materials outlined in Technician's notes 1.6.15. Ask them to **design an investigation** to find out how well different surfaces absorb or reflect sound. If possible supply each group with a decibel meter. [O2]
- Ask groups to share their ideas about how they intend to control key variables, and what they will measure. Discuss any points arising, and establish how to collect accurate, valid and reliable evidence. [O2]
- Allow the groups to **carry out** their investigation and collect results. [O2]
- In their groups, ask the students to **develop their own hypothesis** about why some materials absorb sound and others reflect it. [O1, 2&3]

- The students **share** and **discuss** results and hypotheses. Use the Student Book to explain how materials behave when sound is incident on them and why some are better at absorbing sound than others. Ask them to answer questions 1–3 in the Student Book. [O1, 2&3]

Explain

- Ask the students to answer the questions on Worksheet 1.6.15. Task 2 asks them to draw an annotated diagram of a material that is effective at reflecting sound and one that is effective at absorbing sound. Ask pairs of students to **compare** and **contrast** the diagrams they have drawn, **explaining** the features of the materials that make them effective in what they do. [O2&3]

  Higher-attaining students should use the particle model in their explanation of energy absorption (task 3 of Worksheet 1.6.15). [O3]

Consolidate and apply

- **Pair talk** Ask the students to read the second and third sections of the Student Book. Show some images of concert halls, auditoriums and interiors of cars. Ask them to **discuss** in pairs all the surface features, **describing** the different types of materials and surface shapes they see, and **explaining** how they are used to good effect. [O1, 2&3]

Extend

- Ask students able to progress further to **evaluate** three different car interiors, **explaining** how effective each is at reducing sound and what improvements could be made. [O3]

Plenary suggestions

Learning triangle Ask the students to draw a large triangle with a smaller inverted triangle that just fits inside it (so they have four triangles). Ask them to **reflect on their learning** from the lesson and write in the outer three triangles: something they've seen, something they've done, something they've discussed. Then ask them to add in the central triangle something they've learned.

Alternatively, ask the students to tell a partner three things they have learned today, two things they have found hard and one thing they can put into practice from today's lesson.

Answers to Student Book questions

1. Sound waves do not travel through nor bounce back; energy from the waves is transferred to the surface material.
2. a) There would be an echo nearly as loud as the original sound.
   b) You would probably hear no echo; only the original sound.
3. For example: to stop too many echoes in places like concert halls; to reduce engine noise in cars and planes; to reduce traffic noise in houses and buildings.
4. a) a quieter reflected sound b) hardly any reflected sound
5. It is transferred to air particles and particles in the absorbing material by heat.
6. Any suitable design with different types of sound-absorbing material.

Answers to Worksheet 1.6.15

1. *Good absorbers*: cloth, egg boxes, foam, bubble wrap *Good reflectors*: concrete, metal, wood, glass, ceramic tiles
2. a) Hard, flat materials are good at reflecting sound.
   b) Materials with lots of air pockets are good at absorbing sound; the energy from the sound waves is trapped in the air pockets.
3. The idea of energy of sound transferring to heat as sound waves bounce around the air pockets; causing the particles of air to move around randomly, colliding with one another.

6.16 Hearing sounds

Lesson overview

Learning objectives

- Describe the structure and function of different parts of the ear.
- Explain how the ear is able to hear and detect sounds.

Learning outcomes

- Name different parts of the ear. [O1]
- Explain how parts of the ear are adapted to enable us to hear. [O2]
- Compare and contrast detection of sound by the ear and by a microphone. [O3]

Skills development

- Thinking scientifically: use models
- Working scientifically: develop explanations
- Learner development: collaborate effectively

Resources needed mini-whiteboards; equipment and materials as detailed in the Technician's notes; Worksheet 1.6.16; Practical sheet 1.6.16; Technician's notes 1.6.16

Common misconceptions The ear is simply the part outside our head that we can see.

Key vocabulary ear canal, ear drum, ossicles, cochlea, auditory nerve

Teaching and learning

Engage

- Ask for silence. When it is quiet, ask the students to **identify** any noises they can hear, and if possible the direction from which the sound is coming from, and write these on a mini-whiteboard. This should demonstrate how sensitive their hearing is, and that we are surrounded by background noise all the time. Point out that two ears used together allow us to identify the direction from which a sound is coming. [O1]

Challenge and develop

- Show the students a model of the ear. Point out how the outer ear (the visible part) is linked to the middle ear by the ear canal and the ear drum, and how the middle ear connects to the inner ear. Use the Student Book to discuss all the different parts of the ear and their functions. [O1&2]

  Give extra support if needed, using an online animation of how the ear works.

- Ask the students to complete task 1 of Worksheet 1.6.16. [O1]
- Give out Practical sheet 1.6.16, which asks students to **make a model** of the ear. This lends itself to small group work. Provide each group with a balloon, a sheet of card, a cardboard tube and some sticky tape. The practical sheet also has some questions. [O1&2]
- Ask the students to **read** about the adaptations of the ear and how it works, in the third section of the Student Book, complete task 2 of Worksheet 1.6.16 and question 5 in the Student Book. [O2]

  Higher-attaining students can attempt task 3 of Worksheet 1.6.16, which gives a diagram of a microphone and asks them to **compare** and **contrast** the ear and the microphone. You may want them to produce a presentation to **explain** and **compare** the two systems of receiving and processing sound. [O3]

- Select different students to show their ear models. Ask those who have compared the ear with the microphone to **present their ideas** and take questions. [O1, 2&3]

Explain

- Ask the students to **imagine** they are a sound wave. Ask them to write a story to **explain** what happens to them as they pass through each part of the ear. They can refer to the flow chart in Figure 1.6.16c in the Student Book to help them. [O1&2]

Lower-attaining students should name all the parts of the ear correctly. [O1]

Higher-attaining students should **explain** how each part of the ear is adapted to do its job. [O2]

Consolidate and apply

- Ask the students to think about which parts of the ear can be affected when people become deaf, and about possible causes of deafness. They can **discuss** this in pairs. [O1]
- **Pairs to fours** Ask the pairs to share their ideas with another pair. Then take feedback from selected groups.

Extend

- Ask students able to progress further to **research** how an animal without an outer ear, such as an insect or a fish, detects sound and to **compare** their hearing system with ours. [O2&3]

Plenary suggestions

What am I? Think of a part of the ear. Prompt students to ask questions that can only be answered by 'Yes' or 'No', to try to guess which part of the ear it is. [O1]

Answers to Student Book questions

1. *outer ear*: to receive sound waves; *middle ear*: to make the vibrations bigger; *inner ear*: to convert sound vibrations into electrical signals
2. For example: so they are near the brain, for electrical signals to be interpreted quickly; so we can capture as many sounds as possible because they are high up.
3. Some sound vibrations are very small; energy will be lost in travelling through the ear.
4. a) cochlea b) ossicles c) ear drum
5. When the sound vibrations go from a large surface area to a small surface area, they are amplified.

Answers to Worksheet 1.6.16

1. A: ear canal; B: ossicles; C: semicircular canals; D: auditory nerve; E: cochlea; F: ear drum
2. a) Ear drum: very tight but slightly elastic; so it can move according to the vibrations given; the tighter it is the more sensitive it will be to fine vibrations.

   b) Ossicles: these three bones are connected but able to move; the movement of one bone affects the others. They have a much smaller surface area compared to the ear drum, enabling the sound waves to be amplified.

   c) Cochlea: filled with fluid which moves with vibrations of the sound waves. Tiny hairs on the surface send electrical signals to the auditory nerve.
3. a) *Ear*: sound waves are funnelled into the ear canal

   Microphone: sound waves are incident on the diaphragm

   b) *Ear*: vibrations of the ear drum are passed on to the ossicles

   Microphone: sound waves are converted an electrical signal; and passed on to an electronic amplifying unit

   c) *Ear*: vibrations of the ossicles are passed to the cochlea; where special cells convert the vibrations to an electric signal; for transmitting to the brain via the auditory nerve

   Microphone: vibrations of the diaphragm cause a coil of wire to vibrate in the field of a magnet; which produces an electrical signal for transmission onwards

6.17 Understanding factors affecting hearing

Lesson overview

Learning objectives

- Describe factors which affect hearing.
- Explain how to prevent damage to ears.
- Understand the term hearing range.

Learning outcomes

- Describe what is meant by the loudness of sound and how we can protect ourselves from loud sounds. [O1]
- Describe different ways the ear may become damaged and possible solutions to these problems. [O2]
- Use a knowledge of the structure of the ear to explain how to prevent damage to the ear; use data to identify the hearing ranges of different organisms [O3]

Skills development

- Thinking scientifically: ask questions
- Working scientifically: develop explanations
- Learner development: respect others

Resources needed mini-whiteboards; signal generator; loudspeaker; model ear; Worksheet 1.6.17

Common misconceptions Noise pollution is annoying but harmless.

Key vocabulary loudness, ear defenders, frequency, hearing range

Teaching and learning

Engage

- Hand out mini-whiteboards or pieces of paper. Write a list of sounds on the board and ask the students, working in pairs, to put them in order of loudness. For example the following sounds, but jumbled in order of loudness:
    - rock concert
    - MP3 player
    - heavy traffic nearby
    - average road traffic at 25 m
    - classroom between lessons
    - normal conversation
    - whisper

  Compare the opinions of different groups as a class. [O1&2]
- Recap what is meant by the 'loudness' of a sound, and its unit. Show the actual loudness values of the sounds listed above (respectively, roughly 120 dB, 100 dB, 90 dB, 70 dB, 60 dB, 45 dB, 40 dB). (A fuller list is given on page 2 of Worksheet 1.6.17.) Remind the students how the loudness of sound waves depends on their amplitude. [O1&2]
- Show a video of workers in a quarry or other noisy workplace. Discuss safety aspects that prevent them from being exposed to too high a level of noise. The website www.dangerousdecibels.org can be referred to throughout this lesson. It has information, animations, games and photographs. [O2]

Challenge and develop

- Show the model of the ear again, and ask the students to use this and their knowledge of the ear's structure developed in the previous lesson, together with ideas from the Student Book, to **explore** what might go wrong in the ear and what might be done to prevent this. [O2&3]
- Recap what is meant by the 'frequency' of a wave (the number of waves produced per second, with the unit hertz (Hz) where 1 Hz = 1 wave per second). Demonstrate the (frequency) hearing range of people. Connect a signal generator to a loudspeaker and change the frequency of the signal produced. The students should be able to hear signals between 20 Hz (a low rumble) and 20 kHz (a high, faint sound). Introduce the term 'threshold' as the minimum pure sound that can be heard with no other sounds present. Avoid sustained loud low frequencies and high frequencies because both can cause some individuals to experience unpleasant sensations. You may not hear as high a frequency as the students can, because the ability to hear high frequencies decreases with age. Record the hearing range of the class. [O3]
- Show the students data about different hearing ranges for different animals (see Figure 1.6.17b in the Student Book). Ask the students to answer questions 5–7 from the Student Book. [O3]

Explain

- Ask the students to complete tasks 1 and 2 on Worksheet 1.6.17, **explaining** and **summarising** how our ears can be damaged. [O1&2]

Consolidate and apply

- Working in pairs, ask the students to **design** a leaflet or poster to inform people of the risks of hearing damage if exposed to loud noise, and how to minimise the risks (task 3 of Worksheet 1.6.17). They should incorporate learning from other lessons on sound, and on the structure of the ear. [O2&3]

Extend

- Ask students able to progress further to **evaluate** all the methods we have of reducing noise. They should **explain** the strengths of each method and its limitations. [O3]

Plenary suggestions

Hot seat Ask each student to **think up a question**, based on what has been covered in the sound topics. Select someone to put in the hot seat, and get the students to ask their question and say whether the given answer is correct or incorrect. [O1, 2&3]

Answers to Student Book questions

1. To avoid the ears being damaged by loud sounds.
2. sensible measures as identified in the Student Book
3. There is no way to replace damaged nerve cells or hair cells in the cochlea.
4. Elderly people and those who have been exposed to loud noise or have suffered ear infections.
5. 20 Hz to 20 000 Hz
6. One diagram showing many waves of short wavelength; the other with just a few waves of long wavelength, correctly annotated to explain frequency.
7. 10 Hz to just over 100 000 Hz

Answers to Worksheet 1.6.17

1. Suitable annotations and possible additional drawings – for example a ruptured ear drum.
2. a) As the decibel level increases, hearing is more likely to be damaged.
   b) As exposure time increases, hearing damage worsens.
   c) Hearing protection will prevent their employees developing hearing loss.
3. Posters or leaflets should include all relevant points relating to noisy environments – using ear defenders and so on.

6.18 Finding out about sounds we cannot hear

Lesson overview

Learning objectives

- Recognise what is meant by ultrasound and infrasound.
- Describe some applications for ultrasound and infrasound.
- Explain how some applications work.

Learning outcomes

- Describe the range of sounds relating to ultrasound and infrasound. [O1]
- Describe a wide range of applications for ultrasound and infrasound. [O2]
- Explain why these waves are suitable for their applications. [O3]

Skills development

- Thinking scientifically: ask questions
- Working scientifically: develop explanations
- Learner development: communicate effectively

Resources needed mini-whiteboards; signal generator; loudspeaker; oscilloscope; poster paper; sticky notes; Worksheet 1.6.18

Common misconceptions Ultrasound is very loud sound.

Key vocabulary infrasound, ultrasound, scan

Teaching and learning

Engage

- Use a signal generator, loudspeaker and oscilloscope to demonstrate the ultrasound and infrasound regions. Do not play sounds of very high or low frequency for more than brief periods. Explore the fact that ultrasound and infrasound are sounds that humans cannot hear, but other animals can hear and use effectively. [O1]
- Hand out mini-whiteboards or pieces of paper. Ask the students to draw waves to represent infrasound, 'normal' sound that we can hear and ultrasound. [O1]

Challenge and develop

- Show a video of bats or dolphins using ultrasound and, if possible, one of elephants or giraffes using infrasound. [O2]
- **Pair work** Ask pairs of students to carry out tasks 1 and 2 on Worksheet 1.6.18. Task 2 requires them to **research** one use of ultrasound or infrasound and prepare a poster. They can use information from the Student Book and you can direct them to suitable websites, such as www.gcse.com/waves/ultrasound.htm, which covers some basic uses and is not too advanced. Ensure that all the uses (cleaning teeth / jewellery / components; medical scanning; physiotherapy; inspecting pipes/metal components; predicting volcanoes and earthquakes) are covered by the class. The emphasis should be on accurate information presented in an accessible way. Good use of pictures is important, and enforce an absence of text copied from a website. You could show students good examples of educational posters as exemplars. [O2]

  Higher-attaining students should **explain** why these waves are effective for their jobs (task 3 on Worksheet 1.6.18). [O3]
- Ask the students to display their posters. Provide pairs with sticky notes and ask them to write a comment about what is good in each of the posters and one thing that could be improved. Provide some 'improvement time' for students to address the comments. [O2]

Explain

- Ask the students to **explain** the answer to the question 'Which is the most useful type of sound wave in our everyday lives – ultrasound or infrasound?'. Ask for the inclusion of evidence to support answers. [O2&3]

Consolidate and apply

- Ask the students to **write a summary** of all the applications of ultrasound and infrasound. [O2&3]

Extend

- Ask students able to progress further to **research** piezoelectric crystals (ultrasound transducers) further and to **design** a model to explain how they work.

Plenary suggestions

Mind map Ask the students to produce a mind map of all their learning about sound, using all the key vocabulary from the Student Book and linking the ideas together.

Answers to Student Book questions

1. a) 20 times lower than the lowest frequency a human can hear; 1 Hz b) infrasound
   c) Our ears are not sensitive enough.
2. Two of: scanning unborn babies for problems; scanning aircraft parts; removing kidney stones; detecting vocanic eruptions; tracking meteors
3. 'Normal' sound has a lower frequency; there are not enough waves per second; so not enough energy is transferred to carry these tasks out.
4. Energy by electric current is transferred to energy by vibration; the reflected ultrasound waves transfer energy by vibration to the crystal; which transfers this to energy by electric current. The energy by electric current is transferred to energy by light in forming the image.
5. They can be detected as as vibrations by a quartz (piezoelectric) crystal and displayed on an oscilloscope.

Answers to Worksheet 1.6.18

1. range; 20 000; frequency; pitch; dogs; ultrasound; infrasound

6.19 Checking students' progress

The *Checking your progress* section in the Student Book indicates the key ideas developed in this chapter and shows how students progress to more complex levels. It is provided to support students in:

- identifying those ideas
- developing a sense of their current level of understanding
- developing a sense what the next steps in their learning are.

It is designed either to be used at the end of a chapter to support an overall view of the progress, or alternatively during the teaching of the chapter. Students can self assess or peer assess using this as a basis.

It would be helpful if students can be encouraged to provide evidence from their understanding or their notes to support their judgments. In some cases it may be useful to explore the difference in the descriptors for a particular idea so that students can see what makes for a 'higher outcome'.

It may be useful with some descriptors to provide examples from the specific work done, such as an experiment undertaken or an explanation developed and recorded. If marking and feedback uses similar ideas and phrases this will enable students to relate specific marking to a more general sense of progress.

To make good progress in understanding science students need to focus on these ideas and skills:

Students who are making modest progress will be able to:	**Students who are making good progress will be able to:**	**Students who are making excellent progress will be able to:**
Recognise that energy is transferred by a range of different processes.	Interpret and draw energy transfer diagrams for a range of different energy transfers, including gravitational potential energy, elastic potential energy, chemical energy and electrical energy.	Use Sankey diagrams to explain a range of energy changes and demonstrate that all energy is always accounted for.
Identify simple energy transfers which involve gravitational potential energy, elastic potential energy and chemical energy.	Explain how energy is transferred using elastic, gravitational and chemical potential energy.	Analyse changes in gravitational potential energy in different situations, and compare the energy per gram of different fuels.
Recognise that work can be done by a force, and that the work done is equal to the energy transferred.	Calculate the work done in different situations, given the size of the force and the distance moved.	Explain how simple machines transfer energy in a way that offers an advantage.
Recognise what is meant by temperature and how it is measured.	Explain and make predictions about the direction of heat flow in different situations.	Explain the difference between temperature and heat.
Recognise that sound energy is transferred by waves and describe how sound waves are made in different situations.	Explain how longitudinal waves carry sound. Relate the terms frequency and amplitude to sounds.	Interpret and devise wave diagrams to represent sounds of different wavelength and amplitude.
Recognise an echo as a reflection of sound.	Describe how to measure the speed of sound, and how the speed of sound can be used in different applications to measure distances.	Use calculations to measure the speed of sound and the distance of objects in different applications, applying ideas about echoes.
Recognise that some materials are good at reflecting sound and others can absorb it.	Use the particle model to explain why sound cannot travel through a vacuum. Explain what is meant by reflection and absorption of sound.	Use the particle model to explain why the speed of sound is different in solids, liquids and gases, and how energy is transferred in the reflection and absorption of sound.
Recognise that different organisms hear differently. Name different parts of the human ear.	Explain how parts of the ear are adapted to enable us to hear. Describe what is meant by the term hearing range.	Compare and contrast the detection of sound by an ear and a microphone.
Describe what is meant by infrasound and ultrasound.	Describe a wide range of applications for ultrasound and infrasound.	Explain why these waves are suitable for their applications.

6.20 Answers to Student Book Questions

This table provides answers to the *Questions* section at the end of Chapter 6 of the Student Book. It also shows how different questions assess attainment in terms of the focus and style of a question as well as the context. Question level analysis can indicate students' proficiency in approaching different aspects of scientific understanding and different types of answer.

Q	**Answer**		**Focus**			**Style**			**Context**			
		Marks available	Knowledge & understanding	Application	Evaluation of evidence	Objective test question	Short written answer	Longer written answer	Energy transfers and work done	Fuels, combustion, heat and temperature	Sound waves	Applications of using sound waves
1	b	1	x			x			x			
2	d	1	x			x				x		
3	c	1	x			x					x	
4	Energy stored as gravitational potential energy is transferred by movement	1 1	x x				x x		x x			
5	Any two from: • making scans of foetuses • scanning other organs in the body • physiotherapy • cleaning equipment/ jewellery • identifying cracks in metal objects	2	x				x					x
6	Any two from: • gravitational potential energy; using height • elastic potential energy; stretching or compressing elastic materials or springs • chemical potential energy; combustion of chemicals transfers stored energy	2	x				x		x			
7	• Place a solid flat surface a known distance away and make a sound • Record the time taken for the echo to return • speed = distance ÷ time • Double the distance between the sound source and the wall	1 1 1 1	x x x x					x x x x				x x x x
8	c	1		x		x			x			
9	b	1		x		x					x	
10	d	1		x		x					x	

Chapter 6: Energy Transfers and Sound

Q	Answer		Focus			Style			Context			
		Marks available	Knowledge & understanding	Application	Evaluation of evidence	Objective test question	Short written answer	Longer written answer	Energy transfers and work done	Fuels, combustion, heat and temperature	Sound waves	Applications of using sound waves
11	Distance = speed × time = 330 × 0.5 = 165 m Distance from bat to prey = 165 ÷ 2 = 82.5 m	1 1		x x			x x					x x
12	Any two from: • gravitational potential energy is transferred by movement to the water • energy is transferred by movement of the turbine • energy is transferred by movement in the generator to energy by electricity	2		x			x		x			
13	a) Work done by top lever = 250 N × 0.1 m = 25 J work done by lower lever = 50 N × 0.5 m = 25 J b) The lower lever makes the work easier because the effort force is 5 times smaller	1 1 1 1		x x x x				x x x x	x x x x			
14	Hydrogen; with two reasons from: • high value of energy per gram • no carbon dioxide emission; carbon dioxide is a greenhouse gas that contributes to global warming • availability compared with fossil fuels	2			x		x			x		
15	Any four from: • Graph for age 60 years shows over 40% hearing loss at about 5000 Hz • There is no hearing loss up to age 20 • Graphs for ages 30–50 show less hearing loss at all frequencies than respective graphs for ages 40–60 • Nerves in the cochlea are most likely to be damaged as we get older • Hairs of the cochlea cells are most likely to be damaged as we get older • Ossicles can fuse as we get older	4			x			x			x	
	Total possible:	**30**	**13**	**11**	**6**	**6**	**12**	**12**	**12**	**3**	**7**	**8**

Scheme of Work

Teaching Key Stage 3 in three years

The following pages show the full plan out the scheme of work for Collins Key Stage 3 Science Teacher Pack 1 taught over 3 years.

Teaching Key Stage 3 in two years?

If you are using the Collins KS3 Science scheme to deliver the Programme of Study in two years there are three ways you can do it:

1. Focus on the lessons shaded in the table. By so doing you will have visited all the key ideas.
2. Use the shaded lessons as a starting point but draw on ideas, activities and questions as necessary, i.e., 'swapping out' the occasional activity on an indicated lesson.
3. Use the introductory lesson and/or the 'Applying key ideas' lesson to see what students are more confident with and what time would be better spent on.

Collins Connect is our digital learning platform that offers a range of linked resources to enhance your lessons.

Chapter 1: Cells – the Building Blocks of Life

Lesson	Lesson title	Overarching objectives	Learning objectives	CD-ROM resources	Collins Connect resources	Notes for two-year scheme
1.1.2	Historical ideas about living things	Cells as the fundamental unit of living organisms, including how to observe and record cell structure using a light microscope	Summarise some historical ideas about living things; explain how evidence can change ideas; select evidence to support or disprove ideas.	Worksheet 1.1.2	Quick starter; Slideshow: Historical ideas about living things; The Naked Scientist: How do plants know where to grow?	
1.1.3	Comparing plant and animal cells	Cells as the fundamental unit of living organisms, including how to observe and record cell structure using a light microscope The functions of the cell wall, cell membrane, cytoplasm, nucleus, vacuole, mitochondria and chloroplasts The similarities and differences between animal and plant cells	Develop models to explain the differences between animal and plant cells; record evidence using a microscope; communicate ideas about cells effectively using scientific terminology.	Worksheet 1.1.3a Worksheet 1.1.3b Practical sheet 1.1.3a Practical sheet 1.1.3b Technician's notes 1.1.3	Quick starter; Video: Common structures in animal and plant cells; Slideshow: Differences between animal and plant cells; Interactive activity: Animal or plant?; Ice-cream splat: Key vocabulary game	
1.1.4	Describing cells	The functions of the cell wall, cell membrane, cytoplasm, nucleus, vacuole, mitochondria and chloroplasts The similarities and differences between animal and plant cells	Classify specialised cells as animal or plant cells; describe different specialised animal and plant cells; explain the structure and function of specialised cells using models.	Worksheet 1.1.4	Quick starter; Interactive activity: Match the animal cells to their functions; Video: Specialised plant cells	
1.1.5	Understanding unicellular organisms	The structural adaptations of some unicellular organisms	Recognise different types of unicellular organisms; describe differences in unicellular organisms; compare and contrast the features of unicellular organisms.	Worksheet 1.1.5	Quick starter; Interactive activity: Prokaryotes and Eukaryotes ; Ice-cream splat: Key vocabulary game	May be reduced in scope

1.1.6	Understanding diffusion	The role of diffusion in the movement of materials in and between cells Diffusion in liquids and gases driven by differences in concentration	Describe the process of diffusion and its relation to the cell; plan a fair test investigation to explore the factors affecting diffusion; explain how the different factors speed up or slow down diffusion.	Worksheet 1.1.6 Practical sheet 1.1.6a Practical sheet 1.1.6b Practical sheet 1.1.6c Technician's notes 1.1.6	Quick starter; Interactive activity: How molecules of perfume move across a room; Slideshow: Understanding how factors affect the rate of diffusion; Interactive activity: Diffusion	
1.1.7	Understanding organisation in multicellular organisms	Hierarchical organisation of multicellular organisms: from cells to tissues to organs to systems to organisms	Define the terms tissues, organs and organ systems; explain the organisational structure in multicellular organisms; compare the strengths and weaknesses of multicellular organisms and single-celled organisms.	Worksheet 1.1.7	Quick starter; Interactive activity: Organisation in multicellular organisms; Interactive activity: How did cells evolve?; Ice-cream splat: Key vocabulary game	
1.1.8	Applying key ideas		Extract ideas about the structure of plant and animal cells from earlier topics using the context of skin; apply ideas about the adaptations of specialised animal cells using examples from cells in the skin; use ideas about information to explain the structure and differences between multicellular and unicellular organisms.	Worksheet 1.1.8a Worksheet 1.1.8b		
1.1.9	Comparing flowering plants	Reproduction in plants, including flower structure, wind and insect pollination	Describe the structure and function of parts in the flowering plant; explain why different plants have such diverse structures; evaluate the differences between wind-pollinated and insect-pollinated plants.	Worksheet 1.1.9	Quick starter; Interactive activity: Reproductive organs of flowers; Video: Attracting insects: bees collecting pollen	

1.1.10	Knowing how pollination leads to fertilisation	Reproduction in plants, including flower structure, wind and insect pollination, fertilisation	Describe the processes of pollination and fertilisation; analyse and present data on the growth of pollen tubes; explain factors that affect the growth of pollen tubes.	Worksheet 1.1.10 Practical sheet 1.1.10a Practical sheet 1.1.10b Technician's notes 1.1.10	Quick starter ; Interactive activity: How the fertilisation of a plant takes place	
1.1.11	Understanding the changes facing pollinators	The importance of plant reproduction through insect pollination in human food security	Describe the role of insects in crop production, using data; explain why bee populations are declining; make suggestions for increasing insect populations and hence crop production.	Worksheet 1.1.11	Quick starter; Video: What causes hay fever?; Interactive activity: Problems for Bees; Ice-cream splat: Key vocabulary game	
1.1.12	Understanding how seeds are dispersed by the wind	Reproduction in plants, including seed and fruit formation and dispersal	Recognise the variety of different structures shown by different seeds; describe the need for plants to disperse their seed; plan an investigation into seed dispersal by wind.	Worksheet 1.1.12a Worksheet 1.1.12b	Quick starter; Interactive activity: Seed dispersal; Video: A dandelion opens up and the seeds disperse	
1.1.13	Understanding how fruits disperse seeds	Reproduction in plants, including seed and fruit formation and dispersal, including quantitative investigation of some dispersal mechanisms	Describe how fruits are used in seed dispersal; compare evidence about seed dispersal by wind and by fruit formation; use data to evaluate different seed dispersal mechanisms.	Worksheet 1.1.13	Quick starter	
1.1.14	Understanding the male reproductive system	Reproduction in humans (as an example of a mammal), including the structure and function of the male and female reproductive systems	Describe the structure and function of different parts of the male reproductive system; compare plant and human male reproductive structures; summarise the strengths and weaknesses of the human and plant male reproductive systems.	Worksheet 1.1.14a Worksheet 1.1.14b	Quick starter	

1.1.15	Understanding the female reproductive system and fertility	Reproduction in humans (as an example of a mammal), including the structure and function of the male and female reproductive systems, menstrual cycle (without details of hormones), gametes, fertilisation, gestation and birth	Describe the structure and function of different parts of the female reproductive system; explain the process of fertilisation; explain problems of infertility and how they might be treated.	Worksheet 1.1.15a Worksheet 1.1.15b	Quick starter; Interactive activity: The process of fertilisation in humans; Interactive activity: In vitro fertilisation; Video: IVF ethics; Ice-cream splat: Key vocabulary game	
1.1.16	Learning about changes in puberty	Reproduction in humans (as an example of a mammal), including the menstrual cycle (without details of hormones)	Recognise changes in the male and female body during puberty; describe the process of menstruation; explain how some problems with menstruation occur.	Worksheet 1.1.16	Quick starter; Interactive activity: What changes happen in puberty?; Slideshow: Infertility problems and solutions	
1.1.17	Learning how a foetus develops	Reproduction in humans (as an example of a mammal), fertilisation, gestation and birth	Recognise the process of growth; use data to show how the embryo grows during gestation; compare and contrast the pregnant uterus with normal uterus.	Worksheet 1.1.17	Quick starter; Interactive activity: Different stages of human development; Slideshow: The menstrual cycle	
1.1.18	Understanding factors affecting a developing foetus	Reproduction in humans (as an example of a mammal), to include the effect of maternal lifestyle on the foetus through the placenta	Describe the effects of different factors on the developing foetus; evaluate the strength of data.	Worksheet 1.1.18	Quick starter; Slideshow: The effects of substances on the foetus; Ice-cream splat: Key vocabulary game	

Chapter 2: Eating, Drinking and Breathing						
1.2.2	Exploring a healthy diet	Content of a healthy human diet: carbohydrates, lipids (fats and oils), proteins, vitamins, minerals, dietary fibre and water, and why each is needed	Describe the components of a healthy diet; examine the importance of each component of a healthy diet; evaluate the quality of evidence contained in advertising about a healthy diet.	Worksheet 1.2.2	Quick starter Slideshow: The seven food groups; Interactive activity: Drag the foods into the correct food groups; The Naked Scientist: How does the digestive system work?	

1.2.3	Testing foods		Test foods for starch, sugars, protein and fat; predict the results of food tests for a range of foods; evaluate the risks involved in carrying out food tests.	Worksheet 1.2.3 Practical sheet 1.2.3 Technician's notes 1.2.3	Quick starter; Slideshow: Food tests; Interactive activity: Match the food group to the test	
1.2.4	Comparing energy needs	Calculations of energy requirements in a healthy daily diet Comparing energy values of different foods (from labels) (kJ)	Describe how we use energy from food; compare the energy requirements of people of different ages and lifestyles; analyse numerical data about energy contents of foods.	Worksheet 1.2.4	Quick starter; Interactive activity: How much energy? ; Video: Sugary drinks	
1.2.5	Exploring obesity and starvation	The consequences of imbalances in the diet including obesity, starvation and deficiency diseases	Describe the physical effects of eating too much and eating too little; explain the physical effects of obesity and starvation; compare how deaths from obesity and starvation have changed over time.	Worksheet 1.2.5	Quick starter; Interactive activity: Starvation and obesity; Video: Eating disorders	
1.2.6	Understanding deficiency diseases		Identify the causes and effects of some deficiencies in the diet; suggest which foods could prevent well-known deficiencies; plan ways of communicating ideas about preventing deficiency diseases.	Worksheet 1.2.6	Quick starter; Slideshow: Vitamin and mineral deficiencies; Interactive activity: Deficiency diseases; Ice-cream splat: Key vocabulary game	
1.2.7	Understanding the human digestive system	The tissues and organs of the digestive system, including adaptations to function	Identify the organs of the human digestive system; explain the role of digestion; analyse links between digestion and the circulatory system.	Worksheet 1.2.7	Quick starter; Interactive activity: Foods' journey through the body; Video: Rotating model of the human digestion system	

1.2.8	Investigating the start of digestion	The tissues and organs of the digestive system, including adaptations to function and how the digestive system digests food (enzymes simply as biological catalysts)	Describe what is meant by chemical and physical digestion; explain how teeth and saliva are adapted to digestion; suggest how results can demonstrate that digestion begins in the mouth.	Worksheet 1.2.8	Quick starter; Slideshow: Types of teeth; Interactive activity: Match the type of teeth to their function	
1.2.9	Understanding the roles of the digestive system	The tissues and organs of the digestive system, including adaptations to function	Describe the roles of the oesophagus, stomach, intestine and pancreas in digestion; explain how the structure of each of the organs is adapted to its function.	Worksheet 1.2.9 Technician's notes 1.2.9	Quick starter; Slideshow: Movement of food through the digestive system; Interactive activity: Drag the adaptation into the correct organ; Ice-cream splat: Key vocabulary game	
1.2.10	Applying key ideas		Extract ideas from the text about diet and digestion in other animals; use information about the structure of other digestive systems to show how they are adapted to their function; apply ideas about digestive systems to the efficiency of digestion in different animals.	Worksheet 1.2.10		
1.2.11	Introducing enzymes	How the digestive system digests food (enzymes simply as biological catalysts)	Describe role of different enzymes in digestion; analyse a model of the digestive system; explain observations of a practical activity to explore the role of enzymes.	Worksheet 1.2.11 Practical sheet 1.2.11 Technician's notes 1.2.11	Quick starter; Slideshow: The role of enzymes in digestion; Interactive activity: Digestive enzymes	
1.2.12	Recognising the role of bacteria	The importance of bacteria in the human digestive system	Describe the role of bacteria in our digestive system; explain how the natural flora of bacteria can be disturbed; analyse data about the effects of antibiotics on gut bacteria.	Worksheet 1.2.12	Quick starter; Interactive activity: Bacteria in the gut; Video: Fighting the superbugs; Ice-cream splat: Key vocabulary game	

1.2.13	Understanding how we breathe	The mechanism of breathing to move air in and out of the lungs, using a pressure model to explain the movement of gases	Describe the mechanism of breathing in and out; evaluate a model of breathing; calculate changes in pressure and explain how these help us breathe.	Worksheet 1.2.13 Technician's notes 1.2.13	Quick starter; Slideshow: How do you breathe in and out?; Interactive activity: Breathing in and out; Interactive activity: A bell jar model to demonstrate breathing	Include the practical activity exploring lung volume from lesson 1.2.14
1.2.14	Measuring breathing	The mechanism of breathing to move air in and out of the lungs, including simple measurements of lung volume	Describe what is meant by lung volume and identify some simple methods to measure it; identify independent, dependent and control variables in a lung-volume investigation; interpret and evaluate data linked to lung volume.	Worksheet 1.2.14 Technician's notes 1.2.14 Practical sheet 1.2.14	Quick starter; Interactive activity: A method you can use to measure lung volume	
1.2.15	Evaluating gas exchange in humans	The structure and functions of the gas exchange system in humans, including adaptations to function	Describe the features of the human gas exchange system; explain how the features enable gases to be exchanged; evaluate how well adapted the human gas exchange system is to its function.	Worksheet 1.2.15	Quick starter ; Interactive activity: How oxygen gets into the bloodstream; Video: Our gas exchange system	
1.2.16	Investigating diffusion	The structure and functions of the gas exchange system in humans, including adaptations to function Diffusion in liquids and gases driven by differences in concentration Diffusion in terms of the particle model	Explain how diffusion makes breathing possible; observe the effects of diffusion; apply diffusion to our breathing system and ask questions to develop understanding.	Worksheet 1.2.16 Technician's notes 1.2.16	Quick starter; Interactive activity: Diffusion: Match the term to its meaning; Slideshow: Diffusion: An explanation	

1.2.17	Exploring the effects of disease and lifestyle	The impact of exercise, asthma and smoking on the human gas exchange system	Describe the physical effects of disease and lifestyle on the breathing system; explain the physical effects of disease and lifestyle on the breathing system; describe how our understanding of the effects of smoking has changed over time.	Worksheet 1.2.17 Technician's notes 1.2.17	Quick starter; Interactive activity: The symptoms caused by smoking and asthma; Video: Hospital patients smoking; Ice-cream splat: Key vocabulary game	
Chapter 3: Mixing, Dissolving and Separating						
1.3.2	Working safely in a laboratory		Recognise and reduce risks when working in a laboratory; name and select appropriate equipment.	Worksheet 1.3.2	Quick starter; Video: Scientists working in a laboratory; Interactive activity: Measuring, mixing or heating; The Naked Scientist: What causes my kettle to fur up?	
1.3.3	Recording experiments		Represent scientific experiments clearly; make and record accurate measurements.	Worksheet 1.3.3	Quick starter; Slideshow: Representing laboratory equipment; Interactive activity: Match the quantities to the correct apparatus	
1.3.4	Recognising materials, substances and elements	Differences between atoms, elements and compounds Chemical symbols and formulae for elements and compounds The concept of a pure substance	Recognise the difference between materials, substances and elements; identify elements by their names and symbols; explain what is meant by a chemically pure substance.	Worksheet 1.3.4	Quick starter; Interactive activity: Order the elements from most to least abundant	
1.3.5	Understanding water	The concept of a pure substance	Recognise the importance and different sources of water; explain the differences between types of water.	Worksheet 1.3.5 Practical sheet 1.3.5 Technician's notes 1.3.5	Quick starter; Interactive activity: Water facts; Slideshow: Ice, water and steam	

1.3.6	Dissolving	Mixtures, including dissolving	Explain the terms solvent, solution, solute and soluble; identify factors that affect dissolving; explain the difference between a dilute solution and a concentrated solution.	Worksheet 1.3.6 Practical sheet 1.3.6 Technician's notes 1.3.6	Quick starter; Interactive activity: Sucrose solutions; Ice-cream splat: Key vocabulary game	
1.3.7	Separating mixtures	Mixtures, including dissolving Simple techniques for separating mixtures: filtration	Recognise the differences between substances and use these to separate them.	Worksheet 1.3.7	Quick starter; Video: Using size to separate mixtures: Panning for gold; Slideshow: Sieving for a reason; Interactive activity: Steps for separating a mixture of salt and sand	
1.3.8	Dissolving and evaporating	Mixtures, including dissolving Simple techniques for separating mixtures: evaporation	Separate a soluble substance from water; form crystals from solutions; explain solubility.	Worksheet 1.3.8	Quick starter; Video: Salt crystallizing under microscope; Interactive activity: Drag the quantity into the saturated solution	
1.3.9	Extracting salt		Identify sources of salt and describe how it is extracted; recognise the uses and importance of salt; obtain pure salt from a mixture.	Worksheet 1.3.9 Practical sheet 1.3.9a Practical sheet 1.3.9b Practical sheet 1.3.9c Technician's notes 1.3.9	Quick starter; Slideshow: Seawater and salt mines; Interactive activity: Extracting salt	
1.3.10	Understanding distillation	Simple techniques for separating mixtures: distillation	Use distillation to separate substances; explain why distillation can purify substances.	Worksheet 1.3.10a Worksheet 1.3.10b Practical sheet 1.3.10 Technician's notes 1.3.10	Quick starter; Interactive activity: Order the steps for distillation; Ice-cream splat: Key vocabulary game	

1.3.11	Applying key ideas		Extract ideas about water being hard from the text; extract ideas about solubility to explain some of the implications of the concept; use ideas and information about elements, compounds and formulae to explain the properties of chemicals.			
1.3.12	Finding out what air is made of	Simple techniques for separating mixtures: distillation The composition of the atmosphere	Describe the composition of air; separate gases from air.	Worksheet 1.3.12	Quick starter; Slideshow: Discovering the gases that make up air; Interactive activity: What is air made of?; Video: Ash cloud from Iceland volcano	
1.3.13	Exploring chromatography	Simple techniques for separating mixtures: chromatography The identification of pure substances	Use chromatography to separate dyes.	Worksheet 1.3.13	Quick starter; Interactive activity: Chromatography; Slideshow: Useful chromatography	
1.3.14	Using chromatography	Simple techniques for separating mixtures: chromatography	Use chromatography to identify unknown substances; draw conclusions from evidence.	Worksheet 1.3.14 Practical sheet 1.3.14 Technician's notes 1.3.14	Quick starter; Video: Chromatography and King Richard III	May be combined with 1.3.13
1.3.15	Finding the best solvent	Mixtures, including dissolving Simple techniques for separating mixtures: chromatography	Choose the best solvent; recognise hazards when using solvents.	Worksheet 1.3.15 Technician's notes 1.3.15	Quick starter; Interactive activity: Solvents	
1.3.16	Modelling mixtures and separation	Mixtures, including dissolving Conservation of mass, changes of state and chemical reactions	Explain what happens to mass during dissolving; use a circle model to explain dissolving and separation.	Worksheet 1.3.16	Quick starter; Slideshow: Dissolving: A simple model; Interactive activity: Modelling dissolving; Ice-cream splat: Key vocabulary game	

Chapter 4: Elements, Compounds and Reactions

1.4.2	Finding elements and building the Periodic Table	Chemical symbols and formulas for elements and compounds	Identify where and how different elements were found; recognise differences between elements; recognise that the Periodic Table has changed over time.	Worksheet 1.4.2	Quick starter; Slideshow: When were elements discovered?; Interactive activity: Abundance by mass in the Earth's crust; The Naked Scientist: What are atoms and elements?	
1.4.3	Looking at the Periodic Table of elements	The principles underpinning the Mendeleev Periodic Table The Periodic Table: periods and groups; metals and non-metals	Navigate the Periodic Table and identify some of the elements; identify features of the Periodic Table and describe how it is organised; explain why the Periodic Table is useful.	Worksheet 1.4.3a Worksheet 1.4.3b Practical sheet 1.4.3 Technician's notes 1.4.3	Quick starter; Interactive activity: Match elements to their chemical symbol	
1.4.4	Understanding elements and atoms	Differences between atoms, elements and compounds Chemical symbols and formulae for elements and compounds	Interpret chemical symbols; explain what is meant by 'element' and 'atom'; work out the composition of different substances based on their names.	Worksheet 1.4.4 Practical sheet 1.4.4 Technician's notes 1.4.4	Quick starter; Interactive activity: Match elements to their atomic number; Slideshow: Names, symbols, numbers and masses; Ice-cream splat: Key vocabulary game	
1.4.5	Understanding metals	The varying physical and chemical properties of different elements The properties of metals and non-metals	Recognise the properties and uses of metals; identify differences between metals.	Worksheet 1.4.5 Practical sheet 1.4.5 Technician's notes 1.4.5	Quick starter; Video; Interactive activity: Match each element to how it reacts with air and water	
1.4.6	Understanding non-metals	The varying physical and chemical properties of different elements The properties of metals and non-metals	Identify uses of common non-metals; describe the properties of non-metals.	Worksheet 1.4.6 Practical sheet 1.4.6 Technician's notes 1.4.6	Quick starter; Slideshow: Allotropes of sulfur; Interactive activity: Drag the non-metals into the correct groups	

1.4.7	Identifying metalloids	The varying physical and chemical properties of different elements	Describe semi-metals and their properties; identify some common uses of semi-metals.	Worksheet 1.4.7	Quick starter; Slideshow: Sand and computers; Interactive activity: Metal, metalloid or non-metal?	
1.4.8	Discovering the origin of metals	The varying physical and chemical properties of different elements The properties of metals and non-metals Chemical symbols and formulae for elements and compounds	Recognise that metals have to be extracted from ores; evaluate the impact of extracting metals from the Earth.	Worksheet 1.4.8a Worksheet 1.4.8b Practical sheet 1.4.8 Technician's notes 1.4.8	Quick starter; Slideshow: Metals from their ores; Interactive activity: Metals are obtained from their ores	
1.4.9	Choosing elements for a purpose	The varying physical and chemical properties of different elements	Recognise the elements and their differences from physical data; use data and the properties of elements to choose suitable materials.	Worksheet 1.4.9	Quick starter; Ice-cream splat: Key vocabulary game	
1.4.10	Applying key ideas		Extract ideas about tin or other elements from the text, including earlier sections of the chapter; apply ideas about the properties of tin to explain some of its applications; use ideas and information about elements, compounds and formulas to explain the properties of chemicals.	Worksheet 1.4.10		
1.4.11	Combining elements	Differences between atoms, elements and compounds Chemical symbols and formulae for elements and compounds	Explain what is meant by a compound; recognise how compounds are formed and named; interpret the ratio of atoms and formula of compounds.	Worksheet 1.4.11 Practical sheet 1.4.11 Technician's notes 1.4.11	Quick starter; Interactive activity: Chlorides, oxides or carbonates; Interactive activity: Match the compounds to the correct atom ratio	
1.4.12	Using models to understand chemistry		Use a simple model to show the differences between atoms and molecules; use models to represent compounds.	Worksheet 1.4.12 Practical sheet 1.4.12	Quick starter; Interactive activity: Match the oxide to its coloured circle model	

1.4.13	Understanding what happens when an element burns	Chemical reactions as the rearrangement of atoms Representing chemical reactions using formulae and using equations Combustion	Make observations during chemical reactions; write word equations to demonstrate chemical changes; explain chemical changes using a model.	Worksheet 1.4.13 Practical sheet 1.4.13 Technician's notes 1.4.13	Quick starter; Interactive activity: Elements and compounds	
1.4.14	Observing how elements react in different ways	The varying physical and chemical properties of different elements Representing chemical reactions using formulae and using equations The chemical properties of metal and non-metal oxides with respect to acidity	Draw conclusions to explain observations; use symbols and models to describe a chemical reaction.	Worksheet 1.4.14a Worksheet 1.4.14b Practical sheet 1.4.14 Technician's notes 1.4.14	Quick starter; Video; Interactive activity: Reversible or irreversible; Ice-cream splat: Key vocabulary game	
1.4.15	Identifying the special features of carbon	The varying physical and chemical properties of different elements	Explain the importance of carbon in our lives; identify and explain the differences between an element and its compounds.	Worksheet 1.4.15 Practical sheet 1.4.15a Practical sheet 1.4.15b Technician's notes 1.4.15	Quick starter; Video; Slideshow: Hydrocarbons: What are they and what are they used for?; Interactive activity: Hydrocarbon, carbohydrate or carbonate?; Video: Plastic bags: Why might they cause problems?	
1.4.16	Understanding oxidation	Representing chemical reactions using formulae and using equations Oxidation	Describe oxidation; recognise the effects of oxidation; use data to support conclusions.	Worksheet 1.4.16 Practical sheet 1.4.16a Practical sheet 1.4.16b Technician's notes 1.4.16	Quick starter; Interactive activity: Most to least reactive	

1.4.17	Investigating carbonates	Conservation of mass changes of state and chemical reactions Combustion, thermal decomposition, oxidation Chemical symbols and formulae for elements and compounds Thermal decomposition	Describe the composition and uses of carbonate compounds; recognise and explain thermal decomposition reactions; identify carbon dioxide.	Worksheet 1.4.17 Practical sheet 1.4.17a Practical sheet 1.4.17b Technician's notes 1.4.17	Quick starter; Slideshow: Modelling the thermal decomposition of carbonates	
1.4.18	Explaining changes	Differences between atoms, elements and compounds Chemical symbols and formulae for elements and compounds Conservation of mass changes of state and chemical reactions Chemical reactions as the rearrangement of atoms Thermal decomposition, oxidation	Observe and explain mass changes; use scientific terms and simple models to explain chemical processes.	Worksheet 1.4.18	Quick starter; Interactive activity: Oxidation, thermal decomposition or dissolving; Interactive activity: Match the missing mass to the chemical equation; Ice-cream splat: Key vocabulary game	

Chapter 5: Forces and their Effects

1.5.2	Discovering forces	Forces as pushes or pulls arising from the interaction between two objects Using force arrows in diagrams	Recognise different examples of forces; list main types of force; represent forces using arrows.	Worksheet 1.5.2	Quick starter; Slideshow: Examples of forces and magnetism; Video: Felix Baumgartner's freefall from space; Interactive activity: Balanced or unbalanced?; The Naked Scientist: What does it take to put a man on the Moon?	
1.5.3	Measuring forces	Forces measured in newtons	Measure forces using newtonmeters; use correct unit for force; explain difference between mass and weight.	Worksheet 1.5.3 Practical sheet 1.5.3	Quick starter; Interactive activity: Forces definitions; Slideshow: How do we measure mass, and what is it?	May be combined with 1.5.2

1.5.4	Understanding weight on other planets	Gravity forces acting at a distance on Earth and in space	Explain the meaning of 'weightless'; investigate weight on the Moon and on different planets; identify the link between weight and gravitational attraction.	Worksheet 1.5.4	Quick starter; Slideshow: A look at Isaac Newton and his laws of gravity; Video: Diving on Earth and in space; Interactive activity: Order your weight on each planet	
1.5.5	Exploring the effects of forces	Forces being needed to cause objects to stop or start moving, or to change their speed or direction of motion	Identify and describe the effects of forces of different sizes and directions; predict and explain the changes caused by forces; explain the concept of force pairs (action and reaction).	Worksheet 1.5.5 Practical sheet 1.5.5 Technician's notes 1.5.5	Quick starter; Interactive activity: True or false?	
1.5.6	Understanding stretch and compression	Forces associated with deforming objects Measurements of stretch or compression as force is changed	Explain the relationship between applied force and the change of shape of an object; investigate forces involved in compressing and stretching materials; identify applications for compressible and stretchable materials.	Worksheet 1.5.6 Practical sheet 1.5.6 Technician's notes 1.5.6	Quick starter; Interactive activity: Stretch and compress	
1.5.7	Investigating Hooke's Law	Forces associated with deforming objects; stretching and squashing – springs Measurements of stretch or compression as force is changed Force–extension linear relation; Hooke's Law as a special case	Investigate the effects of applied forces on springs; generate data to produce a graph and analyse outcomes.	Worksheet 1.5.7 Practical sheet 1.5.7 Technician's notes 1.5.7	Quick starter; Slideshow: An introduction to Robert Hooke; Interactive activity: Match forces to the masses; Ice-cream splat: Key vocabulary game	
1.5.8	Understanding friction	Rubbing and friction forces between surfaces	Identify the force of friction between two objects; describe the effects of friction; understand that friction acts in the opposite direction to the direction of movement.	Worksheet 1.5.8	Quick starter; Interactive activity: Order the frictional forces	

1.5.9	Exploring the benefits of friction		Describe applications that make use of friction; design procedures for investigating the force of friction.	Worksheet 1.5.9	Quick starter; Slideshow: Get a grip; Video: Situations where sliding is bad; Interactive activity: Friction	
1.5.10	Understanding air and water resistance	Forces: pushing things out of the way; resistance to motion of air and water	Link frictional forces between surfaces to 'drag' between objects in a fluid; discuss examples of frictional drag in air and in water; consider the effects of friction on sky divers.	Worksheet 1.5.10	Quick starter; Slideshow: How about that: Galileo and his thought experiment; Interactive activity: Describe terminal velocity	
1.5.11	Discovering streamlining		Recognising natural and man-made examples of streamlining; link streamlining to fuel efficiency in vehicles; evaluate the use of data collected from investigations of drag.	Worksheet 1.5.11 Practical sheet 1.5.11 Technician's notes 1.5.11	Quick starter; Interactive activity: Streamlined or not streamlined?; Video: Fastest bike in the world; Ice-cream splat: Key vocabulary game	
1.5.12	Applying key ideas		Identify and represent forces in a range of situations, including less familiar ones; apply ideas about elastic behaviour; use ideas about forces and air resistance in an unfamiliar context to analyse problems.			
1.5.13	Exploring forces and motion	Forces being needed to cause objects to stop or start moving, or to change their speed or direction Balanced and unbalanced forces	Recognise that for an object to start moving there must be a force applied; describe the effects of balanced and unbalanced forces; explain the significance of balanced and unbalanced forces on a moving object.	Worksheet 1.5.13 Practical sheet 1.5.13	Quick starter; Interactive activity: Match the descriptions about speed	

1.5.14	Exploring how forces affect speed and direction	Change depending on direction of force and its size	Recognise that the size of a force determines the effect; recognise that the direction of a force determines the effect; provide examples to illustrate where a force of precise strength and direction is needed.	Worksheet 1.5.14	Quick starter; Slideshow: May the force be with you; Video: The arrow and the apple; Interactive activity: Drag the forces into the correct group	
1.5.15	Understanding speed calculations	Change depending on direction of force and its size Speed and the quantitative relationship between average speed, distance and time (speed = distance ÷ time)	List the factors involved in defining speed; explain a simple method to measure speed; use the speed formula.	Worksheet 1.5.15 Practical sheet 1.5.15	Quick starter; Slideshow: What is speed and how is it measured?; Interactive activity: Order the objects from fastest to slowest; Ice-cream splat: Key vocabulary game	
1.5.16	Understanding turning forces	Moment as the turning effect of a force	Describe the forces acting on a see-saw; understand that the forces turn about the fulcrum; explain how to balance different weights on a see-saw.	Worksheet 1.5.16 Practical sheet 1.5.16 Technician's notes 1.5.16	Quick starter; Interactive activity: Turning forces; Video: Seesaw tricks and a 949 seesaw	
1.5.17	Discovering moments		State and use the law of moments; describe how turning forces can be increased; list some examples of levers used as force multipliers.	Worksheet 1.5.17 Practical sheet 1.5.17 Technician's notes 1.5.17	Quick starter; Interactive activity: Order the size of the moments	
1.5.18	Understanding the application of moments		Link the law of moments to the design of cranes; explain why counterweights are needed by cranes; investigate the lifting capacity of a crane.	Worksheet 1.5.18 Practical sheet 1.5.18 Technician's notes 1.5.18	Quick starter; Interactive activity: Counterweights; Ice-cream splat: Key vocabulary game	Include the definition of 'moment' and the law of moments from lesson 1.5.17

Chapter 6: Energy Transfers and Sound

1.6.2	Exploring energy transfers	Other processes that involve energy transfer: changing motion, dropping an object, completing an electrical circuit, burning fuels Energy as a quantity that can be quantified and calculated; the total energy has the same value before and after a change	Recognise what energy is and its unit; describe a range of energy transfers using simple diagrams; use a Sankey diagram as a model to represent simple energy changes.	Worksheet 1.6.2	Quick starter; Slideshow: Most of our energy comes from the Sun, but how?; Interactive activity: Energy transfers in a washing machine; Video: How does home insulation reduce energy use?; How do thunder and lightning work?	
1.6.3	Understanding potential energy and kinetic energy	Other processes that involve energy transfer: changing motion, dropping an object	Recognise energy transfers due to falling objects; describe factors affecting energy transfers related to falling objects; explain how energy is conserved when objects fall.	Worksheet 1.6.3	Quick starter; Slideshow: How do roller coasters work?; Interactive activity: Energy true and false	
1.6.4	Doing work	Work done; simple machines give bigger force but at the expense of smaller movement (and vice versa): product of force and displacement unchanged	Recognise situations where work is done; describe the relationship work done = force × distance; apply the equation for work done to different situations.	Worksheet 1.6.4	Quick starter; Interactive activity: Order the work done from largest to smallest	
1.6.5	Looking at dynamos	Other processes that involve energy transfer: changing motion, completing an electrical circuit	Describe the energy changes in a dynamo; explain how a dynamo works.	Worksheet 1.6.5 Technician's notes 1.6.5	Quick starter; Slideshow: Dynamos and motors; Interactive activity: Dynamos	
1.6.6	Understanding elastic potential energy	Other processes that involve energy transfer: stretching a spring. Work done and energy changes on deformation Comparing the starting with the final conditions of a system and describing increases and decreases in the amounts of energy in elastic distortions	Describe different situations that use the energy stored in compressing and stretching elastic materials; describe how elastic potential energy in different materials can be compared; explain how elastic potential energy is transferred.	Worksheet 1.6.6 Practical sheet 1.6.6 Technician's notes 1.6.6	Quick starter; Interactive activity: Complete the sentences about elastic potential energy; Slideshow: Springs and clockwork; Video: The world's oldest bungee jumper is 96!; Ice-cream splat: Key vocabulary game	

1.6.7	Knowing the difference between heat and temperature	Heating and thermal equilibrium: temperature difference between two objects leading to energy transfer from the hotter to the cooler one Comparing the starting with the final conditions of a system and describing increases and decreases in the amounts of energy associated with temperatures	Recognise what we mean by temperature; describe how temperature differences lead to energy transfer; explain the difference between heat and temperature.	Worksheet 1.6.7 Practical sheet 1.6.7 Technician's notes 1.6.7	Quick starter; Interactive activity: Order the temperatures from highest to lowest	
1.6.8	Thinking about fuels	Fuels and energy resources; other processes that involve energy transfer: burning fuels, metabolism of food	Identify examples of fuels and their uses; describe combustion of fuels and recognise that different fuels transfer different amounts of energy; describe the advantages and disadvantages of using different fuels.	Worksheet 1.6.8 Technician's notes 1.6.8	Quick starter; Slideshow: How fuels got their energy; Interactive activity: Gas, liquid or solid; Video: Green cars	May be combined with 1.6.9
1.6.9	Investigating fuels	Fuels and energy resources; other processes that involve energy transfer: burning fuels Comparing the starting with the final conditions of a system and describing increases and decreases in the amounts of energy in chemical compositions	Describe how to measure the energy of fuels; collect evidence to investigate the energy of different fuels; present data using appropriate graphs and evaluate the quality of evidence collected.	Worksheet 1.6.9 Practical sheet 1.6.9 Technician's notes 1.6.9	Quick starter; Interactive activity: Match the fuels to their correct uses; Ice-cream splat: Key vocabulary game	
1.6.10	Applying key ideas		Extract ideas about energy transfers and fuels from earlier sections of the chapter; apply ideas about how energy is transferred to explain its application in making electricity; use ideas and information about electricity generation to compare different energy transfers.	Worksheet 1.6.10		

1.6.11	Exploring sound	Sound produced by vibrations of objects; sound waves are longitudinal	Identify how sounds are made; describe how sound waves transfer energy; explain how loud and quiet sounds are made.	Worksheet 1.6.11 Practical sheet 1.6.11 Technician's notes 1.6.11	Quick starter; Video: Vegetable orchestra; Interactive activity: Order the sounds from loudest to quietest	
1.6.12	Describing sound	Sound produced by vibrations of objects, in loudspeakers; detected by their effect on microphone diaphragm and the ear drum Frequencies of sound waves, measured in hertz (Hz)	Describe how the pitch of a sound wave can be changed; apply the terms frequency, wavelength and amplitude to different waveforms.	Worksheet 1.6.12 Technician's notes 1.6.12	Quick starter; Slideshow: Tuning up an orchestra: What does 'in tune' mean?; Interactive activity: Match the 'sound' term to the correct definition	Include the nature of sound as a longitudinal wave, as introduced in lesson 1.6.11
1.6.13	Measuring the speed of sound	Echoes; the speed of sound in air	Describe what an echo is; describe how the speed of sound can be measured using echoes; calculate distances using ideas about echoes.	Worksheet 1.6.13 Practical sheet 1.6.13	Quick starter; Interactive activity: Sound' statements; Ice-cream splat: Key vocabulary game	May be combined with 1.6.14
1.6.14	Understanding how sounds travels through materials	Sound needs a medium to travel; the speed of sound in air, in water, in solids	Recognise how the speed of sound changes in different substances; use the particle model to explain why there are differences when sound travels through solids, liquids and gases.	Worksheet 1.6.14 Practical sheet 1.6.14 Technician's notes 1.6.14	Quick starter; Interactive activity: Speed of sound; Slideshow: Mach numbers and air density	
1.6.15	Learning about the reflection and absorption of sound	Echoes, reflection and absorption of sound	Recognise which materials affect the quality of sound; analyse the effects of different materials on sound waves; use ideas about energy transfer to explain how soundproofing works.	Worksheet 1.6.15 Practical sheet 1.6.15 Technician's notes 1.6.15	Quick starter; Interactive activity: Good absorbers of sound?	May be reduced in scope

1.6.16	Hearing sounds	Sound produced by vibrations of objects, detected by their effects on microphone diaphragm and the ear drum Waves transferring information for conversion to electrical signals by microphone	Describe the structure and function of different parts of the ear; explain how the ear is able to hear and detect sounds.	Worksheet 1.6.16 Practical sheet 1.6.16 Technician's notes 1.6.16	Quick starter; Interactive activity: The passage of sound through the ear	
1.6.17	Understanding factors affecting hearing	Auditory range of humans and animals	Describe factors which affect hearing; explain how to prevent damage to ears; understand the term hearing range.	Worksheet 1.6.17	Quick starter; Slideshow: What are hearing aids and how do they work?; Interactive activity: Ear damage and solutions	
1.6.18	Finding out about sounds we cannot hear	Auditory range of humans and animals Pressure waves transferring energy; use for cleaning and physiotherapy by ultrasound	Recognise what is meant by ultrasound and infrasound; describe some applications for ultrasound and infrasound; explain how some applications work.	Worksheet 1.6.18	Quick starter; Interactive activity: Ultrasound; Video: Using ultrasound to examine a pregnant woman; Ice-cream splat: Key vocabulary game	Include the meaning of hearing range as presented in 1.6.17

Teaching route: Cells

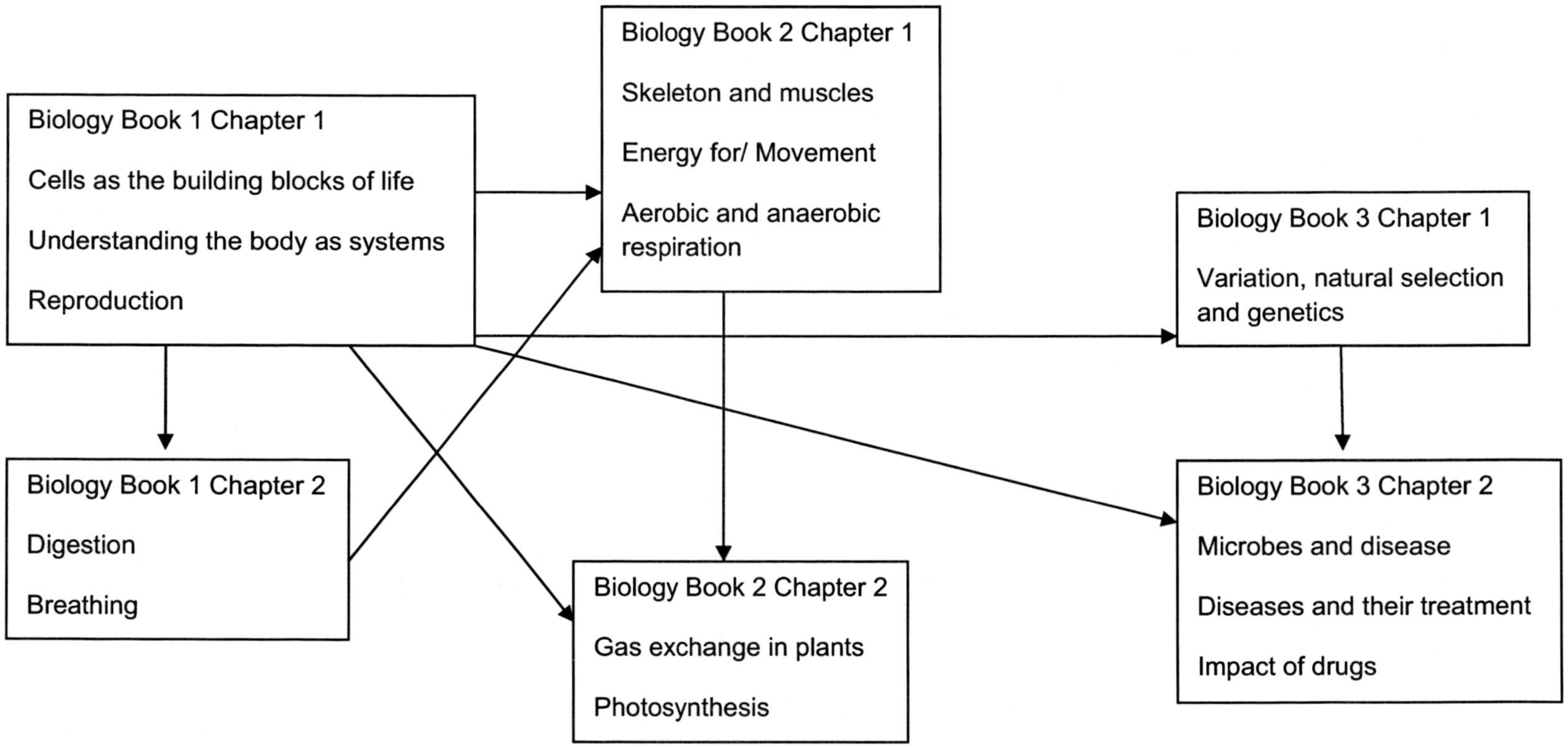

Teaching route: Energy

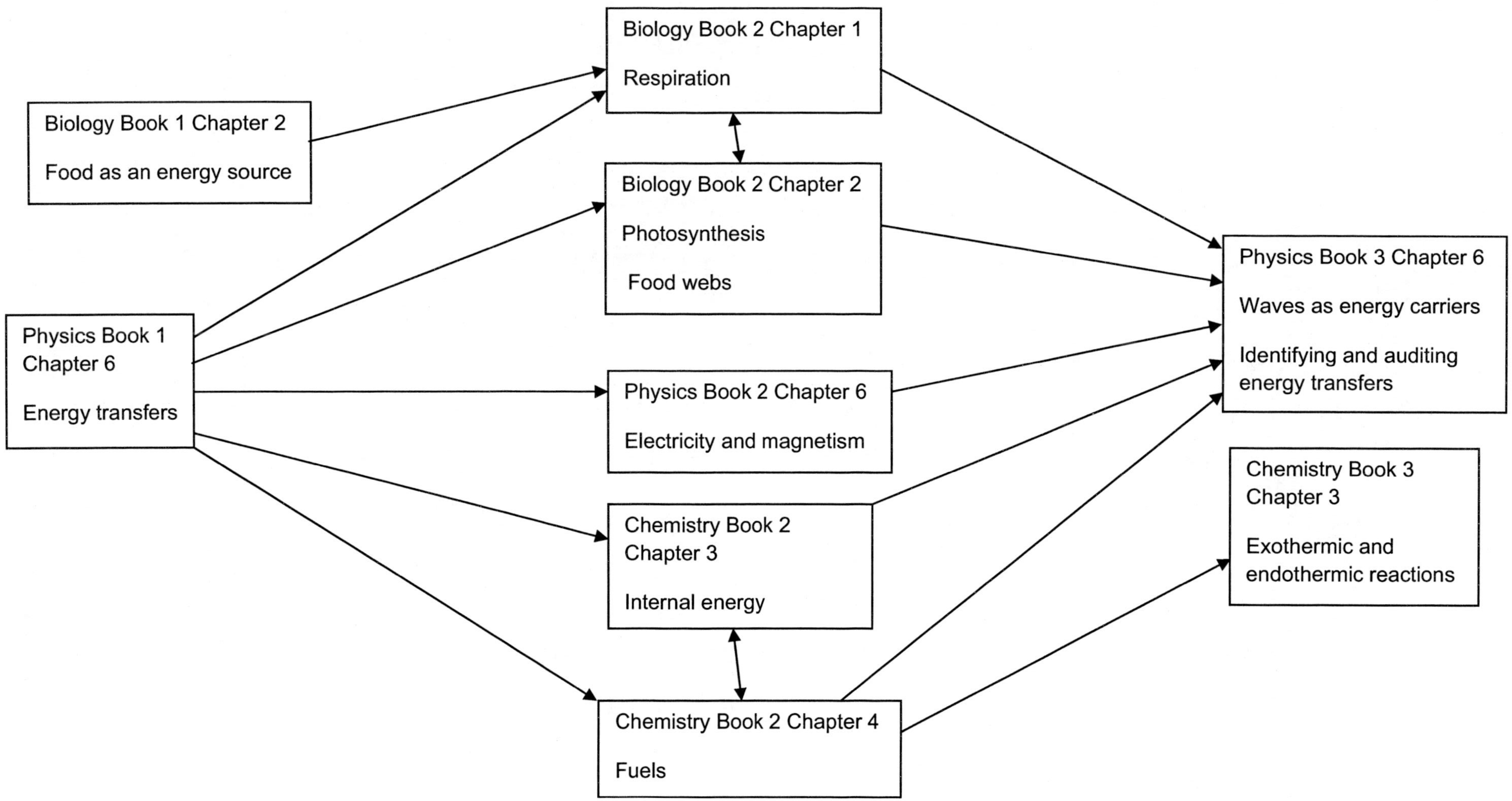

Teaching route: Forces

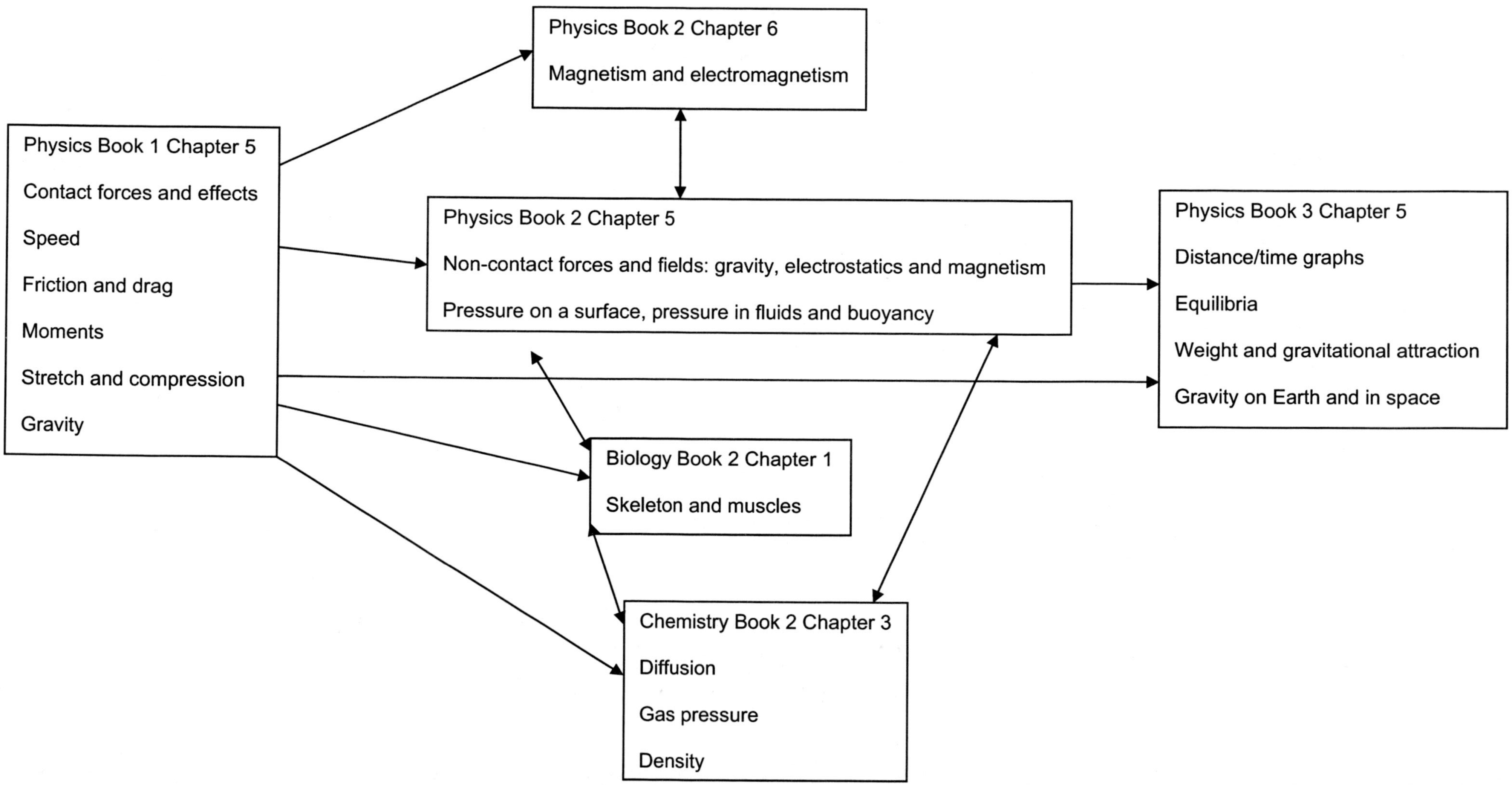

Teaching route: Particles and elements

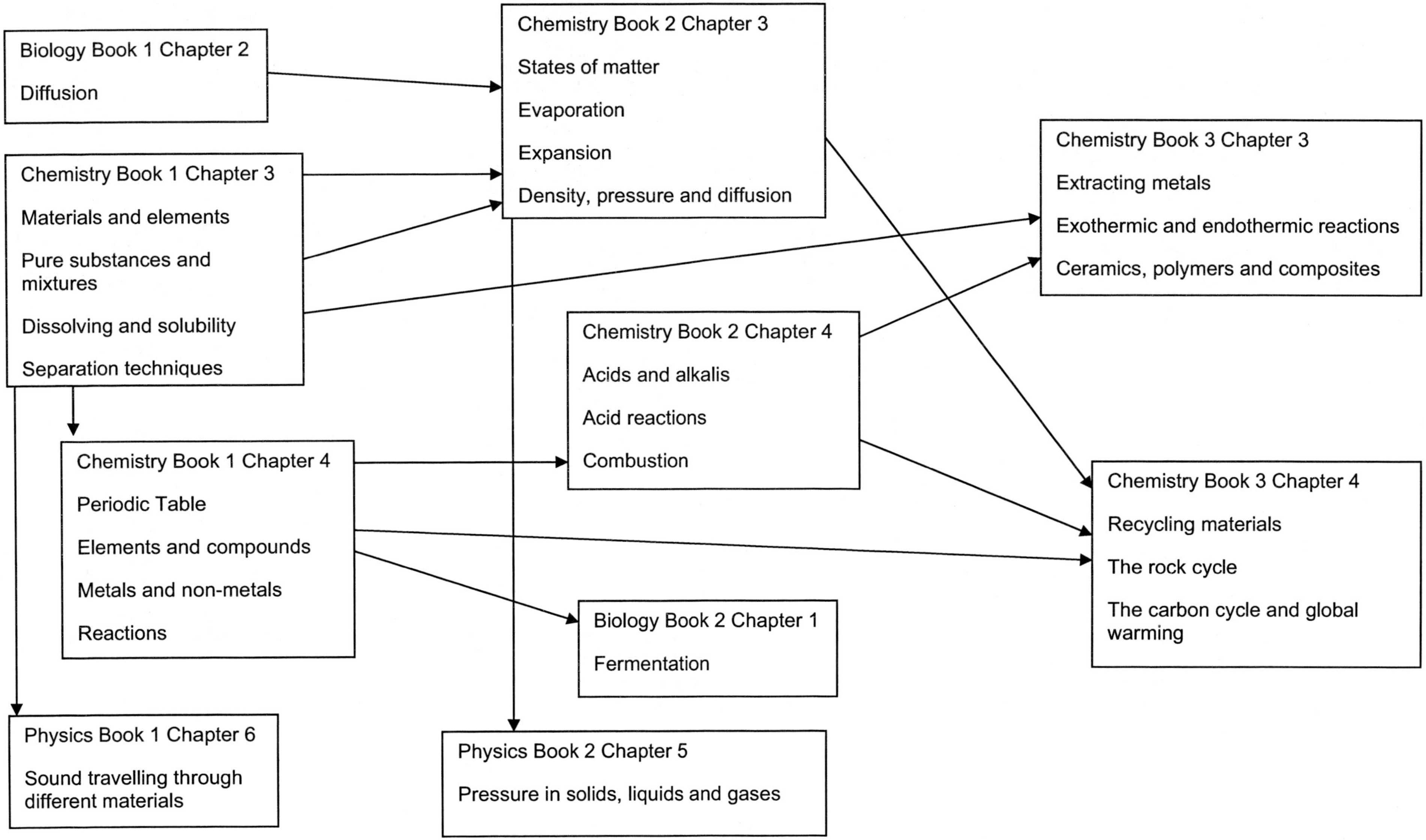

Teaching route: Interdependence

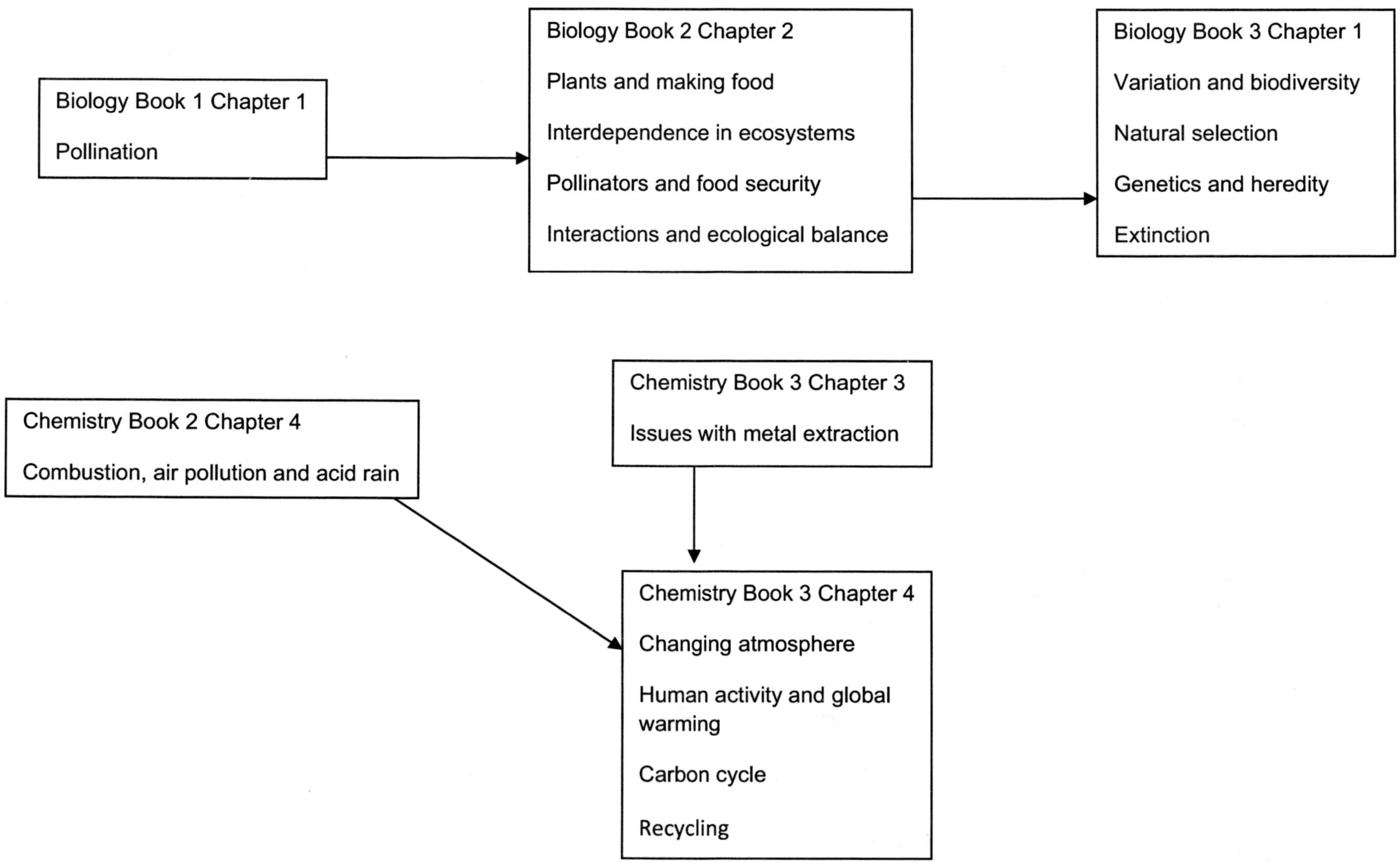

